BEOWULF:
TRANSLATION AND COMMENTARY

BEOWULF

TRANSLATION AND COMMENTARY

Translated by
TOM SHIPPEY

Edited with an Introduction and Commentary by
LEONARD NEIDORF

REVISED AND EXPANDED

UPPSALA BOOKS
London

UPPSALA BOOKS

London, England

www.uppsalabooks.com

First Edition © Uppsala Books 2023
Second Edition © Uppsala Books 2024

ISBN 978-1-961361-14-0 Hardback

ISBN 978-1-961361-15-7 Paperback

ISBN 978-1-961361-02-7 eBook

CONTENTS

ACKNOWLEDGMENTS

We thank Robert Fulk and Rafael Pascual for providing us with essential materials and invaluable correspondence. We thank Zixuan Wei, Na Xu, Kexin Zhang, and Chenyun Zhu for helping us with the preparation of the manuscript. We thank Nirada Chitrakara, Jonathan Chua, Ning He, Ted Morrissey, Sam Newton, Stephen Pollington, and Phyllis Wicks for various forms of support received during the book's composition.

A note on authorship: the translations of *Beowulf*, *Finnsburg*, *Waldere*, and *Hildebrandslied* were composed by Tom Shippey; the commentary was composed by Leonard Neidorf. Shippey composed the "Translator's Preface," "Appendix I: Tolkien and *Beowulf*," and the introduction to "Appendix II: *Finnsburg*, *Waldere*, *Hildebrandslied*;" Neidorf composed the "Introduction," "The Editor on the Translator," the "Note on the *Beowulf* Text," and the "Bibliography."

INTRODUCTION

Beowulf occupies a unique and altogether improbable position in contemporary culture. It is widely regarded as the first great work of English literature, the beginning of the English canon, included in every major anthology and taught annually to millions of students at the high school and college level. *Beowulf* has also come to be considered one of the great epics of world literature, a foundational text from time immemorial, which might be mentioned in the same breath as the *Iliad,* the *Odyssey*, the *Aeneid*, the *Ramayana*, and the *Epic of Gilgamesh*. In addition to being widely taught and read, *Beowulf* continues to be intensively studied, with a steady stream of new monographs, articles, and notes on the poem published every year. Outside of academia, a veritable industry has formed around the poem, which now serves as the basis for motion pictures, television shows, video games, action figures, comic books, and other products intended more for entertainment than education. Because it left a notable mark on J. R. R. Tolkien's best-selling work, *The Lord of the Rings, Beowulf* now serves, directly or indirectly, as one of the principal sources of inspiration for fantasy literature and for any creative endeavor that reimagines the medieval past. No other work of medieval English literature has made such an impact on academic and popular culture; few literary works of any time or place have ever managed to garner such intense and multifaceted interest. It is thus rather disturbing to consider that the entire *Beowulf* industry—all the products sold, all the careers built on the poem's back—would never have existed were it not for the chance preservation of a single medieval manuscript.[1]

Manuscript and Date

All modern editions, translations, and adaptations of *Beowulf* are ultimately and necessarily based on the text of the poem transmitted in one manuscript (London, British Library, Cotton MS Vitellius A.xv) because this manuscript contains the only text of the poem to survive from the medieval period. The handwriting of the two scribes who produced it indicates that they worked around the year 1000. In the same manuscript that preserves *Beowulf*, the scribes also copied down texts of three prose works concerned with fantastical beings (*The Life of St. Christopher, The Wonders of the East,* and *Alexander's Letter to Aristotle*) and the poetic *Judith*, which retells the scene of the heroine's beheading of the tyrannical Holofernes. The texts surrounding *Beowulf* suggest that the poem might owe its preservation to a compiler's interest in things monstrous and lurid. In view of the company that the poem kept, one may reasonably doubt whether this compiler appreciated *Beowulf* as a literary masterpiece or a foundational epic. It would be mistaken, however, to imagine that *Beowulf* never existed outside of its single extant manuscript context. Hundreds of transcription errors in the transmitted text of *Beowulf* indicate that the scribes were working from an earlier written text of the poem, which they mechanically reproduced with minimal comprehension. The virtually certain existence of this earlier manuscript raises the possibility that *Beowulf* might once have been appreciated for rather different reasons. Though there are no indications that *Beowulf* was ever regarded by the early English as a literary work of central importance, it is clear that the poem was considered valuable enough to have it committed to writing on at least two occasions, a fate that rarely befell lengthy poetic narratives in a culture where such narratives circulated predominantly in oral form.[2]

Beowulf itself is doubtless the final product of an extensive oral tradition, but the language of the poem, as we now have it, suggests that it was first composed and committed to parchment within a few decades of the year 700. The language of *Beowulf* differs in many respects from the language of Old English works known to have been composed during the ninth, tenth, and eleventh centuries. There are many verses in *Beowulf* that would be metrically deficient unless the seventh- or eighth-century form of a word is substituted for the form that the scribe wrote down. Such verses shed invaluable light on the language of the *Beowulf* poet, who exhibits awareness of phonological distinctions that became indistinct during the eighth century. There are also many words in *Beowulf* that exhibit meanings different from those they possess in later works, which suggests that the poem's composition antedated semantic changes that took place early in the Old English period. Furthermore, the transcription errors evident in the transmitted text of *Beowulf* seem to have arisen in many places due to the difficulties that the scribes experienced with the spellings and letterforms that were used in the earliest English manuscripts. The most decisive chronological evidence is thus remarkably uniform in suggesting that *Beowulf*, in the form in

3

which we know it, existed in written form around the year 700. Many other considerations, which are less decisive but nonetheless significant, support the dating of the poem to this period. For example, as we note below, the *Beowulf* poet seems to know a lot about sixth-century historical events, significantly more than any later medieval author knows. One cannot precisely articulate the chronological significance of this consideration, but it is plainly consistent with an early date of composition.[3]

Authorship and Structure

Like many writers on *Beowulf*, we refer to the poem's anonymous author as "the *Beowulf* poet." Though some would assert that the poem has no author, and others would argue that the poem has three or more authors, there are compelling reasons to believe that *Beowulf* is essentially the work of a single author. The most compelling reason to believe this is the linguistic homogeneity of the transmitted text of *Beowulf*. The archaic linguistic features mentioned above are not confined to a single portion of the poem but are distributed more or less evenly throughout it. There are also various subtle linguistic regularities that distinguish *Beowulf* from other Old English poems, pertaining to such minutiae as the use of conjunctions and the formation of relative clauses, and these regularities are maintained throughout *Beowulf*. The preservation of archaic features and subtle regularities in the transmitted text of *Beowulf* tells strongly against the supposition that later scribes might have substantially interfered with the work of the earlier poet. It appears, rather, that the extant manuscript of *Beowulf* faithfully preserves the text that one poet composed and committed to parchment three centuries earlier. Whether this poet held a pen in his hand or dictated it to an amanuensis cannot be determined and ultimately does not matter; many pre-modern authors preferred to dictate rather than write their works. In any event, *Beowulf* is not merely unified in terms of its language and meter. It is also an aesthetically coherent poem, the considered product of a single author's engagement with antecedent tradition. Though readers today might be inclined to regard *Beowulf* as an unfiltered expression of a collective tradition, the poem everywhere bears the mark of its author's distinct perspective.[4]

The peculiar structure of *Beowulf* has sometimes been thought to support arguments for multiple authorship. Lines 1-2199 are set during the period of the hero's youth: the Geatish prince Beowulf travels to Denmark, slays two monsters, and is rewarded for his heroic deeds. Lines 2200-3182 are set fifty years later, when an elderly Beowulf is king of Geatland: he is mortally wounded while slaying a dragon, then fittingly mourned at his funeral. Woven into the narrative of the hero's three monster fights are numerous digressions concerning the legendary heroes of the Danes, Geats, Swedes, Frisians, Jutes, Wulfings, Angles, Goths, and other migration-period peoples. This imbalanced and irregular structure, which violates classical theories of aesthetic unity, has naturally given rise to arguments that *Beowulf* is an amalgamation of multiple poems, whether of two long poems on the hero's youth and age or a dozen short poems that a scribal editor has brought together. Such arguments no longer appear credible, in part because of the poem's linguistic homogeneity and in part because of its aesthetic coherence. Yet even when *Beowulf* is viewed as the work of a single author, there is disagreement about its structure: the poem has been considered to have a bipartite structure, organized around youth and age, a tripartite structure, organized around the hero's three monster fights, or a unitary structure, organized around various themes perceived to run through the main narrative and the digressions. Whichever view one favors, it is clear that *Beowulf* possesses its unique structure because one poet fused together history, legend, folklore, and mythology into a complex whole, pregnant with meaning, yet resistant to simplistic attempts to reduce its meaning to a single theme or statement.[5]

History and Legend

Though *Beowulf* deals with a hero's fights against fantastical monsters, its action takes place in front of an ostensibly historical background that is verifiably historical in at least one instance. According to *Beowulf*, king Hygelac of the Geats, the hero's uncle, died during a failed raid in Frankish territory. According to Gregory of Tours' *Historia Francorum* (History of the Franks), a certain Chlochilaicus (a name approximating Proto-Germanic *Hugilaikaz*, the ancestral form of Old English *Hygelac*) from Scandinavia died in precisely the same manner around the year 525. Other Frankish historiographers corroborate and augment Gregory's account of Hygelac's unsuccessful raid. The foregrounded action of *Beowulf* is thus situated in sixth-century Scandinavia. Archaeological evidence indicates that the sixth century was a catastrophic period for Scandinavia, which experienced natural disasters, internecine warfare, and a dramatic reduction in living standards. These indications broadly agree with the characterization of the century that emerges from *Beowulf*, which hints at terrible times ahead for the Geats and the Danes. Furthermore, the demonstrable historicity of Hygelac raises the possibility that other people and events mentioned in *Beowulf* might also possess a genuine historical basis. It is striking, for instance, that the Frankish champion whom Beowulf boasts of killing bears the name *Dæghrefn*, a name that consists of two elements that were uncommon in Anglo-Saxon names yet were entirely characteristic of Frankish names. The mismatch between the names preserved in *Beowulf* and the names that were commonly formed on English soil strengthens the possibility that the poem preserves names that were borne by real people in northern Europe during the fifth and sixth centuries. The potential historicity of *Beowulf* should not be underestimated.[6]

History, however, tends to evolve into legend. In Germanic legendary tradition, a historical core is usually preserved, but events are altered so as to make them conform to certain narrative patterns. The process is well illustrated by the fate that befell king Eormenric of the Goths, another verifiably historical figure who is mentioned in a digression in *Beowulf*. According to the Roman historiographer Ammianus Marcellinus, this Gothic equivalent of Alexander the Great committed suicide when the Huns invaded his vast territory. Legendary tradition preserved Eormenric's name and a memory of his imperial power, but it attributed to him an entirely different sort of death. A narrative developed around Eormenric wherein he kills his son and his wife and is then killed by his wife's kinsmen. This narrative exemplifies the tendency of poets to transmute history into stories of strife between kinsmen or in-laws, which culminate in scenes of kin-slaying and oath-breaking. The allusions in *Beowulf* to future strife between members of the Danish royal family suggest a narrative that conforms to this pattern, in which history has become, or was in the process of becoming, a conventional legendary narrative. The digressions concerning Ingeld and Hengest are more obviously legendary, as the former tells of renewed strife between in-laws after a failed marriage and the latter tells of Hengest's need to break his oath and kill his current lord in order to avenge his former lord. These conventional legendary plots, which focus on transgressions committed under compulsion, are notably absent from the life of Beowulf, who rejoices in his dying words that he killed no kinsmen and broke no oaths. Beowulf, it is clear, was not taken from history or legend; he is rooted, rather, in folklore and mythology.[7]

Folklore and Mythology

Compared to other ancient and medieval heroes of epic poetry, Beowulf is a rather unusual figure. He was considered unpromising in his youth; he prefers to fight without weapons; he has the strength of thirty men; he is famous for a swimming contest; and his defining achievements result from struggles not against other mortals, but against monstrous creatures. This profile identifies Beowulf as a figure drawn not from historical or legendary tradition, but from folkloric tradition, where heroes with similar profiles perform similar deeds. A folktale type known as "the Bear's Son" has been identified as a possible source for *Beowulf*, since some versions of this folktale exhibit extraordinary resemblances to the narrative of Beowulf's fight against Grendel and Grendel's mother. Perhaps the *Beowulf* poet decided to construct his epic around a figure extracted from folkloric tradition because these figures were more morally malleable than those from history or legend, who could not be detached from the narratives of kin-slaying and oath-breaking that developed around them.

8

Folkloric narrative was flexible, as it consisted of mobile collections of variable motifs, which could be adapted to novel moral purposes. Beowulf thus resembles a conventional folkloric hero in certain salient respects, yet he possesses other characteristics not conventionally found in either legendary or folkloric heroes. Beowulf is an unusually courteous and pious hero, who demonstrates concern for the feelings of those around him and cognizance of divine intervention in his life. The hero's courtly dexterity and moral conscientiousness are qualities that the poet evidently took pains to impose upon the partially blank slate that folkloric tradition offered.[8]

Germanic mythology constitutes another possible source for Beowulf's monster-slaying career. Beowulf kills several monsters described as giants (Old English *eoten*) and is mortally wounded while slaying a dragon. A similar career is attributed to Thor in the extant sources for Norse mythology. Thor is depicted in many myths as the principal antagonist of the giants (Old Norse *jǫtunn*, cognate with Old English *eoten*), and he takes various trips with the express purpose of killing giants, much as Beowulf travels to Denmark to rid the kingdom of a troublesome *eoten*. Note that Beowulf, before killing Grendel, boasts that he "exterminated a tribe of giants" (*yðde eotena cyn*, l. 421a) in his youth; the wise men of the Geats encouraged Beowulf to take on Grendel because they knew of his prowess in giant-slaying. Famous antipathy towards giants and other monstrous threats to social order is thus a quality that Beowulf shares with Thor. At Ragnarǫk, Thor is killed not by a giant, but by a dragon: he kills the world-serpent, but is mortally wounded while doing so, and dies shortly thereafter, much as Beowulf dies from wounds incurred while killing a dragon. The striking resemblance between the careers of Beowulf and Thor raises the possibility that the *Beowulf* poet (or one of his predecessors) drew in part on a mythological arche-type while constructing his hero. There is at least one other case in *Beowulf* where an originally mythological narrative appears to have been attributed to human characters. One digression in the poem tells of the Geatish prince Hæthcyn accidentally killing his brother Herebeald with an arrow; the inconsolable grief that this accident causes their father results in his death. The story recalls the account of the death of Baldr recorded in Snorri Sturluson's *Prose Edda*: Hǫðr kills Baldr with an arrow made of mistletoe, which brings unprecedented grief to the gods and takes them closer to their demise at Ragnarǫk. The onomastic connection between the deities and the Geatish princes—Baldr is cognate with the second element of Herebeald, Hǫðr is cognate with the first element of Hæthcyn—leaves little room for doubt that mythology has been converted into legendary history in this case. It is possible that other narratives preserved in *Beowulf* reflect a similar transference of mythological material from the divine realm into the human realm.[9]

Christianity and Paganism

A disproportionate amount of ink has been spilled about the relationship between Christianity and paganism in *Beowulf*. Much of the debate that has arisen among scholars, however, has less to do with the text of *Beowulf* itself and more to do with modern assumptions about what medieval Christians could have believed about their pagan ancestors, what attitudes toward pagans were acceptable for Christians to adopt, and so forth. The theological predicament we confront in *Beowulf* is peculiar, but nevertheless internally consistent. The

Beowulf poet was a Christian; the characters depicted in the poem were not. The conversion of the Anglo-Saxons began in 597, roughly a century before the poem was composed; Scandinavia was not converted until centuries later, so the Danes, Geats, Swedes, and the rest were certainly pagans during the historical period when the action of the poem took place. We thus have a Christian poet telling a story about historically pagan characters. The *Beowulf* poet, disregarding historical accuracy in this respect, takes the liberty of representing the main characters of his narrative as if they were intuitive monotheists. Though they have received neither Mosaic law nor the Christian revelation, these characters have somehow intuited the existence of the one true God of Judeo-Christian tradition. Explicitly Christian language is kept out of the mouths of these characters, who never speak of Christ and are never called Christians, yet their speeches contain abundant references to a single omnipotent deity, whom they revere and thank. Conceptions of providence, covenant, salvation, and damnation are likewise expressed in their speeches. The *Beowulf* poet's decision to represent historically pagan characters as if they were intuitive monotheists and adherents to natural law might seem rather unorthodox, but it is not theologically indefensible. It has been suggested that the poet's conception derives its scriptural justification from certain ideas about pagans expressed in the Pauline epistles.[10]

When scholars write of "Christian and pagan elements" in *Beowulf*, they might identify the reference to Cain and Abel as an example of the former and the description of Scyld Scefing's elaborate ship funeral as an example of the latter. Some devise theories about the interaction of these purportedly distinct elements, suggesting that the poet contrasts one with the other or strikes a delicate balance between them. Yet it is clear from the analogues of *Beowulf* that the poet has taken great pains to sanitize his inherited material and either eliminate or obfuscate its most objectionable aspects. Names of pagan gods are kept out of *Beowulf*, as are direct references to incest, shape-shifting, and human sacrifice. The kin-slayers and oath-breakers of antecedent tradition are relegated to the poem's periphery, while its central narrative focuses on a benevolent monster-slayer with exceptional courtesy and piety. Idol worship is mentioned once and is immediately condemned for imperiling the souls of characters who otherwise follow their better intuitions. In view of the *Beowulf* poet's evident censoriousness, it is likely that most of the ostensibly pagan elements that remain in the poem were simply those that the poet did not consider to be objectionably pagan. We might think that a ship funeral, or a totemic boar-emblem on a helmet, are pagan elements that should offend Christian sensibilities, but the *Beowulf* poet evidently regarded them as innocuous details that need not be erased from the traditions he inherited. A wealth of information about Germanic paganism is thus preserved in *Beowulf* in these traditional details that did not perturb the poet enough to warrant their omission. For example, Hrothgar is twice called the "lord of the friends of Ing" (*eodor Ingwina*, l. 1044a; *frea Ingwina*, l. 1319a). To the *Beowulf* poet, *Ingwine* might have been a semantically opaque (and therefore inoffensive) name, but to the scholar of Germanic paganism, the *Ingwine* ethnonym offers valuable information about the religious orientation of Denmark during the migration period, as it implies descent from or devotion to the fertility deity Yngvi-Freyr. *Beowulf* can be said to be a Christian poem, but it is necessarily and fundamentally indebted to pre-Christian narrative traditions. The reader interested in these traditions can learn much by reading between the lines.[11]

Hero and Theme

Beowulf, as noted above, is a rather unconventional hero. He is unconventional by the standards of ancient and medieval epics, but he seems even more unconventional when he is compared to the heroes of modern action films based on these epics. Readers coming to *Beowulf* after watching the 2007 animated film, where the hero screams "I am Beowulf!" and makes other terse pronouncements, will be surprised to find that Beowulf never delivers these aggressive one-liners. He tends, rather, to deliver lengthy speeches, and he actually spends much of the poem talking. His speeches, moreover, are carefully crafted and highly considerate of those around him. Beowulf takes pains, for instance, not to offend Hrothgar when offering his help, and he makes clear to Hygelac that he respects the authority of his king and uncle even though his own heroic achievements now surpass those of his uncle. Beowulf is courteous: he goes out of his way to thank Unferth for lending him a sword and he praises the sword even though it proved useless against Grendel's mother. Beowulf is also pious: he perceives God's intervention in his life, attributes his survival to God, and worries about the possibility of upsetting God. Though distinguished by his courtesy and piety, Beowulf is still a conventional epic hero in other respects. He comes to Denmark in pursuit of fame and adventure; he boasts proudly of his heroic exploits; he values vengeance and treasure; and he is resolutely unafraid of death. The final line of the poem conveys the peculiar nature of the hero, who is there said to be both kindest to his people and most generous. Beowulf has no children; if he ever married or fell in love, the poet does not tell us. By all appearances, the poet sought to construct a wholly admirable hero, and he omitted details that could complicate this picture.[12]

Not every reader of *Beowulf* sees the hero this way. For certain readers in search of a controlling theme in the poem, the hero is viewed as fatally flawed for one reason or another: he is too proud, too materialistic, too vengeful, and too reckless; his failure to have children might be a strike against him; and he should not have risked his life fighting the dragon alone. Such views tend to emerge when readers assume that *Beowulf* should possess a single theme or that its content should be reducible to a thesis statement or a direct moral exhortation. So, if the poem is a warning against heroic excess or a lamentation on the cyclicality of feuding, then Beowulf should be implicated in the poem's anti-heroic enterprise. There is, however, no compelling reason to assume that *Beowulf* must be structured around a single theme. Efforts to interpret *Beowulf* as an anti-heroic poem appear, moreover, to misconstrue the import of the poem's elegiac passages, which seem intended not to critique the heroic world depicted but to express how much it is valued. Beowulf is mourned at the poem's end not because he was a failed king, but because he was a beloved king and a selfless hero, and his passing from the world is a tremendous loss. The poem does not have a happy ending, but this is a standard feature of early Germanic heroic poetry, which usually culminates in the spectacular demise of the protagonist. *Beowulf* is perhaps better read not so much as a poem with a theme than as a narrative expression of an ethos. Through the exemplary figures of Beowulf and the other foregrounded characters, the poet articulates his peculiar ethical vision, which combines traditional heroic values with values pertaining to courtly restraint, dexterous speech, and monotheistic piety.[13]

Beowulf and Beyond

Beowulf is a great literary work. If it were not, it would not be so widely read by people who are under no compulsion to read it. Any reader can pick up a translation of *Beowulf* and enjoy the poem as an entertaining narrative. Yet what really draws readers into *Beowulf* is the sense that it is a window into a lost world, a time-capsule from a lost civilization, which tells us about a people's hopes, dreams, and fears during a period for which there are no comparable records. This sense is accurate. *Beowulf* is the only poem of its kind to survive. The Old English *Waldere* fragments suggest that other poems like *Beowulf* existed, but these have not been preserved. *Beowulf* is the earliest epic poem not only in the English language, but also in any Germanic language and perhaps also in any western European vernacular language. Consequently, *Beowulf* is a precious source, which sheds unparalleled light on the culture of the peoples whom Greeks and Romans considered barbarians. Classical authors record observations, sometimes admiring though often deprecatory, of their barbarian neighbors, but in *Beowulf* we finally have an extended account of barbarian life from a barbarian's mouth. Because of its unique status, *Beowulf* is a poem that rewards the reader who approaches it with minimal preconceptions. Readers who imagine that barbarian kings, queens, and heroes must resemble those depicted on film will find much to surprise them in the figures of Hrothgar, Wealhtheow, and Beowulf. *Beowulf* is far from the simple, chest-thumping poetry that one might imagine ancient and medieval barbarians to have cultivated. It is a sophisticated heroic-elegiac poem, composed by a philosophical author, who weaved history, legend, folklore, and mythology into a complex whole that is much greater than the sum of its parts.[14]

NOTES

[1] On the reception of *Beowulf* within and beyond the academy, see *Beowulf: The Critical Heritage*, ed. Tom Shippey and Andreas Haarder (London: Routledge, 1998); Kathleen Forni, *Beowulf's Popular Afterlife in Literature, Comic Books, and Film* (New York: Routledge, 2018); David Clark, *Beowulf in Contemporary Culture* (Newcastle upon Tyne: Cambridge Scholars, 2020); and *Beowulf as Children's Literature*, ed. Bruce Gilchrist and Britt Mize (Toronto: University of Toronto Press, 2021). On the film adaptations of *Beowulf*, see Nickolas Haydock and E. L. Risden, *Beowulf on Film: Adaptations and Variations* (Jefferson: McFarland, 2013); and Leonard Neidorf, "*Beowulf*," in *Books to Film: Cinematic Adaptations of Literary Works*, vol. 1, ed. Barry Keith Grant (Farmington Hills: Gale-Cengage, 2018), 21–24. On the influence of *Beowulf* on the works of J. R. R. Tolkien, see Tom Shippey, *The Road to Middle Earth: How J. R. R. Tolkien Created a New Mythology*, 4th ed. (Boston: Houghton Mifflin, 2003).

[2] On the dating of the sole extant manuscript of *Beowulf*, see David N. Dumville, "Beowulf Come Lately: Some Notes on the Paleography of the Nowell Codex," *Archiv für das Studium der neueren Sprachen und Literaturen* 225 (1988): 49–63. For an edition and translation of the texts preserved alongside *Beowulf* in this manuscript, see *The Beowulf Manuscript: Complete Texts and The Fight at Finnsburg*, ed. and trans. R. D. Fulk (Cambridge: Harvard University Press, 2010). On the possible links between these texts and *Beowulf*, see Andy Orchard, *Pride and Prodigies: Studies in the Monsters of the Beowulf-Manuscript* (Cambridge: D. S. Brewer, 1995). On the transcription errors in the extant manuscript and the earlier

manuscript(s) of the poem that they indicate, see Michael Lapidge, "The Archetype of *Beowulf*," *Anglo-Saxon England* 29 (2000): 5–41; and Leonard Neidorf, "The Archetype of *Beowulf*," *English Studies* 99 (2018): 229–242.

[3] On the differences between the language of *Beowulf* and the language of Old English works dated to the ninth, tenth, and eleventh centuries, see the overviews presented in R. D. Fulk, "Archaisms and Neologisms in the Language of *Beowulf*," in *Studies in the History of the English Language III*, ed. Christopher M. Cain and Geoffrey Russom (Berlin: Mouton de Gruyter, 2007), 267–287; and Leonard Neidorf, "Philology, Allegory, and the Dating of *Beowulf*," *Studia Neophilologica* 88 (2016): 97–115. For technical discussion of the metrical evidence bearing on the poem's date of composition, see R. D. Fulk, *A History of Old English Meter* (Philadelphia: University of Pennsylvania Press, 1992); and Leonard Neidorf and Rafael J. Pascual, "The Language of *Beowulf* and the Conditioning of Kaluza's Law," *Neophilologus* 98 (2014): 657–673. On the lexical and semantic indications of the poem's antiquity, see Dennis Cronan, "Poetic Words, Conservatism, and the Dating of Old English Poetry," *Anglo-Saxon England* 33 (2004): 23–50; and Leonard Neidorf, "Lexical Evidence for the Relative Chronology of Old English Poetry," *SELIM* 20 (2013–2014): 7–48. For wide-ranging discussion of various forms of evidence bearing on the poem's date, see the essays in *The Dating of Beowulf: A Reassessment*, ed. Leonard Neidorf (Cambridge: D. S. Brewer, 2014).

[4] On the linguistic evidence for the unitary authorship of *Beowulf*, see Janet Bately, "Linguistic Evidence as a Guide to the Authorship of Old English Verse: A Reappraisal, with Special Reference to *Beowulf*," in *Learning and Literature in Anglo-Saxon England: Studies Presented to Peter Clemoes on the Occasion of His Sixty-Fifth Birthday,*

ed. Michael Lapidge and Helmut Gneuss (Cambridge: Cambridge University Press, 1985), 409–431; Tom Shippey, "Old English Poetry: The Prospects for Literary History," in *Proceedings of the Second International Conference of SELIM (Spanish Society for English Medieval Language and Literature)*, ed. A. León Sendra (Córdoba: SELIM, 1993), 164–179; Daniel Donoghue, "On the Non-Integrity of *Beowulf*," *SELIM* 1 (1991): 29–44; John D. Sundquist, "Relative Clause Variation and the Unity of *Beowulf*," *Journal of Germanic Linguistics* 14 (2002): 243–269; R. D. Fulk, "Old English Þa 'Now that' and the Integrity of *Beowulf*," *English Studies* 88 (2007): 623–631; and Aaron Ecay and Susan Pintzuk, "The Syntax of Old English Poetry and the Dating of *Beowulf*," in *Old English Philology: Studies in Honour of R. D. Fulk*, ed. Leonard Neidorf, Rafael J. Pascual, and Tom Shippey (Cambridge: D. S. Brewer, 2016), 144–171. For an extended defense of the structural homogeneity of the transmitted text of *Beowulf* and an argument against substantial scribal interference, see Leonard Neidorf, *The Transmission of Beowulf: Language, Culture, and Scribal Behavior* (Ithaca: Cornell University Press, 2017).

[5] For an overview of the history of ideas about the poem's structure, see Tom Shippey, "Structure and Unity," in *A Beowulf Handbook*, ed. Robert E. Bjork and John D. Niles (Lincoln: University of Nebraska Press, 1997), 149–174. For the most recent incarnation of the improbable claim that *Beowulf* consists of two or more poems joined by a scribal editor, see Kevin S. Kiernan, *Beowulf and the Beowulf Manuscript*, 2nd ed. (Ann Arbor: University of Michigan Press, 1996). For further discussion of the poem's structure, see John Leyerle, "The Interlace Structure of *Beowulf*," *University of Toronto Quarterly* 37 (1967): 1–17; Kathryn Hume, "The Theme and Structure of *Beowulf*," *Studies in Philology* 72 (1975): 1–27; Jane Chance, "The Structural Unity of *Beowulf*: The Problem of Grendel's

Mother," in *New Readings on Women in Old English Literature*, ed. Helen Damico and Alexandra Hennessy Olsen (Bloomington: Indiana University Press, 1990), 248–261; Gale R. Owen-Crocker, *The Four Funerals in Beowulf and the Structure of the Poem* (Manchester: Manchester University Press, 2000); Yvette Kisor, "Numerical Composition and *Beowulf*: A Reconsideration," *Anglo-Saxon England* 38 (2009): 41–76; and Francis Leneghan, *The Dynastic Drama of Beowulf* (Cambridge: D. S. Brewer, 2020), 1–32.

[6] For a multifaceted defense of the poem's potential historicity, see Tom Shippey, *Beowulf and the North before the Vikings* (Leeds: Arc Humanities Press, 2022). On the archaeological evidence for sixth-century Scandinavia, see Lotte Hedeager, *Iron-Age Societies: from Tribe to State in Northern Europe, 500 BC to AD 700*, trans. John Hines (Oxford: Blackwell, 1992), 239–255; Bo Gräslund, "Fimbulvintern, Ragnarök och klimatkrisen år 536–537 e. Kr.," *Saga och Sed* (2007): 93–123; Frands Herschend, *The Idea of the Good in Late Iron Age Society* (Uppsala: Institutionen för arkeologi och antikens historia, Uppsala Universitet, 1998); and Martin Rundkvist, *Mead-halls of the Eastern Geats: Elite Settlements and Political Geography AD 375–1000 in Östergötland, Sweden* (Stockholm: KVHAA, Royal Swedish Academy, 2012). On names as evidence for the historicity and antiquity of *Beowulf*, see Tom Shippey, "The Merow(ich)ingian Again: *damnatio memoriae* and the *usus scholarum*," in *Latin Learning and English Lore: Studies in Anglo-Saxon Literature for Michael Lapidge*, ed. Katherine O'Brien O'Keeffe and Andy Orchard, 2 vols. (Toronto: University of Toronto Press, 2005), I: 389–406; and Tom Shippey, "Names in *Beowulf* and Anglo-Saxon England," in *The Dating of Beowulf: A Reassessment*, ed. Leonard Neidorf (Cambridge: D. S. Brewer, 2014), 58–78.

[7] On the evolution of historical material into legendary narrative, see Theodore M. Andersson, *A Preface to the Nibelungenlied* (Stanford: Stanford University Press, 1987), 3–16. On the figure of Ermanaric in particular, see Caroline Brady, *The Legends of Ermanaric* (Berkeley: University of California Press, 1943). For the similar case of Attila the Hun, see Michael A. Babcock, *The Stories of Attila the Hun's Death: Narrative, Myth, and Meaning* (Lewiston: Edwin Mellen Press, 2001). For further discussion of Germanic legend, see Edward Haymes and Susann T. Samples, *Heroic Legends of the North: An Introduction to the Nibelung and Dietrich Cycles* (New York: Garland, 1996); and Carolyne Larrington, "Eddic Poetry and Heroic Legend," in *A Handbook to Eddic Poetry: Myths and Legends of Early Scandinavia*, ed. Carolyne Larrington, Judy Quinn, and Brittany Schorn (Cambridge: Cambridge University Press, 2016), 147–172. On the tendency for legendary narratives to be structured around strife between kinsmen or in-laws, see especially Bertha S. Phillpotts, "Wyrd and Providence in Anglo-Saxon Thought," *Essays and Studies* 13 (1928): 7–27; and Leonard Neidorf, "Goths, Huns, and *The Dream of the Rood*," *Review of English Studies* 72 (2021): 821–835. For an argument that Beowulf's last words highlight this character's departure from the norms of legendary tradition, see Thomas D. Hill, "The Confession of Beowulf and the Structure of *Volsunga Saga*," in *The Vikings: Papers from the Cornell Lecture Series Held to Coincide with the Viking Exhibition 1980–1981*, ed. Robert T. Farrell (London: Phillimore, 1982), 165–179.

[8] On the folkloric dimensions of *Beowulf*, see Tom Shippey, "The Fairy-Tale Structure of *Beowulf*," *Notes and Queries* 16 (1969): 2–11; Daniel R. Barnes, "Folktale Morphology and the Structure of *Beowulf*," *Speculum* 45 (1970): 416–434; Bruce A. Rosenberg, "Folktale Morphology and the Structure of *Beowulf*: A Counterproposal," *Journal of the Folklore Institute* 11 (1975): 199–209; and Kent

Gould, "*Beowulf* and Folktale Morphology: God as Magical Donor," *Folklore* 96 (1985): 98–103. On Beowulf as a hero derived from antecedent folkloric tradition, see Larry D. Benson, "The Originality of Beowulf," in *The Interpretation of Narrative: Theory and Practice*, ed. Morton W. Bloomfield (Cambridge: Harvard University Press, 1970), 1–43; and Leonard Neidorf, "Beowulf before *Beowulf*: Anglo-Saxon Anthroponymy and Heroic Legend," *Review of English Studies* 64 (2013): 553–573. On "the Bear's Son" folktale and its relationship to *Beowulf*, see J. Michael Stitt, *Beowulf and the Bear's Son: Epic, Saga, and Fairytale in Northern Germanic Tradition* (New York: Garland, 1992).

[9] On the connections between Beowulf and Thor, see Ursula Dronke, "*Beowulf* and Ragnarǫk," *Saga-Book* 17 (1969): 302–325; and Andy Orchard, *A Critical Companion to Beowulf* (Cambridge: D. S. Brewer, 2003), 119–123. On the relationship between the story of Herebeald and Hæthcyn and the myth of the death of Baldr, see Joseph Harris, "A Nativist Approach to *Beowulf*: The Case of Germanic Elegy," in *Companion to Old English Poetry*, ed. Henk Aertsen and Rolf H. Bremmer Jr. (Amsterdam: VU University Press, 1994), 45–62; Richard North, *Heathen Gods in Old English Literature* (Cambridge: Cambridge University Press, 1997), 198-202; and Heather O'Donoghue, "What Has Baldr to Do with Lamech? The Lethal Shot of a Blind Man in Old Norse Myth and Jewish Exegetical Traditions," *Medium Ævum* 72 (2003): 82–107. The story of Scyld Scefing's mysterious arrival and departure is another episode in the poem evidently derived from a mythological tradition; see Clive Tolley, "Beowulf's Scyld Scefing Episode: Some Norse and Finnish Analogues," *Arv* 52 (1996): 7–48.

[10] For an overview of scholarly opinion, see Edward B. Irving Jr., "Christian and Pagan Elements," in *A Beowulf Handbook*, ed. Robert

E. Bjork and John D. Niles (Lincoln: University of Nebraska Press, 1997), 175–192; and Paul Cavill, "Christianity and Theology in *Beowulf*," in *The Christian Tradition in Anglo-Saxon England: Approaches to Current Scholarship and Teaching*, ed. Paul Cavill (Woodbridge: D. S. Brewer, 2004), 15–40. Earlier discussions that remain useful include Arthur Gilchrist Brodeur, *The Art of Beowulf* (Berkeley: University of California Press, 1959),182–219; and Betty S. Cox, *Cruces of Beowulf* (The Hague: Mouton, 1971), 12–32. For examples of some of the divergent views that have formed, see Larry D. Benson, "The Pagan Coloring of *Beowulf*," in *Old English Poetry: Fifteen Essays*, ed. Robert P. Creed (Providence: Brown University Press, 1967), 193–213; and Margaret E. Goldsmith, *The Mode and Meaning of Beowulf* (London: The Athlone Press, 1970). On the characters' intuitive monotheism, see Charles Donahue, *"Beowulf* and Christian Tradition: A Reconsideration from a Celtic Stance," *Traditio* 21 (1965): 55–116; Thomas D. Hill, "The Christian Language and Theme of *Beowulf*," in *Companion to Old English Poetry*, ed. Rolf H. Bremmer Jr. and Henk Aertsen (Amsterdam: VU University Press, 1994), 63–77; Dennis Cronan, "Beowulf, the Gaels, and the Recovery of the Pre-Conversion Past," *Anglo-Saxon* 1 (2007): 137–180. On the Pauline source for the poet's theology, see A. D. Horgan, "Religious Attitudes in *Beowulf*," in *Essays and Poems Presented to Lord David Cecil*, ed. W. W. Robson (London: Constable, 1970), 9–17; and Marijane Osborn, "The Great Feud: Scriptural History and Strife in *Beowulf*," *PMLA* 93 (1978): 973–981.

[11] For the notion that pagan and Christian elements are deliberately contrasted in *Beowulf*, see Fred C. Robinson, *Beowulf and the Appositive Style* (Knoxville: University of Tennessee Press, 1985). For a contrary view, see Edward B. Irving, Jr., "The Nature of Christianity in *Beowulf*," *Anglo-Saxon England* 13 (1984): 7–21. On the question of whether the poet perceived pagan elements as genuinely

pagan, see C. E. Fell, "Paganism in *Beowulf*: A Semantic Fairy-Tale," in *Pagans and Christians: The Interplay between Christian Latin and Traditional Germanic Cultures in Early Medieval Europe*, edited by T. Hofstra, L. A. J. R. Houwen, and A. A. MacDonald (Groningen: Egbert Forsten, 1995), 9–34. On the idol worship of the Danes, see Karl P. Wentersdorf, "*Beowulf*: The Paganism of Hrothgar's Danes," *Studies in Philology* 78 (1981): 91–119; and Geoffrey Russom, "Historicity and Anachronism in *Beowulf*," in *Epic and History*, ed. David Konstan and Kurt A. Raaflaub (Malden: Wiley-Blackwell, 2010), 243–261. On the poet's selective censoriousness, see James W. Earl, "The Forbidden *Beowulf*: Haunted by Incest," *PMLA* 125 (2010): 289–305; and Leonard Neidorf, "The *Beowulf* Poet's Sense of Decorum," *Traditio* 76 (2021): 1–28. On the implications of the *Ingwine* ethnonym, see E. O. G. Turville-Petre, *Myth and Religion of the North: The Religion of Ancient Scandinavia* (New York: Holt, Reinhart and Winston, 1964), 170–172; and Stephen Pollington, *The Elder Gods: Religion and the Supernatural in Early England* (Ely: Anglo-Saxon Books, 2011), 213–216.

[12] On the carefully crafted speeches delivered by Beowulf and other characters, see Tom Shippey, "Principles of Conversation in Beowulfian Speech," in *Techniques of Description: Spoken and Written Discourse: A Festschrift for Malcolm Coulthard*, ed. John M. Sinclair, Michael Hoey, and Gwyneth Fox (London: Routledge, 1993), 109–126; Michael R. Kightley, "Reinterpreting Threats to Face: The Use of Politeness in *Beowulf*, ll. 407–472," *Neophilologus* 93 (2009): 511–520; and A. Keith Kelly, "Teaching Good Manners: Civil Discourse Patterns in *Beowulf* and *Sir Gawain and the Green Knight*," in *Literary Speech Acts of the Medieval North: Essays Inspired by the Works of Thomas A. Shippey*, ed. Eric Shane Bryan and Alexander Vaughan Ames (Tempe, AZ: ACMRS, 2020), 223–242. On Beowulf's courteousness toward Unferth, see Graham Williams, "*Wine*

Min Unferð: Courtly Speech and a Reconsideration of (Supposed) Sarcasm in *Beowulf*," *Journal of Historical Pragmatics* 18 (2017): 175–194. For wide-ranging discussion of courtliness in the poem, see E. G. Stanley, "Courtliness and Courtesy in *Beowulf* and Elsewhere in English Medieval Literature," in *Words and Works: Studies in Medieval English Language and Literature in Honour of Fred C. Robinson*, ed. Peter S. Baker and Nicholas Howe (Toronto: University of Toronto Press, 1998), 67–104; and Leonard Neidorf, *The Art and Thought of the Beowulf Poet* (Ithaca: Cornell University Press, 2022). On Beowulf's overall character and biography, see Sherman Kuhn, "*Beowulf* and the Life of Beowulf: A Study in Epic Structure," in *Studies in the Language, Literature, and Culture of the Middle Ages and Later*, ed. E. Bagby Atwood and Archibald A. Hill (Austin: University of Texas at Austin, 1969), 243–264.

[13] For an overview of thematic readings, see George Clark, "The Hero and the Theme," in *A Beowulf Handbook*, ed. Robert E. Bjork and John D. Niles (Lincoln: University of Nebraska Press, 1997), 271–290. For examples of readings of *Beowulf* as a poem designed to expose flaws in the hero or in heroic culture more generally, see John Leyerle, "Beowulf the Hero and the King," *Medium Ævum* 34 (1965): 89–102; Martin Camargo, "The Finn Episode and the Tragedy of Revenge in *Beowulf*," *Studies in Philology* 78 (1981): 120–134; and Linda Georgianna, "King Hrethel's Sorrow and the Limits of Heroic Action in *Beowulf*," *Speculum* 62 (1987): 829–850. On the connection between elegy and heroic poetry, see Joseph Harris, "Elegy in Old English and Old Norse: A Problem in Literary History," in *The Old English Elegies: New Essays in Criticism and Research*, ed. Martin Green (Rutherford: Fairleigh Dickinson University Press, 1983), 46–56; and Harris, "Hadubrand's Lament: On the Origin and Age of Elegy in Germanic," in *Heldensage und Heldendichtung im Germanischen*, ed. Heinrich Beck (Berlin: Walter de Gruyter, 1988),

81–114. For the suggestion that *Beowulf* is an expression of an ethos, see Tom Shippey, "'The Fall of King Hæðcyn': Or, Mimesis 4a, the Chapter Auerbach Never Wrote," in *On the Aesthetics of Beowulf and Other Old English Poems*, ed. John M. Hill (Toronto: University of Toronto Press, 2010), 247–265.

[14] On the *Waldere* fragments, see *The Old English Epic of Waldere*, ed. Jonathan B. Himes (Newcastle upon Tyne: Cambridge Scholars Publishing, 2009). On the use of "barbarian" in ancient and medieval writings, see Shami Ghosh, *Writing the Barbarian Past: Studies in Early Medieval Historical Narrative* (Leiden: Brill, 2016). On the need to read *Beowulf* on its own terms, with minimal cultural or aesthetic preconceptions, the classic statement is J. R. R. Tolkien, "*Beowulf*: The Monsters and the Critics," *Proceedings of the British Academy* 22 (1936): 245–295.

THE EDITOR ON THE TRANSLATOR

Translation is a form of interpretation. That is a truth universally acknowledged in contemporary literary studies. A translation is a continuous interpretation, in which the translator registers with the choice of every word an interpretation of the denotation and connotations of the text. It is therefore remarkable to consider how rarely distinguished interpreters of *Beowulf* have taken it upon themselves to publish translations of the poem. Many translations of *Beowulf* have been produced by people who show no interest at all in the poem's interpretation, people who have never published one significant article on *Beowulf*, let alone a significant book on the poem. The most widely read translations of *Beowulf* are by professional translators and creative writers, who cannot really comprehend the poem in its original language and must therefore cobble together a translation that combines previously published translations with the miscellaneous suggestions of a scholarly advisor and their own arbitrary intuitions. Even the translations of *Beowulf* that have been produced by university professors, it must be said, have rarely been produced by professors who are distinguished interpreters of *Beowulf*. Some notable exceptions come to mind (J. R. R. Tolkien, Marijane Osborn, R. D. Fulk), but in general, readers holding a random

Beowulf translation in their hands will search in vain for evidence that the translator of *Beowulf* is a significant interpreter of the poem. Most translations of *Beowulf* are not by people who publish dozens of articles and books on *Beowulf*, but by people who have made no substantial contribution to our understanding of this obscure and recalcitrant poem.

The state of affairs is unfortunate, since *Beowulf* is an exceptionally challenging poem. Experts can debate for hours about what one line or one word *really* means. The literal meaning might be easy enough to figure out, but what is the subtext, what is the sense conveyed through the words? The innumerable problems of interpretation that arise when reading the poem in its original language force its readers to turn to translators for guidance. I can think of no person more qualified to guide readers through the interpretation of *Beowulf* than Thomas A. Shippey. Shippey has demonstrated a lifelong commitment to the study of *Beowulf*: his first paper on *Beowulf* was published in 1969, and his most recent book on *Beowulf* was published in 2022. For more than 50 years, Shippey has been teaching and writing about *Beowulf* and related Old English and Old Norse literary works. Shippey's wide-ranging studies of *Beowulf* include works on the poem's structure and unity, its relationship with its analogues, its potential historicity, its narrative style, its speech acts, its names, its proverbs, its ethos, and its reception history. His 1972 book, *Old English Verse*, considered *Beowulf* within the context of the extant corpus of Old English poetry. His 1978 book, *Beowulf*, remains one of the great attempts to confront the poem on its own peculiar terms. His 1998 book, *Beowulf: The Critical Heritage*, explores the history of ideas about the poem and translates into English the most significant German and Scandinavian writing about *Beowulf* from the nineteenth century. His 2022 book, *Beowulf and the North before the Vikings*, demonstrates how sixth-century Scandinavian history and archaeology illuminate *Beowulf* and are, in turn, illuminated by *Beowulf*.

One feature of Shippey's *Beowulf* criticism that especially qualifies him to translate the poem is the attention it consistently pays to the poem's subtexts. No scholar or critic of *Beowulf* has done more to illuminate the subtle implications of the poem's many speeches than Shippey, whose groundbreaking article on "Principles of Conversation in Beowulfian Speech" influenced a generation of scholars. Shippey's insights into the poem's speeches, evident in this article, in his 1978 book, and in various other publications, have borne considerable fruit, even giving rise to a festschrift in 2020 (one of three festschrifts dedicated to Shippey) entitled *Literary Speech Acts of the Medieval North: Essays Inspired by the Works of Thomas A. Shippey*. In addition to his work on speech acts, Shippey has been the rare *Beowulf* scholar to write penetrating studies of the poem's relationship to both its folkloric and its heroic-legendary analogues. His first publication, "The Fairy-Tale Structure of *Beowulf*" (1969), pioneered the analysis of the poem through the lens of Vladimir Propp's *Morphology of the Folktale*. It demonstrated that the presence or absence of certain folktale motifs in the poem reveals much about the priorities of the *Beowulf* poet, who evidently sought to reduce the magical dimensions of his inherited material. Shippey's work on the heroic-legendary analogues, meanwhile, reaches the striking conclusion that the account of migration-period history that can be inferred from *Beowulf* appears considerably more coherent and plausible than the more partial accounts found in its analogues. The internally consistent nature of what is reported about Danes, Geats, Swedes, and the rest in *Beowulf* raises the distinct possibility that the poem's account is genuinely based on memories of historical events from the migration period.

Shippey began his career as Assistant Lecturer and then Lecturer at the University of Birmingham, 1965-72. He became a Fellow of St John's College, Oxford, 1972-79, and subsequently Professor of English Language and Medieval English Literature at Leeds University, 1979-93. He then took up the Walter J. Ong Jr. Chair of Humanities at Saint Louis University, until retirement in 2008. In addition to his work on *Beowulf* and medieval literature, Shippey is the leading authority on the works of J. R. R. Tolkien. He consulted on Peter Jackson's *Lord of the Rings* films and is well known for his books *The Road to Middle Earth: How J. R. R. Tolkien Created a New Mythology* and *J. R. R. Tolkien: Author of the Century*. Overall, Shippey's interests in medieval literature, fantasy literature, science fiction, and medievalism have resulted in him publishing more than 100 articles on these topics. He has also edited or co-edited a dozen essay-collections, and in recent years has written more than 200 reviews on fantasy and science fiction for *The Wall Street Journal*, as well as many contributions, often on archaeology, to *The London Review of Books*. Finally, it must be said that a brief overview cannot convey the brilliance of Shippey's writings, which are never dull or uninspired and always have something provocative in them. Shippey's literary and media footprint is simply a marvellous thing to ponder. Whether lecturing at a conference, speaking in a documentary, or writing for an academic or popular audience, Shippey is a master of grabbing an audience's attention and holding it with wit, humor, cogent arguments, and original insights. He is invariably interesting. I am honored to be here and elsewhere the James Boswell to this Dr. Johnson.

TRANSLATOR'S PREFACE

In the more than two hundred years since the first edition of *Beowulf* was published in 1815, hundreds of thousands of hours, possibly millions, have been spent in translating the poem. It has been translated by scholars, by poets, most of all by students undergoing a *rite de passage* of the educational system. Almost no time at all, by contrast, has been spent in explaining why this is such a difficult exercise, and sometimes an unrewarding one.

The main reason is that quite a lot of the poem simply *does not mean very much*. This is such a terrible thing to say about poetry, to modern thinking, that it needs to be unpacked carefully.

The clearest sign of its truth comes from the geographical locations offered for the Danes. In the poem they are called *Norð-Dene* once, *Suð-Dene* twice, *East-Dene* three times and *West-Dene* twice. It is quite possible that all these designations *could* once have meant something—"North-Danes" for instance might mean people like Wulfgar the door-ward, who comes from Vendil at the north end of Jutland, while "East-Danes" might well be the people who live at or near Heorot, opposite Sweden across the Øresund.

However, this is not the case. In *Beowulf, they are all the*

31

same Danes. It might make sense for Hygelac to refer to the "South-Danes" when talking to Beowulf about his expedition (line 1996), for the Danes who suffer from Grendel's attacks are certainly to the south of Hygelac's country. But exactly the same Danes are the "North-Danes" listening in terror to the sound of Grendel screaming (line 783). At line 392 Wulfgar describes Hrothgar as "lord of the East-Danes," but just nine lines earlier Hrothgar himself identifies "us" with "the West-Danes."

The explanation for these apparent contradictions is once again obvious. The Old English poetic line consists of two half-lines, which are linked by alliteration, that is to say, by syllables which begin with the same sound. In the case of North-, South-, East-, and West-Danes, the compass-point word invariably takes alliteration: in every case it links with a syllable in the other half-line. That is what it is there for. And the same goes for *Gar-Dene, Beorht-Dene, Hring-Dene.* They are a poetic convenience. What they "mean" is not much more than, respectively, n-, s-, vowel- (all vowels are allowed to alliterate with each other), w-, g-, b-, h-.

This hardly matters, and translators are usually content to leave the words as they are, even if they appear contradictory. It becomes more difficult when one considers other first-elements of some other compound words. In Old English, the verb *sceþþan* means "to cause harm or injury," while the noun *sceaþa* means someone with those intentions, as in line 4 of the poem. (The word survives in modern English only as the adjective "scathing" —a scathing critique is one which means to hurt.)

It is reasonable, then, if also tautologous, for Grendel to be described as a *hearm-sceaþa* (line 766). He is a *syn-sceaþa* in line 801, and a *man-sceaþa* four times, beginning with line

712. The first elements mean, respectively, "harm," "sin," and "crime" or "guilt": or one might say, see above, they "mean" h-, s-, m-. Should they be differentiated by the translator? And if so, how? The editors of the fourth edition of *Klaeber's Beowulf* (K4 for short, now effectively the poem's authorised version) offer respectively "pernicious enemy," "hostile attacker," "guilty ravager," and no criticism of the new editors, Messrs. Bjork, Fulk and Niles, is here intended: they have thought about the meaning of every single word in the poem, and their glosses are of the greatest value. They are doing what translators have had to do ever since 1815: do their best for the poet, in very different literary circumstances. Nevertheless, I have contented myself with the relatively undifferentiated "evil one," "evil-doer," "malefactor," which I think are closer to the facts of the case.

One might add that the element *sceapa* actually has *eleven* different elements prefixed to it in the poem as a whole, and some of these *do* have particular meaning. The dragon is an *attor-sceapa* at line 2839, which makes perfect sense, as *attor* means "poison" and the dragon-bite is poisonous. At line 707 Grendel, as the word stands in the MS, is described once more as a *syn-sceapa*, but editors have corrected this to *scyn-sceapa*, to improve the line's alliteration, and since a *scynn* or *scinna* is a demon, this too can make sense and add something: K4 "demonic foe," here "monster foe." But on the whole the prefixed elements are vague, or synonymous.

It gets more difficult still when one comes across elements which appear to be, or are, downright inappropriate. The word *sige* means "victory." In Beowulf's confrontation with Unferth, he ends his reply by saying that if Unferth were all that he claims to be, then he, Beowulf, would not need to be there in Heorot: but Grendel has found out that he need have no fear "of your people, the *Sige-Scyldinga*," that is, "the Victory-Scyldings." This sounds very like sarcasm, indeed it sounds like a sneer—"call yourselves victorious, you can't even handle a single monster!" And Beowulf seems to be capable of sarcasm, as by calling Unferth "my friend" right at the start of his speech. But in this particular context sarcasm against the whole nation would seem a dangerous tactic, and contrary to Beowulf's careful courtesy so far. So is the word meant?

There is another example much later in the poem which is easier to evaluate, if not to translate. This comes at line 2204. Here the poet looks on from Beowulf's adventures in Denmark to the sad history of his people, the Geats, and in particular the killing of their king, Heardred, Hygelac's son and Beowulf's cousin, at the hands of the Swedes, when they sought him out *on sigeþeode*, "among his victorious people." But his people at this moment are definitely *not* victorious, they are about to suffer humiliating defeat. This time, though, there is no point in sarcasm: the word *sige* must be used only as a general honorific, and, of course, it alliterates with *gesohtan*, "sought out." So how should one translate it, to get round the evident "loose semantic fit," as I call such cases? The K4 editors, doing their best for the poet once again, suggest "victorious or glorious" people, in this case the latter: you can be glorious without being victorious. But that is not what the word actually means.

One other word which seems similarly discrepant (though there are many to choose from) comes in line 2959. Here the Swedes, initially triumphant in their battle with the Geats, are now falling back, and the banners of Hygelac go forward across the *freoðowong*: literally, the "peace-plain." But it is nothing like a peace-plain. As the poet has just said, it is a *swatswaðu*, a "swathe of blood." So what on earth does he mean? The editors of K4 suggest "field of refuge, fastness"? If so, it is not much of a refuge for the Swedes or their king Ongentheow, who will be killed on it. Elsewhere in the poem, the word *freoðoburh* is also less than clear, and indeed gets a more substantial if tentative explanation from the editors when they gloss it in K4.

One may sum up by saying that, rather oddly, the words in the poem which receive the greatest sonic emphasis are sometimes the ones which carry the least information. They are there to help the poet with the first of his major aims: which is, one might say, *to maintain the beat* and the meter of his poetic lines.

This seems a rather humble aim to us, for our idea of poetry is that its wording should be exact, unexpected, provocative—to paraphrase the Savage in Aldous Huxley's *Brave New World*, who has just been introduced to Shakespeare—words which make you feel like you'd sat on a pin. But we emphasize novelty, originality, surprise: and accordingly we fail to feel the power of reinforcement, familiarity, recognition. And it is this which satisfied the poet's second major aim: *to express the ethos of a social group.*

That social group is, very clearly in the poem, the lord and his armed male retainers, though it might well have been the case that this applied also to what we would call "wannabes"— people who admired that social group and its values, aspired to become members of it or at least to identify or be associated with it. Its ethos is in any case unmistakably expressed by the poem's maxims, which recommend very directly the virtues of generosity (lord to retainers), loyalty (retainers to lord), determination, and family solidarity: with at its firmest Wiglaf's no-exceptions statement, "For every nobleman, death is better than a life of shame."

The ethos shows up as well in the poet's readiness to work in a few lines of a battle-scene: Hrothgar's saddle is mentioned, and right away we get a brief cameo of the play of swords and dead men falling; similarly in Hrothgar's obituary for Æschere we have the foot-soldiers clashing, the helmets being struck. Naturally enough, then, interest is taken in swords: Hrunting, Nægling, the giant sword used to behead Grendel's mother, the sword which sparks murder at the Heathobard court, Hrethel's sword donated to Beowulf, and not least: Wiglaf's sword, *Eanmundes laf*.

However, as one reads though the poem, it is hard to resist the thought that the real icon of the heroic ethos for the poet (and his audience) is the armor, the ring-mail shirt. He has some thirty synonyms for this item, *hringnet*, *beadohrægl*, *fyrdsearo*, *guðbyrne* (etc.), putting some strain on a translator's modern vocabulary, which runs to little more that "war-gear," "battle-dress" (etc.), even with the addition of obsolete expressions, like "corslet," "harness," "panoply."

The poet also has a habit of focusing on some aspect of mail-shirts for no apparent reason: Beowulf and his men arrive at Heorot, and much of the description in lines 320-31 is devoted to their armour, hard, hand-linked, shining, ringing; he starts to speak to Hrothgar, and once again "on him the armor shone, the cunning net stitched by the craft of the smith" (405b-6); the phrase *secg(as) on searwum*, "man/men in armor" is used three times (249, 2200, 2530), the last time somewhat inappositely, as Beowulf is there addressing his companions, who for all their armor will shortly abandon him to the dragon. Even the K4 editors are puzzled by what might be meant by *on frætewum* at line 962—elsewhere the word means "precious things," including armor, but here it refers to Grendel, who in his raid on Heorot has neither (apart from his troll-glove, of which we hear only later). Similarly uncertain is *on searwum* at line 1557—this usually means armor, but here it seems to mean whatever is lying around in the underwater lair. Items left behind by previous victims?

The focus on armor is moreover apparent several times in the narrative in a way which seems obsessive. Both Beowulf and Breca wear their mail in their swimming-contest, though since a mail-shirt weighed some twenty to thirty pounds, and must moreover have been the exact opposite of a wetsuit in terms of heat-retention, this does not make much sense. Later on Beowulf tells Hrothgar not to worry about the disposal of his body: his mailshirt, however, must go back to Hygelac. Still later, the sting of total defeat in the Netherlands is moderated by Beowulf's rescue, not of thirty men, but of thirty mailshirts. Perhaps the strangest remark comes from the man who buries the treasure later found by the dragon. Among the vanished joys he regrets are the hawk and the horse, the now-rusting and unpolished swords and helmets, but at most length (2260b–2262a), "The ringed shirt cannot walk widely (*wide feran*) with the champion, along with the hero." Is this not somehow the wrong way round? Armor here and elsewhere seems to trump people.

There is again a probable explanation. Modern craftsmen reckon that it takes anything up to a thousand hours to make a good mail-shirt, all rings riveted, and that takes no account of the man-hours spent on creating the material, the metal strips to be made into rings. In Anglo-Saxon society such items must have been very rare, and consequently much envied, much admired. If a sword with ivory hilt, golden collar-rings and jewelled pommel was the Rolex of the eighth century, one might say, the top-quality full-length mail-shirt would have been the Ferrari.

The original audience of *Beowulf* liked to hear about them, even if they played little part in the narrative. They were an important part of the poetic vocabulary, of victory and war, of peace and wealth, of rank and nobility, treasure and weapons, all playing their part in the creation of the heroic ethos—even if here and there only loosely related to context. The translator has then not only to find a suitable vocabulary to match the poet's, but also to cover up, as far as possible, any discrepancies or irrelevancies. A large part of what editors do—and once again I must express my gratitude to the three editors of K4—is give translators a lead in the difficult exercise of "doing one's best for the poet": in, I repeat, very much-changed literary circumstances, which have created very different literary expectations.

Having said so much, I would like to say what my intentions have been, and a little of what I hope makes this translation different from many others. Faced with what I call above "loose semantic fit," it is a temptation for translators to respond with a kind of "loose fit" of their own, which I call "translationese": using obsolete or rare words whose meaning is rather vague, thus fuzzing over uncertainty about the original. It affects everybody. I caught myself (faced with the "war-gear" issue mentioned above) using words like "harness" (Shakespearean) and "panoply" (classical Greek). I have taken these out and hope no more have crept in.

Long ago a reviewer said of an earlier volume of mine, containing translations of then little-known Old English poems, that he did not always agree with me about what the poems meant, but at least he always knew what I *thought* they meant. I took this as a compliment and have tried to deserve it again.

One other issue is that all too many translators, I fear, owe their knowledge of Old English to looking words up in the dictionary. This ignores cultural context and affects interpretation. Thus, a great deal of nonsense has been written for many years about words like *wyrd, dom, lof.* Look these up in the dictionary and it will probably tell you "fate," "doom," "praise," creating an image of Anglo-Saxons as gloomy, passive, unrealistic, and, frankly, not too bright—as an undergraduate I was told repeatedly about "the Anglo-Saxon Tragic Vision."

Much of this is our mistake, not theirs. The word "fate" for instance derives from Latin *fari,* "to speak," and it means "what is spoken"—not by us, by some supernatural power which we cannot affect. *Wyrd* on the other hand derives from the verb *weorþan,* "to become, to happen," and it means "what happens, what has happened"—the Old English word for a historian is *wyrd-writere,* someone who writes down what's happened.

When the poet of another Old English poem writes, then, *wyrd bi∂ ful aræd,* the Internet will tell you that this means "Fate is totally inexorable." But it doesn't. It means "what's happened is now fixed," or more briefly, "what's done is done." In many circumstances this certainly is a gloomy thought, but the response to it may well be, not "Gosh, might as well sit down and give up, then!" as the Internet version would have it, but rather, "so suck it up and move on!"

"Fate" looks forward, *wyrd* looks back. Big difference. Interestingly, there is a very parallel semantic development in modern English from the Old English word *gelingan,* which also means "to happen," and from which we get our word "luck"—the sound-change is just like German *Drücke* from *dringen,* both words meaning "press."

It's true, certainly, that sometimes in *Beowulf*, *wyrd* feels like a personification, which sweeps people and peoples away: but note that this is apparent only after it has happened. I have accordingly kept the translation "fate" six times out of twelve, but elsewhere I use "luck," "chance," "what would happen." When Beowulf says to Hrothgar, *Gæð a wyrd swa hio scel* (line 455), meaning obviously that he does not know what will be the result of his fight with Grendel, I translate "Things will always go as they must." When he says (line 572), *Wyrd oft nereð unfægne eorl, þonne his ellen deah*, this seems on the face of it perplexing—how can Fate spare a man who is not doomed? If he's not doomed surely Fate doesn't come into it? I translate, "Luck often spares a man not marked for death, as long as his courage holds." So, you never know your luck, and it may be bad luck or good luck, but you have to keep going anyway. That seems very sensible, good advice, and nothing supernatural about it.

Much the same can be said about *lof*, which causes trouble early in the poem at line 24, *lofdædum*, and in the poem's last word, *lofgeornost*. If we take *lof* to mean "praise" (as it says in the dictionary), then that last word, *lofgeornost*, "most eager for praise," sounds almost critical. The poet has just said that Beowulf was the gentlest, kindest, most loving—did he just do that to flatter his own ego? Did he, like his uncle Hygelac, go raiding to boost his own reputation? No, because *lof* describes a reciprocal relationship, praise from people to lord, generosity from lord to people. So *lofgeornost* is here the latter and there is no contradiction: Beowulf was gentle, kind, loving and gen-erous.

In the same way, at the start of the poem, the poet is not saying that "praiseworthy deeds" are always the road to suc-cess—anyone who thinks that is so has not really noticed the way of the world—it is, much more in line with what the poet has in fact just said, about buying loyalty, and it means, much more realistically, "Among people everywhere, generous deeds will get a man on"—or, one might say, more cynically, "everyone loves a bung." "Bung" is vulgar English for bribe or backhander, so I have not used it in my translation, but the ethos of *Beowulf* is more hard-headed about rewards than people often think—even if the rewards are not expressed in money.

Clarity, cultural context, and a bit of common sense: that's what this translation aims at. I think that's what the poet aimed at too.

Tom Shippey

NOTE ON THE BEOWULF TEXT

Because *Beowulf* is preserved in a single medieval manuscript (London, British Library, Cotton MS Vitellius A.xv), editions of the Old English text of the poem are necessarily based on this manuscript and are consequently identical in the vast majority of cases. There are, however, many minor respects in which editions differ, and at times these differences can create a substantially different experience for the reader. In Howell Chickering's *Beowulf: A Dual-Language Edition*, for instance, the words transmitted in the manuscript as *eotenum* and *eotena* are edited as forms of *eoten* ("giant") and translated as such, with the result that Heremod meets his end "among the giants" (902b), Hildeburh has no need to praise "the faith of the giants" (1072a), and Hengest's hall is to be shared "with the sons of giants" (1088a).[1] Other editors construe *eotenum* and *eotena* as forms of the Jutish ethnonym, and they are surely right to do so, since sources external to *Beowulf* provide good reasons to expect Jutes to appear in precisely those places where Chickering finds giants (see §20 and §24 in the present book's commentary). The differences between *Beowulf* editions arise principally due to manuscript readings that are defective or ambiguous. In most cases, there are straightforward and satisfactory solutions to the problems that the manuscript

43

presents, but in certain cases, there is no obvious solution. Compromises must be made, and the text must continuously be evaluated on a case-by-case basis.

The principles of this compromise-oriented approach to the textual criticism of *Beowulf* are well articulated by R. D. Fulk in his exposition of the principles governing the treatment of the text in Frederick Klaeber's edition of *Beowulf*.[2] This approach proceeds from the recognition that the extant manuscript of *Beowulf* is a copy of a copy and thus a layered text, which preserves archaic and Anglian spellings within a textual matrix otherwise conforming to the artificial Late West Saxon written standard. The editor, recognizing the futility of reconstructing the original archetype or achieving absolute consistency with respect to orthography, aims merely to correct substantive errors that scribes have committed in the course of the poem's transmission. The identification of substantive errors is, of course, a matter of editorial judgment. On account of its sound judgment and magisterial apparatus, Klaeber's edition became the standard scholarly edition for much of the twentieth century, and it remains the standard edition in the twenty-first century on account of the revised (fourth) edition that Fulk produced in collaboration with Robert E. Bjork and John D. Niles.[3] The text of *Beowulf* printed in the present edition remains firmly within the Klaeberian tradition. Besides the exceptions indicated below, we follow the text of the fourth edition in nearly all places and offer no further comment on its emendations. Readers interested in the errors requiring emendation can learn more about them in the commentary of *Klaeber's Beowulf* or in the present editor's *Transmission of Beowulf* (henceforth *TOB*).[4] Our relatively few departures from *Klaeber's Beowulf* are enumerated and justified below.

l. 6a: MS *eorl* emended to *Eorle*
The manuscript reading (*eorl*) is manifestly defective, as it generates metrical and grammatical problems. Editors conventionally resolve these problems by emending *eorl* to *eorlas* ("warriors"). We prefer to emend it to *Eorle* and construe it as a form of the Herulian ethnonym for reasons made clear in recent scholarship, especially Michael D. C. Drout and Nelson Goering, "The Emendation *Eorle* (Heruli) in *Beowulf*, Line 6a: Setting the Poem in 'The Named Lands of the North,'" *Modern Philology* 117 (2020): 285–300; see also Tom Shippey, *Beowulf and the North before the Vikings* (Leeds: Arc Humanities Press, 2022), 23–24.

l. 467b: MS *Heregār* emended to *Heorogār*
A scribe has trivialized the name Heorogar (cf. *Heorogār* in l. 61a and *Hiorogār* in l. 2158b) by writing its first element (*heoro*, "sword") as if it were the more common element *here* ("army"). The two elements are distinct, however, and the distinction is significant: the repeated use of the *heoro* element in the names of Heorogar and his son Heoroweard reflects their kinship. For further discussion, see Neidorf, *TOB*, 166.

ll. 902b, 1145a: MS *eotenum* emended to *Ēotum*
The dative plural form of the Jutish ethnonym was apparently altered in the course of transmission to the dative plural form of *eoten* ("giant"). The editors of *Klaeber's Beowulf* retain the manuscript readings but register their recognition of the Jutish ethnonym by capitalizing them. We emend to *Ēotum* instead. For further discussion, see Neidorf, *TOB*, §103, but see also Dennis Cronan, "*Eotena, Eotenum* 'Jutes' in the Finnsburg Episode in *Beowulf*," *Modern Philology* 116 (2018): 1–19.

ll. 1418b, 1638b, 1721b: MS *weorc* emended to *wærc*

Anglian *wærc* ("pain") is consistently transmitted as West Saxon *weorc* ("labor"). Since these are two distinct words, it seems best to distinguish them by emending *weorc* to *wærc*. This is a question of lexical identity rather than phonological regularity. For further discussion, see Neidorf, *TOB*, §60; and R. D. Fulk, "Old English *weorc*: Where Does It Hurt? South of the Thames," *ANQ* 17 (2004): 6–12.

l. 1537a: MS *eaxle* emended to *feaxe*

Beowulf seizes Grendel's mother not by the shoulder (*eaxle*, the manuscript reading) but by the hair (*feaxe*). The emendation is encouraged not only by the line's alliteration but also by the sense of the off-verse (*nalas for fæhðe mearn*), which must mean that Beowulf "did not regret the transgression" he committed by resorting in desperation to the disreputable tactic of hair-pulling. For further discussion, see Neidorf, *TOB*, §82; and E. G. Stanley, "Did Beowulf Commit 'Feaxfeng' against Grendel's Mother?," *Notes and Queries* 23 (1976): 339–40.

l. 1710a: MS *eaforum* emended to *eafora*

The transmitted reading (*eaforum Ecgwelan*) apparently refers to the Danes as the "sons of Ecgwela," a name otherwise unknown in Danish legendary tradition. Due to the improbability that the Danes would be so designated, it is likely that the original phrase was singular (*eafora*) and referred instead to Heremod. Scribal confusions of *a* and *u* are relatively common. For further discussion, see Neidorf, *TOB*, §53.

l. 1809b: MS *lēanes* emended to *lǣnes*

Beowulf thanks Unferth for the "loan" (*lǣn*) of his sword rather than the "reward" (*lean*, the transmitted reading) of it. Emendation therefore appears justified. The emendation indicates that although *lǣn* is normally a feminine noun, it was originally a neuter noun like all of its Germanic cognates. For further discussion, see Neidorf, *TOB*, §50.

l. 407: MS *wæs* emended to *wes*
l. 411b: MS *þæs* emended to *þes*
l. 1171b: MS *spræc* emended to *sprec*
In these three cases, the scribal substitution of *æ* for *e* alters the grammar of the sentence: it changes imperative *wes* to preterit *wæs*, nominative *þes* to genitive *þæs*, and imperative *sprec* to preterit *spræc*. In all three cases, it is preferable to emend and reverse the scribal alteration, thereby registering the presence of error and clarifying the grammar of the text. For further discussion, see Neidorf, *TOB*, §65.

l. 63a MS *Heaðo-Scilfingas* emended to *Heaðo-Scilfinges*
l. 519a: MS *Heaþo-Rǣmes* emended to *Heaþo-Rǣmas*
l. 2453a: MS *yrfeweardas* emended to *yrfeweardes*
l. 2921a: MS *Merewīoingas* emended to *Merewīoinges*
Confusion of *-as* and *-es* desinences is evident in these four cases. Editors conventionally refrain from emending away the confusion in the belief that it provides a genuine reflection of scribal pronunciation. This belief now seems rather improbable, however, and the extreme rarity of the confusion suggests, rather, that in all four we are dealing with scribal errors that have little to do with the spoken Old English. For further discussion, see Neidorf, *TOB*, §111.

NOTES

[1] Howell D. Chickering, Jr., ed. and trans., *Beowulf: A Dual-Language Edition*, 2nd ed. (New York: Anchor Books, 2006).

[2] R. D. Fulk, "The Textual Criticism of Frederick Klaeber's *Beowulf*," in *Constructing Nations, Re-constructing Myths: Essays in Honour of T. A. Shippey*, ed. Andrew Wawn with Graham Johnson and John Walter (Turnhout: Brepols, 2007), 131–153. See also R. D. Fulk, "Inductive Methods in the Textual Criticism of Old English Verse," *Medievalia et Humanistica* 23 (1996): 1–24.

[3] R. D. Fulk, Robert E. Bjork, and John D. Niles, ed., *Klaeber's Beowulf and The Fight at Finnsburg*, 4th ed. (Toronto: University of Toronto Press, 2008). For a review that places this edition in the context of the history of *Beowulf* studies, see Tom Shippey, "Review Article: Klaeber's *Beowulf* Eighty Years On: A Triumph for a Triumvirate," *Journal of English and Germanic Philology* 108 (2009): 360–376.

[4] Leonard Neidorf, *The Transmission of Beowulf: Language, Culture, and Scribal Behavior* (Ithaca, NY: Cornell University Press, 2017). On the early *Beowulf* scholars responsible for most of the emendations adopted in recent editions, see Birte Kelly, "The Formative Stages of *Beowulf* Textual Scholarship: Part I," *Anglo–Saxon England* 11 (1982): 247–274; and Kelly, "The Formative Stages of *Beowulf* Textual Scholarship: Part II," *Anglo–Saxon England* 12 (1983): 239–275.

BEOWULF

Hwæt, wē Gār-Dena   in ġeārdagum,
þēodcyninga   þrym ġefrūnon,
hū ðā æþelingas   ellen fremedon.
Oft Scyld Scēfing   sceaþena þrēatum,
5 monegum mǣġþum   meodosetla oftēah,
eġsode Eorle,   syððan ǣrest wearð
fēasceaft funden.   Hē þæs frōfre ġebād:
wēox under wolcnum,   weorðmyndum þāh,
oð þæt him ǣġhwylċ   þāra ymbsittendra
10 ofer hronrāde   hȳran scolde,
gomban ġyldan.   Þæt wæs gōd cyning.
Ðǣm eafera wæs   æfter cenned
ġeong in ġeardum,   þone God sende
folce tō frōfre;   fyrenðearfe onġeat —
15 þæt hīe ǣr drugon   aldor(l)ēase
lange hwīle.   Him þæs līffrēa,
wuldres wealdend   woroldāre forġeaf:
Bēow wæs brēme   — blǣd wīde sprang —
Scyldes eafera   Scedelandum in.
20 Swā sceal ġe(ong) guma   gōde ġewyrċean,
fromum feohġiftum   on fæder (bea)rme,
þæt hine on ylde   eft ġewuniġen
wilġesīþas,   þonne wīġ cume,
lēode ġelǣsten;   lofdǣdum sceal
25 in mǣġþa ġehwǣre   man ġeþēon.

BEOWULF

Well, we have heard of the power of the Spear-Dane kings,
how in days gone by they did great deeds.
   Shield-with-the-Sheaf, he often stripped away
the mead-benches from many tribes,
from hosts of enemies, struck fear into the Heruls,
since he was first picked up, a naked foundling.
He got comfort for that, throve beneath the sky,
gained prestige, grew in reputation,
until all the peoples round about him,
across the sea-roads, had to obey him,
give him tribute. He was a good king.
To him in time a child was born,
a young one for his home, sent by God
as relief for his people. God saw the dire need
they had endured so long without a king.
So the Lord of Life, the Ruler of Glory
granted them to have success in this world.
Shield's son Barley became famous,
his reputation spread wide in the lands of the North.
That's how a young man should make a good start,
by giving splendid gifts while his father is alive,
so that when he's older and war comes on him,
he has willing companions there to support him,
stand by their prince. Among people everywhere
generous deeds will get a man on.

Him ðā Scyld ġewāt   tō ġescæphwīle
felahrōr fēran   on frēan wǣre.
Hī hyne þā ætbǣron   tō brimes faroðe,
swǣse ġesīþas,   swā hē selfa bæd
30 þenden wordum wēold.   Wine Scyldinga,
lēof landfruma   lange āhte —
þǣr æt hȳðe stōd,   hrinġedstefna
īsiġ ond ūtfūs —   æþelinges fær;
ālēdon þā   lēofne þēoden,
35 bēaga bryttan   on bearm scipes,
mǣrne be mæste.   Þǣr wæs mādma fela
of feorwegum   frætwa ġelǣded.
Ne hȳrde iċ cȳmlicor   ċēol ġeġyrwan
hildewǣpnum   ond heaðowǣdum,
40 billum ond byrnum;   him on bearme lǣġ
mādma mæniġo,   þā him mid scoldon
on flōdes ǣht   feor ġewītan.
Nalæs hī hine lǣssan   lācum tēodan,
þēodġestrēonum,   þonne þā dydon
45 þē hine æt frumsceafte   forð onsendon
ǣnne ofer ȳðe   umborwesende.
Þā ġȳt hīe him āsetton   seġen gy(l)denne
hēah ofer hēafod,   lēton holm beran,
ġēafon on gārsecg;   him wæs ġeōmor sefa,
50 murnende mōd.   Men ne cunnon
secgan tō sōðe,   selerǣdende,
hæleð under heofenum,   hwā þǣm hlæste onfēng.

Ðā wæs on burgum   Bēow Scyldinga,
lēof lēodcyning   longe þrāge
55 folcum ġefrǣġe   — fæder ellor hwearf,
aldor of earde —   oþ þæt him eft onwōc
hēah Healfdene;   hēold þenden lifde
gamol ond gūðrēouw   glæde Scyldingas.
Ðǣm fēower bearn   forðġerīmed

At his appointed time Shield passed on,
a very old man, into the Lord's keeping.
As he had ordered while he held rule,
his loyal companions carried him to the shore.
The friend of the Scyldings, beloved leader of the land,
had long owned a vessel fit for a prince –
the ring-prowed ship stood ice-rimed in the harbor,
ready to sail. They placed their dear lord,
famous ring-divider, in the hull of the ship,
beside the mast. Many treasures and valuables
from far-off lands were laid down there.
I have heard of no ship more splendidly loaded
with battle-dress and weapons of war,
with swords and armor. Many precious things
lay on his breast, to go far with him
into the power of the sea. They certainly did not provide him
with fewer offerings from the nation's wealth
than those ones did who first sent him out
in the beginning, just an infant,
alone over the waves. And then they raised
a golden ensign, high over his head,
let the waves take him, gave him to the ocean.
Their minds were sad, they mourned in their hearts.
No-one can say for sure, not councillors in hall,
not heroes under the sky, who would receive that cargo.

Then Barley, son of Shield, ruled the homesteads
once his father had passed away from the world.
He was a popular king, dear to his people,
until in his turn Healfdene the high
came to succeed him. He ruled lifelong
old and fierce, the fortunate Scyldings.
To him in their turn four children were born

60 in worold wōcun,   weoroda rǣswa[n],
Heorogār ond Hrōðgār   ond Hālga til;
hȳrde iċ þæt [. . . . .   wæs On]elan cwēn,
Heaðo-Scilfinges   healsġebedda.

    Þā wæs Hrōðgāre   herespēd ġyfen,
65 wīġes weorðmynd,   þæt him his winemāgas
ġeorne hȳrdon,   oðð þæt sēo ġeogoð ġewēox,
magodriht miċel.   Him on mōd bearn
þæt healreċed   hātan wolde,
medoærn miċel   men ġewyrċean
70 þon[n]e yldo bearn   ǣfre ġefrūnon,
ond þǣr on innan   eall ġedǣlan
ġeongum ond ealdum   swylċ him God sealde,
būton folcscare   ond feorum gumena.
Ðā iċ wīde ġefræġn   weorc ġebannan
75 maniġre mǣġþe   ġeond þisne middanġeard,
folcstede frætwan.   Him on fyrste ġelomp,
ǣdre mid yldum,   þæt hit wearð eal ġearo,
healærna mǣst;   scōp him Heort naman
sē þe his wordes ġeweald   wīde hæfde.
80 Hē bēot ne ālēh: bēagas dǣlde,
sinċ æt symle.   Sele hlīfade
hēah ond hornġēap;   heaðowylma bād,
lāðan līġes —   ne wæs hit lenġe þā ġēn
þæt se ecghete   āþumswēoran
85 æfter wælnīðe   wæcnan scolde.
    Ðā se ellengǣst   earfoðlīċe
þrāge ġeþolode,   sē þe in þȳstrum bād,
þæt hē dōgora ġehwām   drēam ġehȳrde
hlūdne in healle.   Þǣr wæs hearpan swēġ,
90 swutol sang scopes.   Sæġde sē þe cūþe
frumsceaft fīra   feorran reċċan,
cwæð þæt se ælmihtiga   eorðan worh(te),
wlitebeorhtne wang,   swā wæter bebūgeð,
ġesette siġehrēþiġ   sunnan ond mōnan,

into the world, leaders of war-bands,
Heorogar and Hrothgar and Halga the good.
I was told that Yrse was Onela's queen,
consort of the warlike Scylfing.
                                     Success in battle
was given to Hrothgar, glory in war,
so that friends and family obeyed him eagerly,
till the young men grew up to be a great troop of retainers.
It came into his mind to have a mead-hall built,
bigger than the children of men had ever heard of,
and from it he would share out whatever God sent him
to young and old alike, everything except
the common land and human lives.
I heard that across middle-earth there were many tribes
set to work, to make splendid the great seat of the people.
It happened quickly, as time goes among men,
that it was all ready, the greatest of halls.
He whose word ruled widely gave it the name
of Heorot, Staghall. Nor did he belie his word,
he gave out rings and treasure at the feast.
The hall towered, high and wide-gabled.
It was waiting for the fire of war, hateful flame –
but not for a long time yet would be woken
after deadly spite, the armed hatred
between father and daughter's husband.
    Then the monster who waited in darkness
suffered torment, constant pain,
hard to bear, hearing every day
loud merriment in hall – the sound of the harp,
the poet's sweet song. He knew how to tell
of the origin of us all in far-off days.
He said that the Almighty created the Earth,
the plain of bright beauty, beringed by water.

95   lēoman tō lēohte   landbūendum,
      ond ġefrætwade   foldan scēatas
      leomum ond lēafum,   līf ēac ġesceōp
      cynna ġehwylcum   þāra ðe cwice hwyrfaþ.
      Swā ðā drihtguman   drēamum lifdon,
100 ēadiġlīċe,   oð ðæt ān ongan
      fyrene fre(m)man   fēond on helle;
      wæs se grimma gǣst   Grendel hāten,
      mǣre mearcstapa,   sē þe mōras hēold,
      fen ond fæsten;   fīfęlcynnes eard
105 wonsǣlī wer   weardode hwīle,
      siþðan him scyppen   forscrifen hæfde
      in Cāines cynne —   þone cwealm ġewræc
      ēċe drihten,   þæs þe hē Ābel slōg;
      ne ġefeah hē þǣre fǣhðe,   ac hē hine feor forwræc,
110 metod for þȳ māne   mancynne fram.
      Þanon untȳdras   ealle onwōcon,
      eotenas ond ylfe   ond orcnēas,
      swylċe ġī(ga)ntas,   þā wið Gode wunnon
      lange þrāge;   hē him ðæs lēan forġeald.

115   Ġewāt ðā nēosian,   syþðan niht becōm,
      hēan hūses,   hū hit Hring-Dene
      æfter bēorþeġe   ġebūn hæfdon.
      Fand þā ðǣr inne   æþelinga ġedriht
      swefan æfter symble;   sorge ne cūðon,
120 wonsceaft wera.   Wiht unhǣlo,
      grim ond grǣdiġ,   ġearo sōna wæs,
      rēoc ond rēþe,   ond on ræste ġenam
      þrītiġ þeġna;   þanon eft ġewāt
      hūðe hrēmiġ   tō hām faran,
125 mid þǣre wælfylle   wīca nēosan.
      Ðā wæs on ūhtan   mid ǣrdæġe
      Grendles gūðcræft   gumum undyrne;
      þā wæs æfter wiste   wōp up āhafen,

Triumphant, He set in place the Sun and Moon
as lights for all that live on Earth,
made fair Earth's surface with leaves and trees,
created life for all that live and move.
So the warriors lived in happiness and prosperity –
until a fiend from Hell began to do ill deeds.
The grim spirit was called Grendel,
famous prowler of the borderland,
ruling the marshes, the fen-fastness.
For a long time he had lived in the land
of the monster-races, miserable creature,
ever since the Creator had condemned him
among the race of Cain – the eternal Lord
avenged Cain's crime, the murder of Abel.
Cain got no joy from that enmity,
the Lord exiled him for that ill deed
far from humanity. From him awoke
all unnatural creatures, the ogres and elves,
the walking-dead, and the giants as well,
who fought against God for many years:
He paid them their reward for it.

   When night came, then, Grendel made his way
to seek the high hall, how the Ring-Danes
had settled into it after their beer-drinking.
Inside he found there a troop of nobles,
sleeping after their banquet – they did not know sorrow,
sad human condition. The uncanny creature,
grim and greedy, wasted no time
but, cruel and savage, he snatched thirty thanes
from their beds, went back home
exulting in his prey, reaching his lair
with his fill of the dead.
               Then at daybreak
Grendel's skill in battle became obvious to all.

micel morgenswēġ.   Mǣre þēoden,
130 æþeling ǣrgōd,   unblīðe sæt,
þolode ðrȳðswȳð,   þeġnsorge drēah,
syðþan hīe þæs lāðan   lāst scēawedon,
werġan gāstes;   wæs þæt ġewin tō strang,
lāð ond longsum.   Næs hit lengra fyrst,
135 ac ymb āne niht   eft ġefremede
morðbeala māre,   ond nō mearn fore,
fǣhðe ond fyrene;   wæs tō fæst on þām.
Þā wæs ēaðfynde   þē him elles hwǣr
ġerūmlicor   ræste [sōhte],
140 bed æfter būrum,   ðā him ġebēacnod wæs,
ġesæġd sōðlīċe   sweotolan tācne
healðeġnes hete;   hēold hyne syðþan
fyr ond fæstor   sē þǣm fēonde ætwand.
Swā rīxode   ond wið rihte wan,
145 āna wið eallum,   oð þæt īdel stōd
hūsa sēlest.   Wæs sēo hwīl micel:
twelf wintra tīd   torn ġeþolode
wine Scyldinga,   wēana ġehwelcne,
sīdra sorga.   Forðām [ġesȳne] wearð
150 ylda bearnum,   undyrne cūð
ġyddum ġeōmore   þætte Grendel wan
hwīle wið Hrōþgār,   hetenīðas wæġ,
fyrene ond fǣhðe   fela missera,
singāle sæce;   sibbe ne wolde
155 wið manna hwone   mæġenes Deniġa,
feorhbealo feorran,   fēa þingian,
nē þǣr nǣniġ witena   wēnan þorfte
beorhtre bōte   tō banan folmum,
(ac se) æġlǣċa   ēhtende wæs,
160 deorc dēaþscua,   duguþe ond ġeogoþe,
seomade ond syrede;   sinnihte hēold,
mistiġe mōras;   men ne cunnon
hwyder helrūnan   hwyrftum scrīþað.

Then lamentation was raised after the feasting,
great outcry in the morning. Once they could see
the track of the evil one, the cursed spirit,
the good king, famous lord, sat unhappily, felt bitter pain,
sorrow for his thanes. That strife was too strong,
too hateful, too lasting. Nor was it long,
before the next night Grendel did more murders,
more crimes, remorseless, too rooted in hostility.
Then it was easy to see who chose to sleep
further away, make their beds in the out-buildings,
once they had been shown, by sure token,
the hatred of the visitor who haunted the hall.
To escape the fiend, the further the better.
So one against all fought against right
until the best of buildings stood empty.
It lasted a long time. The lord of the Scyldings
suffered torment for twelve winters,
much pain, many sorrows, because to all children of men,
it was clear, known for certain, through sad songs,
that Grendel was for long at war with Hrothgar,
waged hatred and spite for many seasons,
never-ending warfare, enmity and evil.
He did not want a deal with any of the Danes,
no removal of the deadly plague,
nor any pay-off through negotiation,
nor did any counsellor have cause to expect
any better cure from the hands of the killer,
but the dark death-shadow dogged young and old,
with plot and ambush. In perpetual night
he ruled misty marshlands. No man can know
where these hell-hags hold their circuits.

Swā fela fyrena   fēond mancynnes,
165 atol āngenġea   oft ġefremede,
heardra hȳnða;   Heorot eardode,
sinċfāge sel   sweartum nihtum.
Nō hē þone ġifstōl   grētan mōste,
māþðum for metode,   nē his myne wisse.
170 Þæt wæs wræc miċel   wine Scyldinga,
mōdes brecða.   Moniġ oft ġesæt,
rīċe tō rūne;   ræd eahtedon,
hwæt swīðferhðum   sēlest wære
wið færgryrum   tō ġefremmanne.
175 Hwīlum hīe ġehēton   æt *hæ*rgtrafum
wīġweorþunga,   wordum bædon
þæt him gāstbona   ġēoce ġefremede
wið þēodþrēaum.   Swylċ wæs þēaw hyra,
hæþenra hyht;   helle ġemundon
180 in mōdsefan,   metod hīe ne cūþon,
dæda dēmend,   ne wiston hīe drihten God,
nē hīe hūru heofena helm   herian ne cūþon,
wuldres waldend.   Wā bið þæm ðe sceal
þurh slīðne nīð   sāwle bescūfan
185 in fȳres fæþm,   frōfre ne wēnan,
wihte ġewendan;   wēl bið þæm þe mōt
æfter dēaðdæġe   drihten sēċean
ond tō fæder fæþmum   freoðo wilnian.

Swā ðā mælċeare   maga Healfdenes
190 singāla sēað;   ne mihte snotọr hæleð
wēan onwendan;   wæs þæt ġewin tō swȳð,
lāþ ond longsum,   þē on ðā lēode becōm,
nȳdwracu nīþgrim,   nihtbealwa mæst.
Þæt fram hām ġefræġn   Hiġelāces þeġn
195 gōd mid Ġēatum,   Grendles dæda;
sē wæs moncynnes   mæġenes strenġest
on þæm dæġe   þysses līfes,

So for many years the enemy of mankind,
the terrible lone-walker committed many crimes,
imposed deep humiliation. In the dark night
he haunted Staghall, shining with treasure.
The Lord would not let him go up to the gift-throne,
nor did he know the favor of the Lord.
That was a great grief for the lord of the Scyldings,
a mental torment. Often many wise ones
sat in council, considered plans,
what would be best for the brave ones to do
against the sudden terror. Sometimes they sacrificed
at shrines to pagan idols, prayed the soul-slayer
for help in this calamity. Such was their custom,
hope of the heathens. They remembered Hell
in their hearts, did not know the Ruler, Judge of deeds,
knew nothing of the Lord God, had no way to praise
the Guardian of Heaven, the Ruler of Glory.
Woe to him who must through terrible malice
deliver his soul into the embrace of fire,
without hope of relief, any change at all.
Well for him who after his death
may be allowed to seek out the Lord
and ask for peace in the Father's embrace.

So the son of Healfdene seethed internally
over the trouble of the time, not to be turned aside
by the wise man. The woe and the strife
which had struck his people was too severe, too hateful,
too long-lasting, greatest of night-evils,
fierce persecution forced by spite.
The thane of Hygelac, good man of the Geats,
heard at his home of Grendel's deeds.
Of all men in the world living at that time,

æþele ond ēacen.   Hēt him ȳðlidan
gōdne ġeġyrwan;   cwæð, hē gūðcyning
200 ofer swanrāde   sēċean wolde,
mǣrne þēoden,   þā him wæs manna þearf.
Ðone sīðfæt him   snotere ċeorlas
lȳthwōn lōgon,   þēah hē him lēof wǣre;
hwetton hiġe(r)ōfne,   hǣl scēawedon.
205 Hæfde se gōda   Ġēata lēoda
cempan ġecorone,   þāra þe hē cēnoste
findan mihte.   Fīftȳna sum
sundwudu sōhte;   secg wīsade,
lagucræftiġ mon   landġemyrċu.
210 Fyrst forð ġewāt;   flota wæs on ȳðum,
bāt under beorge.   Beornas ġearwe
on stefn stigon.   Strēamas wundon,
sund wið sande.   Secgas bǣron
on bearm nacan   beorhte frætwe,
215 gūðsearo ġeatoliċ;   guman ūt scufon,
weras on wilsīð   wudu bundenne.
Ġewāt þā ofer wǣġholm   winde ġefȳsed
flota fāmīheals   fugle ġelīcost,
oð þæt ymb āntīd   ōþres dōgọres
220 wundenstefna   ġewaden hæfde,
þæt ðā līðende   land ġesāwon,
brimclifu blīcan,   beorgas stēape,
sīde sǣnæssas;   þā wæs sund liden,
eoletes æt ende.   Þanon up hraðe
225 Wedera lēode   on wang stigon,
sǣwudu sǣldon,   syrċan hrysedon,
gūðġewǣdo;   Gode þancedon
þæs þe him ȳþlāde   ēaðe wurdon.
      Þā of wealle ġeseah   weard Scildinga,
230 sē þe holmclifu   healdan scolde,
beran ofer bolcan   beorhte randas,
fyrdsearu fūslicụ;   hine fyrwyt bræc

he was the strongest, noble and mighty.
He ordered a good ship to be made ready,
vowed to seek the war-king over the swans' road,
now the famous prince had need of men.
Though he was dear to them, the wise councillors
did not dissuade him. They took the omens,
encouraged the valiant one. From the Geats
he chose the boldest champions he could find,
with fourteen others he made for the ship,
an experienced sailor showed the landmarks.
Time passed, the ship waited on the water,
at the shoreline. The warriors readily
went aboard, where currents met,
sea against sand, stored in the hold
shining equipment, splendid war-gear.
Glad of their expedition, the men pushed out
their high-prowed vessel. Impelled by the wind,
with foaming bow-wave, the ship sped like a bird
over the sea, until, on time next day,
the ring-prowed ship had sped so far
that the travellers saw land: steep hills, broad headlands,
sea-cliffs shining. The sea was crossed,
their journey was over. Quickly the Weders
disembarked on shore, shook out their mail-shirts,
their battle-armor, tied up the boat,
thanked God that their crossing had been an easy one.
    The Scylding warden, whose job it was
to guard the sea-cliffs, saw from his rampart
men bearing bright shields and ready war-gear
across the gang-plank. He was on the alert,

mōdġehyġdum   hwæt þā men wǣron.

    Ġewāt him þā tō waroðe   wicge rīdan

235 þeġn Hrōðgāres,   þrymmum cwehte

mæġenwudu mundum,   meþelwordum fræġn:

'Hwæt syndon ġē   searohæbbendra,

byrnum werede,   þē þus brontne ċēol

ofer lagustrǣte   lǣdan cwōmon,

240 hider ofer holmas?   [Iċ hwī]le wæs

endesǣta,   ǣġwearde hēold,

þē on land Dena   lāðra nǣniġ

mid scipherġe   sceðþan ne meahte.

Nō hēr cūðlicor   cuman ongunnon

245 lindhæbbende,   nē ġē lēafnesword

gūðfremmendra   ġearwe ne wisson,

māga ġemēdu.   Nǣfre iċ māran ġeseah

eorla ofer eorþan   ðonne is ēower sum,

secg on searwum;   nis þæt seldguma,

250 wǣpnum ġeweorðad,   næfne him his wlite lēoge,

ǣnliċ ansȳn.   Nū iċ ēower sceal

frumcyn witan,   ǣr ġē fyr heonan

lēasscēaweras   on land Dena

furþur fēran.   Nū ġē feorbūend,

255 merelīðende,   mīn[n]e ġehȳrað

ānfealdne ġeþōht: ofost is sēlest

tō ġecȳðanne   hwanan ēowre cyme syndon.'

    Him se yldesta   andswarode,

werodes wīsa,   wordhord onlēac:

260 'Wē synt gumcynnes   Ġēata lēode

ond Hiġelāces   heorðġenēatas.

Wæs mīn fæder   folcum ġecȳþed,

æþele ordfruma,   Ecgþēow hāten;

ġebād wintra worn,   ǣr hē on weġ hwurfe,

265 gamol of ġeardum;   hine ġearwe ġeman

witena wēlhwylċ   wīde ġeond eorþan.

he had to know what these men were.
The thane of Hrothgar rode down to the shore,
brandished a mighty spear, spoke words of challenge:
"What warriors are you, armored in mail-shirts,
who have brought your proud ship across the sea-road,
from over the waves? I have long been
the border-guard, kept watch on the sea,
so that no enemies, no sea-raiders
can do any harm to the land of the Danes.
No shield-warriors have come more brazenly,
nor have you asked leave from the war-leaders,
consent from the kinsmen. One of you, in all his gear,
is the largest on earth that I have ever seen.
He is no kitchen-boy, kitted out with fine armor –
unless his looks belie him, his imposing appearance.
Now I need to know what people you belong to,
before you go any further as spies into Denmark.
Listen, seafarers, strangers from afar, to what I tell you straight:
Best you tell me quickly where you come from."

   The eldest of them gave him answer,
the war-band's leader unlocked his store of words:
"We are men of the race of the Geatish people,
and belong to Hygelac's household guard.
My father was a great champion. He was called Ecgtheow,
well-known to all peoples. He lived many winters
before in old age from his homestead
he passed away. Many wise men
all over the world well remember him.

65

Wē þurh holdne hiġe   hlāford þīnne,
sunu Healfdenes   sēċean cwōmon,
lēodġebyrġean.   Wes þū ūs lārena gōd.
270 Habbað wē tō þǣm mǣran   miċel ǣrende
Deniġa frēan.   Ne sceal þǣr dyrne sum
wesan, þæs iċ wēne: þū wāst, ġif hit is
swā wē sōþlīċe   secgan hȳrdon,
þæt mid Scyldingum   sceaðona iċ nāt hwylċ,
275 dēogol dǣdhata   deorcum nihtum
ēaweð þurh eġsan   uncūðne nīð,
hȳnðu ond hrāfyl.   Iċ þæs Hrōðgār mæġ
þurh rūmne sefan   rǣd ġelǣran
hū hē frōd ond gōd   fēond oferswȳðeþ —
280 ġyf him edwenden   ǣfre scolde
bealuwa bisigu,   bōt eft cuman —
ond þā ċearwylmas   cōlran wurðaþ;
oððe ā syþðan   earfoðþrāge,
þrēanȳd þolað   þenden þǣr wunað
285 on hēahstede   hūsa sēlest.'
    Weard maþelode   ðǣr on wicge sæt,
ombeht unforht: 'Ǣġhwæþres sceal
scearp scyldwiga   ġescād witan,
worda ond worca,   sē þe wēl þenċeð.
290 Iċ þæt ġehȳre,   þæt þis is hold weorod
frēan Scyldinga.   Ġewītaþ forð beran
wǣpen ond ġewǣdu;   iċ ēow wīsiġe.
Swylċe iċ maguþeġnas   mīne hāte
wið fēonda ġehwone   flotan ēowerne,
295 nīwtyrwydne   nacan on sande
ārum healdan,   oþ ðæt eft byreð
ofer lagustrēamas   lēofne mannan
wudu wundenhals   tō Wedermearce,
gōdfremmendra   swylcum ġifeþe bið
300 þæt þone hilderǣs   hāl ġedīġeð.'
    Ġewiton him þā fēran;   flota stille bād,

We have come to seek your lord, son of Healfdene,
protector of the people, with peaceful intentions.
Give us good advice. We are here on grave errand
to the lord of the Danes, in no way a dark one,
so I believe. But you will know,
if things are as we honestly have heard it said –
that there is a scourge among the Scyldings.
In the dark nights some secret malefactor
is causing terror, hostility unheard of,
shame and slaughter. I can show Hrothgar
a plan I have devised, how he in his wisdom
and benevolence can overcome his enemy –
if a cure and change can ever be found
for his turmoil of griefs, his surge of sorrows
ever become cool – or else he must suffer
this time of troubles ever after,
this awful emergency, as long as he lives
in his high seat, the best of halls."
    The coastguard spoke, a fearless officer,
as he sat there upon his steed.
"A shield-warrior with his wits about him
must know how to decide, from deeds or from words.
What I have heard is that this war-band
comes as friends to the lord of the Danes.
Carry on with your armor and your weapons.
I will show you the way. I will also
tell my companions to guard against enemies
your new-tarred boat there on the sand,
take good care of it, until the ring-prowed ship
carries its crew back across the sea-currents
to Wedermark – those of the warlike ones
to whom it is given to survive the battle."
    They moved off. The broad-beamed ship

seomode on sāle   sīdfæþmed scip,
on ancre fæst;   eoforlīċ scionon
ofer hlēorber[g]an   ġehroden golde,
305 fāh ond fȳrheard;   ferhwearde hēold
gūþmōd grimmon.   Guman ōnetton,
sigon ætsomne,   oþ þæt hȳ [s]æl timbred
ġeatoliċ ond goldfāh   onġyton mihton;
þæt wæs foremǣrost   foldbūendum
310 reċeda under roderum,   on þǣm se rīċa bād;
līxte se lēoma   ofer landa fela.
Him þā hildedēor   [h]of mōdiġra
torht ġetǣhte,   þæt hīe him tō mihton
ġeġnum gangan;   gūðbeorna sum
315 wicg ġewende,   word æfter cwæð:
'Mǣl is mē tō fēran;   fæder alwalda
mid ārstafum   ēowiċ ġehealde
sīða ġesunde.   Iċ tō sǣ wille,
wið wrāð werod   wearde healdan.'

320   Strǣt wæs stānfāh,   stīġ wīsode
gumum ætgædere.   Gūðbyrne scān
heard hondlocen;   hrinġīren scīr
song in searwum.   Þā hīe tō sele furðum
in hyra gryreġeatwum   gangan cwōmon,
325 setton sǣmēþe   sīde scyldas,
rondas reġnhearde   wið þæs reċedes weal;
bugon þā tō benċe.   Byrnan hringdon,
gūðsearo gumena;   gāras stōdon,
sǣmanna searo   samod ætgædere,
330 æscholt ufan grǣġ;   wæs se īrenþrēat
wǣpnum ġewurþad.
                Þā ðǣr wlonc hæleð
ōretmecgas   æfter æþe/um fræġn:
'Hwanon feriġeað ġē   fǣtte scyldas,
grǣġe syrċan,   ond grīmhelmas,

remained where it was, firmly anchored.
Boar-shapes shone, adorned with gold,
on the cheek-protectors, shining, tempered.
The warriors escorted them. On they went together,
until they could see the timbered hall,
splendid, gold-shining. Where the great one lived
was of all buildings beneath the skies,
the one best-known to dwellers on earth.
Its light shone out over many lands.
The bold man showed them the brave ones' hall,
so that they could approach it directly.
He turned his horse, and said these words:
"Time for me to go. May the Almighty Father
give you His favor and keep you safe
in your exploit. I will go back to the sea,
to keep my watch against fierce war-bands."

    The street showed the way, shining, stone-paved,
to the men together. Their armor gleamed,
bright iron mail, hard, hand-clinched,
war-gear ringing. When they came then,
striding to the hall in all their battle-armor,
the sea-wearied men set down broad shields,
round and hardened, by the building's wall,
sat down on benches. Battle-armor rang,
the men's mail-shirts. Spears stood in a clump,
the seamen's weapons, a wood of ash-shafts
tipped with grey. The whole troop
was well provided with iron armament.

    Then a proud hero asked the warriors
about their lineage. "Where have you brought
your gilded shields from, your grey mail-shirts
and visored helmets, the stack of war-shafts?

335   heresceafta hēap?   Iċ eom Hrōðgāres
ār ond ombiht.   Ne seah iċ elþēodiġe
þus maniġe men   mōdiġlīcran.
Wēn' iċ þæt ġē for wlenċo,   nalles for wræcsīðum
ac for hiġeþrymmum,   Hrōðgār sōhton.'
340 Him þā ellenrōf   andswarode,
wlanc Wedera lēod,   word æfter spræc
heard under helme: 'Wē synt Hiġelāces
bēodġenēatas;   Bēowulf is mīn nama.
Wille iċ āsecgan   sunu Healfdenes,
345 mærum þēodne   mīn ǣrende,
aldre þīnum,   ġif hē ūs ġeunnan wile
þæt wē hine swā gōdne   grētan mōton.'
Wulfgār maþelode;   þæt wæs Wendla lēod;
wæs his mōdsefa   manegum ġecȳðed,
350 wīġ ond wīsdōm: 'Iċ þæs wine Deniġa,
frēan Scildinga   frīnan wille,
bēaga bryttan,   swā þū bēna eart,
þēoden mærne   ymb þīnne sīð,
ond þē þā andsware   ǣdre ġecȳðan
355 ðē mē se gōda   āġifan þenċeð.'
     Hwearf þā hrædlīċe   þær Hrōðgār sæt
eald ond anhār   mid his eorla ġedriht;
ēode ellenrōf,   þæt hē for eaxlum ġestōd
Deniġa frēan;   cūþe hē duguðe þēaw.
360 Wulfgār maðelode   tō his winedrihtne:
'Hēr syndon ġeferede,   feorran cumene
ofer ġeofenes begang   Ġēata lēode;
þone yldestan   ōretmecgas
Bēowulf nemnað.   Hȳ bēnan synt
365 þæt hīe, þēoden mīn,   wið þē mōton
wordum wrixlan.   Nō ðū him wearne ġetēoh
ðīnra ġeġncwida,   glædman Hrōðgār.
Hȳ on wīġġetawum   wyrðe þinċeað
eorla ġeæhtlan;   hūru se aldor dēah,
370 sē þǣm heaðorincum   hider wīsade.'

I am Hrothgar's servant and his herald.
Never have I seen so many strangers
look any bolder. It is my belief
that you sought Hrothgar, not as exiles
hoping for refuge, but as heroes
seeking adventure."
                        Answer was given
by the brave one, speaking proudly,
the man of the Weders said these words,
hard under helmet: "We are King Hygelac's
close companions. I am called Beowulf.
I will tell my errand to your lord, son of Healfdene,
the famous prince, if he is prepared
to grant us permission to address the great one."
Wulfgar replied, a man of the Wendels,
many knew his character, his courage and wisdom:
"I will ask the famous prince, lord of the Scyldings,
friend of the Danes, divider of treasure,
about your business, as you request,
and quickly bring you whatever response
the gracious one decides to give me."
   He went in haste to where Hrothgar sat,
old and very grey amidst his group of heroes,
went boldly to stand directly before
the lord of the Danes: he knew the rules of court.
"There have arrived from far across the sea
men of the Geats. The eldest of them
is called Beowulf by the warriors.
My lord, they request leave to speak with you.
Gracious Hrothgar, do not refuse
to give them answer. Judging by their war-gear
they are worthy of men's respect;
the one who leads them, who brought the warriors here,
is beyond question a man of consequence."

TEXT

Hrōðgār maþelode,   helm Scyldinga:
'Iċ hine cūðe   cnihtwesende;
wæs his ealdfæder   Ecgþēo hāten,
ðǣm tō hām forġeaf   Hrēþel Ġēata
375 āngan dohtor;   is his eafora nū
heard hēr cumen,   sōhte holdne wine.
Đonne sæġdon þæt   sǣlīþende,
þā ðe ġifsceattas   Ġēata fyredon
þyder tō þance,   þæt hē þrītiġes
380 manna mæġencræft   on his mundgripe
heaþorōf hæbbe.   Hine hāliġ God
for ārstafum   ūs onsende,
tō West-Denum,   þæs iċ wēn hæbbe,
wið Grendles gryre.   Iċ þǣm gōdan sceal
385 for his mōdþræce   mādmas bēodan.
Bēo ðū on ofeste,   hāt in gân
sēon sibbeġedriht   samod ætgædere;
ġesaga him ēac wordum,   þæt hīe sint wilcuman
Deniġa lēodum.'   *   *   *
390   [Wedera lēodum]   word inne ābēad:
'Ēow hēt secgan   siġedrihten mīn,
aldor Ēast-Dena,   þæt hē ēower æþelu can,
ond ġē him syndon   ofer sǣwylmas
heardhicgende   hider wilcuman.
395 Nū ġē mōton gangan   in ēowrum gūðġetawum
under heregrīman   Hrōðgār ġesēon;
lætað hildebord   hēr onbīdan,
wudu wælsceaftas   worda ġeþinġes.'
    Ārās þā se rīca,   ymb hine rinċ maniġ,
400 þrȳðliċ þeġna hēap;   sume þǣr bidon,
heaðorēaf hēoldon,   swā him se hearda bebēad.
Snyredon ætsomne,   þā secg wīsode,
under Heorotes hrōf;   [ēode hildedēor]
hear(d) under helme,   þæt hē on heo[r]ðe ġestōd.

72

Hrothgar spoke, protector of the Scyldings:
"I knew him before, when he was a boy.
His father was Ecgtheow, to whom, at his own court,
Hrethel of the Geats gave his only daughter.
Now his bold child has arrived here
to visit a dear friend. The seafarers
who took our gifts to the Geats as thanks,
said he was supposed to have the strength
of thirty heroes in his handgrip,
the battle-bold one. It is my belief
that holy God has sent him now
as a sign of favor for the West-Danes
against Grendel's terror. I shall give the good man
reward for his courage. Be quick, tell him
to come in and see the troop of kinfolk
all together. Tell him also
that they are welcome to the men of the Danes."
    Wulfgar took the reply to the men of the Weders:
"My victorious lord, prince of the East-Danes,
bids me tell you he knows your birth,
and you are welcome, you valiant ones
from across the sea-surges. Now you may go
in your armor and your helmets, to see Hrothgar.
Let your war-shields and battle-spears
wait here, for what may be the outcome of your words."
    The mighty one got up, many men round him,
a splendid troop of thanes. Some stayed where they were,
to watch over the weapons, as the wise one ordered.
They hastened together, as the herald showed them,
under the roof of Heorot. The hard man went forward

405 Bēowulf maðelode;   on him byrne scān,
     searonet seowed   smiþes orþancum:
     'Wes þū, Hrōðgār, hāl!   Iċ eom Hiġelāces
     mæġ ond magoðeġn;   hæbbe iċ mærða fela
     ongunnen on ġeogoþe.   Mē wearð Grendles þinġ
410 on mīnre ēþeltyrf   undyrne cūð;
     secgað sǣlīðend   þæt þes sele stande,
     reċed sēlesta   rinca ġehwylcum
     īdel ond unnyt,   siððan ǣfenlēoht
     under heofenes haðor   beholen weorþeð.
415 Þā mē þæt ġelǣrdon   lēode mīne
     þā sēlestan,   snotere ċeorlas,
     þēoden Hrōðgār,   þæt iċ þē sōhte,
     forþan hīe mæġenes cræft   mīn[n]e cūþon;
     selfe ofersāwon   ðā iċ of searwum cwōm
420 fāh from fēondum,   þǣr iċ fīfe ġeband,
     ȳðde eotena cyn,   ond on ȳðum slōg
     niceras nihtes,   nearoþearfe drēah,
     wræc Wedera nīð   — wēan āhsodon —
     forgrand gramum;   ond nū wið Grendel sceal,
425 wið þām āglǣcan   āna ġehēġan
     ðinġ wið þyrse.   Iċ þē nūða,
     brego Beorht-Dena,   biddan wille,
     eodor Scyldinga,   ānre bēne,
     þæt ðū mē ne forwyrne,   wīġendra hlēo,
430 frēowine folca,   nū iċ þus feorran cōm,
     þæt iċ mōte āna,   mīnra eorla ġedryht,
     ond þes hearda hēap   Heorot fǣlsian.
     Hæbbe iċ ēac ġeāhsod   þæt se ǣġlǣċa
     for his wonhȳdum   wǣpna ne reċċeð;
435 iċ þæt þonne forhicge,   swā mē Hiġelāc sīe,
     mīn mondrihten   mōdes blīðe,
     þæt iċ sweord bere   oþðe sīdne scyld,
     ġeolorand tō gūþe,   ac iċ mid grāpe sceal
     fōn wið fēonde   ond ymb feorh sacan,

under his helmet till he stood on the hearth.
Beowulf made his address. On him his armor shone,
the cunning net stitched by the craft of the smith:
"Hail to you, Hrothgar. I am Hygelac's
kinsman and servant. I have carried out
many famous deeds in youth. The matter of Grendel
became known to me in my homeland.
Seafarers say this hall, best of buildings,
stands empty and useless for every warrior,
once the evening light is lost beneath the sky.
Lord Hrothgar, the wise ones, best of my people,
advised me to seek you, because they knew
my strength and power. They had seen themselves
how I came bloodstained from the traps of my enemies,
where I dealt with five of them, destroyed the giant-race,
killed sea-monsters by night in the waves.
I survived great danger, avenged the Weders' distress,
crushed our enemies – they caused it themselves.
And now it is up to me to venture alone
against Grendel's terror, try conclusions
against the ogre. Lord of the Bright-Danes,
prince of the Scyldings, protector of warriors,
friend of the peoples, I ask one boon,
that you will not deny me, now I have come so far,
leave to cleanse Heorot myself, with my troop
of noblemen, this hardy band.
I have also been told that in his temerity
the terrible one takes no heed of weapons.
To please my lord Hygelac I therefore renounce
carrying to battle sword or broad shield
of yellow lindenwood, but I shall grapple the fiend

440 lāð wið lāþum;   ðǣr ġelȳfan sceal
dryhtnes dōme   sē þe hine dēað nimeð.
Wēn' iċ þæt hē wille,   ġif hē wealdan mōt,
in þǣm gūðsele   Ġeatena lēode
etan unforhte,   swā hē oft dyde
445 mæġenhrēð manna.   Nā þū mīnne þearft
hafalan hȳdan,   ac hē mē habban wile
d[r]ēore fāhne,   ġif meċ dēað nimeð:
byreð blōdiġ wæl,   byrġean þenċeð,
eteð āngenġa   unmurnlīċe,
450 mearcað mōrhopu —   nō ðū ymb mīnes ne þearft
līċes feorme   lenġ sorgian.
Onsend Hiġelāce,   ġif meċ hild nime,
beaduscrūda betst   þæt mīne brēost wereð,
hræġla sēlest;   þæt is Hrǣdlan lāf,
455 Wēlandes ġeweorc.   Gǣð ā wyrd swā hīo scel.'

Hrōðgār maþelode,   helm Scyldinga:
'Fore †fyhtum þū,   wine mīn Bēowulf,
ond for ārstafum   ūsiċ sōhtest.
Ġeslōh þīn fæder   fǣhðe mǣste;
460 wearþ hē Heaþolāfe   tō handbonan
mid Wilfingum;   ðā hine Wedera cyn
for herebrōgan   habban ne mihte.
Þanon hē ġesōhte   Sūð-Dena folc
ofer ȳða ġewealc,   Ār-Scyldinga;
465 ðā iċ furþum wēold   folce Deniga
ond on ġeogoðe hēold   ġinne rīċe,
hordburh hæleþa,   ðā wæs Heorogār dēad,
mīn yldra mǣġ   unlifiġende,
bearn Healfdenes;   sē wæs betera ðonne iċ!
470 Siððan þā fǣhðe   fēo þingode:
sende iċ Wylfingum   ofer wæteres hrycg
ealde mādmas;   hē mē āþas swōr.
Sorh is mē tō secgannẹ   on sefan mīnum

76

and fight for life, one foe against the other.
He whom death takes must trust then to God's judgement.
I expect, if he can do it, he will devour with impunity
the men of the Geats in the hall where we fight,
as he has often done to a fine host of men.
If death takes me, you will have no need
to bury my head for he will have me
stained with blood. The lone strider
will bear off the bloody corpse,
mean to eat it, feast remorselessly,
staining the fastnesses in the fenlands.
No cause for you to care any longer
for tending my body. If battle should take me,
send to Hygelac that best of tunics
which guards my breast, best of war-shirts.
It is Hrethel's legacy, the work of Weland.
Things will always go as they must."

 Hrothgar spoke, protector of the Scyldings:
"My friend Beowulf, you came to us
to fight for glory. Your father began
the greatest of feuds with a killing.
Among the Wylfings, he was the bane
of Heatholaf, killed hand-to-hand,
so that for fear of war the Weder people
could not shelter him. From them he sought out
the South Dane people, the honored Scyldings,
over the tossing waves. That was in my youth
when I ruled the Danes, guarded the broad kingdom
and the city of heroes, after the death
of Heorogar, child of Healfdene,
my elder brother. He was better than I.
Then I paid off the feud, sent ancient treasures
over the water's back to the Wylfings.
He swore oaths to me. It saddens my heart

gumena ǣngum   hwæt mē Grendel hafað
475   hȳnðo on Heorote   mid his heteþancum,
fǣrnīða ġefremed;   is mīn fletwerod,
wīġhēap ġewanod;   hīe wyrd forswēop
on Grendles gryre.   God ēaþe mæġ
þone dolscaðan   dǣda ġetwǣfan!
480   Ful oft ġebēotedon   bēore druncne
ofer ealowǣġe   ōretmecgas
þæt hīe in bēorsele   bīdan woldon
Grendles gūþe   mid gryrum ecga.
Đonne wæs þēos medoheal   on morgentīd,
485   drihtsele drēorfāh   þonne dæġ līxte,
eal benċþelu   blōde bestȳmed,
heall heorudrēore;   āhte iċ holdra þȳ lǣs,
dēorre duguðe,   þē þā dēað fornam.
Site nū tō symle   ond onsǣl meoto,
490   siġehrēð secgum,   swā þīn sefa hwette.'
Þā wæs Ġēatmæcgum   ġeador ætsomne
on bēorsele   benċ ġerȳmed;
þǣr swīðferhþe   sittan ēodon,
þrȳðum dealle.   Þeġn nytte behēold,
495   sē þe on handa bær   hroden ealowǣġe,
scencte scīr wered.   Scop hwīlum sang
hādor on Heorote.   Þǣr wæs hæleða drēam,
duguð unlȳtel   Dena ond Wedera.

Ūnferð maþelode,   Ecglāfes bearn,
500   þē æt fōtum sæt   frēan Scyldinga,
onband beadurūne.   Wæs him Bēowulfes sīð,
mōdġes merefaran,   miċel æfþunca,
forþon þe hē ne ūþe   þæt ǣniġ ōðer man
ǣfre mǣrða þon mā   middanġeardes
505   ġehēdde under heofenum   þonne hē sylfa:
'Eart þū se Bēowulf,   sē þe wið Brecan wunne
on sīdne sǣ,   ymb sund flite,

to tell to anyone what humiliations
Grendel's hatred and sudden attacks
have inflicted on me. My household guard,
my troop of warriors, is diminished.
Fate swept them away through the terror of Grendel.
God can easily put final end
to this ravager's deeds. Often, drunk with beer,
my warriors would boast over the ale-cup
that they would wait with terrible swords
for Grendel's attack in the beer-hall.
Then when day dawned over the retainers,
and morning came, the mead-hall here
was stained with blood, bench-planks soaked in it,
the whole hall awash. I had the fewer
loyal retainers among my veterans,
once death took them. Sit now to eat,
and open your thoughts, of glory and victory,
to all men here, as your mind urges you."
    Then in the beer-hall a bench was cleared
for the Geats together, where the great ones
seated themselves, proud of their strength.
The servant who carried the decorated ale-cup
did his duty, poured out bright drink.
The poet sang, clear in Heorot. Heroes were merry,
no small band of Danes and Weders.

    Unferth spoke, child of Ecglaf,
who sat at the feet of the lord of the Scyldings,
hostile words, to provoke strife.
The arrival of Beowulf, the brave seafarer,
displeased him greatly, because he would not admit
that any other man in middle-earth
had been more concerned under the sky
with famous deeds than he had himself:
"Are you that Beowulf, the one who is said

ðǣr ġit for wlenċe   wada cunnedon
ond for dolġilpe   on dēop wæter
510 aldrum nēþdon?   Nē inċ ǣniġ mon,
nē lēof nē lāð,   belēan mihte
sorhfullne sīð,   þā ġit on sund rēon.
Þǣr ġit ēagorstrēam   earmum þehton,
mǣton merestrǣta,   mundum brugdon,
515 glidon ofer gārsecg;   ġeofon ȳþum wēol,
wintrys wylm[um].   Ġit on wæteres ǣht
seofonniht swuncon;   hē þē æt sunde oferflāt,
hæfde māre mæġen.   Þā hine on morgentīd
on Heaþo-Rǣmas   holm up ætbær;
520 ðonon hē ġesōhte   swǣsne ēþel,
lēof his lēodum,   lond Brondinga,
freoðoburh fæġere,   þǣr hē folc āhte,
burh ond bēagas.   Bēot eal wið þē
sunu Bēanstānes   sō(ð)e ġelǣste.
525 Ðonne wēne iċ tō þē   wyrsan ġeþinġea,
ðēah þū heaðorǣsa   ġehwǣr dohte,
grimre gūðe,   ġif þū Grendles dearst
nihtlongne fyrst   nēan bīdan.'
    Bēowulf maþelode,   bearn Ecgþeowes:
530 'Hwæt, þū worn fela,   wine mīn Ūnferð,
bēore druncen   ymb Brecan sprǣce,
sæġdest from his sīðe.   Sōð iċ taliġe,
þæt iċ merestrenġo   māran āhte,
*ea*feþo on ȳþum,   ðonne ǣniġ ōþer man.
535 Wit þæt ġecwǣdon   cnihtwesende
ond ġebēotedon   — wǣron bēġen þā ġīt
on ġeogoðfēore —   þæt wit on gārsecg ūt
aldrum nēðdon,   ond þæt ġeæfndon swā.
Hæfdon swurd nacod,   þā wit on sund rēon,
540 heard on handa;   wit unc wið hronfixas
werian þōhton.   Nō hē wiht fram mē
flōdȳþum feor   flēotan meahte,

to have competed against Breca
in a swimming match on the open sea,
when the two of you tested the waves
out of vainglory, and with foolish boast
risked your lives out on deep water?
No man, friend or foe, could dissuade you
from that sorrowful trip, when the two of you
struck out swimming. With arms you swept
ocean-currents, struck out with hands,
measured out sea-roads, cruised across the surface.
The ocean-waves surged with wintry swells.
For seven nights you two toiled
in the power of the water. He beat you at swimming,
he was the stronger. The sea bore him up
in the morning to the land of the Ræmas.
From there he returned, gladly received,
to his own country, the land of the Brondings,
with its fine stronghold, where he had kin,
wealth and homestead. The son of Beanstan
certainly made good his boast against you.
So I expect a worse outcome for you,
though you succeeded in grim war everywhere,
in battle-charges, if you dare wait
the whole night long for Grendel's coming."
  Beowulf, son of Ecgtheow, gave him answer:
"Well, my friend Unferth, you have said a great deal
about Breca, drunk on beer,
telling of his feat. Truth is, I had greater strength,
power in the water, than any other man.
When we were boys the two of us boasted –
we were both still young – that we would risk our lives
out on the sea, and so we did.
We had hard swords drawn in our hands
when we set out swimming, meant to defend ourselves
against the whale-fish. He could not swim

hraþor on holme, nō iċ fram him wolde.
Ðā wit ætsomne on sǣ wǣron
545 fīfnihta fyrst, oþ þæt unc flōd tōdrāf,
wado weallende, wedera ċealdost,
nīpende niht, ond norþan wind
heaðogrim ondhwearf; hrēo wǣron ȳþa.
Wæs merefixa mōd onhrēred;
550 þǣr mē wið lāðum līċsyrċe mīn
heard hondlocen helpe ġefremede;
beadohræġl brōden on brēostum læġ
golde ġeġyrwed. Mē tō grunde tēah
fāh fēondscaða, fæste hæfde
555 grim on grāpe; hwæþre mē ġyfeþe wearð
þæt iċ āglǣċan orde ġerǣhte,
hildebille; heaþorǣs fornam
mihtiġ meredēor þurh mīne hand.

Swā meċ ġelōme lāðġetēonan
560 þrēatedon þearle. Iċ him þēnode
dēoran sweorde, swā hit ġedēfe wæs.
Næs hīe ðǣre fylle ġefēan hæfdon,
mānfordǣdlan, þæt hīe mē þēgon,
symbel ymbsǣton sǣgrunde nēah,
565 ac on merġenne mēċum wunde
be ȳðlāfe uppe lǣgon,
sweo[r]dum āswefede, þæt syðþan nā
ymb brontne ford brimlīðende
lāde ne letton. Lēoht ēastan cōm,
570 beorht bēacen Godes, brimu swaþredon,
þæt iċ sǣnæssas ġesēon mihte,
windiġe weallas. Wyrd oft nereð
unfǣġne eorl, þonne his ellen dēah!
Hwæþere mē ġesǣlde þæt iċ mid sweorde ofslōh
575 niceras nigene. Nō iċ on niht ġefræġn
under heofones hwealf heardran feohtan,

further out than me, or swim faster in the sea.
I would not leave him. Five nights in the sea
we were together until we were parted
by surging waves and by the flood.
Cold storms, night falling, strong wind from the north
all turned against us. The waves were rough,
the temper of the fish was stirred up also,
so that my body-armor, hard hand-clinched,
had to help me against my enemies,
the battle-shirt with gilded links, which lay on my breast.
A deadly enemy dragged me down
to the sea-bottom, the savage one
had me in his grip. But it was granted me
to pierce the monster with the point of my sword.
The rush of battle took off the sea-beast,
the mighty creature, by my hand.

   So the evil-doers attacked me fiercely.
I paid them out for it, as was only right,
with my good sword. The guilty ones
did not get their fill, feasting on me
at the sea-bottom, instead in the morning
they lay cast up on shore, killed with the sword,
so that never again would they hinder
seafarers' passage across the high sea,
Light came from the east, God's bright beacon,
the waves subsided, so that I saw the windy cliffs
of the sea-headlands. Luck often spares a man
not marked for death, as long as his courage holds.
So it was given to me to kill with my sword
nine of the monsters. I have never heard

nē on ēgstrēamum   earmran mannon;
hwæþere iċ fāra fenġ   fēore ġedīġde,
sīþes wēriġ.   Đā meċ sæ oþbær,
580 flōd æfter faroðe   on Finna land,
wadu weallendu.   Nō iċ wiht fram þē
swylcra searonīða   secgan hȳrde,
billa brōgan.   Breca næfre ġīt
æt heaðolāce,   nē ġehwæþer inċer,
585 swā dēorlīċe   dæd ġefremede
fāgum sweordum   — nō iċ þæs [fela] ġylpe —
þēah ðū þīnum brōðrum   tō banan wurde,
hēafodmǣgum;   þæs þū in helle scealt
werhðo drēogan,   þēah þīn wit duge.
590 Secge iċ þē tō sōðe,   sunu Ecglāfes,
þæt næfre Gre[n]del swā fela   gryra ġefremede,
atol ǣġlǣċa,   ealdre þīnum,
hȳnðo on Heorote,   ġif þīn hiġe wǣre,
sefa swā searogrim   swā þū self talast;
595 ac hē hafað onfunden   þæt hē þā fǣhðe ne þearf,
atole ecgþrǣce   ēower lēode
swīðe onsittan,   Siġe-Scyldinga;
nymeð nȳdbāde,   nǣnegum ārað
lēode Deniġa,   ac hē lust wiġeð,
600 swefeð, ondsendeþ,   seċċe ne wēneþ
tō Gār-Denum.   Ac iċ him Ġēata sceal
eafoð ond ellen   unġēara nū,
gūþe ġebēodan.   Gǣþ eft sē þe mōt
tō medo mōdiġ,   siþþan morgenlēoht
605 ofer ylda bearn   ōþres dōgores,
sunne sweġlwered   sūþan scīneð.'
    Þā wæs on sālum   sinċes brytta
gamolfeax ond gūðrōf;   ġēoce ġelȳfde
brego Beorht-Dena;   ġehȳrde on Bēowulfe
610 folces hyrde   fæstrǣdne ġeþōht.

of a harder fight at night under heaven,
nor of men harder pressed in the water.
Yet I got away with life from my enemies' grip,
wearied from the struggle. The surging waves
carried me to shore on the coast of the Finns.
I have never heard tell of such hard-fought struggles
from you, with terrible blades. Nor has Breca ever yet
done any such famous deed in battle
with bloody sword – I do not mean to boast of it –
nor you either, even though you were
the death of your brothers, your closest kinsmen:
for which you must endure damnation in Hell,
clever though you may be. I tell you for sure,
son of Ecglaf, that the monster Grendel
would never have inflicted such fear and humiliation
to your lord in Heorot, if your heart and mind
were as fierce in battle as you yourself boast.
But he has realized that he has no need to fear
the enmity and the swords of your people,
the Victory-Scyldings. He takes his toll,
he has no dread of the Danish people,
but does as he likes, kills and drags off,
not expecting resistance from the Spear-Danes.
But soon now I will show him the strength and valor
of the Geats in battle. Let he who may go bravely
to the mead-drinking, once dawn-light next day,
the sun in splendor, shines from the south
over the children of men."
                         At that the treasure-sharer,
grey-haired and warlike prince of the Bright-Danes,
took heart once more. Hearing Beowulf's
determined intention, he believed help had come.

Ðǣr wæs hæleþa hleahtọr,   hlyn swynsode,
word wǣron wynsume.   Ēode Wealhþēo forð,
cwēn Hrōðgāres   cynna ġemyndiġ,
grētte goldhroden   guman on healle,
615 ond þā frēoliċ wīf   ful ġesealde
ǣrest Ēast-Dena   ēþelwearde,
bæd hine blīðne   æt þǣre bēorþeġe,
lēodum lēofne;   hē on lust ġeþeah
symbel ond seleful,   siġerōf kyning.
620 Ymbēode þā   ides Helminga
duguþe ond ġeogoþe   dǣl ǣġhwylcne,
sinċfato sealde,   oþ þæt sǣl ālamp
þæt hīo Bēowulfe,   bēaghroden cwēn
mōde ġeþungen   medoful ætbær;
625 grētte Ġēata lēod,   Gode þancode
wīsfæst wordum   þæs ðe hire se willa ġelamp
þæt hēo on ǣniġne   eorl ġelȳfde
fyrena frōfre.   Hē þæt ful ġeþeah,
wælrēow wiga   æt Wealhþêon,
630 ond þā ġyddode   gūþe ġefȳsed.
Bēowulf maþelode,   bearn Ecgþeowes:
'Iċ þæt hogode,   þā iċ on holm ġestāh,
sǣbāt ġesæt   mid mīnra secga ġedriht,
þæt iċ ānunga   ēowra lēoda
635 willan ġeworhte   oþðe on wæl crunge
fēondgrāpum fæst.   Iċ ġefremman sceal
eorliċ ellen,   oþðe endedæġ
on þisse meoduhealle   mīnne ġebīdan.'
Ðām wīfe þā word   wēl līcodon,
640 ġilpcwide Ġēates;   ēode goldhroden
frēolicu folccwēn   tō hire frēan sittan.
Þā wæs eft swā ǣr   inne on healle
þrȳðword sprecen,   ðēod on sǣlum,
siġefolca swēġ,   oþ þæt semninga
645 sunu Healfdenes   sēċean wolde

Men were laughing, noise and clamor,
words were cheerful. Then Wealhtheow,
queen of Hrothgar, came out to her kinfolk.
The gold-adorned queen greeted the men in hall,
the noble woman gave the cup first
to him who guarded the land of the East-Danes,
urged him to be happy and dear to his people
at the beer-drinking. The victorious king
gladly enjoyed both food and drink.
The Helming woman went round the hall,
shared out the treasure-cup to young and old,
until the time came for the queen in her coronet
to carry politely the mead-cup to Beowulf.
She greeted the Geat, gave thanks to God
with wise words that her wish was granted,
to trust in a cure for the crimes committed
from any nobleman. He took the cup,
the fierce warrior, from Wealhtheow,
and then made a speech, eager for battle:
"When I took to sea with my troop of men,
boarded the boat, I had it in mind
that I would either fulfill the wish of your people,
or else I would fall among the dead,
fast in the grip of my foeman.
I shall do a noble deed, or else endure
the day of my death here in this mead-hall."
The Geat's promise greatly pleased the lady.
In her gold ornaments the excellent queen
went to sit by her lord.
                              Then again as before
brave words were spoken within the hall,
the voices rose of a victorious people
in good cheer, until abruptly
the son of Healfdene would seek his bed

æfenræste;　wiste þǣm āhlǣċan
tō þǣm hēahsele　hilde ġeþinġed,
siððan hīe sunnan lēoht　ġesēon meahton
oþ ðe nīpende　niht ofer ealle,
650　scaduhelma ġesceapu　scrīðan cwōman
wan under wolcnum.　Werod eall ārās.
[Ġe]grētte þā　guma ōþerne,
Hrōðgār Bēowulf,　ond him hǣl ābēad,
wīnærnes ġeweald,　ond þæt word ācwæð:
655　'Nǣfre iċ ǣnegum men　ǣr ālȳfde,
siþðan iċ hond ond rond　hebban mihte,
ðrȳþærn Dena　būton þē nūða.
Hafa nū ond ġeheald　hūsa sēlest,
ġemyne mǣrþo,　mæġenellen cȳð,
660　waca wið wrāþum!　Ne bið þē wilna gād
ġif þū þæt ellenweorc　aldre ġedīġest.'

Ðā him Hrōþgār ġewāt　mid his hæleþa ġedryht,
eodur Scyldinga　ūt of healle;
wolde wīġfruma　Wealhþēo sēċan,
665　cwēn tō ġebeddan.　Hæfde kyningwuldor
Grendle tōġēanes,　swā guman ġefrungon,
seleweard āseted;　sundọrnytte behēold
ymb aldor Dena,　eotonweard' ābēad.
Hūru Ġēata lēod　ġeorne truwode
670　mōdgan mæġnes,　metodes hyldo.
Ðā hē him of dyde　īsernbyrnan,
helm of hafelan,　sealde his hyrsted sweord,
īrena cyst,　ombihtþeġne,
ond ġehealdan hēt　hildeġeatwe.
675　Ġespræc þā se gōda　ġylpworda sum,
Bēowulf Ġēata,　ǣr hē on bed stiġe:
'Nō iċ mē an herewæsmun　hnāgran taliġe
gūþġeweorca　þonne Grendel hine;
forþan iċ hine sweorde　swebban nelle,

88

for the night: he knew that battle
had been intended by the ogre
against the high hall, from the hour they could see
the light of the sun until night began to fall
over everything, and there came striding
beneath the skies shapes from under
the cloak of darkness. The whole band stood up.
Hrothgar spoke to Beowulf, one man to another,
wished him good luck, and said these words:
"Never before, since I was able to lift hand and shield,
have I entrusted the Danes' great hall
to any man, except you now. Keep and protect
this best of houses, think of glory,
prove your strength, keep watch against foes!
Reward for you will not fall short
of what you wish if you come away
from this noble deed still with your life."

Then Hrothgar, prince of the Scyldings,
went out of the hall with his troop of heroes:
the war-leader wished to join Wealhtheow,
his queen and consort. The King of Glory,
as men had heard, had set a hall-guardian;
he filled a special role for the lord of Danes,
appointed a giant-watch.
　　　　　　　　　　The man of the Geats
indeed had good faith in the Lord's favor,
and his strength and courage. He took off his iron shirt,
helmet from his head, gave his ornamented sword,
the best of blades, to his attendant thane,
telling him to take charge of all his war-gear.
Before he took to his bed Beowulf of the Geats,
good man that he was, said words of valor:
"I do not rate myself weaker in warlike strength
and deeds of battle than Grendel does himself.
Therefore I do not wish to kill him with the sword,

680   aldre benēotan,   þēah iċ eal mǣġe.
      Nāt hē þāra gōda   þæt hē mē onġēan slêâ,
      rand ġehēawe,   þēah ðe hē rōf sîê
      nīþġeweorca;   ac wit on niht sculon
      secge ofersittan   ġif hē ġesēċean dear
685   wīġ ofer wǣpen,   ond siþðan wītiġ God
      on swā hwæþere hond,   hāliġ dryhten
      mǣrðo dēme,   swā him ġemet þinċe.'
      Hylde hine þā heaþodēor,   hlēorbolster onfēng
      eorles andwlitan,   ond hine ymb moniġ
690   snelliċ sǣrinċ   selereste ġebēah.
      Nǣniġ heora þōhte   þæt hē þanon scolde
      eft eardlufan   ǣfre ġesēċean,
      folc oþðe frēoburh   þǣr hē āfēded wæs;
      ac hīe hæfdon ġefrūnen   þæt hīe ǣr tō fela micles
695   in þǣm wīnsele   wældēað fornam,
      Deniġea lēode.   Ac him dryhten forġeaf
      wīġspēda ġewiofu,   Wedera lēodum,
      frōfor ond fultum,   þæt hīe fēond heora
      ðurh ānes cræft   ealle ofercōmon,
700   selfes mihtum.   Sōð is ġecȳþed
      þæt mihtiġ God   manna cynnes
      wēold (w)īdeferhð.
                   Cōm on wanre niht
      scrīðan sceadugenġa.   Scēotend swǣfon,
      þā þæt hornreċed   healdan scoldon,
705   ealle būton ānum   — þæt wæs yldum cūþ
      þæt hīe ne mōste,   þā metod nolde,
      se s[c]ynscaþa   under sceadu breġdan —
      ac hē wæċċende   wrāþum on andan
      bād bolgenmōd   beadwa ġeþinġes.

710   Ðā cōm of mōre   under misthleoþum
      Grendel gongan,   Godes yrre bær;
      mynte se mānscaða   manna cynnes

deprive him of life, though I doubtless could.
Fierce though he may be in hostile deeds,
he knows nothing of how to slash at me,
chop at my shield, so in the night,
if he dares to face war without weapons,
we will both do without, and may wise God,
the holy Lord, decide the issue
for either side, as He may see fit."
The fierce one lay down, his head on the pillow,
round him there lay on his bed in the hall
many a bold seaman. Not one expected
that he would ever return to the homeland he loved,
his family and the place where he was brought up.
They had all heard that already too many
of the Danish people had been taken
in the wine-hall by death in battle.
But the Lord wove for the Weder people
success in war, support and help,
so that they all overcame their enemy,
through one man's strength, his might alone.
The truth is revealed: the human race
is always ruled by the might of God.

In the dark night there came striding
the shadow-walker. The shooters all slept,
those who were to guard the gabled hall –
all except one. It was known to men
that against God's will the monster-foe
would not be permitted to drag them off
under the shadow. In despite of his foe
the one who was awake, waited enraged
for what would be the result of battle.

    Then from the marsh below the misty slopes,
Grendel came striding, he bore God's anger.

sumne besyrwan   in sele þām hēan.
Wōd under wol(c)num   tō þæs þe hē wīnreċed,
715 goldsele gumena   ġearwost wisse
fæ*t*um fāhne.   Ne wæs þæt forma sīð
þæt hē Hrōþgāres   hām ġesōhte;
næfre hē on aldọrdagum   ær nē siþðan
heardran hæle,   healðeġnas fand.
720 Cōm þā tō reċede   rinċ sīðian
drēamum bedæled.   Duru sōna onarn
fȳrbendum fæst,   syþðan hē hire folmum (æt)hrān;
onbræd þā bealohȳdiġ,   ðā (hē ġe)bolgen wæs,
reċedes mūþan.   Raþe æfter þon
725 on fāgne flōr   fēond treddode,
ēode yrremōd;   him of ēagum stōd
liġġe ġelīcost   lēoht unfæġer.
Ġeseah hē in reċede   rinca maniġe,
swefan sibbẹġedriht   samod ætgædere,
730 magorinca hēap.   Þā his mōd āhlōg;
mynte þæt hē ġedælde,   ær þon dæġ cwōme,
atol āglæċa   ānra ġehwylċes
līf wið līċe,   þā him ālumpen wæs
wistfylle wēn.   Ne wæs þæt wyrd þā ġēn
735 þæt hē mā mōste   manna cynnes
ðicgean ofer þā niht.   Þrȳðswȳð behēold
mæġ Hiġelāces   hū se mānscaða
under færgripum   ġefaran wolde.
Nē þæt se āglæċa   yldan þōhte,
740 ac hē ġefēng hraðe   forman sīðe
slæpendne rinċ,   slāt unwearnum,
bāt bānlocan,   blōd ēdrum dranc,
synsnædum swealh;   sōna hæfde
unlyfiġendes   eal ġefeormod,
745 fēt ond folma.   Forð nēar ætstōp,
nam þā mid handa   hiġeþīhtiġne
rinċ on ræste.   Hē hi(m) ræhte onġēan,

The evil one meant to trap one of the race of men
in the high hall. Under the clouds he strode
to where he knew full well the wine-hall was,
the golden hall of men shining with plate.
It was not the first time he had ventured
to Hrothgar's home. Never before or since
in all the days of his life did he meet harder welcome
from thanes in the hall. Exiled from happiness
the warrior came striding to the hall.
The door, reinforced with forged iron bands
flew wide open at his first touch.
Intent on evil, now he was enraged,
he swept open the hall-gateway.
Quickly then the monster trod the mosaic floor,
came forward angrily. From his eyes there shone
an ugly light most like fire.
In the hall he saw a host of men,
a troop of kinsmen asleep together,
a band of retainers. In his heart he laughed.
The monster reckoned that before day broke
he would snatch the life of each one of them
from his body, now that the hope
of a fill of feasting had fallen to him.
It was no longer fated that he should be free
to take at night any more of the race of men.
Hygelac's mighty kinsman watched to see
how the evil one would act in his sudden attack.
Not that the monster had any mind to delay,
but quickly seized a sleeping man
straight away, tore him irresistibly,
bit through his joints, drank blood from his veins,
in great gobbets gulped him down.
In an instant he had eaten all of the dead man,
feet and fists too. He advanced further in,
seized with his hands the mighty one on his bed,

fēond mid folme;   hē onfēng hraþe
inwitþancum   ond wið earm ġesæt.
750 Sōna þæt onfunde   fyrena hyrde,
þæt hē ne mētte   middanġeardes,
eorþan scēata   on elran men
mundgripe māran.   Hē on mōde wearð
forht on ferhðe;   nō þȳ ǣr fram meahte.
755 Hyġe wæs him hinfūs,   wolde on heolster flēon,
sēċan dēofla ġedræ̇ġ;   ne wæs his drohtoð þǣr
swylċe hē on ealderdagum   ǣr ġemētte.
Ġemunde þā se gōda,   mǣġ Hiġelāces,
ǣfensprǣċe,   uplang āstōd
760 ond him fæste wiðfēng;   fingras burston;
eoten wæs ūtweard,   eorl furþur stōp.
Mynte se mǣra   (hw)ǣr hē meahte swā
wīdre ġewindan   ond on weġ þanon
flēon on fenhopu;   wiste his fingra ġeweald
765 on grames grāpum.   Þæt wæs ġeocor sīð
þæt se hearmscaþa   tō Heorute ātēah.
Dryhtsele dynede;   Denum eallum wearð,
ċeasterbūendum,   cēnra ġehwylcum,
eorlum ealuscerwen.   Yrre wǣron bēġen,
770 rēþe renweardas.   Reċed hlynsode.
Þā wæs wundor miċel   þæt se wīnsele
wiðhæfde heaþodēorum,   þæt hē on hrūsan ne fēol,
fæġer foldbold;   ac hē þæs fæste wæs
innan ond ūtan   īrenbendum
775 searoþoncum besmiþod.   Þǣr fram sylle ābēag
medubenċ moniġ,   mīne ġefrǣġe,
golde ġereġnad,   þǣr þā graman wunnon.
Þæs ne wēndon ǣr   witan Scyldinga
þæt hit ā mid ġemete   manna ǣniġ
780 betliċ ond bānfāg   tōbrecan meahte,
listum tōlūcan,   nymþe līġes fæþm
swulge on swaþule.   Swēġ up āstāg

the fiend reached out to him. The sleeper seized his arm
quickly, angrily, pulled himself up.
Very soon he realized, the keeper of crimes,
that he had never met a greater grip
from any other man of middle-earth,
anywhere across the expanse of the world.
He was struck with terror in heart and mind.
Not for that could he get free. He was set on escape,
wanted to flee into the darkness,
get back to the company of the devils.
What he felt there was not what he had ever met
in his life before. The good kinsman of Hygelac
remembered his words in the evening.
He stood up and gripped the monster firmly.
Fingers snapped, the fiend turned to flee,
the nobleman followed him. The infamous one meant
to get outside, if he only could,
and then flee away into the depths of the fen.
He knew his fingers were held in the grip of the fierce one.
It was a sad journey for him that the evil-doer
took to Heorot. The feasting-hall echoed.
All of the Danes, all the nobles,
all the bold ones in buildings round about
were struck with fear. Both were enraged,
the fierce ones fighting in the hall.
The building resounded. It was a great marvel
that the wine-hall resisted the fighters,
that the fair building did not fall to earth,
but it was firmly strengthened inside and outside
with iron bands, cunningly forged.
As I have heard, many a mead-bench
decorated with gold was dislodged from its setting,
where the fierce ones fought. The Scylding counsellors
had never imagined that any clash of men
should break them, excellent, set with bone,
unless embrace of fire should eat them up.

nīwe ġeneahhe;   Norð-Denum stōd
ateliċ eġesa,   ānra ġehwylcum
785 þāra þe of wealle   wōp ġehȳrdon,
gryreleōð galan   Godes andsacan,
siġeleāsne sang,   sār wāniġean
helle hæfton.   Hēold hine fæste
sē þe manna wæs   mæġene strenġest
790 on þǣm dæġe   þysses līfes.

Nolde eorla hlēo   æniġe þinga
þone cwealmcuman   cwicne forlǣtan,
nē his līfdagas   lēoda ǣngum
nytte tealde.   Þǣr ġenehost brǣgd
795 eorl Bēowulfes   ealde lāfe,
wolde frēadrihtnes   feorh ealgian,
mǣres þēodnes,   ðǣr hīe meahton swā.
Hīe þæt ne wiston,   þā hīe ġewin drugon,
heardhicgende   hildemecgas,
800 ond on healfa ġehwone   hēawan þōhton,
sāwle sēċan: þone synscaðan
æniġ ofer eorþan   īrenna cyst,
gūðbilla nān,   grētan nolde,
ac hē siġewǣpnum   forsworen hæfde,
805 ecga ġehwylcre.   Scolde his aldorġedāl
on ðǣm dæġe   þysses līfes
earmliċ wurðan,   ond se ellorgāst
on fēonda ġeweald   feor sīðian.
Ðā þæt onfunde   sē þe fela ǣror
810 mōdes myrðe   manna cynne,
fyrene ġefremede   — hē [wæs] fāg wið God —
þæt him se līchoma   lǣstan nolde,
ac hine se mōdega   mǣġ Hyġelāces
hæfde be honda;   wæs ġehwæþer ōðrum
815 lifiġende lāð.   Līcsār ġebād
atol ǣġlǣċa;   him on eaxle wearð

Noise was renewed. The North-Danes were struck
with fear and horror, every one of those
who from the walls heard the wailing,
God's enemy singing a song of fear,
a dirge of defeat, the captive of Hell
lamenting his pain. The one who held him fast
was the greatest in might of all men who ever lived.

  By no means did the protector of nobles
wish to let the evildoer escape alive,
nor did he reckon his life of value to any man.
Close around him Beowulf's men
drew their ancient swords, wanting if they could
to protect the life of their famous prince and lord.
They did not know, the brave companions,
when they joined the fight, aiming to kill,
tried to strike from every side, that no sword on earth,
not the best of blades, would bite on the malefactor,
but he had put a spell on all sword-edges,
all weapons of victory. Wretched would be
his parting from this life, the alien spirit
would travel far into the power of the fiends.
He who had once committed many crimes against men
with a glad heart – he was God's enemy –
found his body failing because the bold
kinsman of Hygelac had him by the hand.
Each of them was loath to let the other live.
The terrible brute felt a body-wound.
A great tear could be seen in his shoulder,

syndolh sweotol,   seonowe onsprungon,
burston bānlocan.   Bēowulfe wearð
gūðhrēð ġyfeþe.   Scolde Grendel þonan
820 feorhsēoc flēon   under fenhleoðu,
sēċean wynlēas wīċ;   wiste þē ġeornor
þæt his aldres wæs   ende ġegongen,
dōgera dæġrīm.   Denum eallum wearð
æfter þām wælrǣse   willa ġelumpen:
825 hæfde þā ġefǣlsod   sē þe ǣr feorran cōm,
snotor ond swyðferhð,   sele Hrōðgāres,
ġenered wið nīðe.   Nihtweorce ġefeh,
ellenmǣrþum.   Hæfde Ēast-Denum
Ġēatmecga lēod   ġilp ġelǣsted,
830 swylċe oncȳþðe   ealle ġebētte,
inwidsorge   þe hīe ǣr drugon
ond for þrēanȳdum   þolian scoldon,
torn unlȳtel.   Þæt wæs tācen sweotol
syþðan hildedēor   hond āleġde,
835 earm ond eaxle   — þǣr wæs eal ġeador
Grendles grāpe —   under ġēapne hr(ōf).

Ðā wæs on morgen   mīne ġefrǣġe
ymb þā ġifhealle   gūðrinċ moniġ;
fērdon folctogan   feorran ond nēan
840 ġeond wīdwegas   wundor sċēawian,
lāþes lāstas.   Nō his līfġedāl
sārliċ þūhte   secga ǣnegum
þāra þe tīrlēases   trode sċēawode,
hū hē wēriġmōd   on weġ þanon,
845 nīða ofercumen,   on nicera mere
fǣge ond ġeflȳmed   feorhlāstas bær.
Ðǣr wæs on blōde   brim weallende;
atol ȳða ġeswinġ   eal ġemenġed
hāton heolfre   heorodrēore wēol.
850 Dēaðfǣġe dēog   siððan drēama lēas

sinews sprang, joints snapped.
Glory in battle was given to Beowulf.
It was Grendel who had to go from there,
mortally wounded, to the marshy slopes,
back to his home, bereft of hope.
He knew all too well that his life was over,
the number of his days. After the deadly clash,
the wish of all the Danes had been granted.
He who had come from afar, wise and resolute,
had cleansed Hrothgar's hall, saved it from hate.
His night's work pleased him, his proof of valor.
The man of the Geats had made good his boast
to the East-Danes, and also found
a cure for the distress they had endured,
the heartfelt sorrow they had had to suffer,
through dire necessity, no small grief.
There was a clear sign of it when the bold one
laid down the hand, the arm and shoulder,
beneath the hall's high-gabled roof,
Grendel's grasp all together.

Then in the morning, as I have heard,
there was many a warrior round the gift-hall,
the folk-chiefs came from far and near,
along the wide ways, to see the wonder,
the traces of the evil one. Not one of those
who viewed the track of the defeated
regretted his passing, how he, beaten and despairing,
doomed and flying, left bloody footprints
to the monsters' lake. There the mere
was full of blood, the churning waves
stained with hot gore, seething with gush of battle.
He hid, death-doomed, once in despair,

in fenfreoðo   feorh āleġde,
hǣþene sāwle;   þǣr him hel onfēng.
Panon eft ġewiton   ealdġesīðas
swylċe ġeong maniġ   of gomenwāþe
855 fram mere mōdġe   mēarum rīdan,
beornas on blancum.   Ðǣr wæs Bēowulfes
mǣrðo mǣned;   moniġ oft ġecwæð
þætte sūð nē norð   be sǣm twēonum
ofer eormengrund   ōþer nǣniġ
860 under sweġles begong   sēlra nǣre
rondhæbbendra,   rīċes wyrðra.
Nē hīe hūru winedrihten   wiht ne lōgon,
glædne Hrōðgār,   ac þæt wæs gōd cyning.
Hwīlum heaþorōfe   hlēapan lēton,
865 on ġeflit faran   fealwe mēaras,
ðǣr him foldwegas   fæġere þūhton,
cystum cūðe.   Hwīlum cyninges þeġn,
guma ġilphlæden,   ġidda ġemyndiġ,
sē ðe eal fela   ealdġeseġena
870 worn ġemunde,   word ōþer fand
sōðe ġebunden;   secg eft ongan
sīð Bēowulfes   snyttrum styrian
ond on spēd wrecan   spel ġerāde,
wordum wrixlan;   wēlhwylċ ġecwæð
875 þæt hē fram Siġemunde[s]   secgan hȳrde
ellendǣdum,   uncūþes fela,
Wælsinges ġewin,   wīde sīðas,
þāra þe gumena bearn   ġearwe ne wiston,
fǣhðe ond fyrena,   būton Fitela mid hine,
880 þonne hē swulċes hwæt   secgan wolde,
êam his nefan,   swā hīe ā wǣron
æt nīða ġehwām   nȳdġesteallan;
hæfdon eal fela   eotena cynnes
sweordum ġesǣġed.   Siġemunde ġesprong
885 æfter dēaðdæġe   dōm unlȳtel

100

in the fen-fastness, he had forfeited his life,
his heathen soul. There Hell took him.
    Back from the lake many bold veterans
rode their mounts cheerfully, and young ones too,
men on white horses. There they proclaimed
the fame of Beowulf, many men often said
that south or north, between the seas,
across the whole earth beneath the sky's expanse,
there was no man better among the shield-bearers,
none worthier to rule. Nor did they in any way
find any fault with their friend and lord,
the gracious Hrothgar, for he was a good king.
Sometimes the warriors raced their roan horses,
let them gallop where the going was good,
they knew the paths. Sometimes a king's thane,
skilled in verse-craft, who knew many songs,
had in his mind many old stories,
put words together, properly linked,
began to tell cunningly the quest of Beowulf,
put a tale together, weaving his words.
He said a great deal of the glorious deeds
that he had heard of Sigemund, the strife of the Volsung,
much that was not known, the wide adventures,
feuds and troubles, of which the children of men
knew nothing clearly, except for Fitela,
who was with him, whenever he wished
to say anything as uncle to nephew,
companions in need as they always were.
Their swords had ended many of the giant-race.
After his death, no little fame
was given to Sigemund, once, hard in battle,

syþðan wīġes heard   wyrm ācwealde,
hordes hyrde.   Hē under hārne stān,
æþelinges bearn,   āna ġenēðde
frēcne dǣde,   nē wæs him Fitela mid;
890 hwæþre him ġesǣlde   ðæt þæt swurd þurhwōd
wrǣtlicne wyrm,   þæt hit on wealle ætstōd,
dryhtliċ īren;   draca morðre swealt.
Hæfde āglǣċa   elne ġegongen
þæt hē bēahhordes   brūcan mōste
895 selfes dōme;   sǣbāt ġehlēod,
bær on bearm scipes   beorhte frætwa
Wælses eafera;   wyrm hāt ġemealt.
Sē wæs wreċċena   wīde mǣrost
ofer werþēode,   wīġendra hlēo,
900 ellendǣdum   — hē þæs ǣr onðāh —
siððan Heremōdes   hild sweðrode,
eafoð ond ellen.   Hē mid Ēotum wearð
on fēonda ġeweald   forð forlācen,
snūde forsended.   Hine sorhwylmas
905 lemedon tō lange;   hē his lēodum wearð,
eallum æþellingum   tō aldorċeare;
swylċe oft bemearn   ǣrran mǣlum
swīðferhþes sīð   snotor ċeorl moniġ,
sē þe him bealwa tō   bōte ġelȳfde,
910 þæt þæt ðēodnes bearn   ġeþēon scolde,
fæderæþelum onfōn,   folc ġehealdan,
hord ond hlēoburh,   hæleþa rīċe,
ēþel Scyldinga.   Hē þǣr eallum wearð,
mǣġ Hiġelāces,   manna cynne,
915 frēondum ġefæġra;   hine fyren onwōd.
Hwīlum flītende   fealwe strǣte
mēarum mǣton.   Ðā wæs morgenlēoht
scofen ond scynded.   Ēode scealc moniġ
swīðhicgende   tō sele þām hēan
920 searowundor sēon;   swylċe self cyning

he had killed the dragon, guardian of the hoard.
Alone the prince's child dared the valiant deed
beneath grey stone: Fitela was not with him.
Yet it was granted him that his sword pierced
right through the shining worm, so it stood in the wall,
the splendid blade. From the cruel stroke
the dragon died. By valor the fierce one
had brought it about that he could enjoy
at his own will the whole of the ring-hoard.
The son of Völsi loaded his boat,
carried bright treasures into the ship's hold.
    The worm melted in its own heat.
The protector of nobles became the most famous
for deeds of valor of all adventurers
among the peoples – he had profited by them –
ever since the warfare of King Heremod,
his might and glory, became diminished.
Among the Jutes he was betrayed
into enemies' power, swiftly put an end to.
Waves of sorrow oppressed him too long.
To his people he became a deadly danger,
to all the noble ones. In times gone by
many a wise man lamented what happened
to the mighty one, men who had trusted him
as a cure for their cares, thinking the prince's child
would flourish for them, follow his father's line,
and guard the people, their wealth and citadel,
the whole kingdom and land of the Scyldings.
To his friends and all others Hygelac's kinsman
became ever more pleasing. Evil possessed Heremod.
    Sometimes the racers galloped their horses
along the bare pathways. Then the light of morning
was up and far advanced. To the high hall
went many a wise man to see the strange wonder.
As did the king himself, the keeper of treasure,

of brȳdbūre,   bēahhorda weard,
tryddode tīrfæst   ġetrume micle,
cystum ġecȳþed,   ond his cwēn mid him
medostiġġe mæt   mæġþa hōse.

925   Hrōðgār maþelode — hē tō healle ġēong,
stōd on stapole,   ġeseah stēapne hrōf
golde fāhne,   ond Grendles hond:
'Ðisse ansȳne   alwealdan þanc
lungre ġelimpe.   Fela iċ lāþes ġebād,
930 grynna æt Grendle;   ā mæġ God wyrċan
wunder æfter wundre,   wuldres hyrde.
Ðæt wæs unġeāra   þæt iċ æniġra mē
wēana ne wēnde   tō wīdan feore
bōte ġebīdan,   þonne blōde fāh
935 hūsa sēlest   heorodrēoriġ stōd,
wēa wīdscofen   witena ġehwylc*um*,
ðāra þe ne wēndon   þæt hīe wīdeferhð
lēoda landġeweorc   lāþum beweredon
scuccum ond scinnum.   Nū scealc hafað
940 þurh drihtnes miht   dǣd ġefremede
ðē wē ealle   ǣr ne meahton
snyttrum besyrwan.   Hwæt, þæt secgan mæġ
efne swā hwylċ mæġþa   swā ðone magan cende
æfter gumcynnum,   ġyf hēo ġȳt lyfað,
945 þæt hyre ealdmetod   ēste wǣre
bearnġebyrdo.   Nū iċ, Bēowulf, þeċ,
secg bet[e]sta,   mē for sunu wylle
frēoġan on ferhþe;   heald forð tela
nīwe sibbe.   Ne bið þē [n]æniġrę gād
950 worolde wilna   þe iċ ġeweald hæbbe.
Ful oft iċ for lǣssan   lēan teohhode,
hordweorþunge   hnāhran rinċe,
sǣmran æt sæcce.   Þū þē self hafast
dǣdum ġefremed   þæt þīn [dōm] lyfað

known for his goodness, stepping nobly
with a great company from his wife's chamber.
The queen as well walked along the path
to the mead-hall with her handmaidens.

   Hrothgar spoke. He went to the hall,
stood on the steps, looked at the steep roof
shining with gold, and Grendel's hand:
"May thanks for this sight rise swift to the Almighty.
Many injuries I endured, much evil from Grendel.
God can always perform, the Guardian of Glory,
miracle after miracle. I could not imagine
how I could ever expect cure for any of my cares,
when this best of houses stood stained with blood
and the marks of battle, a pain far-reaching
for all my counsellors, who could not hope
ever to protect the people's house
from the evil ones, demons and monsters.
Now one man has, through the might of the Lord,
performed a deed which none of us
in all our wisdom could ever have thought of.
Indeed, whichever it was of womankind
who brought forth this man to be among us,
she may well say, if she still lives,
that the God of old was gracious to her
when she bore her child. Now, Beowulf, best of men,
I will hold you in my heart as a son:
from now on, keep well your new kinship.
Whatever in the world that you wish for,
I will hold back nothing that I own.
I have often given rewards for less,
valuable treasure to a lesser man,
one weaker in battle. You have performed
such deeds that your fame will live forever.

955 āwa tō aldre.   Alwalda þeċ
gōde forġylde,   swā hē nū ġȳt dyde!'
    Bēowulf maþelode,   bearn Ecþeowes:
'Wē þæt ellenweorc   ēstum miclum,
feohtan fremedon,   frēcne ġenēðdon
960 eafoð uncūþes.   Ūþe iċ swīþor
þæt ðū hine selfne   ġesēon mōste,
fēond on frætewum   fylwēriġne.
Iċ hine hrædlīċe   heardan clammum
on wælbedde   wrīþan þōhte,
965 þæt hē for mundgripe   mīnum scolde
licgean līfbysiġ,   būtan his līċ swice;
iċ hine ne mihte,   þā metod nolde,
ganges ġetwǣman,   nō iċ him þæs ġeorne ætfealh,
feorhġenīðlan;   wæs tō foremihtiġ
970 fēond on fēþe.   Hwæþere hē his folme forlēt
tō līfwraþe   lāst weardian,
earm ond eaxle.   Nō þǣr æniġe swā þēah
fēasceaft guma   frōfre ġebohte:
nō þȳ lenġ leofað   lāðġetēona
975 synnum ġeswenċed,   ac hyne sār hafað
in nīðgripe   nearwe befongen,
balwon bendum;   ðǣr ābīdan sceal
maga māne fāh   miclan dōmes,
hū him scīr metod   scrīfan wille.'
980   Ðā wæs swīgra secg,   sunu Eclāfes,
on ġylpsprǣċe   gūðġeweorca,
siþðan æþelingas   eorles cræfte
ofer hēanne hrōf   hand sċēawedon,
fēondes fingras;   foran ǣġhwylċ wæs,
985 steda næġla ġehwylċ   stȳle ġelīcost,
hǣþenes handsporu,   hilderinċes,
eġl' unhēoru.   Ǣġhwylċ ġecwæð
þæt him heardra nān   hrīnan wolde
īren ǣrgōd   þæt ðæs āhlǣċan
990 blōdġe beadufolme   onberan wolde.

May the Almighty grant you good fortune,
as he has done already just now."
   Beowulf spoke, son of Ecgtheow:
"Very willingly did we venture
on this exploit, fought the fight,
boldly tested the strength of the unknown.
I would rather have it that you saw for yourself
the demon lying dead in his trappings.
I meant to hold him swiftly with hard grasp
on his deathbed, so he should lie dying
from my handgrip, had not his body slipped me.
But against God's will I could not stop his going,
no matter how eagerly I grappled my deadly foe.
The fiend was too strong in his flight away.
Still, to save his life, he left his hand behind,
his arm and shoulder, to mark his track.
Nor did the wretch buy any relief by it.
The ill-doer marked by sins will live no longer for it,
his wound has him tightly gripped
in unforgiving fetters of pain.
There the sinful creature will have to abide
the great judgment, the bright Lord's sentence."
   Then the son of Ecglaf was quieter in speech,
in his boasting about battle-deeds,
once the princes could see, up in the rafters,
won by the strength of the noble one,
the hand and fingers of the fiend.
The hand-spur of the heathen warrior
was tipped with nails just like steel,
a monstrous claw. Everyone said
that not the best of iron blades
would strike harder, do more damage,
than the monster's bloody talon.

Ðā wæs hāten hreþe   Heort innanweard
folmum ġefrætwod;   fela þæra wæs,
wera ond wīfa   þe þæt wīnreċed,
ġestsele ġyredon.   Goldfāg scinon
995 web æfter wāgum,   wundọrsīona fela
secga ġehwylcum   þāra þe on swylċ starå.
Wæs þæt beorhte bold   tōbrocen swīðe,
eal inneweard   īrẹnbendum fæst,
heorras tōhlidene;   hrōf āna ġenæs
1000 ealles ansund,   þē se āglǣċa
fyrendǣdum fāg   on flēam ġewand,
aldres orwēna.   Nō þæt ȳðe byð
tō beflēonne   — fremme sē þe wille —
ac ġesēċan sceal   sāwlberendra
1005 nȳde ġenȳdde,   niþ̊a bearna,
grundbūendra   ġearwe stōwe,
þǣr his līċhoma   leġerbedde fæst
swefeþ æfter symle.
Þā wæs sǣl ond mǣl
þæt tō healle gang   Healfdenes sunu;
1010 wolde self cyning   symbel þicgan.
Ne ġefræġen iċ þā mǣġþe   māran weorode
ymb hyra sinċġyfan   sēl ġebǣran.
Bugon þā tō benċe   blǣdāgande,
fylle ġefǣgon;   fæġere ġeþǣgon
1015 medoful maniġ   māgas þāra
swīðhicgende   on sele þām hēan,
Hrōðgār ond Hrōþulf.   Heorot innan wæs
frēondum āfylled;   nalles fāċẹnstafas
Þēod-Scyldingas   þenden fremedon.
1020 Forġeaf þā Bēowulfe   brand Healfdenes,
seġen gyldenne   sigores tō lēane,
hroden hildecumbọr,   helm ond byrnan.
Mǣre māðþumsweord   maniġe ġesāwon
beforan beorn beran.   Bēowulf ġeþāh

Quickly it was ordered that Heorot the wine-hall
be refurnished internally. Many men and women
replaced the decorations of the guest-hall.
Coloured tapestries shone with gold
along the walls, many wonderful sights
for all who look at them. Locked together within
by iron bands, the bright building,
was much damaged, doors off their hinges.
Only the roof was left entirely untouched,
when the monster stained with crimes
turned away in flight, despairing of life.
It is hard to flee, try it who will,
for every one of the children of men,
every soul alive on earth
must go to the place appointed for it,
where the body after the banquet
will sleep in its grave.
                              Then it was time
for the son of Healfdene to enter the hall,
the king himself wished to join the feast.
I have never heard of people bearing themselves better
with a greater company around their treasure-giver.
The famous ones sat down on benches,
enjoyed their fill. As was proper,
the mighty kinsmen drank many a mead-cup
in the high hall, Hrothgar and Hrothulf.
Heorot was filled with friends. At that time the Scyldings
did not commit deeds of treachery.
As reward for victory, Beowulf was given
the sword of Healfdene, a golden ensign,
a decorated battle-banner, helmet and mail-shirt.
Many saw the sword, famous and valuable,
carried before the warrior. Beowulf took the cup

1025 ful on flette;   nō hē þǣre feohġyfte
for sc[ē]oten[d]um   scamiġan ðorfte.
Ne ġefrǣġn iċ frēondlicor   fēower mādmas
golde ġeġyrede   gummanna fela
in ealobenċe   ōðrum ġesellan.

1030 Ymb þæs helmes hrōf   hēafodbeorge
wīrum bewunden   walu ūtan hēold,
þæt him fē[o]la lāf   frēcne ne meahte
scūrheard sceþðan,   þonne scyldfreca
onġēan gramum   gangan scolde.

1035 Heht ðā eorla hlēo   eahta mēaras
fǣtedhlēore   on flet tēon,
(in) under eoderas;   þāra ānum stōd
sadol searwum fāh,   sinċe ġewurþad;
þæt wæs hildesetl   hēahcyninges

1040 ðonne sweorda ġelāc   sunu Healfdenes
efnan wolde —   nǣfre on ōre læġ
wīdcūþes wīġ   ðonne walu fēollon.
Ond ðā Bēowulfe   bēga ġehwæþres
eodor Ingwina   onweald ġetēah,

1045 wicga ond wǣpna;   hēt hine wēl brūcan.
Swā manlīċe   mǣre þēoden,
hordweard hæleþa,   heaþorǣsas ġeald
mēarum ond mādmum,   swā hȳ nǣfre man lȳhð,
sē þe secgan wile   sōð æfter rihte.

1050   Ðā ġȳt ǣġhwylcum   eorla drihten
þāra þe mid Bēowulfe   brimlāde tēah
on þǣre medubenċe   māþðum ġesealde,
yrfelāfe,   ond þone ǣnne heht
golde forġyldan,   þone ðe Grendel ǣr

1055 māne ācwealde —   swā hē hyra mā wolde,
nefne him wītiġ God   wyrd forstōde
ond ðæs mannes mōd.   Metod eallum wēold
gumena cynnes,   swā hē nū ġīt dēð.

for all to see. He had no need
to feel ashamed of the gifts he was given
before the warriors. I have never heard
of four treasures, gold-adorned,
given by many more generously
to another man on the ale-bench.
Around the helmet-crest a head-protection,
a ridge of twisted wires kept out the death-stroke,
so that no sword, tempered in battle,
and filed with care, could cause great harm,
when the shield-warrior must face his enemies.
The protector of warriors then had eight mares
brought into the precinct, on to the hall-floor.
One of them bore a saddle shiningly adorned,
the high-king's war-seat when the son of Healfdene
wished to take part in the play of swords.
The famous one was ever at the front
when men were falling. And then the ruler
of the friends of Ing gave to Beowulf
possession of both, horses and weapons,
told him, use them well. In this manly way
the famous prince, hoard-guardian of heroes,
rewarded the battle-clash with horses and treasures,
undeniable by anyone who will tell the true story.

   Yet in addition did the lord of nobles
give a valuable gift, an heirloom from the past,
on the mead-bench to each man of those
who had with Beowulf crossed the sea
and ordered compensation to be paid in gold
for the one whom Grendel had criminally killed –
as he would have killed more, if God in his wisdom
had not curbed that chance, and one man's courage.
God ruled the whole of all humanity,

Forþan bi'ð andġit   ǽġhwǽr sēlest,
1060 ferh'ðes foreþanc: fela sceal ġebīdan
lēofes ond lāþes   sē þe longe hēr
on 'ðyssum windagum   worolde brūce'ð.
    Þǽr wæs sang ond swēġ   samod ætgædere
fore Healfdenes   hildewīsan,
1065 gomenwudu grēted,   ġid oft wrecen,
'ðonne Healgamen,   Hrōþgāres scop
æfter medobenċe   mǽnan scolde
Finnes eafer*an;*   'ðā hīe se fǽr beġeat,
hǽle'ð Healf-Dena,   Hnæf Scyldinga
1070 in Frēswǽle   feallan scolde.
    Nē hūru Hildeburh   herian þorfte
Ēotena trēowe;   unsynnum wear'ð
beloren lēofum   æt þām *li*ndplegan
bearnum ond brō'ðrum;   hīe on ġebyrd hruron
1075 gāre wunde;   þæt wæs ġeōmuru ides!
Nalles hōlinga   Hōces dohtor
meotodsceaft bemearn   syþ'ðan morgen cōm,
'ðā hēo under sweġle   ġesēon meahte
morþorbealo māga,   þǽr hē[o] ǽr mǽste hēold
1080 worolde wynne.   Wīġ ealle fornam
Finnes þeġnas   nemne fēaum ānum,
þæt hē ne mehte   on þǽm me'ðelstede
wīġ Henġeste   wiht ġefeohtan,
nē þā wēalāfe   wīġe forþringan,
1085 þēodnes 'ðeġne;   ac hiġ him ġeþinġo budon,
þæt hīe him ō'ðer flet   eal ġerȳmdon,
healle ond hēahsetl,   þæt hīe healfre ġeweald
wi'ð Ēotena bearn   āgan mōston,
ond æt feohġyftum   Folcwaldan sunu
1090 dōgra ġehwylċe   Dene weorþode,
Henġestes hēap   hringum wenede
efne swā swī'ðe   sinċġestrēonum

as still He does. So it is always best
to be aware, take thought for the future.
Anyone who lives long here in the world,
in these days of strife, is bound to experience
many events, both good and bad.
   Then song and music rose together
before Healfdene's commander, the harp was played,
a lay often sung, once Healgamen,
Hrothgar's court-poet, told on the mead-bench
of the child of Finn. When the attack came,
Hnæf of the Scyldings, hero of the Half-Danes,
was to fall in battle.
                Certainly Hildeburh
had no cause to praise the good faith of the Jutes.
At the play of shields she was to lose
her dear son and brother, both without cause.
They were fated to fall, wounded by spears:
that was a sad lady. Not without reason
did the daughter of Hoc lament her destiny,
when morning came and she could see
under the sky, where before she had felt
the world's greatest joy, the fatal battle
between kinsmen. War claimed all Finn's thanes,
except for a few, so that he could not
fight to a finish the feud with Hengest,
nor could he wipe out the sad survivors
of the prince's thanes. So they were offered a deal,
that they would vacate another building for them,
a hall and a high-seat, so that they could have
joint possession with the children of the Jutes,
and at the gift-giving the son of Folcwalda
would every day honor the Danes,
the followers of Hengest, pay them as much
in rings and treasures of ornamented gold

fǣttan goldes swā hē Frēsena cyn
on bēorsele byldan wolde.
1095 Ðā hīe ġetruwedon on twā healfa
fæste frioðuwǣre. Fin Henġeste
elne unflitme āðum benemde
þæt hē þā wēalāfe weotena dōme
ārum hēolde, þæt ðǣr ǣniġ mon
1100 wordum nē worcum wǣre ne brǣce,
nē þurh inwitsearo ǣfre ġemǣnden,
ðēah hīe hira bēagġyfan banan folgedon
ðēodenlēase, þā him swā ġeþearfod wæs;
ġyf þonne Frȳsna hwylċ frēcnen sprǣċe
1105 ðæs morþorhetes myndgiend wǣre,
þonne hit sweordes ecg syððan scēde.
Ād wæs ġeæfned ond icge gold
āhæfen of horde; Here-Scyldinga
betst beadorinca wæs on bǣl ġearu.
1110 Æt þǣm āde wæs ēþġesȳne
swātfāh syrċe, swȳn eal gylden,
eofer īrenheard, æþeling maniġ
wundum āwyrded; sume on wǣle crungon.
Hēt ðā Hildeburh æt Hnæfes āde
1115 hire selfre sunu sweoloðe befæstan,
bānfatu bærnan, ond on bǣl dôn
ēame on eaxle. Ides gnornode,
ġeōmrode ġiddum. Gūðrēċ āstāh,
wand tō wolcnum; wælfȳra mǣst
1120 hlynode for hlāwe. Hafelan multon,
benġeato burston ðonne blōd ætspranc,
lāðbite līċes; līġ ealle forswealg,
gǣsta ġīfrost, þāra ðe þǣr gūð fornam
bēga folces. Wæs hira blǣd scacen.

1125 Ġewiton him ðā wīġend wīca neosian
frēondum befeallen, Frȳsland ġesēon,

as he gave out to gladden the Frisians
in the beer-hall. Then on both sides
they made a firm compact of peace.
Finn swore Hengest oaths, strongly, incontestably,
that he would, by the advice of his councillors
treat the sad survivors with due respect,
and that if any man should break the compact
by word or deed, or ever speak of them
with ill intent, even though they followed
their ring-giver's killer, as they were compelled to,
without a lord – if, then, any Frisian
brought up the deadly strife with provoking speech,
then it would be settled by the edge of the sword.
A pyre was raised, and shining gold
brought out from hoard. The best warrior
of the Raider-Scyldings was ready for the flame.
There on the pyre it was plain to see
bloodstained mail, boar-images
in gold and iron, many a prince
dead of wounds; they died in battle.
At the pyre of Hnæf Hildeburh had her son
committed to the flames, his corpse cremated,
burned with his uncle, side by side.
The woman mourned, sang a lament.
Smoke rose up, circling to the sky,
a great death-fire roaring before the barrow.
Skulls melted, wounds broke open so the blood gushed out
from the corpse-gashes. Fire, greediest of spirits,
swallowed them all, all those from both sides
whom war had taken. Their lives were over.

The warriors dispersed, went back friendless,
to their homes in Frisia, towns and villages.

hāmas ond hēaburh.   Henġest ðā ġȳt
wælfāgne wintẹr   wunode mid Finne;
h[ē] unhlitme   eard ġemunde,
1130 þēah þe *ne* meahte   on mere drīfan
hrinġedstefnan   — holm storme wēol,
won wið winde,   wintẹr ȳþe belēac
īsġebinde —   oþ ðæt ōþer cōm
ġēar in ġeardas,   swā nū ġȳt dêð,
1135 þā ðe syngāles   sēle bewitiað,
wuldọrtorhtan weder.   Ðā wæs winter scacen,
fæġer foldan bearm.   Fundode wreċċa,
ġist of ġeardum;   hē tō gyrnwræce
swīðor þōhte   þonne tō sǣlāde,
1140 ġif hē tornġemōt   þurhtēon mihte,
þæt hē Ēotena bearn   inne ġemunde —
swā hē ne forwyrnde   woroldrǣdenne —
þonne him Hūnlāfing   hildelēoman,
billa sēlest   on bearm dyde,
1145 þæs wǣron mid Ēotum   ecge cūðe.
Swylċe ferhðfrecan   Fin eft beġeat
sweordbealo slīðen   æt his selfes hām,
siþðan grimne gripe   Gūðlāf ond Ōslāf
æfter sǣsīðe   sorge mǣndon,
1150 ætwiton wēana dǣl;   ne meahte wǣfre mōd
forhabban in hreþre.   Ðā wæs heal *r*oden
fēonda fēorum,   swilċe Fin slæġen,
cyning on corþre,   ond sēo cwēn numen.
Scēotend Scyldinga   tō scypon feredon
1155 eal inġesteald   eorðcyninges,
swylċe hīe æt Finnes hām   findan meahton
siġla searoġimma.   Hīe on sǣlāde
drihtliċe wīf   tō Denum feredon,
lǣddon tō lēodum.
                    Lēoð wæs āsungen,
1160 glēomannes ġyd.   Gamen eft āstāh,

Hengest stayed with Finn, a winter haunted
by the killings. He thought of home
with deep longing, though he could not launch
his ring-prowed ship – the sea raged with storm,
wrestled against wind, winter's ice locked the waves
– until a new year came, weather fine and bright,
obeying the seasons, as it still does.
Winter had gone, earth's surface was fair.
The exile longed to leave, to quit his place
as guest of Finn, but more he thought
of desired revenge than any sea-journey,
if he could bring about a bitter clash,
remember in it the children of the Jutes.
So he did not reject the role of leader,
when the son of Hunlaf laid in his lap
Battle-light, the best of swords.
Well did the Jutes know its edges.
So cruel death came upon Finn,
the bold-hearted one in his own home,
once Guthlaf and Oslaf, arrived by sea,
spoke of their sorrow and the fierce attack,
brought up the injuries they had suffered.
The troubled spirit could not hold back.
Then the hall was reddened by the blood of enemies,
Finn killed as well, the king amidst his guards,
his queen taken back to her own people.
The Scylding warriors carried to their ships
all they could find in the home of Finn,
all of his goods, gems and treasures.
To Denmark they took the noble lady
by sea-journey.
                    The song was sung
the minstrel had finished. Merriment rose again,

beorhtode benċswēġ;   byrelas sealdon
wīn of wundẹrfatum.   Þā cwōm Wealhþēo forð
gān under gyldnum bēage   þǣr þā gōdan twēġen
sǣton suhterġefæderan;   þā ġȳt wæs hiera sib ætgædere,
ǣġhwylċ ōðrum trȳwe.   Swylċe þǣr Ūnferþ þyle
æt fōtum sæt frēan Scyldinga;   ġehwylċ hiora his ferhþe trēowde,
þæt hē hæfde mōd miċel,   þēah þe hē his māgum nǣre
ārfæst æt ecga ġelācum.   Spræc ðā ides Scyldinga:
'Onfōh þissum fulle,   frēodrihten mīn,
1170 sinċes brytta.   Þū on sǣlum wes,
goldwine gumena,   ond tō Ġēatum sprec
mildum wordum,   swā sceal man dôn.
Bēo wið Ġēatas glæd,   ġeofena ġemyndiġ,
nēan ond feorran   [þā] þū nū hafast.
1175 Mē man sæġde   þæt þū ðē for sunu wolde
hereri[n]ċ habban.   Heorot is ġefǣlsod,
bēahsele beorhta;   brūc þenden þū mōte
maniġra mēdo,   ond þīnum māgum lǣf
folc ond rīċe   þonne ðū forð scyle,
1180 metodsceaft sêon.   Iċ mīnne can
glædne Hrōþulf,   þæt hē þā ġeogoðe wile
ārum healdan   ġyf þū ǣr þonne hē,
wine Scildinga,   worold oflǣtest;
wēne iċ þæt hē mid gōde   ġyldan wille
1185 uncran eaferan   ġif hē þæt eal ġemon,
hwæt wit tō willan   ond tō worðmyndum
umbọrwesendum ǣr   ārna ġefremedon.'
Hwearf þā bī benċe,   þǣr hyre byre wǣron,
Hrēðrīċ ond Hrōðmund,   ond hæleþa bearn,
1190 ġiogoð ætgædere;   þǣr se gōda sæt,
Bēowulf Ġēata   be þǣm ġebrōðrum twǣm.

Him wæs ful boren,   ond frēondlaþu
wordum bewæġned,   ond wunden gold
ēstum ġeēawed,   earmrēade twā,

talk brightened up on the benches,
servants gave out wine in splendid cups.
Then Wealhtheow came forward, wearing her golden coronet,
to where they sat, the two good men,
uncle and nephew. At this time
the family was united, each true to the other.
Their counsellor Unferth sat at the feet
of the Scyldings' lord. Each of them trusted him,
thought he had great courage, although to his kinsmen
he had not been merciful in the play of blades.
The Scylding lady spoke: "Take this cup, my noble lord,
gold-friend of men, and to the Geats
speak kind words as is only right.
Be generous to the Geats, think of gifts for them,
all that you have from far and near.
I was told, you wished to have the warrior as your son.
Heorot has been cleansed, the bright ring-hall.
Enjoy the praise of many as long as permitted to you,
and leave folk and kingdom to your own sons,
when you must pass on and see destiny.
I know my gracious Hrothulf will honor the young ones,
if it should happen, friend of the Scyldings,
that you leave the world before he should do so.
I expect he will repay your sons and mine
with all good things, if he remembers
the favors we have done to honor and please him,
while he was a child." Then she went to the bench
where her sons sat, Hrethric and Hrothmund,
with the young men, children of heroes.
The gallant man sat there also,
Beowulf the Geat, by the two brothers.

   The cup was then carried to him,
a friendly welcome given in words,
and twisted gold given with good will:

1195 hræġl ond hringas,   healsbēaga mǣst
þāra þe iċ on foldan   ġefræġen hæbbe.
Nǣniġne iċ under sweġle   sēlran hȳrde
hordmāðð<u>u</u>m hæleþa   syþðan Hāma ætwæġ
tō þǣre byrhtan byriġ   Brōsinga mene,
1200 siġle ond sinċfæt —   searonīðas *flēah*
Eormenrīċes,   ġeċēas ēċne rǣd.
Þone hrinġ hæfde   Hiġelāc Ġēata,
nefa Swertinges   nȳhstan sīðe,
siðþan hē under seġne   sinċ ealgode,
1205 wælrēaf werede;   hyne wyrd fornam
syþðan hē for wlenċo   wēan āhsode,
fǣhðe tō Frȳsum.   Hē þā frætwe wæġ,
eorclanstānas   ofer ȳða ful,
rīċe þēoden;   hē under rande ġecranc.
1210 Ġehwearf þā in Francna fæþm   feorh cyninges,
brēostġewǣdu,   ond se bēah somod.
Wyrsan wīġfrecan   wæl rēafeden
æfter gūðsceare;   Ġēata lēode
hrēawīċ hēoldon.   Heal swēġe onfēng.
1215 Wealhðēo maþelode;   hēo fore þǣm werede spræc:
'Brūc ðisses bēages,   Bēowulf lēofa,
hyse, mid hǣle,   ond þisses hræġles nēot,
þēo[d]ġestrēona,   ond ġeþēoh tela,
cen þeċ mid cræfte,   ond þyssum cnyhtum wes
1220 lāra līðe.   Iċ þē þæs lēan ġeman.
Hafast þū ġefēred   þæt ðē feor ond nēah
ealne wīdeferhþ   weras ehtiġað,
efne swā sīde   swā sǣ bebūgeð,
windġeard, weallas.   Wes þenden þū lifiġe,
1225 æþeling, ēadiġ.   Iċ þē an tela
sinċġestrēona.   Bēo þū suna mīnum
dǣdum ġedēfe,   drēamhealdende.
Hēr is ǣġhwylċ eorl   ōþrum ġetrȳwe,
mōdes milde,   mandrihtne hol[d];

two bracelets, mail-shirt and rings,
and the greatest neck-ring ever told of in the world.
Never have I heard of a better hoarded
treasure of heroes since Hama stole away
the Brosings' necklace to the bright city,
jewel and treasure-cup. He was flying
from the crafty malice of Eormenric,
he chose instead a lasting benefit.
Hygelac of the Geats, on his last venture,
Swerting's nephew, wore that neck-ring,
when he defended treasure and battle-loot
beneath his banner; bad luck overtook him,
when out of pride he sought out disaster,
fighting the Frisians. The lord of power
carried his treasures and precious stones
across the waves, fell beneath his shield.
The king's life left him in the land of the Franks,
and with it his armor and the neck-ring.
It was the worse warriors who robbed the dead
after the carnage. The killing-ground
held for ever the host of the Geats.
Merriment resumed in the mead-hall.
Wealhtheow spoke again, before the war-band:
"Dear Beowulf, young warrior,
enjoy this ring, use this mail-shirt,
live in prosperity, know your strength,
and give these boys your kind guidance.
I will remember to reward you for it.
You have so borne yourself that men everywhere,
from far and near, wherever the sea
and wind wrap the coasts, all respect you.
Prince, good luck to you as long as you live,
and I will grant you many treasures.
Be kind in your deeds to my sons,
hold them in joy. Here every noble
is true to the other, in good temper,
loyal to their lord. The thanes are united,

1230 þeġnas syndon ġeþwǣre,   þēod eal ġearo;
     druncne dryhtguman   dōð swā iċ bidde.'
        Ēode þā tō setle.   Þǣr wæs symbla cyst,
     druncon wīn weras.   Wyrd ne cūþon,
     ġeōsceaft grim*me*,   swā hit āgangen wearð
1235 eorla manegum,   syþðan ǣfen cwōm,
     ond him Hrōþgār ġewāt   tō hofe sīnum,
     rīċe tō ræste.   Reċed weardode
     unrīm eorla,   swā hīe oft ǣr dydon.
     Benċþelu beredon;   hit ġeondbrǣded wearð
1240 beddum ond bolstrum.   Bēorscealca sum
     fūs ond fǣġe   fletræste ġebēag.
     Setton him tō hēafdon   hilderandas,
     bordwudu beorhtan;   þǣr on benċe wæs
     ofer æþelinge   ȳþġesēne
1245 heaþostēapa helm,   hringed byrne,
     þrecwudu þrymliċ.   Wæs þēaw hyra
     þæt hīe oft wǣron   anwīġġearwe,
     ġē æt hām ġē on herġe,   ġē ġehwæþer þāra
     efne swylċe mǣla   swylċe hira mandryhtne
1250 þearf ġesǣlde;   wæs sēo þēod tilu.

        Sigon þā tō slǣpe.   Sum sāre anġeald
     ǣfenræste,   swā him ful oft ġelamp
     siþðan goldsele   Grendel warode,
     unriht æfnde,   oþ þæt ende becwōm,
1255 swylt æfter synnum.   Þæt ġesȳne wearþ,
     wīdcūþ werum,   þætte wrecend þā ġȳt
     lifde æfter lāþum,   lange þrāge,
     æfter gūðċeare;   Grendles mōdor,
     ides āglǣċwīf   yrmþe ġemunde,
1260 sē þe wæterġesan   wunian scolde,
     ċealde strēamas,   siþðan Cā*in* wearð
     tō ecgbanan   āngan brēþer,

the people all ready, as is right and proper,
the drinking warriors do as I ask them."
   She went to her seat. That was the best of feasts,
men drank wine. They did not know
what would happen – grim destiny,
as it has come about to many men –
once evening came, and Hrothgar left
for his chambers, the powerful one
went to his bed. A great number of nobles
stayed in the hall, as they often used to.
They cleared the floor, so it was spread
with pillows and bedrolls. One of those beer-drinkers
went to his rest marked for death.
They put their shields down by their heads,
bright paint on wood. There on the bench
it was easy to see by each nobleman
the steep-coned helmet, the ring-mail shirt,
the splendid spear. It was their habit
to be always ready for war, whether at home or on service,
on every occasion, just as need dictated
for their prince. They were a good people.

   They lay down to sleep. One of them paid sorely
for his evening rest, as had often happened,
before, when Grendel haunted the gold-hall,
did evil deeds, until an end came to him,
death for his sins. It was soon seen,
became widely known, that for the hateful one
an avenger still lived, long after that sad strife.
Grendel's mother, the monster-woman,
remembered her loss, she who had to live
in the cold currents, in dangerous water,
ever since Cain killed his only brother

fæderenmǣġe;   hē þā fāg ġewāt,
morþre ġemearcod   mandrēam flēon,
1265 wēsten warode.   Þanon wōc fela
ġeōsceaftgāsta;   wæs þǣra Grendel sum,
heorowearh heteliċ,   sē æt Heorote fand
wæċċendne wer   wīġes bīdan.
Þǣr him āglǣċa   ætgrǣpe wearð;
1270 hwæþre hē ġemunde   mæġenes strenġe,
ġimfæste ġife   ðe him God sealde,
ond him tō anwaldan   āre ġelȳfde,
frōfre ond fultum;   ðȳ hē þone fēond ofercwōm,
ġehnǣġde helle gāst.   Þā hē hēan ġewāt,
1275 drēame bedǣled   dēaþwīċ sēon,
mancynnes fēond,   ond his mōdor þā ġȳt
ġīfre ond galgmōd   ġegān wolde
sorhfulne sīð,   sunu *dēoð* wrecan.
     Cōm þā tō Heorote,   ðǣr Hrinġ-Dene
1280 ġeond þæt sæld swǣfun.   Þā ðǣr sōna wearð
edhwyrft eorlum,   siþðan inne fealh
Grendles mōdor.   Wæs se gryre lǣssa
efne swā micle   swā bið mæġþa cræft,
wīġgryre wīfes   be wǣpnedmen,
1285 þonne heoru bunden,   hamere ġeþrū*en,
sweord swāte fāh   swīn ofer helme
ecgum dyhttiġ   andweard scireð.
Þā wæs on healle   heardecg togen
sweord ofer setlum,   sīdrand maniġ
1290 hafen handa fæst;   helm ne ġemunde,
byrnan sīde,   þā hine se brōga anġeat.
Hēo wæs on ofste,   wolde ūt þanon,
fēore beorgan,   þā hēo onfunden wæs;
hraðe hēo æþelinga   ānne hæfde
1295 fæste befangen,   þā hēo tō fenne gang.
Sē wæs Hrōþgāre   hæleþa lēofost
on ġesīðes hād   be sǣm twēonum,

with the sword-edge, his father's son.
Guilty, he went away, marked by murder,
fleeing the joys of men, to live in the wilderness.
From him there awoke many ill-fated spirits.
One such was Grendel, grim and hateful outcast,
who at Heorot found one waiting to fight him.
There man and monster grappled together,
but the man remembered his strength and power,
the mighty gift which God gave him,
trusted too in the favor of the Almighty,
His help and comfort, by which he overcame the fiend,
laid low the hell-spirit. Mankind's enemy fled away,
defeated and joyless, to find his deathbed;
and his mother now meant to make
a painful visitation, avenge her son's death,
bitter and ravenous.
                              Where the Ring-Danes slept,
throughout the hall, she came to Heorot.
Suddenly fortune changed for the warriors,
when Grendel's mother broke her way in.
Less was her terror, in the same proportion
as the strength in war of a woman
against an armed man, when ringed swords
forged by hammers hack powerfully,
stained with blood, at men's boar-helmets.
There in the hall many hard-edged swords
were seized from the benches, many broad shields
grasped firmly in hand. When the horror hit them,
they did not think of helmets or stout armor.
Once discovered she desired only
to get out swiftly and save her life.
When she fled to the fen she had firmly seized
one of the nobles. The one she snatched
from his bed of rest, rich shield-warrior,
a man of renown, was to Hrothgar the dearest

rīċe randwiga,   þone ðe hēo on ræste ābrēat,
blǣdfæstne beorn.   Næs Bēowulf ðǣr,
1300 ac wæs ōþer in   ǣr ġeteohhod
æfter māþðu̯mġife   mǣrum Ġēate.
    Hrēam wearð on Heorote;   hēo under heolfre ġenam
cūþe folme;   cearu wæs ġenīwod,
ġeworden in wīcun.   Ne wæs þæt ġewrixle til,
1305 þæt hīe on bā healfa   bicgan scoldon
frēonda fēorum.
             Þā wæs frōd cyning,
hār hilderinċ   on hrēon mōde
syðþan hē aldorþeġn   unlyfiġendne,
þone dēorestan   dēadne wisse.
1310 Hraþe wæs tō būre   Bēowulf fetod,
sigorēadiġ secg.   Samod ǣrdæġe
ēode eorla sum,   æþele cempa
self mid ġesīðum   þǣr se snotera bād
hwæþer him a/walda   ǣfre wille
1315 æfter wēaspelle   wyrpe ġefremman.
    Gang ðā æfter flōre   fyrdwyrðe man
mid his handscale   — healwudu dynede —
þæt hē þone wīsan   wordum nǣġde
frēan Ingwina,   fræġn ġif him wǣre
1320 æfter nēodlaðu[m]   niht ġetǣse.

    Hrōðgār maþelode,   helm Scyldinga:
'Ne frīn þū æfter sǣlum!   Sorh is ġenīwod
Deniġea lēodum: dēad is Æschere,
Yrmenlāfes   yldra brōþor,
1325 mīn rūnwita   ond mīn rǣdbora,
eaxlġestealla   ðonne wē on orleġe
hafelan weredon,   þonne hniton fēþan,
eoferas cnysedan.   Swy(lċ) scolde eorl wesan,
[æþeling] ǣrgōd,   swylċ Æschere wæs.
1330 Wearð him on Heorote   tō handbanan

of all his men and his companions.
Beowulf was not there. After the gift-giving
another sleeping-place had been appointed
for the famous Geat. In Heorot there was tumult.
She took to the darkness the arm that she knew.
Sorrow was renewed, brought home again.
That was no fair exchange, that they should pay
two times over with the lives of friends.

Then the wise king, the grey-haired warrior,
was in a troubled mood, once he heard
that his chief thane, most cherished servant
had lost his life. Beowulf, the victorious one,
was quickly called to the king's chamber.
At dawn the noble champion, warrior with his comrades,
went to where he knew the wise one waited,
to see if the Almighty would ever change things
for the better, after the bad news.
With his picked troop the valiant man
trod the hall floor – its planks creaked –
so that he could greet the wise lord
of the friends of Ing. He asked if he had passed
a pleasant night, according to his wish.

    Hrothgar spoke, protector of the Scyldings:
"Don't talk about good! Grief has come back
to the people of the Danes. Æschere is dead,
Yrmenlaf's elder brother.
He was my confidant and my counsellor,
he stood beside me when in battle
we defended our heads, when dead men fell,
boar-helmets clashed. All that a noble should be,
a long-trusted prince, so Æschere was.
Now some drifting demon of death
has bare-handed killed him in Heorot.

127

wælgǣst wǣfre;   iċ ne wāt hwæðer
atol ǣse wlanc   eftsīðas tēah,
fylle ġefrēcnod.   Hēo þā fǣhðe wræc
þē þū ġystran niht   Grendel cwealdest
1335 þurh hǣstne hād   heardum clammum,
forþan hē tō lange   lēode mīne
wanode ond wyrde.   Hē æt wīġe ġecrang
ealdres scyldiġ,   ond nū ōþer cwōm
mihtiġ mānscaða,   wolde hyre mǣġ wrecan,
1340 ġē feor hafað   fǣhðe ġestǣled —
þæs þe þinċean mæġ   þeġne monegum,
sē þe æfter sinċġyfan   on sefan grēoteþ —
hreþerbealo hearde;   nū sēo hand liġeð,
sē þe ēow wēlhwylcra   wilna dohte.
1345 Iċ þæt londbūend,   lēode mīne,
selerǣdende   secgan hȳrde
þæt hīe ġesāwon   swylċe twēġen
micle mearcstapan   mōras healdan,
ellorgǣstas.   Ðǣra ōðer wæs,
1350 þæs þe hīe ġewislicost   ġewitan meahton,
idese onlīcnæs;   ōðer earmsceapen
on weres wæstmum   wræclāstas træd,
næfne hē wæs māra   þonne ǣniġ man ōðer;
þone on ġeārdagum   Grendel nemdo(n)
1355 foldbūende;   nō hīe fæder cunnon,
hwæþer him ǣniġ wæs   ǣr ācenned
dyrnra gāsta.   Hīe dȳġel lond
wariġeað, wulfhleoþu,   windiġe næssas,
frēcne fenġelād,   ðǣr fyrġenstrēam
1360 under næssa ġenipu   niþer ġewīteð,
flōd under foldan.   Nis þæt feor heonon
mīlġemearces   þæt se mere standeð;
ofer þǣm hongiað   hrinde bearwas,
wudu wyrtum fæst   wæter oferhelmað.

I do not know where she has gone,
gloating over her prey, pleased with her feast.
She was avenging the feud you began
when yester-night you killed Grendel
violently, with hard grip, because for too long
he had preyed on and destroyed my people.
He fell in the fight, forfeited his life.
And now another mighty ravager
has come, wanting to avenge her son,
indeed it will seem to many a man
that in this feud she has gone further –
anyone who grieves in heart for the treasure-giver,
feels bitter sorrow. Now the hand lies dead,
who would have given all that you desire.
   I have heard my people say, who live on the land,
talking in the hall, they have seen two such,
gigantic prowlers of the borderlands,
haunting the marshes, alien creatures.
As near as they could tell, one of them was
in the shape of a woman. The other misshapen wretch
trod the paths of exile in the form of a man,
except that he was bigger than any other.
The local people in days gone by
named him Grendel. Whether he was begotten
by any father from the dark spirits,
they do not know. They dwell, the giant pair,
in the hidden country, wolf-haunted slopes,
windy nesses, dangerous fenland,
where the stream pours down under the dark cliffs
from the mountain, to sink underground.
The mere lies from here not far in miles.
Over it there hang frosty-bound groves,
fast-rooted woods overshadow the water.

1365 Þǣr mæġ nihta ġehwǣm   nīðwundor sēon,
fȳr on flōde.   Nō þæs frōd leofað
gumena bearna   þæt þone grund wite.
Ðēah þe hǣðstapa   hundum ġeswenċed,
heorot hornum trum   holtwudu sēċe,
1370 feorran ġeflȳmed,   ǣr hē feorh seleð,
aldor on ōfre,   ǣr hē in wille,
hafelan [beorgan];   nis þæt hēoru stōw.
Þonon ȳðġeblond   up āstīgeð
won tō wolcnum   þonne wind styreþ
1375 lāð ġewidru,   oð þæt lyft ðrysmaþ,
roderas rēotað.   Nū is se rǣd ġelang
eft æt þē ānum.   Eard ġīt ne const,
frēcne stōwe,   ðǣr þū findan miht
sinniġne secg;   sēċ ġif þū dyrre!
1380 Iċ þē þā fǣhðe   fēo lēaniġe,
ealdġestrēonum,   swā iċ ǣr dyde,
wundnan golde,   ġyf þū on weġ cymest.'

Bēowulf maþelode,   bearn Ecgþeowes:
'Ne sorga, snotor guma.   Sēlre bið ǣġhwǣm
1385 þæt hē his frēond wrece   þonne hē fela murne.
Ūre ǣġhwylċ sceal   ende ġebīdan
worolde līfes;   wyrċe sē þe mōte
dōmes ǣr dēaþe;   þæt bið drihtguman
unlifġendum   æfter sēlest.
1390 Ārīs, rīċes weard,   uton hraþe fēran,
Grendles māgan   gang scēawiġan.
Iċ hit þē ġehāte,   nō hē on helm losaþ,
nē on foldan fæþm   nē on fyrġenholt
nē on ġyfenes grund,   gā þǣr hē wille.
1395 Ðȳs dōgor þū   ġeþyld hafa
wēana ġehwylċes,   swā iċ þē wēne tō.'
Āhlēop ðā se gomela,   Gode þancode,
mihtigan drihtne,   þæs se man ġespræc.

130

Every night you can see a dreadful sight there,
fire in the flood. No child of men
is so wise as to know what lies beneath.
Although the proud-horned stag, the heath-treader,
is pressed by hounds, hunted from afar,
and seeks shelter in the wood, he will on the shore
give up life and breath, before, to save his head,
he will plunge in. That is an uncanny place.
When the wind stirs up foul weather,
the tossing waves rise dark to the clouds,
until the air drizzles, the heavens weep.
Now the decision is up to you alone.
You do not know the land, the dangerous place
where you can find the sinful creature.
Seek if you dare! As I did before,
I will repay you for the pursuit
with ancient treasures, with twisted gold,
with many riches – if you return again."

   Beowulf spoke, child of Ecgtheow:
"Do not grieve, wise man. It is better for everyone
to avenge his friend than to mourn overmuch.
Every one of us will have to endure
an end of life in the world. Let he who may
gain himself glory before he dies.
That is best in the end for the dead warrior.
Guardian of the kingdom, stand up, let's go quickly
to follow the track of Grendel's kinsman.
I promise you, she will not find shelter,
not in the depths of the earth nor the mountain wood
nor at the sea-bottom, go where she will.
Today be patient in all your sorrows,
as I expect of you."
               The old man leapt up,
he thanked God, the mighty Lord, for what the man said.

Þā wæs Hrōðgāre   hors ġebǣted,
1400 wicg wundenfeax.   Wīsa fenġel
ġeatoliċ gende;   gumfēþa stōp
lindhæbbendra.   Lāstas wǣron
    æfter waldswaþum   wīde ġesȳne,
    gang ofer grundas,   [þǣr] ġeġnum fōr
1405 ofer myrċan mōr,   magoþeġna bær
    þone sēlestan   sāwollēasne
    þāra þe mid Hrōðgāre   hām eahtode.
    Oferēode þā   æþelinga bearn
    stēap stānhliðo,   stīġe nearwe,
1410 enġe ānpaðas,   uncūð ġelād,
    neowle næssas,   nicorhūsa fela;
    hē fēara sum   beforan gengde
    wīsra monna   wong scēawian,
    oþ þæt hē fǣringa   fyrġenbēamas
1415 ofer hārne stān   hleonian funde,
    wynlēasne wudu;   wæter under stōd
    drēoriġ ond ġedrēfed.   Denum eallum wæs,
    winum Scyldinga,   wærc on mōde
    tō ġeþolianne,   ðeġne monegum,
1420 oncȳð eorla ġehwǣm,   syðþan Æscheres
    on þām holmclife   hafelan mētton.
    Flōd blōde wēol   — folc tō sǣgon —
    hātan heolfre.   Horn stundum song
    fūsliċ (fyrd)lēoð.   Fēþa eal ġesæt.
1425 Ġesāwon ðā æfter wætere   wyrmcynnes fela,
    selliċe sǣdracan   sund cunnian,
    swylċe on næshleoðum   nicras licgean,
    ðā on undernmǣl   oft bewitiġað
    sorhfulne sīð   on seġlrāde,
1430 wyrmas ond wildēor.   Hīe on weġ hruron,
    bitere ond ġebolgne;   bearhtm onġēaton,
    gūðhorn galan.   Sumne Ġēata lēod
    of flānbogan   fēores ġetwǣfde,

Hrothgar's horse was bridled, with its braided hair,
then the wise lord rode off in splendor.
A troop of shield-bearers advanced on foot.
The traces were obvious along the forest path,
the trail across the ground where Grendel's mother had gone
directly across the dark moorland,
carrying the body of the best of all thanes
who made their home with Hrothgar the king.
The prince's child crossed steep, stony cliffs,
a narrow path, trails in single file,
unknown territory, precipitous promontories,
home to many monsters; he and a few others
showed the way in front for the wise men following,
until suddenly he came upon the mountain trees
leaning over grey stone, a cheerless wood.
Beneath it the water was bloody and turbid.
To all the Danes, to the friends of the Scyldings,
to many a thane, it was hard to bear,
a grief to all of them, when they encountered,
on the lakeside, the head of Æschere.
The lake welled with blood, as they looked at it,
with hot gore. Again and again a horn
sent out its war-song. The troop all sat down.
They saw in the water many snake-like creatures,
strange sea-dragons swimming there,
and on the banks of the lake monsters lying,
worms and wild beasts, which in the mornings often watch
for unfortunate seafarers. They scattered away,
bitterly angry, when they heard the bright call
of the war-horn. The hero of the Geats
put an end to the life of one of them,

ȳðġewinnes,   þæt him on aldre stōd
1435 herestrǣl hearda;   hē on holme wæs
sundes þē sǣnra   ðē hyne swylt fornam.
Hræþe wearð on ȳðum   mid eofersprēotum
heorohōcyhtum   hearde ġenearwod,
nīða ġenǣġed,   ond on næs togen,
1440 wundọrliċ wǣgbora;   weras scēawedon
gryrelicne ġist.

        Ġyrede hine Bēowulf
eorlġewǣdum,   nalles for ealdre mearn;
scolde herebyrne   hondum ġebrōden,
sīd ond searofāh,   sund cunnian,
1445 sēo ðe bāncofan   beorgan cūþe,
þæt him hildegrāp   hreþre ne mihte,
eorres inwitfenġ,   aldre ġesceþðan;
ac se hwīta helm   hafelan werede,
sē þe meregrundas   menġan scolde,
1450 sēcan sundġebland   sinċe ġeweorðad,
befongen frēawrāsnum,   swā hine fyrndagum
worhte wǣpna smið,   wundrum tēode,
besette swīnlīcum,   þæt hine syðþan nō
brond ne beadomēċas   bītan ne meahton.
1455 Næs þæt þonne mǣtost   mæġenfultuma
þæt him on ðearfe lāh   ðyle Hrōðgāres;
wæs þǣm hæftmēċe   Hrunting nama;
þæt wæs ān foran   ealdġestrēona;
ecg wæs īren,   ātẹrtānum fāh,
1460 āhyrded heaþoswāte;   nǣfre hit æt hilde ne swāc
manna ǣngum   þāra þe hit mid mundum bewand,
sē ðe gryresīðas   ġegān dorste,
folcstede fāra;   næs þæt forma sīð
þæt hit ellenweorc   æfnan scolde.
1465 Hūru ne ġemunde   mago Ecglāfes,
eafoþes cræftiġ,   þæt hē ǣr ġespræc
wīne druncen,   þā hē þæs wǣpnes onlāh

and to his swimming, with a shot from a bow.
The hard war-shaft stood in his heart.
He was the slower at swimming in the water
once death took him. He was attacked
quickly in the waves with boar-spears,
with hooked gaffs, violently dealt with,
the wonderful sea-pig dragged out on shore.
They stared at the strange and fearsome thing.

Beowulf did not care about his life.
He made ready in his armor.
The patterned ring-mail, stout and cunningly made,
which would guard his body, so that no malicious grip
of enraged enemies could reach heart or life,
it was to dive with him. And the shining helmet
which guarded his head, adorned with gold,
circled with chains, just as in days gone by
the weapon-smith had wonderfully forged it,
put boar-shapes on it, so that no brands,
no swords of battle could bite on it,
this too was to plumb the surging waters,
stir the lake-depths. That was not the least
of mighty aids which Hrothgar's herald
lent him in his need. The hilted sword
was called Hrunting. It was an ancient,
pre-eminent treasure. Its iron blade was covered
in serpent-patterns and tempered in blood.
It had never failed any man in battle
who took it in hand and dared to venture boldly
on his enemies' ground. This was not the first time
that it should do a deed of valor.
The son of Ecglaf, strong and mighty as he was,
certainly did not think of what he had said earlier,
drunk then with wine, when he lent the weapon

sēlran sweordfrecan;　selfa ne dorste
under ȳða ġewin　aldre ġenēþan,
1470　drihtscype drēogan;　þǣr hē dōme forlēas,
ellenmǣrðum.　Ne wæs þǣm ōðrum swā
syðþan hē hine tō gūðe　ġeġyred hæfde.

　　Bēowulf maðelode,　bearn Ecgþeowes:
'Ġeþenċ nū, se mǣra　maga Healfdenes,
1475　snottra fenġel,　nū iċ eom sīðes fūs,
goldwine gumena,　hwæt wit ġeō sprǣcon,
ġif iċ æt þearfe　þīnre scolde
aldre linnan,　þæt ðū mē ā wǣre
forðġewitenum　on fæder stǣle.
1480　Wes þū mundbora　mīnum magoþeġnum,
hondġesellum,　ġif meċ hild nime;
swylċe þū ðā mādmas　þe þū mē sealdest,
Hrōðgār lēofa,　Hiġelāce onsend.
Mæġ þonne on þǣm golde onġitan　Ġeata dryhten,
1485　ġesēon sunu Hrǣdles,　þonne hē on þæt sinċ starað,
þæt iċ gumcystum　gōdne funde
bēaga bryttan,　brēac þonne mōste.
Ond þū Ūnferð lǣt　ealde lāfe,
wrǣtliċ wǣġsweord　wīdcūðne man
1490　heardecg habban;　iċ mē mid Hruntinge
dōm ġewyrċe,　oþðe meċ dēað nimeð.'
　　Æfter þǣm wordum　Weder-Ġeata lēod
efste mid elne,　nalas andsware
bīdan wolde;　brimwylm onfēng
1495　hilderinċe.　Ðā wæs hwīl dæġes
ǣr hē þone grundwong　onġytan mehte.
Sōna þæt onfunde　sē ðe flōda begong
heoroġīfre behēold　hund missera,
grim ond grǣdiġ,　þæt þǣr gumena sum
1500　ǣlwihta eard　ufan cunnode.
Grāp þā tōġēanes,　gūðrinċ ġefēng

to a better swordsman. He himself did not dare
to risk his life beneath the waves,
to endure bravely. There he lost his fame
for deeds of valor. It was not like that
with the other man, once he was battle-ready.

    Beowulf spoke, son of Ecgtheow:
"Famous one, son of Healfdene,
wise ruler, gold-friend of men,
now I am about to go on my venture,
remember now what we said before:
if in your need I should lose my life,
you would always be as a father to me
once I had passed away. If battle should take me,
be a protector for my thanes,
my close companions. Also, dear Hrothgar,
send to Hygelac the treasures you gave me.
The lord of the Geats, son of Hrethel,
can then understand, seeing the treasure,
when he looks at the gold, that I found a good
and generous ring-sharer, enjoy them who may.
And let Unferth, the famous man,
have the ancient heirloom, my hard-edged, splendid
wave-patterned sword. I will win glory
with Hrunting now, or death shall take me."
    After those words the man of the Geats
was quick and purposeful, would wait for no answer.
The surging lake took the warrior.
It was some time then before he saw the bottom.
She who had watched avidly for fifty years
over the reach of the floods soon realized,
grim and greedy, that a man from above
was making trial of the monsters' land.
She seized the warrior, gripped him then

atolan clommum;   nō þȳ ǣr in ġescōd
hālan līċe;   hrinġ ūtan ymbbearh,
þæt hēo þone fyrdhom   ðurhfōn ne mihte,
1505 locene leoðosyrċan   lāþan fingrum.
Bær þā sēo brimwyl[f],   þā hēo tō botme cōm,
hringa þenġel   tō hofe sīnum,
swā hē ne mihte   — nō hē þæs mōdiġ wæs —
wǣpna ġewealdan,   ac hine wundra þæs fela
1510 swe[n]cte on sunde,   sǣdēor moniġ
hildetūxum   heresyrċan bræc,
ēhton āglǣċan.   Ðā se eorl onġeat
þæt hē [in] nīðsele   nāthwylcum wæs,
þǣr him nǣniġ wæter   wihte ne sceþede,
1515 nē him for hrōfsele   hrīnan ne mehte
fǣrgripe flōdes;   fȳrlēoht ġeseah,
blācne lēoman   beorhte scīnan.
    Onġeat þā se gōda   grundwyrġenne,
merewīf mihtiġ;   mæġenrǣs forġeaf
1520 hildebille,   hond swenġ ne oftēah,
þæt hire on hafelan   hrinġmǣl āgōl
grǣdiġ gūðlēoð.   (Ð)ā se ġist onfand
þæt se beadolēoma   bītan nolde,
aldre sceþðan,   ac sēo ecg ġeswāc
1525 ðēodne æt þearfe;   ðolodę ǣr fela
hondġemōta,   helm oft ġescær,
fǣġes fyrdhræġl;   ðā wæs forma sīð
dēorum mādme   þæt his dōm ālæġ.
    Eft wæs ānrǣd,   nalas elnes læt,
1530 mǣrða ġemyndiġ   mǣġ Hȳlāces:
wearp ðā wundenmǣl   wrǣttum ġebunden
yrre ōretta,   þæt hit on eorðan læġ,
stīð ond stȳlecg;   strenġe ġetruwode,
mundgripe mæġenes.   Swā sceal man dôn
1535 þonne hē æt gūðe   ġegān þenċeð
longsumne lof,   nā ymb his līf ċearað.

in terrible clutch. But not for that
could she harm his body, still left unhurt.
The rings prevented her penetrating his armor,
the linked shirt, with her evil fingers.
Reaching the bottom the sea-wolf carried
the lord of rings into her hall,
so that, however brave, he could wield no weapons,
but sea-beasts harassed him in the water,
marvellously many monsters attacked him,
bit his battle-shirt with teeth and fangs.
Then the nobleman realized he was now
in a hostile hall, of some kind,
where he could be harmed no longer by the water,
nor the flood's grip touch him at all,
because of the hall-roof. He saw firelight,
a pale gleam shining brightly.
   Then the good man saw the outcast of the deep,
the mighty lake-woman. He gave a great stroke
with his war-sword, his hand did not
hold back its swing, so that the ringed sword
sang a fierce war-song as it met her head.
Then the intruder found that the light-of-battle
would not bite on her, injure her life,
but the blade betrayed its lord in his need.
Before it had endured many fights hand-to-hand,
often cut through helmets and dead men's armor.
This was the first time for the precious treasure
that its glory failed.
               Still he was resolute,
the kinsman of Hygelac, by no means disheartened,
intent on glory. The angry warrior
threw down the patterned sword, so it lay on the ground,
strong and steel-edged; trusted in his strength
the power of his handgrip. So must a man do
when he means to gain lasting fame in battle,

Ġefēng þā be feaxe   — nalas for fǣhðe mearn —
Gūð-Ġēata lēod   Grendles mōdor;
brægd þā beadwe heard,   þā hē ġebolgen wæs,
1540 feorhġenīðlan,   þæt hēo on flet ġebēah.
    Hēo him eft hraþe   *a*ndlēan forġeald
    grimman grāpum   ond him tōġēanes fēng;
    oferwearp þā wēriġmōd   wigena strenġest,
    fēþecempa,   þæt hē on fylle wearð.
1545 Ofsæt þā þone seleġyst,   ond hyre sea*x* ġetēah
    brād [ond] brūnecg;   wolde hire bearn wrecan,
    āngan eaferan.   Him on eaxle læġ
    brēostnet brōden;   þæt ġebearh fēore
    wið ord ond wið ecge,   ingang forstōd.
1550 Hæfde ðā forsīðod   sunu Ecgþeowes
    under ġynne grund,   Ġēata cempa,
    nemne him heaðobyrne   helpe ġefremede,
    herenet hearde,   ond hāliġ God.
    Ġewēold wīġsigor   wītiġ drihten,
1555 rodera rǣdend;   hit on ryht ġescēd
    ȳðelīċe,   syþðan hē eft āstōd.

    Ġeseah ðā on searwum   siġeēadiġ bil,
    ealdsweord eotenisc   ecgum þȳhtiġ,
    wigena weorðmynd;   þæt [wæs] wǣpna cyst, —
1560 būton hit wæs māre   ðonne ǣniġ mon ōðer
    tō beadulāce   ætberan meahte,
    gōd ond ġeatoliċ,   ġīganta ġeweorc.
    Hē ġefēng þā fetelhilt,   freca Scyldinga
    hrēoh ond heorogrim,   hrinġmǣl ġebrægd
1565 aldres orwēna,   yrringa slōh,
    þæt hire wið halse   heard grāpode,
    bānhringas bræc;   bil eal ðurhwōd
    fǣġne flǣschoman,   hēo on flet ġecrong;
    sweord wæs swātiġ,   secg weorce ġefeh.
1570   Līxte se lēoma,   lēoht inne stōd,

140

not care about his life. The man of the War-Geats
then seized Grendel's mother by the hair,
regretted not the rude deed.
Hard in battle, and now enraged,
he twisted his deadly foe so she bowed to the ground.
She paid him back with fierce grip
and seized him close. The champion,
strongest of men, stumbled in exhaustion,
so that he fell. She sat on the intruder
and drew her seax-knife, broad and shining-edged;
she meant to avenge her child, her only son.
He still wore his linked mail; that saved his life,
withstood penetration by point or edge.
The son of Ecgtheow, champion of the Geats,
would have died there, deep underground,
if his battle-armor had not helped him,
that hard war-net, and holy God.
The wise Lord, Ruler of the skies,
determined victory in battle, decided it rightly,
and easily, as soon as the man
stood up again.   He saw among the remains
an old sword of giants – a victorious blade
with mighty edges, a credit for warriors,
best of weapons – except that it was bigger
than any other man could bear in battle,
good and splendid, the work of giants.
The Scylding's champion seized the ringed-hilt,
fierce and grim, despairing of life,
he swung the sword, struck angrily,
so that the hard edge split her throat,
cut through the neck-bones, went all the way
through the body of the doomed one.
She fell to the ground. The sword was bloody,
the man was pleased at what he had done.
    A gleam shone out, there was light inside,

efne swā of hefene   hādre scīneð
rodores candel.   Hē æfter reċede wlāt;
hwearf þā be wealle,   wǣpẹn hafenade
heard be hiltum   Hiġelāces ðeġn,
1575   yrre ond ānrǣd.   Næs sēo ecg fracod
hilderinċe,   ac hē hraþe wolde
Grendle forġyldan   gūðrǣsa fela
ðāra þe hē ġeworhte   tō West-Denum
oftor micle   ðonne on ǣnne sīð,
1580   þonne hē Hrōðgāres   heorðġenēatas
slōh on sweofote,   slǣpende frǣt
folces Deniġea   fȳftȳne men
ond ōðer swylċ   ūt offerede,
lāðlicu lāc.   Hē him þæs lēan forġeald,
1585   rēþe cempa,   ðæs þe hē on ræste ġeseah
gūðwēriġne   Grendel licgan,
aldorlēasne,   swā him ǣr ġescōd
hild æt Heorote   — hrā wīde sprong
syþðan hē æfter dēaðe   drepe þrōwade,
1590   heoroswenġ heardne —   ond hine þā hēafde beċearf.
    Sōna þæt ġesāwon   snottre ċeorlas,
þā ðe mid Hrōðgāre   on holm wliton,
þæt wæs ȳðġeblond   eal ġemenġed,
brim blōde fāh.   Blondenfeaxe,
1595   gomele ymb gōdne   onġeador sprǣcon
þæt hiġ þæs æðelinges   eft ne wēndon,
þæt hē siġehrēðiġ   sēċean cōme
mǣrne þēoden;   þā ðæs moniġe ġewearð
þæt hine sēo brimwylf   ābroten hæfde.
1600   Ðā cōm nōn dæġes.   Næs ofġēafon
hwate Scyldingas;   ġewāt him hām þonon
goldwine gumena.   Ġistas sētan
mōdes sēoce   ond on mere staredon;
wīston ond ne wēndon   þæt hīe heora winedrihten
1605   selfne ġesāwon.

just like the sky-candle bright-shining above.
He looked round the dwelling, turned to the wall,
Hygelac's thane, angry and resolute,
lifted the hard weapon by its hilt.
Its edge had done well for the warrior,
but he wanted quickly to pay Grendel back
for all the assaults made on the West-Danes,
far more than once, when he had killed
Hrothgar's hearth-companions as they slumbered,
eaten fifteen Danes as they lay asleep,
carried off as many more, a hateful plunder.
The fierce warrior paid him back for that,
when he saw Grendel lying on his bed,
dead and defeated, as had been decided
by battle in Heorot. His body gaped wide,
when after death he suffered a blow,
a hard war-stroke, severing his head.

   The wise men, those with Hrothgar,
looking at the lake, saw what was spreading
in the water, the lake stained with blood.
Old and grey-haired, they spoke together
of the good man, did not expect
the noble to return, to come back with success
to the famous king: it seemed to many
that the water-wolf had destroyed him.
Then it was midday. The bold Scyldings
left the promontory, the gold-friend of men
turned away for home. The strangers sat,
sick at heart, stared at the lake,
wishing but not expecting to see their friend
and lord himself.

Þā þæt sweord ongan
æfter heaþoswāte   hildeġiċęlum,
wīġbil wanian;   þæt wæs wundra sum
þæt hit eal ġemealt   īse ġelīcost,
ðonne forstes bend   fæder onlǣteð,
1610 onwindeð wǣlrāpas,   sē ġeweald hafað
sǣla ond mǣla;   þæt is sōð metod.
Ne nōm hē in þǣm wīcum,   Weder-Ġēata lēod,
māðmǣhta mā,   þēh hē þǣr moniġe ġeseah,
būton þone hafelan   ond þā hilt somod
1615 sinċe fāge;   sweord ǣr ġemealt,
forbarn brōdenmǣl;   wæs þæt blōd tō þæs hāt,
ǣttren ellorgǣst   sē þǣr inne swealt.
Sōna wæs on sunde   sē þe ǣr æt sæċċe ġebād
wīġhryre wrāðra,   wæter up þurhdēaf;
1620 wǣron ȳðġebland   eal ġefǣlsod,
ēacne eardas,   þā se ellorgāst
oflēt līfdagas   ond þās lǣnan ġesceaft.
Cōm þā tō lande   lidmanna helm
swīðmōd swymman;   sǣlāca ġefeah
1625 mæġenbyrþenne   þāra þe hē him mid hæfde.
Ēodon him þā tōġēanes,   Gode þancodon,
ðrȳðliċ þeġna hēap,   þēodnes ġefēgon,
þæs þe hī hyne ġesundne   ġesēon mōston.
Đā wæs of þǣm hrōran   helm ond byrne
1630 lungre ālȳsed.   Lagu drūsade,
wæter under wolcnum,   wældrēore fāg.
Fērdon forð þonon   fēþelāstum
ferhþum fæġne,   foldweġ mǣton,
cūþe strǣte;   cyningbalde men
1635 from þǣm holmclife   hafelan bǣron
earfoðlīċe   heora ǣġhwæþrum
felamōdiġra;   fēower scoldon
on þǣm wælstenġe   wærc ġeferian

Then the bloodstained sword,
the blade of battle began to drip
like metal icicles. It was a marvel
that it all melted away, like ice when the Father,
He who has control of times and seasons,
loosens the bonds of frost, undoes the water-fetters.
He is the true Ruler. The man of the Weder-Geats
took from the hall no more precious things –
though he saw many – than the head and sword-hilt,
shining with treasure. The sword had melted,
the patterned blade had burned away,
so hot and venomous was the blood
of the alien spirit who had died there.
Quickly he who endured the terror in battle
of the angry creatures took to swimming,
dived up through the water. The currents of the lake
and the whole broad region had been cleansed,
now that the alien spirit had departed
the days of his life and this fleeting world.

  The stout-hearted protector of the seamen
came swimming to shore, glad of his lake-plunder,
the great burdens he had with him.
His fine troop of thanes, thanking God,
came towards him, glad to greet their lord
that they might see him safe and sound.
Quickly he was freed of helmet and armor.
The water lay still beneath the skies,
stained with blood. They went off on foot,
glad at heart, tramped the pathway,
the road they knew; brave as kings,
they carried the head, with difficulty
for all the bold ones; it took four of them
to bear Grendel's head painfully on a pole

tō þǣm goldsele   Grendles hēafod,
1640 oþ ðæt semninga   tō sele cōmon
frome fyrdhwate   fēowertȳne
Ġēata gongan;   gumdryhten mid
modiġ on ġemonge   meodowongas træd.
Ðā cōm in gân   ealdor ðeġna,
1645 dǣdcēne mon   dōme ġewurþad,
hæle hildedēor,   Hrōðgār grētan.
Þā wæs be feaxe   on flet boren
Grendles hēafod,   þǣr guman druncon,
eġesliċ for eorlum   ond þǣre idese mid,
1650 wlitesēon wrǣtliċ;   weras on sāwon.

Bēowulf maþelode,   bearn Ecgþeowes:
'Hwæt, wē þē þās sǣlāc,   sunu Healfdenes,
lēod Scyldinga,   lustum brōhton
tīres tō tācne,   þē þū hēr tō lōcast.
1655 Iċ þæt unsōfte   ealdre ġedīġde
wiġġe under wætere,   weorc ġenēþde
earfoðlīċe;   ætrihte wæs
gūð ġetwǣfed,   nymðe meċ God scylde.
Ne meahte iċ æt hilde   mid Hruntinge
1660 wiht ġewyrċan,   þēah þæt wǣpen duge;
ac mē ġeūðe   ylda waldend
þæt iċ on wāge ġeseah   wlitiġ hangian
ealdsweord ēacen;   ofost wīsode
winiġea lēasum,   þæt iċ ðȳ wǣpne ġebrǣd.
1665 Ofslōh ðā æt þǣre sæċċe,   þā mē sǣl āġeald,
hūses hyrdas.   Þā þæt hildebil
forbarn brogdenmǣl,   swā þæt blōd ġesprang,
hātost heaþoswāta.   Iċ þæt hilt þanan
fēondum ætferede,   fyrendǣda wræc,
1670 dēaðcwealm Deniġea,   swā hit ġedēfe wæs.
Iċ hit þē þonne ġehāte   þæt þū on Heorote mōst
sorhlēas swefan   mid þīnra secga ġedryht

to the gold-hall, until eventually
the fourteen eager Geats arrived at the hall;
their brave lord amidst them trod the mead-path.
Then the leader of the retainers,
brave in action, battle-ready hero,
covered in glory, went to greet Hrothgar.
Grendel's head was carried in by the hair,
where men were drinking. A dreadful sight,
a wonderful spectacle for the noble ones
and the lady with them: the men looked at it.

   Beowulf spoke, child of Ecgtheow:
"Well, son of Healfdene, man of the Scyldings,
we brought you gladly these gifts from the sea
that you see here as a sign of victory.
Only with difficulty did I survive
the fight underwater, I found it hard
to finish the deed. The fight would soon
have been decided, without God's protection.
I could do nothing with Hrunting in the fight,
good weapon though it is. But it was granted to me
by the Ruler of men that I saw, old and mighty,
a splendid sword hanging on the wall.
Haste guided me, alone and friendless,
to draw the weapon. Once time was given me,
I killed in battle the guardians of the hall.
Then it burned away, the patterned war-sword,
as the hot blood of battle sprang out.
I took the hilt away from the fiends,
avenging the evil deeds, the deadly plague
upon the Danes, as was right and proper.
So I can promise you now that you may sleep in Heorot
with your troop of men, with every one

 ond þeġna ġehwylċ þīnra lēoda,

 duguðe ond iogoþe, þæt þū him ondrǣdan ne þearft,

1675 þēodẹn Scyldinga, on þā healfe,

 aldọrbealu eorlum, swā þū ǣr dydest.'

 Ðā wæs gylden hilt gamelum rinċe,

 hārum hildfruman on hand ġyfen,

 enta ǣrġeweorc; hit on ǣht ġehwearf

1680 æfter dēofla hryre Deniġea frêan,

 wundọrsmiþa ġeweorc; ond þā þās worold ofġeaf

 gromheort guma, Godes andsaca,

 morðres scyldiġ, ond his mōdor ēac,

 on ġeweald ġehwearf woroldcyninga

1685 ðǣm sēlestan be sǣm twēonum

 ðāra þe on Scedeniġġe sceattas dǣlde.

  Hrōðgār maðelode; hylt scēawode,

 ealde lāfe. On ðǣm wæs ōr writen

 fyrnġewinnes; syðþan flōd ofslōh,

1690 ġifen ġēotende ġīganta cyn,

 frēcne ġefērdon; þæt wæs fremde þēod

 ēċean dryhtne; him þæs endelēan

 þurh wæteres wylm waldend sealde.

 Swā wæs on ðǣm scennum scīran goldes

1695 þurh rūnstafas rihte ġemearcod,

 ġeseted ond ġesǣd, hwām þæt sweord ġeworht,

 īrena cyst ǣrest wǣre,

 wreoþenhilt ond wyrmfāh. Ðā se wīsa spræc

 sunu Healfdenes; swīgedon ealle:

1700 'Þæt, lā, mæġ secgan sē þe sōð ond riht

 fremeð on folce, feor eal ġemon,

 eald ēþelweard, þæt ðes eorl wǣre

 ġeboren betera. Blǣd is ārǣred

 ġeond wīdwegas, wine mīn Bēowulf,

ðīn ofer þēoda ġehwylċe. Eal þū hit ġeþyldum healdest,

mæġen mid mōdes snyttrum. Iċ þē sceal mīne ġelǣstan

frēode, swā wit furðum sprǣcon. Ðū scealt tō frōfre weorþan

of your people's thanes, young and old,
without any care, for, lord of the Scyldings,
you have no need to fear fatal injury
from that quarter, as you did before."
Then the golden hilt, made long ago
by the giants, was given to the hands
of the old warrior, the grey-haired prince.
After the fall of the fiends,
the marvellous work of smiths of old
passed into the possession of the lord of the Danes.
Once the fierce one, enemy of God,
guilty of murder, and his mother too,
had given up this world, it was passed on
into the keeping of the best of kings
in all this world between the two seas,
of all those who in Scandinavia
gave out treasure. Hrothgar spoke,
looking at the hilt, the ancient relic.
On it was engraved the origin of old strife,
when the great flood, the pouring ocean,
drowned the race of giants. That was a people
estranged from the eternal Lord.
The Ruler gave them a final reward for it
through the surge of water. Also it was marked out
on plates of bright gold in runic letters,
stated and said properly, by whom the sword,
best of blades, had first been wrought,
with twist-wrapped hilt and serpent-patterns.
Then the wise son of Healfdene spoke,
all fell silent: "He who speaks truth
and right among the people, an old counsellor
who remembers all things from far away,
he can indeed say that this nobleman
was born to eminence. My friend Beowulf,
your fame is spread across the wide ways,
to every people. Do you keep it all
with moderation, might with wisdom.
I shall be your friend as we said before.

eal langtwīdiġ   lēodum þīnum,
hæleðum tō helpe.
             Ne wearð Heremōd swā
1710 eafora Ecgwelan,   Ār-Scyldingum;
ne ġewēox hē him tō willan   ac tō wælfealle
ond tō dēaðcwalum   Deniġa lēodum;
brēat bolgenmōd   bēodġenēatas,
eaxlġesteallan,   oþ þæt hē āna hwearf,
1715 mǣre þēoden   mondrēamum from.
Ðēah þe hine mihtiġ God   mæġenes wynnum,
eafeþum stēpte   ofer ealle men,
forð ġefremede,   hwæþere him on ferhþe grēow
brēosthord blōdrēow,   nallas bēagas ġeaf
1720 Denum æfter dōme;   drēamlēas ġebād
þæt hē þæs ġewinnes   wærc þrōwade,
lēodbealo longsum.   Ðū þē lǣr be þon,
gumcyste onġit;   iċ þis ġid be þē
āwræc wintrum frōd.
             Wundor is tō secganne̦
1725 hū mihtiġ God   manna cynne
þurh sīdne sefan   snyttru bryttað,
eard ond eorlscipe;   hē āh ealra ġeweald.
Hwīlum hē on lufan   lǣteð hworfan
monnes mōdġeþonc   mǣran cynnes,
1730 seleð him on ēþle   eorþan wynne,
tō healdanne   hlēoburh wera,
ġedēð him swā ġewealde̦ne   worolde dǣlas,
sīde rīċe,   þæt hē his selfa ne mæġ
for his unsnyttrum   ende ġeþenċean.
1735 Wuna(ð) hē on wiste;   nō hine wiht dweleð
ādl nē yldo,   nē him inwitsorh
on sefa(n) sweorceð,   nē ġesacu ōhwǣr,
ecghete eoweð,   ac him eal worold
wendeð on willan;   hē þæt wyrse ne con —

You shall be for many years, a resource for your people,
a support for heroes.
                              Heremod was not like that,
the child of Ecgwela, to the honorable Scyldings.
He did not grow to please the Danish people.
but became a deadly plague, a slaughterer of them.
When he was enraged he would strike down
his close companions, who stood at his side,
until the famous prince turned away alone
from the joys of men. Although mighty God
had advanced him above all men
to enjoy strength and power, his heart and spirit
grew bloodthirsty. He gave no rings
at all to the Danes in return for praise;
he lived without joy until he suffered
grief from the struggle, a lasting affliction.
Take note of that, learn generosity.
I, old in winters, have made this speech
for your sake alone.
                              It is marvellous to see
how mighty God, who rules all things,
has in deep thought distributed wisdom
to the human race, rank and property.
Sometimes he lets the mind of a man of famous stock
turn to gladness. He gives him earthly joy
in his homeland, gives him possession
of his people's citadel, gives him control
of such a share of the world's regions,
a broad kingdom, that in his folly
he cannot imagine any end to it.
He lives happily. He is not held back
by age or sickness, his mind is not darkened
by any sorrow, no strife anywhere
or armed hatred shows itself to him,
but the whole world goes as he pleases,
he has no awareness of anything worse –

1740 oð þæt him on innan   oferhyġda dǣl
weaxe(ð) ond wrīdað;   þonne se weard swefeð,
sāwele hyrde;   bið se slǣp tō fæst,
bisgum ġebunden,   bona swīðe nēah,
sē þe of flānbogan   fyrenum scēoteð.

1745 Þonne bið on hreþre   under helm drepen
biteran strǣle   — him bebeorgan ne con —
wōm wundorbebodum   werġan gāstes;
þinċeð him tō lȳtel   þæt hē lange hēold,
ġȳtsað gromhȳdiġ,   nallas on ġylp seleð

1750 fǣtte bēagas,   ond hē þā forðġesceaft
forġyteð ond forġȳmeð,   þæs þe him ǣr God sealde,
wuldres waldend,   weorðmynda dǣl.
Hit on endestæf   eft ġelimpeð
þæt se līċhoma   lǣne ġedrēoseð,

1755 fǣġe ġefealleð;   fēhð ōþer tō,
sē þe unmurnlīċe   māðmas dǣleþ,
eorles ǣrġestrēon,   eġesan ne ġȳmeð.
Bebeorh þē ðone bealonīð,   Bēowulf lēofa,
secg bet[e]sta,   ond þē þæt sēlre ġeċēos,

1760 ēċe rǣdas;   oferhȳda ne ġȳm,
mǣre cempa.   Nū is þīnes mæġnes blǣd
āne hwīle;   eft sōna bið
þæt þeċ ādl oððe ecg   eafoþes ġetwǣfeð,
oððe fȳres feng,   oððe flōdes wylm,

1765 oððe gripe mēċes,   oððe gāres fliht,
oððe atol yldo;   oððe ēagena bearhtm
forsiteð ond forsworceð;   semninga bið
þæt ðeċ, dryhtguma,   dēað oferswȳðeð.
    Swā iċ Hring-Dena   hund missera

1770 wēold under wolcnum   ond hiġ wiġġe belēac
manigum mǣġþa   ġeond þysne middanġeard,
æscum ond ecgum,   þæt iċ mē ǣniġne
under sweġles begong   ġesacan ne tealde.
Hwæt, mē þæs on ēþle   edwenden cwōm,

until within him arrogance grows
and spreads wider. The watchman sleeps,
guardian of the soul. The sleep is too sound,
wrapped in cares, the killer very close,
who shoots arrows of sin from his bow.
Then in his mind he is struck through the helmet
with a bitter dart – he cannot defend himself –
with the false promptings of the damned spirit.
It seems to him that what he has held
for so long is too little, he turns sullen and miserly,
does not give out rings of gold,
in honorable fashion, forgets and thinks little
of his future state, and the share of honors
which God had given him, Ruler of Glory,
In the end it happens that his mortal body fails him,
he sinks into death. Another one succeeds,
who shares out treasure, the noble's inheritance,
without regrets, and feels no fear.
My dear Beowulf, best of men,
shield yourself from such deadly danger,
choose the better part, famous champion,
counsels of eternity, take no heed of pride.
Your strength is famous, now, for a while.
Soon sickness or the blade will steal your strength,
or the grip of fire or the surge of flood,
or bite of sword or flight of spear,
or terrible old age, or the light of your eyes
will fail and grow dark. Warrior, death
will suddenly be too strong for you.
    In this way I was ruler of the Ring-Danes
beneath the skies for fifty years,
protected them by war from many tribes
throughout the world, with spears and blades,
so that I thought I had no enemy
beneath the sky. Yet in my homeland
a change of fortune came upon me,

153

1775 gyrn æfter gomene, seoþðan Grendel wearð,
ealdġewinna, ingenġa mīn;
iċ þǣre sōcne singāles wǣġ
mōdċeare micle. Þæs siġ metode þanc,
ēċean dryhtne, þæs ðe iċ on aldre ġebād
1780 þæt iċ on þone hafelan heorodrēoriġne
ofer eald ġewin ēagum stariġe.
Gā nū tō setle, symbęlwynne drēoh
wīġġeweorþad; unc sceal worn fela
māþma ġemǣnra siþðan morgen bið.'
1785 Ġēat wæs glædmōd, ġēong sōna tō,
setles nēosan, swā se snottra heht.
Þā wæs eft swā ǣr ellenrōfum,
fletsittendum fæġere ġereorded
nīowan stefne. Nihthelm ġeswearc
1790 deorc ofer dryhtgumum. Duguð eal ārās;
wolde blondenfeax beddes nēosan,
gamela Scylding. Ġēat uniġmetes wēl,
rōfne randwigan, restan lyste;
sōna him seleþeġn sīðes wērgum,
1795 feorrancundum forð wīsade,
sē for andrysnum ealle beweotede
þeġnes þearfe, swylċe þȳ dōgor
heaþolīðende habban scoldon.
Reste hine þā rūmheort; reċed hlīuade
1800 ġēap ond goldfāh; gæst inne swæf,
oþ þæt hrefn blaca heofones wynne
blīðheort bodode. Ðā cōm beorht [lēoma]
[ofer sceadwa] scacan; scaþan ōnetton,
wǣron æþelingas eft tō lēodum
1805 fūse tō farenne; wolde feor þanon
cuma collenferhð, ċēoles nēosan.
Heht þā se hearda Hrunting beran
sunu Ecglāfes, heht his sweord niman,
lēoflīċ īren; sæġde him þæs lǣnes þanc,

sadness followed joy, once Grendel,
that old enemy, became my attacker.
Great grief I suffered from his visitations
without respite. God be praised,
the eternal Lord, that I have lived
so long as to look on his bloodstained head,
old strife over. Go now to your seat,
enjoy the pleasure of the feast
and the glory you have won in battle.
In the morning many treasures
shall be shared between us."

   The Geat was pleased, went quickly to his bench,
as the wise one had told him.
Then as before a feast was prepared
for the brave ones who sat in the hall.
The night shades fell dark upon the retainers.
The troop all got up. The grey-haired Scylding
wished to seek his bed. The Geat, fierce warrior,
very much wished to rest. Weary from his exploit,
the stranger from afar was shown the way quickly
by a servitor, who courteously tended
to all the thane's needs, such as in those days
adventurers used to have.
                    The great-hearted one rested.
The building towered, steep, shining with gold,
the guest slept inside, until the glossy raven
cheerfully announced joy in the sky.
Then bright light came, overtaking the shadows.
The warriors hurried, the noble ones were eager
to return to their people; the spirited visitor
wished to go back to his far-off ship.

   The hard one then ordered Hrunting
to be borne to the son of Ecglaf,
told him to take back his splendid blade.
He thanked him for the loan, said he reckoned it

1810 cwæð, hē þone gūðwine   gōdne tealde,
wīġcræftiġne,   nales wordum lōg
mēċes ecge;   þæt wæs mōdiġ secg.
    Ond þā sīðfrome,   searwum ġearwe
wīġend wæron;   ēode weorð Denum
1815 æþeling tō yppan,   þær se ōþer wæs,
hæle hildedēor   Hrōðgār grētte.

Bēowulf maþelode,   bearn Ecgþeowes:
'Nū wē sælīðend   secgan wyllað
feorran cumene   þæt wē fundiaþ
1820 Hiġelāc sēċan.   Wæron hēr tela,
willum bewenede;   þū ūs wēl dohtest.
Ġif iċ þonne on eorþan   ōwihte mæġ
þīnre mōdlufan   māran tilian,
gumena dryhten,   ðonne iċ ġȳt dyde,
1825 gūðġeweorca,   iċ bēo ġearo sōna.
Ġif iċ þæt ġefricge   ofer flōda begang
þæt þeċ ymbsittend   eġesan þȳwað,
swā þeċ hetende   hwīlum dydon,
iċ ðē þūsenda   þeġna bringe,
1830 hæleþa tō helpe.   Iċ on Hiġelāc wāt,
Ġēata dryhten,   þēah ðe hē ġeong sȳ,
folces hyrde,   þæt hē meċ fremman wile
wordum ond worcum,   þæt iċ þē wēl heriġe
ond þē tō ġēoce   gārholt bere,
1835 mæġenes fultum,   þær ðē bið manna þearf.
Ġif him þonne Hrēþrīċ   tō hofum Ġēata
ġeþinġeð þēodnes bearn,   hē mæġ þær fela
frēonda findan;   feorcȳþðe bēoð
sēlran ġesōhte   þæm þe him selfa dēah.'
1840   Hrōðgār maþelode   him on andsware:
'Þē þā wordcwydas   wiġtiġ drihten
on sefan sende;   ne hȳrde iċ snotorlicor
on swā ġeongum feore   guman þingian.

a good friend in battle, strong in war.
By no means did he dispraise the weapon's edge.
That was a brave man.
              And then the warriors
were ready in their armor, eager to depart.
Their prince went, honored by the Danes,
to the high seat where the other was,
the bold hero greeted Hrothgar.

Beowulf spoke, child of Ecgtheow:
"Now we seafarers, come from afar,
wish to tell you that we intend
to return to Hygelac. Here we have been
hospitably entertained, you have treated us well.
Lord of men, if there is any way on earth
by which I can earn your affection
by warlike deeds, more than I did before,
I will at once be ready. If I should hear
across the sea's expanse that your neighbors
are offering you threat, as enemies did before,
then I can bring thousands of thanes and heroes
to your assistance. I know that Hygelac,
lord of the Geats and keeper of the people,
young though he is, will support me
in word and deed, so that I can honor you
and bring a strong force, a wood of spears,
to come to your aid when you have need of men.
If moreover Hrethric, the prince's child,
should decide to visit the courts of the Geats,
he can find there many friends.
Distant countries are better visited
by those who are in themselves strong."
    Hrothgar replied in answer to him:
"God in his wisdom has put those words
into your mind. I have never heard a man
speak so thoughtfully at so young an age.

TEXT

Þū eart mæġenes strang   ond on mōde frōd,
1845 wīs wordcwida.   Wēn iċ taliġe,
ġif þæt ġegangeð   þæt ðe gār nymeð,
hild heorugrimme   Hrēþles eaferan,
ādl oþðe īren   ealdor ðīnne,
folces hyrde,   ond þū þīn feorh hafast,
1850 þæt þe Sæ-Ġēatas   sēlran næbben
tō ġeċēosenne   cyning æniġne,
hordweard hæleþa,   ġyf þū healdan wylt
māga rīċe.   Mē þīn mōdsefa
līcað lenġ swā wēl,   lēofa Bēowulf.
1855 Hafast þū ġefēred   þæt þām folcum sceal,
Ġēata lēodum   ond Gār-Denum
sib ġemænu,   ond sacu restan,
inwitnīþas   þe hīe ær drugon,
wesan, þenden iċ wealde   wīdan rīċes,
1860 māþmas ġemæne,   maniġ ōþerne
gōdum ġegrētan   ofer ganotes bæð;
sceal hrinġnaca   ofer heaþu bringan
lāc ond luftācen.   Iċ þā lēode wāt
ġē wið fēond ġē wið frēond   fæste ġeworhte,
1865 æġhwæs untæle   ealde wīsan.'
    Ðā ġīt him eorla hlēo   inne ġesealde,
mago Healfdenes,   māþmas twelfe;
hēt [h]ine mid þǣm lācum   lēode swǣse
sēċean on ġesyntum,   snūde eft cuman.
1870 Ġecyste þā   cyning æþelum gōd,
þēoden Scyldinga   ðeġn bet[e]stan
ond be healse ġenam;   hruron him tēaras
blondenfeaxum.   Him wæs bēġa wēn
ealdum infrōdum,   ōþres swīðor,
1875 þæt h[ī]e seoðða(n nō)   ġesēon mōston,
mōdiġe on meþle.   (W)æs him se man tō þon lēof
þæt hē þone brēostwylm   forberan ne mehte,
ac him on hreþre   hyġebendum fæst

You are strong in body and old in mind,
wise in your speech. I expect that if the spear
and grim warfare should take from you
the son of Hrethel, sickness or the blade
take off your lord, keeper of the people,
and you survive him, then the Sea-Geats
will have no-one better to choose as king,
treasure-warden for heroes, if you are willing
to rule the kingdom of your kinfolk.
My dear Beowulf, the more I know you,
the more I admire your mind and spirit.
You have brought it about that there shall be friendship
between the Geat people and the Spear-Danes,
an end to hostilities and the enmity
they once suffered. While I am ruler
of the broad kingdom, we shall exchange treasures,
many will visit with gifts across the gannet's bath,
the ring-prowed ship will carry presents across the sea
and tokens of friendship. I know the peoples
to be firmly united for friend or foe,
in every way blameless in the old fashion."
    Then the son of Healfdene, protector of nobles,
gave him in hall twelve treasures,
told him to take them safely to his own people
and come back soon. Then the king,
lord of the Scyldings, kissed the good prince,
best of thanes, and embraced him.
Tears were shed by the grey-haired one.
The wise old man expected the worse,
that they would not see each other again
as brave men meeting. The man was so dear to him
that he could not restrain the sorrow of his heart,
but hidden longing for the dear one,

æfter dēorum men   dyrne langað

1880 born wið blōde.   Him Bēowulf þanan,
    gūðrinċ goldwlanc   græsmoldan træd
    sinċe hrēmiġ;   sægenġa bād
    āge[n]dfrêan,   sē þe on ancre rād.
    Þā wæs on gange   ġifu Hrōðgāres

1885 oft ġeæhted;   þæt wæs ān cyning
    æġhwæs orleahtre,   oþ þæt hine yldo benam
    mæġenes wynnum,   sē þe oft manegum scōd.
    Cwōm þā tō flōde   felamōdiġra,
    hæġstealdra [hēap],   hringnet bæron,

1890 locene leoðosyrċan.   Landweard onfand
    eftsīð eorla,   swā hē ær dyde;
    nō hē mid hearme   of hliðes nōsan
    gæs(tas) grētte,   ac him tōġēanes rād,
    cwæð þæt wilcuman   Wedera lēodum

1895 scaþan scīrhame   tō scipe fōron.
    Þā wæs on sande   sæġēap naca
    hladen herewædum,   hringedstefna
    mēarum ond māðmum;   mæst hlīfade
    ofer Hrōðgāres   hordġestrēonum.

1900 Hē þæm bātwearde   bunden golde
    swurd ġesealde,   þæt hē syðþan wæs
    on meodubenċe   māþme þȳ weorþra,
    yrfelāfe.   Ġewāt him on naca
    drēfan dēop wæter,   Dena land ofġeaf.

1905 Þā wæs be mæste   merehræġla sum,
    seġl sāle fæst;   sundwudu þunede;
    nō þær wēġflotan   wind ofer ȳðum
    sīðes ġetwæfde;   sægenġa fōr,
    flēat fāmiġheals   forð ofer ȳðe,

1910 bundenstefna   ofer brimstrēamas,
    þæt hīe Ġēata clifu   onġitan meahton,
    cūþe næssas;   ċēol up ġeþrang,
    lyftġeswenċed   on lande stōd.

locked firm in his breast, burned in his blood.
Then Beowulf, like a warrior
proud of his gold, exultant in his treasure,
walked away on the grassy turf.
The ocean-goer riding at anchor,
waited for its owner. As they walked,
the gifts of Hrothgar were greatly praised.
That was a king completely faultless,
until old age, which has so often
injured many, took away from him
the bodily strength he once enjoyed.
   The troop of warriors, young and bold,
came to the sea, wearing their ring-mail,
sleeved shirts, skilfully clinched.
The coastguard spotted the nobles' coming,
as he had before. He did not greet the strangers
with hostility from the steep headland,
but rode towards them, said they were welcome,
the bright-coated warriors of the Geat people,
as they came to their ship. Then on the sand
the broad-beamed ship was loaded up
with war-equipment, the ring-prowed one
with rich gifts and horses. The mast rose high
over Hrothgar's hoarded treasure.
Beowulf gave the boat-guard a sword bound with gold,
so that from then on the precious heirloom
brought him the more honor on the mead-bench.
Once in the ship, they rowed her out
into deep water, left the Danes' land.
Then they made a sail, part of the sea-tackle,
fast on its rope. The wooden ship creaked.
The wind did not hinder the floater on its journey
across the waves, with foam at its prow
the seagoer sped across the water,
the twisted bow over the sea-currents,
until they could see the cliffs of the Geats,
the well-known nesses. Urged by the wind,
the ship drove on, came to the land.

161

Hreþe wæs æt holme   hȳðweard ġeara,
1915 sē þe ǣr lange tīd   lēofra manna
fūs æt faroðe   feor wlātode;
sǣlde tō sande   sīdfæþme scip
onċerbendum fæst,   þȳ lǣs hym ȳþa ðrym
wudu wynsuman   forwrecan meahte.
1920 Hēt þā up beran   æþelinga ġestrēon,
frætwe ond fǣtgold;   næs him feor þanon
tō ġesēċanne   sinċes bryttan,
Hiġelāc Hrēþling,   þǣr æt hām wunað
selfa mid ġesīðum   sǣwealle nēah.
1925 Bold wæs betliċ,   bregorōf cyning,
hēa[h on] healle,   Hyġd swīðe ġeong,
wīs wēlþungen,   þēah ðe wintra lȳt
under burhlocan   ġebiden hæbbe,
Hæreþes dohtor;   næs hīo hnāh swā þēah,
1930 nē tō gnēað ġifa   Ġēata lēodum,
māþmġestrēona.   Mōdþrȳðo wæġ
Fremu, folces cwēn,   firen' ondrysne;
nǣniġ þæt dorste   dēor ġenēþan
swǣsra ġesīða,   nefne sinfrēâ,
1935 þæt hire an dæġes   ēagum starede,
ac him wælbende   weotode tealde
handġewriþene;   hraþe seoþðan wæs
æfter mundgripe   mēċe ġeþinġed,
þæt hit sceādenmǣl   scȳran mōste,
1940 cwealmbealu cȳðan.   Ne bið swylċ cwēnliċ þēaw
idese tō efnanne,   þēah ðe hīo ǣnlicu sȳ,
þætte freoðuwebbe   fēores onsǣċe
æfter liġetorne   lēofne mannan.
Hūru þæt onhōhsnod[e]   Hemminges mǣġ:
1945 ealodrincende   ōðer sǣdan,
þæt hīo lēodbealewa   lǣs ġefremede,
inwitnīða, (s)yððan ǣrest wearð
ġyfen goldhroden   ġeongum cempan,

Quickly the harbor-master was there at the shore,
he who had long been looking out,
anxious on shore for the dear ones from afar.
He moored to the beach the broad-beamed ship
firmly with anchor ropes, so that no force of the waves
could drive the fine vessel to destruction.
Then he ordered to be carried up
the prince's treasures, precious things and plated gold.
It was not far from there to reach
the divider of treasure, Hygelac son of Hrethel,
where he lives at home with his companions,
near the sea-wall. It was a splendid building,
the king a brave lord, high in the hall.
Hygd was very young, Hæreth's daughter,
wise and accomplished, though she had lived at court
for few years only. Yet she was not frugal,
nor too sparing of gifts to the Geat people,
her precious treasures. The people's queen Fremu
showed great pride, committed awful crimes.
There was none so bold of her own companions,
save for her husband, who dared by day
to set eyes on her, knowing his sentence
would be fatal bonds twisted by hand.
All too quickly then after his arrest
the sword would be his fate, the patterned blade
allowed to cut, give the death-blow.
That is no custom for any queen,
any lady to follow, beautiful though she may be,
a peacemaker depriving of life
her own familiars by false accusation.
The son of Hemming indeed put a stop to it.
Men drinking ale told a different story,
that she committed fewer criminal acts,
injuries to the people, once she was first given,
decked with gold, to the young champion

æðelum dīore,   syððan hīo Offan flet
1950 ofer fealone flōd   be fæder lāre
sīðe ġesōhte;   ðǣr hīo syððan well
in gumstōle,   gōde mǣre,
līfġesceafta   lifiġende brēac,
hīold hēahlufan   wið hæleþa brego,
1955 ealles moncynnes   mīne ġefrǣġe
þone sēlestan   bī sǣm twēonum,
eormencynnes;   forðām Offa wæs
ġeofum ond gūðum,   gārcēne man,
wīde ġeweorðod,   wīsdōme hēold
1960 ēðel sīnne;   þonon Ēomēr wōc
hæleðum tō helpe,   Hem[m]inges mǣġ,
nefa Gārmundes,   nīða cræftiġ.

   Ġewāt him ðā se hearda   mid his hondscole
sylf æfter sande   sǣwong tredan,
1965 wīde waroðas.   Woruldcandel scān,
siġel sūðan fūs.   Hī sīð drugon,
elne ġeēodon,   tō ðæs ðe eorla hlēo,
bonan Ongenþeoes   burgum in innan,
ġeongne gūðcyning   gōdne ġefrūnon
1970 hringas dǣlan.   Hiġelāce wæs
sīð Bēowulfes   snūde ġecȳðed,
þæt ðǣr on worðiġ   wīġendra hlēo,
lindġestealla   lifiġende cwōm,
heaðolāces hāl   tō hofe gongan.
1975 Hraðe wæs ġerȳmed,   swā se rīċa bebēad,
fēðeġestum   flet innanweard.

   Ġesæt þā wið sylfne   sē ðā sæċċe ġenæs,
mǣġ wið mǣġe,   syððan mandryhten
þurh hlēoðo̦rcwyde   holdne ġegrētte,
1980 mēaglum wordum.   Meoduscenċum hwearf
ġeond þæt [heal]reċed   Hæreðes dohtor,
lufode ðā lēode,   līðwæġe bær

of noble birth, and by her father's plan
made her way across the dark water
to the home of Offa. She lived from then on
happily enthroned, good and famous,
enjoyed her blessings as long as she lived,
kept up great love with the leader of heroes,
as I have heard, the best of the whole
great race of men between the seas;
for Offa was honored both for his war
and his liberality, a bold spearman,
who ruled his kingdom well and wisely.
From him sprang Eomer, Hemming's kinsman,
Garmund's grandson, strong in fight.

    With his picked men, the hard one set off
from sandy beach to tread the broad shoreline,
the road by the coast. The world-candle shone,
sun from the south. They followed the way,
went on eagerly, to where they knew
the protector of heroes, slayer of Ongentheow,
splendid young war-king, dealt out rings
within his residence. To Hygelac,
Beowulf's arrival was quickly announced
that the protector of warriors, the shield-companion,
was coming alive, unhurt by battle-play,
to the residence. Room on the floor
was quickly made for the marching troop,
by order of the great one.
                        The fight-survivor
sat down by him, two kinsmen together,
once the lord had given his trusted man
formal greeting with friendly words.
The daughter of Hæreth poured out mead,
circled the hall, serving the people,
carrying the drinking-cup to the hands of heroes.

hæ*leð*um tō handa.   Hiġelāc ongan
sīnne ġeseldan   in sele þām hēan
1985 fæġre fricgcean;   hyne fyrwet bræc,
hwylċe Sæ-Ġeata   sīðas wæron:
'Hū lomp ēow on lāde,   lēofa Bīowulf,
þā ðū færinga   feorr ġehogodest
sæċċe sēċean   ofer sealt wæter,
1990 hilde tō Hiorote?   Ac ðū Hrōðgāre
wī*d*cūðne wēan   wihte ġebēttest,
mærum ðēodne?   Iċ ðæs mōdċeare
sorhwylmum sēað,   sīðe ne truwode
lēofes mannes;   iċ ðē lange bæd
1995 þæt ðū þone wælgæst   wihte ne grētte,
lēte Sūð-Dene   sylfe ġeweorðan
gūðe wið Grendel.   Gode iċ þanc secge
þæs ðe iċ ðē ġesundne   ġesēon mōste.'
   Bīowulf maðelode,   bearn Ecgðioes:
2000 'Þæt is undyrne,   dryhten Hiġe(lāc),
(mæru) ġemēting   monegum fīra,
hwyl(ċ) or(leġ)hwīl   uncer Grendles
wearð on ðām wange,   þær hē worna fela
Siġe-Scyldingum   sorge ġefremede,
2005 yrmðe tō aldre;   iċ ðæt eall ġewræc,
swā beġylpan [ne] þearf   Grendeles māga
(æ)n(iġ) ofer eorðan   ūhthlem þone,
sē (ð)e lenġest leofað   lāðan cynnes,
fær(e) bifongen.   Iċ ðær furðum cwōm
2010 tō ðām hrinġsele   Hrōðgār grētan;
sōna mē se mæra   mago Healfdenes,
syððan hē mōdsefan   mīnne cūðe,
wið his sylfes sunu   setl ġetæhte.
Weorod wæs on wynne;   ne seah iċ wīdan feorh
2015 under heofones hwealf   healsittendra
medudrēam māran.   Hwīlum mæru cwēn,
friðusibb folca   flet eall ġeondhwearf,

In the high hall Hygelac began
to question politely his hall-companion.
He was anxious to know how it had gone
with the Sea-Geats' venture.
                              "My dear Beowulf,
what was it happened on your journey,
when you decided suddenly to seek out battle
far away across salt water, a fight in Heorot?
Did you cure at all the woes of Hrothgar,
the famous prince, of which we all know?
I was troubled in mind, filled with anxiety,
was not confident in my dear one's venture.
I asked you often not to go anywhere
near that deadly spirit, but let the South-Danes
wage their own war against Grendel.
I thank God that I see you now safe and sound."
  Beowulf spoke, child of Ecgtheow:
"My lord Hygelac, the famous clash
is now made known to many men,
what a fight I had with Grendel in the place
where he inflicted such a multitude of griefs
on the Victory-Scyldings, so many deadly sorrows.
I avenged them all. Not one on earth
of Grendel's kin, whichever lives longest
of the hateful race, will have any need
to boast of our clash in the night,
seized by sudden attack. I went first of all
to the ring-hall to speak with Hrothgar.
Quickly Healfdene's son, once he knew my spirit,
gave me a seat by his own sons.
The troop was delighted. Never have I seen
beneath the sky in all my life
greater merriment among drinkers in hall.
From time to time the famous queen,
a pledge of peace among the peoples,

bǣdde byre ġeonge;   oft hīo bēahwriðan
secge (sealde)   ǣr hīe tō setle ġēong.
2020 Hwīlum for (d)uguðe   dohtǫr Hrōðgāres
eorlum on ende   ealuwǣġe bær,
þā iċ Frēaware   fletsittende
nemnan hȳrde,   þǣr hīo (næ)ġled sinċ
hæleðum sealde.   Sīo ġehāten (*is*),
2025 ġeong goldhroden,   gladum suna Frōdan;
(h)afað þæs ġeworden   wine Scyldinga,
rīċes hyrde,   ond þæt rǣd talað,
þæt hē mid ðȳ wīfe   wælfǣhða dǣl,
sæċċa ġesette.   Oft seldan hwǣr
2030 æfter lēodhryre   lȳtle hwīle
bongār būgeð,   þēah sēo brȳd duge.
Mæġ þæs þonne ofþynċan   ðēoden Heaðo-Beardna
ond þeġna ġehwām   þāra lēoda
þonne hē mid fǣmnan   on flett gǣð,
2035 dryhtbearn Dena,   duguða biwenede.
On him gladiað   gomelra lāfe,
heard ond hrinġmǣl   Heaða-Bear[d]na ġestrēon,
þenden hīe ðām wǣpnum   wealdan mōston —

oð ðæt hīe forlǣddan   tō ðām lindplegan
2040 swǣse ġesīðas   ond hyra sylfra feorh.
    Þonne cwið æt bēore   sē ðe bēah ġesyhð,
eald æscwiga,   sē ðe eall ġe(ma*n*),
gārcwealm gumena   — him bið grim (se)fa —
onġinneð ġeōmormōd   ġeong(um) cempan
2045 þurh hreðra ġehyġd   hiġes cunnian,
wīġbealu weċċean,   ond þæt word ācwyð:
"Meaht ðū, mīn wine,   mēċe ġecnāwan,
þone þīn fæder   tō ġefeohte bær
under heregrīman   hindeman sīðe,
2050 dȳre īren,   þǣr hyne Dene slōgon,
wēoldon wælstōwe,   syððan Wiðerġyld læġ,

circled the whole hall, encouraged her young sons.
Often she gave a man a twisted ring
before she went back to her seat.
Sometimes Hrothgar's daughter carried the ale-cup
to the nobles in turn, whom I heard
the men sitting there call Freawaru,
as she handed men the embossed treasure.
Young and gold-adorned, she is promised
to the fortunate son of Froda.
The friend of the Scyldings, keeper of the people,
has brought it about, considers it a good plan,
to settle the strife and the deadly feud
through the woman. As a rule it is rare
that the deadly spear rests anywhere for long,
after the fall of a prince, however good the bride.
It can give offence to the lord of the Heathobeards,
and all the thanes of that people,
when some young fellow from the Danish troop
comes into the hall with the maiden,
hosted by the veterans. On him there shine
inherited relics, a hard patterned sword,
a Heathobard treasure when they were able
to wield weapons,
                    until at the shield-play
they lost loyal companions and their own lives.
Then as they drink, an old ash-warrior,
who remembers it all, the dead men speared,
he will notice the precious thing
with grim heart, and in his grief
will start to test the young man's temper
by revealing the thoughts of his heart,
to wake up enmity, and says these words:
'My friend, are you able to recognise that sword,
the precious blade your father bore to battle
beneath his war-mask, on his last journey,
back when the Danes were the death of him,
the bold Scyldings held the battlefield

169

æfter hæleþa hryre,   hwate Scyldungas?
Nū hēr þāra banena   byre nāthwylċes
frætwum hrēmiġ   on flet gǣð,
2055 morðres ġylpe(ð),   ond þone māðþum byreð,
þone þe ðū mid rihte   rǣdan sceoldest."
Manað swā ond myndgað   mǣla ġehwylċe
sārum wordum,   oð ðæt sǣl cymeð
þæt se fǣmnan þeġn   fore fæder dǣdum
2060 æfter billes bite   blōdfāg swefeð,
ealdres scyldiġ;   him se ōðer þonan
losað (li)fiġende,   con him land ġeare.
Þonne bīoð (āb)rocene   on bā healfe
āðsweord eorla;   (syð)ðan Inġelde
2065 weallað wælnīðas,   ond him wīflufan
æfter ċearwælmum   cōlran weorðað.
Þȳ iċ Heaðo-Bear[d]na   hyldo ne telġe,
dryhtsibbe dǣl   Denum unfǣcne,
frēondscipe fæstne.
              Iċ sceal forð sprecan
2070 ġēn ymbe Grendel,   þæt ðū ġeare cunne,
sinċes brytta,   tō hwan syððan wearð
hondrǣs hæleða.   Syððan heofones ġim
glād ofer grundas,   gǣst yrre cwōm,
eatol ǣfengrom   ūser nēosan,
2075 ðǣr wē ġesunde   sæl weardodon.
Þǣr wæs Hondsciō   hild onsǣġe,
feorhbealu fǣgum;   hē fyrmest læġ,
gyrded cempa;   him Grendel wearð,
mǣrum maguþeġne   tō mūðbonan,
2080 lēofes mannes   līċ eall forswealg.
Nō ðȳ ǣr ūt ðā ġēn   īdelhende
bona blōdiġtōð,   bealewa ġemyndiġ,
of ðām goldsele   gongan wolde,
ac hē mæġnes rōf   mīn costode,
2085 grāpode ġearofolm.   Glōf hangode

once Withergyld lay dead after the fall of heroes?
Now some child of the killers, walks the floor here,
proud of his booty, boasts of the killing,
and wears the treasure which by rights
you should possess.' So he prompts
and reminds all the time with bitter words,
until the moment comes that the maiden's thane
for his father's deeds forfeits his life,
lies bloodstained from the bite of sword.
The other one will make his escape
and save his life, he knows the country well.
Then the sworn oaths made on both sides
by the nobles will be broken,
deadly resentment will rise in Ingeld,
love of his wife will grow cooler
from the turmoil of sorrow. So I do not trust
the Heathobards' good faith, their friendship to be firm,
their alliance with the Danes sincere.
    Divider of treasure, I need to say more
about Grendel, so that you know exactly
what came about later in the hand-to-hand
fight of heroes. Once across the earth
the sky-gem sank, a terrible spirit
came in wrath to find us, where we watched
the hall as yet unharmed. Then to Hondscio
came a deadly assault on the doomed man,
the fight was fatal. He was first to fall,
the belted champion. Grendel was the killer,
with mouth and fangs, of the famous thane,
he swallowed whole the dear man's body.
Nor for that would the killer, bloody-toothed,
intent on slaughter, powerful and strong,
mean to leave the hall empty-handed,
but he tried me out, grappled me
with ready hand. From him there hung
a great glove, huge and wonderful

sīd ond sylliċ,   searobendum fæst;
sīo wæs orðoncum   eall ġeġyrwed
dēofles cræftum   ond dracan fellum.
Hē meċ þǣr on innan   unsynniġne,
2090 dīor dǣdfruma   ġedōn wolde
maniġra sumne;   hyt ne mihte swā,
syððan iċ on yrre   upprihte āstōd.
Tō lang ys tō reċċenn̦e   hū i(ċ ð)ām lēodsceaðan
yfla ġehwylċes   *o*ndlēan forġeald;
2095 þǣr iċ, þēoden mīn,   þīne lēode
weorðode weorcum.   Hē on weġ losade,
lȳtle hwīle   līfwynna brē(*a*)c;
hwæþre him sīo swīðre   swaðe weardade
hand on Hiorte,   ond hē hēan ðonan,
2100 mōdes ġeōmor   meregrund ġefēoll.
Mē þone wælrǣs   wine Scildunga
fǣttan golde   fela lēanode,
manegum māðmum,   syððan merġen cōm,
ond wē tō symble   ġeseten hæfdon.
2105 Þǣr wæs ġidd ond glēo;   gomela Scilding,
felafricgende   feorran rehte;
hwīlum hildedēor   hearpan wynne,
gome(*n*)wudu grētte,   hwīlum ġyd āwræc
sōð ond sārliċ,   hwīlum sylliċ spell
2110 rehte æfter rihte   rūmheort cyning;
hwīlum eft ongan   eldo ġebunden,
gomel gūðwiga   ġioguðe cwīðan,
hildestrenġo;   hreðer (*in*)ne wēoll
þonne hē wintrum frōd   worn ġemunde.
2115 Swā wē þǣr inne   andlangne dæġ
nīode nāman,   oð ðæt niht becwōm
ōðer tō yldum.   Þā wæs eft hraðe
ġearo gyrnwræce   Grendeles mōdor,
sīðode sorhfull;   sunu dēað fornam,
2120 wīġhete Wedra.   Wīf unhȳre

clasped with cunning bonds, all craftily made
by devilish skills from dragons' skins.
The fierce malefactor meant to put me in it,
guiltless as I was, one of many.
That could not happen, once I stood upright.
It would be too long to tell you how
I paid the menace back for the evils he had done.
There, my lord, I brought credit to your people
by what I did. He got away,
but did not enjoy life for long;
he left his right hand behind in Heorot,
and sank to the lake-bottom, humiliated, sad at heart.
The friend of the Scyldings repaid me for the fight
with much plated gold, many treasures,
once morning came and we sat to the feast.
There was song and merriment, the old Scylding
who knew so much told tales from far back.
Sometimes the bold man played the harp joyfully,
sometimes made a song, true and painful,
sometimes, great-hearted, he told a tale of wonder
in due order, sometimes, sunk in age,
the old warrior began to tell the young men
of strength in battle; his heart grieved him
when, old in winters, he thought of many things.
So the whole day we did as we pleased,
until another night came upon men.
Then Grendel's mother made a painful attack;
she was quickly eager for vengeance;
death had taken her son, through the battle-hatred
of the Weders. The monster-woman

hyre bearn ġewræc,　beorn ācwealde
ellenlīċe;　þǣr wæs Æschere,
frōdan fyrnwitan　feorh ūðgenġe.
Nōðer hȳ hine ne mōston,　syððan merġen cwōm,
2125 dēaðwēriġne　Denia lēode
bronde forbærnan,　nē on bēl hladan
lēofne mannan;　hīo þæt līċ ætbær
fēondes fæð(m)um　un)der firġenstrēam.
Þæt wæs Hrōðgār(e)　hrēowa tornost
2130 þāra þe lēodfruman　lange beġēate.
Þā se ðēoden meċ　ðīne līfe
healsode hrēohmōd　þæt iċ on holma ġeþrinġ
eorlscipe efnde,　ealdre ġenēðde,
mǣrðo fremede;　hē mē mēde ġehēt.
2135 Iċ ðā ðæs wælmes,　þē is wīde cūð,
grim(n)e gryrelicne　grundhyrde fond;
þǣr unc hwīle wæs　hand ġemǣne;
holm heolfre wēoll,　ond iċ hēafde beċearf
in ðām [gūð]sele　Grendeles mōdor
2140 ēacnum ecgum;　unsōfte þonan
feorh oðferede;　næs iċ fǣġe þā ġȳt,
ac mē eorla hlēo　eft ġesealde
māðma meniġeo,　maga Healfdenes.
Swā se ðēodkyning　þēawum lyfde;
2145 nealles iċ ðām lēanum　forloren hæfde,
mæġnes mēde,　ac hē mē (māðma)s ġeaf,
sunu Healfdenes　on (mīn)ne sylfes dōm;
ðā iċ ðē, beorncyning,　bringan wylle,
ēstum ġeȳwan.　Ġēn is eall æt ðē
2150 lissa ġelong;　iċ lȳt hafo
hēafodmāga　nefne, Hyġelāc, ðeċ.'
Hēt ðā in beran　eaforhēafodseġn,
heaðostēapne helm,　hāre byrnan,
gūðsweord ġeatoliċ,　ġyd æfter wræc:
2155 'Mē ðis hildesceorp　Hrōðgār sealde,

174

avenged her son, violently killed a man.
There Æschere's life departed from him,
the wise counsellor. Nor was it allowed
to the Danish people, once the dawn came,
to burn their dead with brands of fire,
build a funeral pyre for the beloved.
She carried the body off into the embrace
of the fiends beneath the mountain-stream.
That was the greatest of all griefs for Hrothgar,
which had long beset the people's leader.
Then the king in his trouble begged me by your life
to show valor in the tumultuous water,
hazard my life, do a deed of glory.
He promised to repay me. As people know,
I then sought out the savage, terrible
guardian of the gulf. For a good while
we two were hand-to-hand, and where we fought,
in the hall of combat, I cut the head
from Grendel's mother with a giant blade.
It was no soft matter for me to save my life,
but my fated time was not yet come.
The protector of warriors then presented me
with many treasures, the son of Healfdene.
   So the people's king lived courteously.
Nor did I lose my recompense, reward of my strength,
but the son of Healfdene gave me treasures
at my own bidding. I bring them to you,
warrior-king, give them to you freely.
All my delight depends on you.
I have few close kin except you, Hygelac."
   Then he had brought in the boar's head banner,
the high-crowned helmet, the grey corselet
and splendid war-sword, and spoke about them:
"Hrothgar, the wise prince, gave me this war-outfit

snotra fenġel;   sume worde hēt
þæt iċ his ǣrest ðē   ēst ġesæġde:
cwæð þæt hyt hæfde   Hiorogār cyning,
lēod Scyldunga   lange hwīle;
2160 nō ðȳ ǣr suna sīnum   syllan wolde,
hwatum Heorowearde,   þēah hē him hold wǣre,
brēostġewǣdu.   Brūc ealles well!'
Hȳrde iċ þæt þām frætwum   fēower mēaras
lungre, ġelīċe   lāst weardode,
2165 æppelfealu̯we;   hē him ēst ġetēah
mēara ond māðma.   Swā sceal mǣġ dôn,
nealles inwitnet   ōðrum breġdon
dyrnum cræfte,   dēað rēn(ian)
hondġesteallan.   Hyġelāce wæs
2170 nīða heardum   nefa swȳðe hold,
ond ġehwæðer ōðrum   hrōþra ġemyndiġ.
Hȳrde iċ þæt hē ðone healsbēah   Hyġde ġesealde,
wrǣtlicne wundurmāððum,   ðone þe him Wealhðēo ġeaf,
ðēod(nes) dohtor,   þrīo wicg somod
2175 swancor ond sadolbeorht;   hyre syððan wæs
æfter bēahðeġe   br[ē]ost ġeweorðod.
    Swā b(eal)dode   bearn Ecgðeowes,
guma gūð(um) cūð,   gōdum dǣdum,
drēah æfter dōme;   nealles druncne slōg
2180 heorðġenēatas;   næs him hrēoh sefa,
ac hē mancynnes   mǣste cræfte
ġinfæstan ġife   þe him God sealde
hēold hildedēor.   Hēan wæs lange,
swā hyne Ġēata bearn   gōdne ne tealdon,
2185 nē hyne on medobenċe   micles wyrðne
(dry)hten Wedera   ġedōn wolde;
swȳðe (wēn)don   þæt hē slēac wǣre,
æðeling unfrom.   Edwenden cwōm
tīrēadigum menn   torna ġehwylċes.
2190   Hēt ðā eorla hlēo   in ġefetian,

and said shortly that I should tell you
first of his favor. He said that for long
it belonged to King Heorogar, prince of the Scyldings.
Yet he did not wish to give the armor to his son,
the valiant Heoroweard, though he was dear to him.
Use it all well." Then I have heard
that four horses likewise followed hard upon
the precious weapons, dappled and glossy-coated.
Beowulf passed to Hygelac full possession
of horses and treasures. That is how a kinsman
ought to behave, not spreading for others
nets of treachery, plotting the death
of near companions. His nephew was loyal
always to Hygelac, the hard in strife,
each kinsman thought of the other's comfort.
I heard he gave Hygd the great neck-ring,
the wondrous treasure which Wealhtheow gave him,
the prince's daughter, and three horses also,
graceful with gleaming saddles. After that gift,
Hygd bore the torque displayed on her breast
as a sign of honor.
               So Ecgtheow's child,
war-famous man, showed his merit
by good deeds, strove for glory.
By no means did he kill his close companions
overcome by mead. His mind was not cruel,
but he used well, bold in battle,
that great gift which God gave him,
to be of all men the most in might.
For a long time he had no respect,
the tribe of the Geats thought little of him,
the lord of the Weders gave him little honor
on the mead-bench, they believed instead
that he was sluggish, a prince without spark.
For the famous man there would follow
a complete change from all such grief.
    The protector of nobles, the valiant king,

TEXT

heaðorōf cyning   Hrēðles lāfe
golde ġeġyrede;   næs mid Ġēatum ðā
sinċmāðþum sēlra   on sweordes hād;
þæt hē on Bīowulfes   bearm āleġde,
2195 ond him ġesealde   seofan þūsendo,
bold ond bregostōl.   Him wæs (b)ām samod
on ðām lēodscipe   lond ġecynde,
eard ēðelriht,   ōðrum swīðor
sīde rīċe   þām ðǣr sēlra wæs.

2200   Eft þæt ġeīode   ufaran dōgrum
hildehlæmmum,   syððan Hyġelāc læġ,
ond Hear[dr]ēde   hildemēċeas
under bordhrēoðan   tō bonan wurdon,
ðā hyne ġesōhtan   on siġeþēode
2205 hearde hildefrecan,   Heaðo-Scilfingas,
nīða ġenǣġdan   nefan Hererīċes:
syððan Bēowulfe   br(ā)de rīċe
on hand ġehwearf;   hē ġehēold tela
fīftiġ wintr(a)   — wæs ðā frōd cyning,
2210 eald ēþel(w)eard —   oð ðæt (ā)n ongan
deorcum nihtum   draca rīcs[i]an,
sē ðe on hēa(um) h(of)e   hord beweotode,
stānbeorh stēar(c)ne;   stīġ under læġ
eldum uncūð.   Þǣr on innan ġīong
2215 nið[ð]a nāthwyl(ċ,   sē ðe nē)h ġ(eþ[r]on)g
hǣðnum horde;   hond (ēðe ġefēng)
(searo) sinċe fāh.   Nē hē þæt syððan (bemāð),
þ(ēah) ð(e hē) slǣpende   besyre(d wur)de
þēofes cræfte: þæt sīe ðīod (onfand),
2220 b(ū)folc b(i)orn(a),   þæt hē ġebolge(n) wæs.

Nealles (met ġe)wēaldum   wyrmhorda cræft,
sylfes willum,   sē ðe him sāre ġesceōd,
ac for þrēanēdlan   þē(o) nāthwylċes

then had brought in an heirloom of Hrethel,
adorned with gold. Among the Geats
there was no finer treasure in the form of a sword.
He laid it down on Beowulf's lap,
and with it gave him a grant of rule
over seven thousand hides, hall and high-seat.
In that nation, land and country
and ancestral rights, all were inherited
by both together, but the broad kingdom
went to the one who there was senior.

　It came about through the blows of war,
in later days, once Hygelac lay dead,
and war-swords had been, under the shield-rim,
the death of Heardred, when those hard warriors,
the warlike Scylfings, sought him out
among his victor-people, violently attacked
the grandson of Hereric, that then there passed
into Beowulf's hand the broad kingdom.
For fifty winters he defended it well,
now an old guardian of the homeland,
until in the dark nights a dragon began to reign,
who guarded his hoard in a high hall,
a strong stone barrow. Beneath it lay a path
unknown to men. Inside it went
some man or other, creeping in close
to the heathen hoard. His hand seized readily
a treasure-goblet shining with gold.
The dragon did not hide his anger later,
though tricked in sleep by the skill of a thief.
That they found out, those who lived in the land,
once he was enraged.
　　　　　　By no means deliberately,
of his own will, did he who caused
the dragon such harm test the hoard's magic,

TEXT

hæleða bearna   heteswenġeas flē(*a*)h,
2225 ærnes þearf(a),   ond ðǣr inne (*f*)eal(*h*)
secg syn(by)siġ   sōna (*in þ*)ā tīde,
þæt (þǣr) ðām ġyst(e)   g(r)yrebr(ō)g(a) stōd;
hwæðr(e earm)sceapen   (ealdre nēþd)e,
2230 forh(t on ferhðe)   þā hyne se fǣ(*r*) beġeat,
sinċfæt (sōhte).   Þǣr wæs swylcra fela
in ðām eorðse(le)   ǣrġestrēona,
swā hȳ on ġeārdagum   gumena nāthwylċ,
eormenlāfe   æþelan cynnes,
2235 þanchycgende   þǣr ġehȳdde,
dēore māðmas.   Ealle hīe dēað fornam
ǣrran mǣlum,   ond s(ē) ān ðā ġēn
lēoda duguðe,   sē ðǣr lenġest hwearf,
weard wineġeōmor,   (*wēn*)de þæs yl(*c*)an,
2240 þæt hē lȳtel fæc   longġestrēona
brūcan mōste.   Beorh eall ġearo
wunode on wonge   wæterȳðum nēah,
nīwe be næsse,   nearocræftum fæst;
þǣr on inn(*a*)n bær   eorlġestrēona
2245 hringa hyrde   h(*o*)rdwyrðne dǣl,
fǣttan goldes,   fē(*a*) worda cwæð:
'Heald þū nū, hrūse,   nū hæleð ne m(ō)stan,
eorla ǣhte.   Hwæt, hyt ǣr on ðē
gōde beġēaton;   gūðdēað fornam,
2250 (*f*)eorhbeal(*o*) frēcne   fȳra ġe(*h*)wylcne
lēoda mīnra,   þ(*o*)n(*e*) ðe þis [līf] ofġeaf;
ġesāwon seledrēam(as).   Nāh hwā sweord weġe
oððe f(orð bere)   fǣted wǣġe,
drynċfæt dēore;   dug(uð) ellor s[c]eōc.
2255 Sceal se hearda helm   (hyr)stedgolde,
fǣtum befeallen;   feormynd swefað,
þā ðe beadogrīman   bȳwan sceoldon;
ġē swylċe sēo herepād,   sīo æt hilde ġebād
ofer borda ġebræc   bite īrena,

but some slave or other of the sons of heroes
found his way in, flying homeless
from angry lashes, in dire necessity.
The guilty man soon realized
the dreadful risk there for the stranger,
but when the danger came upon him,
the wretch, deeply fearful, risked his life
and took the precious cup. There were many like it,
treasures from of old, in the earth-hall,
as they were hidden, carefully, long ago
by someone unknown, precious treasures,
the mighty legacy of a noble race.
Death took them all in days gone by,
and he who alone lived the longest
of all the men of his company,
saddened by the loss of all his friends,
he reckoned likewise he would be allowed
little time to keep the long-hoarded treasure.
The barrow stood ready on level ground
by the shoreline, unused on a headland,
with cunning crafts to make it safe.
The keeper of the rings carried them in,
a precious hoard of noble relics
plated with gold, and said few words:
"Earth, let you hold, now heroes may not,
the possessions of the princes.
Good men once got them from you.
Death in war, deadly life-peril,
took away every one of my people,
who gave up this life, left the joys of hall.
I have no-one to burnish the sword
or carry plated cup, or precious goblet.
That company has passed away.
The hard helmet shall lose its plates
of decorated gold; the polishers sleep,
who should furbish the war-mask.
Yes, even the battle-dress, which endured the bite
of iron in battle, over the clash of shields,

2260 brosnað æfter beorne.   Ne mæġ byrnan hriṅġ
    æfter wīġfruman   wīde fēran,
    hæleðum be healfe.   Næs hearpan wyn,
    gomen glēobēames,   nē gōd hafoc
    ġeond sæl swingeð,   nē se swifta mearh
2265 burhstede bēateð.   Bealocwealm hafað
    fela feorhcynna   forð onsended.'
    Swā ġiōmormōd   giohðo mǣnde
    ān æfter eallum,   unblīðe hwear(f)
    dæġes ond nihtes,   oð ðæt dēaðes wylm
2270 hrān æt heortan.   Hordwynne fond
    eald ūhtsceaða   opene standan,
    sē ðe byrnende   biorgas sēċeð,
    nacod nīðdraca,   nihtes flēogeð
    fȳre befangen;   hyne foldbūend
2275 (swīðe ondrǣ)da(ð).   Hē ġesēċean sceall
    (hea)r(h on) hrūsan,   þǣr hē hǣðen gold
    warað wintrum frōd;   ne byð him wihte ðȳ sēl.
        Swā se ðēodsceaða   þrēohund wintra
    hēold on hrūsan   hordærna sum
2280 ēacencræftiġ,   oð ðæt hyne ān ābealch
    mon on mōde;   mandryhtne bær
    fǣted wǣġe,   frioðowǣre bæd
    hlāford sīnne.   Ðā wæs hord rāsod,
    onboren bēaga hord,   bēne ġetīðad
2285 fēasceaftum men;   frēa scēawode
    fīra fyrnġeweorc   forman sīðe.
    Þā se wyrm onwōc,   wrōht wæs ġenīwad;
    stonc ðā æfter stāne,   stearcheort onfand
    fēondes fōtlāst;   hē tō forð ġestōp
2290 dyrnan cræfte   dracan hēafde nēah.
    Swā mæġ unfǣġe   ēaðe ġedīgan
    wēan ond wrǣcsīð,   sē ðe waldendes
    hyldo ġehealdeþ.   Hordweard sōhte
    ġeorne æfter grunde,   wolde guman findan,

it will decay with its owner. The ringed shirt
cannot walk widely with the champion,
along with the hero. There is no joy from the harp,
no merriment from the song-wood,
nor does the good hawk swoop through the hall,
nor the swift horse stamp the courtyard.
Death in battle destroyed many races of men."
So the lone man lamented his sorrow
over all things, wandered unhappily
day and night until death's stroke
pierced his heart.
        The old dawn-ravager
found the precious hoard standing open,
the bare-skinned spite-dragon,
he who attacks the towns with fire,
flies at night cloaked with flame:
dwellers in the land dread him greatly.
He will seek out an old shrine in the earth,
where, aged by winters, he guards heathen gold,
none the better for it.
        So for three hundred winters
the people's enemy by mighty power
guarded the treasure in chamber underground,
until a man woke his mind to wrath:
he carried to his lord the plated cup,
asked a pledge of peace from his lord.
Then the hoard had been breached,
ring-store lessened, his request granted
to the destitute man. For the first time
his lord looked at the ancient work of men.
When the worm woke, strife was renewed.
He sniffed at the stone, the strong-hearted one
found the footprint of his enemy;
he had trodden too close, stealthily,
to the dragon's head. That's how a man not doomed,
who has the Ruler's favor, can readily survive
sorrow and exile. The hoard-guardian
looked eagerly all round about,

2395 þone þe him on sweofote   sāre ġetēode;
    hāt ond hrēohmōd   hlǣw oft ymbehwearf
    ealne ūtanweardne;   nē ðǣr ǣniġ mon
    on þ(ām) wēstenne —   hwæðre wīges ġefeh,
    bea(dwe) weorces;   hwīlum on beorh æthwearf,
2300 sinċfæt sōhte;   hē þæt sōna onfand,
    ðæt hæfde gumena sum   goldes ġefandod,
    hēahġestrēona.   Hordweard onbād
    earfoðlīċe   oð ðæt ǣfen cwōm;
    wæs ðā ġebolgen   beorges hyrde,
2305 wolde se lāða   līġe forġyldan
    drinċfæt dȳre.   Þā wæs dæġ sceacen
    wyrme on willan;   nō on wealle læ[n]ġ
    bīdan wolde,   ac mid bǣle fōr,
    fȳre ġefȳsed.   Wæs se fruma eġesliċ
2310 lēodum on lande,   swā hyt lungre wearð
    on hyra sinċġifan   sāre ġeendod.
        Ðā se gǣst ongan   glēdum spīwan,
    beorht hofu bærnan —   brynelēoma stōd
    eldum on andan;   nō ðǣr āht cwices
2315 lāð lyftfloga   lǣfan wolde.
    Wæs þæs wyrmes wīġ   wīde ġesȳne,
    nearofāges nīð   nēan ond feorran,
    hū se gūðsceaða   Ġēata lēode
    hatode ond hȳnde;   hord eft ġescēat,
2320 dryhtsele dyrnne,   ǣr dæġes hwīle.
    Hæfde landwara   līġe befangen,
    bǣle ond bronde;   beorges ġetruwode,
    wīġes ond wealles;   him sēo wēn ġelēah.
        Þā wæs Bīowulfe   brōga ġecȳðed
2325 snūde tō sōðe,   þæt his sylfes hām,
    bolda sēlest,   brynewylmum mealt,
    ġifstōl Ġēata.   Þæt ðām gōdan wæs
    hrēow on hreðre,   hyġesorga mǣst;
    wēnde se wīsa   þæt hē wealdende

184

wanted to find the man who had done him
such an injury in his slumber.
Hot and angry he circled the mound
from the outside, found no man there
in the wilderness – yet he was eager for fight,
for a deed of battle. He criss-crossed the barrow,
looking again for the precious cup.
Soon he was sure that it was some man
who got into his gold, the precious treasures.
Until evening came the hoard-guardian,
keeper of the barrow, waited impatiently;
by then his mood had become enraged,
the evil one wanted to avenge with fire
his precious goblet. The day had gone,
as the worm wanted; he would wait no longer
by his stone cave, but set out aflame,
driven on by fire. His onset was terrifying
for the people of the land, as it was quickly
brought to a finish for their treasure-giver.

    Then the raider began to spew out flame,
to burn the bright halls – the blazing light
struck fear into men; the hateful flier
had no mind to leave anything alive.
The attack of the worm, the hostile spite
of the cruel one was seen far and wide,
how the destroyer hated and humiliated
the people of the Geats. Before day came
he flew back to his hoard, his dark stronghold.
He had engulfed with flame and fire and burning
all who lived there. He trusted in his strength,
and his stone barrow. His hope belied him.

    The terror was told quickly and truly
to Beowulf, that his home, best of buildings,
had been dissolved in flame, gift-throne of the Geats.
That was the greatest of sorrows to the good man,
caused disturbance deep in his mind.
The wise one thought he must have offended

2330 ofer ealde riht,   ēċean dryhtne
bitre ġebulge;   brēost innan wēoll
þēostrum ġeþoncum,   swā him ġeþȳwe ne wæs.
   Hæfde līġdraca   lēoda fæsten,
ēalond ūtan,   eorðweard ðone
2335 glēdum forgrunden;   him ðæs gūðkyning,
Wedera þīoden   wræce leornode.
Heht him þā ġewyrċean   wīġendra hlēo
eall īrenne,   eorla dryhten,
wīġbord wrǣtliċ;   wisse hē ġearwe
2340 þæt him holtwudu   he(lpan) ne meahte,
lind wið līġe.   Sceolde (lī)þend daga,
æþeling ǣrgōd   ende ġebīdan,
worulde līfes,   ond se wyrm somod,
þēah ðe hordwelan   hēolde lange.
2345 Oferhogode ðā   hringa fenġel
þæt hē þone wīdflogan   weorode ġesōhte,
sīdan herġe;   nō hē him þā sæċċe ondrēd,
nē him þæs wyrmes wīġ   for wiht dyde,
eafoð ond ellen,   forðon hē ǣr fela
2350 nearo nēðende   nīða ġedīġde,
hildehlemma,   syððan hē Hrōðgāres,
sigorēadiġ secg,   sele fǣlsode,
ond æt gūðe forgrāp   Grendeles mǣgum
lāðan cynnes.
            Nō þæt lǣsest wæs
2355 hondġemōt(a)   þǣr mon Hyġelāc slōh,
syððan Ġēata cyning   gūðe rǣsum,
frēawine folca   Frēslondum on,
Hrēðles eafora   hiorodrynċum swealt,
bille ġebēaten.   Þonan Bīowulf cōm
2360 sylfes cræfte,   sundnytte drēah;
hæfde him on earme   (ealra) þrītiġ
hildeġeatwa   þā hē tō holme (þron)g.
Nealles Hetware   hrēmġe þorf(t)on

the Ruler bitterly, the eternal Lord,
against ancient right. His breast boiled inside
with dark thoughts, as was not his habit.
The fire-dragon had destroyed with flame
the people's fortress, the guarded land,
whole coastal region: the war-king,
lord of the Weders, would teach him revenge.
The lord of men, protector of warriors,
ordered to be made, all of iron,
a splendid shield; he knew for sure
wood could not help him, linden against fire.
The seafarer, the splendid prince,
was to come to an end of life in this world,
and the worm as well, though he had long held
the wealth of the hoard. The lord of rings scorned
to attack the wide-flier with a war-band,
a great army; he did not fear the fight,
nor did he value the worm's warfare,
its strength and power, for he had survived
many difficult and daring contests,
strokes of battle, since victoriously
he cleansed the hall of Hrothgar the king,
overpowered with his grip Grendel's kinswoman
of evil race.

It was not the least
of hand-to-hand fights when Hygelac was killed,
when the Geat king, son of Hrethel,
peoples' lord and friend, died in Frisia
in the rushes of battle, beaten down by the blade,
by bloody swords. Beowulf escaped
by his own strength, he took to swimming.
In his arms he had thirty suits of armor
when he plunged into the water.
The Hetware who bore their shields against him

fēðewīġes,   þē him foran onġēan
2365 linde bǣron;   lȳt eft becwōm
fram þām hildfrecan   hāmes nīosan.

Oferswam ðā sioleða bigong   sunu Ecgðeowes,
earm ānhaga   eft tō lēodum;
þǣr him Hyġd ġebēad   hord ond rīċe,
2370 bēagas ond bregostōl;   bearne ne truwode,
þæt hē wið ælfylċum   ēþelstōlas
healdan cūðe,   ðā wæs Hyġelāc dēad.
Nō ðȳ ǣr fēasceafte   findan meahton
æt ðām æðelinge   ǣniġe ðinga
2375 þæt hē Heardrēde   hlāford wǣre,
oððe þone cynedōm   ċīosan wolde;
hwæðre hē him on folce   frēondlārum hēold,
ēstum mid āre,   oð ðæt hē yldra wearð,
Weder-Ġēatum wēold.

                Hyne wræcmæcgas
2380 ofer sǣ sōhtan,   suna Ōhteres;
hæfdon hȳ forhealden   helm Scylfinga,
þone sēlestan   sǣcyninga
þāra ðe in Swīorīċe   sinċ brytnade,
mǣrne þēoden.   Him þæt tō mearce wearð:
2385 hē þǣr [f]or feorme   feorhwunde hlēat,
sweordes swenġum,   sunu Hyġelāces,
ond him eft ġewāt   Ongenðioes bearn
hāmes nīosan   syððan Heardrēd læġ,
lēt ðone bregostōl   Bīowulf healdan,
2390 Ġēatum wealdan;   þæt wæs gōd cyning.

Sē ðæs lēodhryres   lēan ġemunde
uferan dōgrum,   Ēadġilse wearð
fēasceaftum frēond;   folce ġestēpte
ofer sǣ sīde   sunu Ōhteres,
2395 wigum ond wǣpnum;   hē ġewræc syððan
ċealdum ċearsīðum,   cyning ealdre binēat.

had little need to boast of that battle on foot;
few would return from the warrior
to see their homes. Then the son of Ecgtheow,
sad and solitary, swam back to his people
across the sea's expanse. There Hygd offered him
hoard and kingdom, rings and throne.
She had no faith in her son to defend
the land against foreigners, and its family seats,
once Hygelac was dead. The hard-pressed ones
could not despite that find by any means
that the prince would be lord to Heardred,
or accept the kingship. Instead he guarded him
among the people with friendship and advice,
willingly and honorably, until he was older
and ruled the Geats.
               Exiles sought him out
across the sea, the sons of Ohthere,
in rebellion against their uncle Onela,
the famous prince, protector of the Scylfings,
best of all sea-kings who shared out treasure
in the land of the Swedes. That cost his life.
For sheltering them, the son of Hygelac
got his death-wound from strokes of swords.
Once he lay dead the child of Ongentheow
went back again to seek his home,
allowed Beowulf to keep the throne,
and rule the Geats. That was a good king.

Later Beowulf would bear in mind
the fall of his prince, exact a pay-back.
He befriended the fugitive Eadgils,
gave support to the son of Ohthere
across the broad water with weapons and war.
In a cold campaign he took the king's life,
claimed his revenge.

Swā hē nīða ġehwane   ġenesen hæfde,
slīðra ġeslyhta,   sunu Ecgðiowes,
ellenweorca,   oð ðone ānne dæġ
2400 þe hē wið þām wyrme   ġewegan sceolde.
Ġewāt þā twelfa sum   torne ġebolgen
dryhten Ġēata   dracan scēawian;
hæfde þā ġefrūnen   hwanan sīo fǣhð ārās,
bealonīð biorna;   him tō bearme cwōm
2405 mā(ð)þumfæt mǣre   þurh ðæs meldan hond.
Sē wæs on ðām ðrēate   þreottēoða secg,
sē ðæs orleġes   ōr onstealde,
hæft hyġeġiōmor,   sceolde hēan ðonon
wong wīsian.   Hē ofer willan ġīong
2410 tō ðæs ðe hē eorðsele   ānne wisse,
hlǣw under hrūsan   holmwylme nēh,
ȳðġewinne;   sē wæs innan full
wrǣtta ond wīra.   Weard unhīore,
ġearo gūðfreca   goldmāðmas hēold
2415 eald under eorðan;   næs þæt ȳðe ċēap
tō ġegangenne   gumena ǣniġum.
Ġesæt ðā on næsse   nīðheard cyning,
þenden hǣlo ābēad   heorðġenēatum,
goldwine Ġēata.   Him wæs ġeōmor sefa,
2420 wǣfre ond wælfūs,   wyrd unġemete nēah,
sē ðone gomelan   grētan sceolde,
sēċean sāwle hord,   sundur ġedǣlan
līf wið līċe;   nō þon lange wæs
feorh æþelinges   flǣsce bewunden.
2425 Bīowulf maþelade,   bearn Ecgðeowes:
'Fela iċ on ġiogoðe   gūðrǣsa ġenæs,
orleġhwīla;   iċ þæt eall ġemon.
Iċ wæs syfanwintre   þā meċ sin(c)a baldor,
frēawine folca   æt mīnum fæder ġenam;
2430 hēold meċ ond hæfde   Hrēðel cyning,
ġeaf mē sinċ ond symbęl,   sibbe ġemunde;

                    So the son of Ecgtheow
had survived every strife,
dangerous battles, deeds of glory,
until the day came when he had to fight
against the worm. Angered and grieving,
the lord of the Geats, with eleven others,
set off to look upon the dragon;
by then he had heard what the feud arose from,
the baleful assault. The one who knew of it,
he who had caused the start of the strife,
handed him the famous treasure-goblet:
he made the thirteenth man in the troop,
as a sad captive he had to show the way
from there, in disgrace. Against his will
he went to where he knew the lonely earth-hall was,
a cave underground near the seashore,
the surging waves. It was stuffed inside
with ornaments and metal strips.
The uncanny guardian, alert and aggressive,
kept the gold treasures, old, under earth,
goods not easy for any man to gain.
The war-hardened king, gold-friend of the Geats,
sat down on the ness while to his companions
he said farewell. His mind was sad,
disturbed, foreboding, the fate very near
which would have to come to the old man,
take the soul within him, separate life from body.
Not long clad in flesh would be the prince's life.
Beowulf spoke, child of Ecgtheow:
"When I was young I survived many battles,
many times of strife. I remember them all.
I was seven winters when the lord of treasures,
friend and lord of peoples, took me from my father.
King Hrethel kept me and brought me up,
gave me feast and treasure, acknowledged our kinship.

næs iċ him tō līfe   lāðra ǫwihte,
beorn in burgum,   þonne his bearna hwylċ,
Herebeald ond Hæðcyn   oððe Hyġelāc mīn.
2435 Wæs þām yldestan   unġedēfelīċe
mǣ ġes dǣdum   morþǫrbed strêd,
syððan hyne Hæðcyn   of hornbogan,
his frēawine   flāne ġeswencte,
miste merċelses   ond his mǣ ġ ofscēt,
2440 brōðǫr ōðerne   blōdigan gāre.
Þæt wæs feohlēas ġefeoht,   fyrenum ġesyngad,
hreðre hyġemēðe;   sceolde hwæðre swā þēah
æðeling unwrecen   ealdres linnan.
   Swā bið ġeōmorlīċ   gomelum ċeorle
2445 tō ġebīdanne,   þæt his byre rīde
ġiong on galgan.   Þonne hē ġyd wrece,
sāriġne sang,   þonne his sunu hangað
hrefne tō hrōðre,   ond hē him helpe ne mæġ
eald ond infrōd   ǣniġe ġefremman,
2450 symble bið ġemyndgad   morna ġehwylċe
eaforan ellorsīð;   ōðres ne ġȳmeð
tō ġebīdanne   burgum in innan
yrfeweardes,   þonne se ān hafað
þurh dēaðes nȳd   dǣda ġefondad.
Ġesyhð sorhċeariġ   on his suna būre
2455 wīnsele wēstne,   windġe reste,
rēot[ġ]e berofene;   rīdend swefað,
hæleð in hoðman;   nis þǣr hearpan swēġ,
gomen in ġeardum,   swylċe ðǣr iū wǣron.

2460 Ġewīteð þonne on sealman,   sorhlēoð gæleð
ān æfter ānum;   þūhte him eall tō rūm,
wongas ond wīċstede.
            Swā Wedra helm
æfter Herebealde   heortan sorge
weallinde wæġ;   wihte ne meahte

While he lived in his courts I was no less welcome
to him than were any of his own children,
Herebeald and Hæthcyn and my Hygelac.
By a kinsman's deed the death-bed was prepared
for the eldest of them, as was unfitting,
when Hæthcyn shot his friend and lord
with an arrow from a horn-bow,
he missed the mark and shot his kinsman,
one brother the other with a bloody dart.
That was a violent deed for which there could be
no compensation, a criminal wrongdoing,
great trouble to the mind. Nevertheless, for all that,
the prince's death had to remain unavenged.

   It's hard likewise for an old man
to bear, that his young son
rides on the gallows. He laments then
with song of grief, when his son hangs
a prey to the raven, and the wise old man
can give no help. Every morning
he always remembers his son's passing,
does not care to wait for another inheritor,
within his home, once the first has come
to an end of deeds by sentence of death.
Sad in his heart, he sees his son's chamber,
the deserted wine-hall, dreary and desolate,
a windswept resting-place, mournful, abandoned.
The riders sleep, heroes in their graves,
there is no joy of the harp, no merriment in the courts
as once there was.

              He takes to his bed,
sings lonely lament, for the one lost,
for him everything now seems empty,
fields and dwelling-place.

              So the protector
of the Weders felt sorrow welling up

2465 on ðām feorhbonan fǣghðe ġebētan;
nō ðȳ ǣr hē þone heaðorinċ hatian ne meahte
lāðum dǣdum, þēah him lēof ne wæs.
Hē ðā mid þǣre sorhge, þē him sīo sār belamp,
gumdrēam ofġeaf, Godes lēoht ġeċēas;
2470 eaferum lǣfde, swā dēð ēadiġ mon,
lond ond lēodbyriġ, þā hē of līfe ġewāt.
  Þā wæs synn ond sacu Swēona ond Ġeata
ofer (w)īd wæter wrōht ġemǣne,
herenīð hearda, syððan Hrēðel swealt,
2475 oð ðe him Ongenðeowes eaferan wǣran
frome fyrdhwate, frēode ne woldon
ofer heafo healdan, ac ymb Hrēosna Beorh
eatolne inwitscear oft ġefremedon.
  Þæt mǣġwine mīne ġewrǣcan,
2480 fǣhðe ond fyrene, swā hyt ġefrǣġe wæs,
þēah ðe ōðer his ealdre ġebohte,
heardan ċēape; Hæðcynne wearð,
Ġeata dryhtne gūð onsǣġe.
  Þā iċ on morgne ġefræġn mǣġ ōðerne
2485 billes ecgum on bonan stǣlan,
þǣr Ongenþēow Eofores nīosað;
gūðhelm tōglād, gomela Scylfing
hrēas [hilde]blāc; hond ġemunde
fǣhðo ġenōge, feorhsweng ne oftēah.
2490 Iċ him þā māðmas þe hē mē sealde
ġeald æt gūðe, swā me ġifeðe wæs,
lēohtan sweorde; hē mē lond forġeaf,
eard ēðelwyn. Næs him ǣniġ þearf
þæt hē tō Ġifðum oððe tō Gār-Denum
2495 oððe in Swīorīċe sēċean þurfe
wyrsan wīġfrecan, weorðe ġeċȳpan;
symle iċ him on fēðan beforan wolde,
āna on orde, ond swā tō aldre sceall
sæċċe fremman, þenden þis sweord þolað

deep in his heart. There was no way for him
to settle the killing with the killer,
nor was he able to hate the warrior
for his ill deed, though he could not love him.
Because of his grief when the tragedy came,
he gave up joys of men, he chose God's light.
As an honest man does, he left to his children
land and citadel, when he passed away.

    After his death, there was dispute and enmity,
warfare all across the wide water
between Swedes and Geats, savage raiding,
once Ongentheow's sons were bold and warlike.
They did not want peace across the water,
but around Hreosna Hill they often carried out
grievous slaughter. For that my kinsmen
took their revenge, for the raids and crimes,
as was proper, although one of them
paid with his life, a hard bargain.
War was fatal to King Hæthcyn,
lord of the Geats.

                  I heard that one kinsman
in the morning avenged the other
on his killer, with the edge of the sword,
when Ongentheow clashed with Eofor.
The war-helmet split, the old Scylfing fell
pale in death. The hand of Eofor
well remembered the vendetta,
did not draw back the fatal stroke.

    I paid back in battle with bright sword
the treasures I was given, as it was granted to me.
He gave me land of my own, a fine estate.
He had no need to look for lesser warriors
among the Swedes, Spear-Danes or Gepids,
pay a price for them. I was always ready
to go on foot before him, alone in the front,
and so I will always do, as long as this sword lasts

2500 þæt meċ ǣr ond sīð   oft ġelǣste,
    syððan iċ for dugeðum   Dæġhrefne wearð
    tō handbonan,   Hūga cempan —
    nalles hē ðā frætwe   Frēscyning[e],
    brēostweorðunge   bringan mōste,
2505 ac in *campe* ġecrong   cumbles hyrde,
    æþeling on elne;   ne wæs ecg bona,
    ac him hildegrāp   heortan wylmas,
    bānhūs ġebræc.   Nū sceall billes ecg,
    hond ond heard sweord   ymb hord wīgan.'
2510 Bēowulf maðelode,   bēotwordum spræc
    nīehstan sīðe: 'Iċ ġenēðde fela
    gūða on ġeogoðe;   ġȳt iċ wylle,
    frōd folces weard   fǣhðe sēcan,
    mǣrð*u* fremman,   ġif meċ se mānsceaða
2515 of eorðsele   ūt ġesēċeð.'
    Ġegrētte ðā   gumena ġehwylcne,
    hwate helmberend   hindeman sīðe,
    swǣse ġesīðas: 'Nolde iċ sweord beran,
    wǣpen tō wyrme,   ġif iċ wiste hū
2520 wið ðām āglǣċean   elles meahte
    ġylpe wiðgrīpan,   swā iċ giō wið Grendle dyde;
    ac iċ ðǣr heaðufȳres   hātes wēne,
    [o]reðes ond āttres;   forðon iċ mē on hafu
    bord ond byrnan.   Nelle iċ beorges weard
2525 oferflēon fōtes trem,   ac unc [feohte] sceal
    weorðan æt wealle,   swā unc wyrd ġetēoð
    metod manna ġehwæs.   Iċ eom on mōde from,
    þæt iċ wið þone gūðflogan   ġylp ofersitte.
    Ġebīde ġē on beorge   byrnum werede,
2530 secgas on searwum,   hwæðer sēl mæġe
    æfter wælrǣse   wunde ġedȳgan
    uncer twēġa.   Nis þæt ēower sīð,
    nē ġemet mannes   nef(*ne*) mīn ānes,
    þæt hē wið āglǣċean   eofoðo dǣle,

which has often helped me early and late,
ever since I was the death of Dayraven,
champion of the Franks, fighting hand-to-hand
before the armies. It was not given to him
to bear the breast-ornament, the great neck-ring,
to the Frisian king. He fell in the fight,
the noble one in his pride. The edge did not kill him,
but my warlike grasp crushed his bone-house
and his heart's beating. Now the blade's edge,
hand and hard sword shall fight for the hoard."
   Beowulf spoke out, pledged his word
for the last time: "I lived through
many battles when I was young.
Old guardian now of the people,
I will still offer fight, do a famous deed,
if the marauder, marked with guilt,
will come out to me from his earth-hall."
He gave a greeting to each of his men,
bold ones in their helmets, his own companions
for the last time: "I would not carry sword
or any weapon against the worm,
if I knew how else I could come with honor
to grips with the monster, as with Grendel
I did long ago. But here I expect
hot hostile blaze, breath of poison.
So I must carry shield and armor.
I will not give way the space of a foot
to the mound-guardian, but by the stone
there will be battle between the two of us
however fate, which rules all men,
shall dictate for us. My spirit is strong,
so that I will waste no words on the battle-flier.
Warriors in armor, wait by the mound
to see which of us both will better survive,
after the deadly clash, the wounds dealt out.
This is no venture for you, nor is it right
for any man except myself
to test his might against the monster,

2535 eorlscype efne. Iċ mid elne sceall
gold ġegangan,   oððe gūð nimeð,
feorhbealu frēcne   frēan ēowerne.'
Ārās ðā bī ronde   rōf ōretta,
heard under helme,   hioroserċean bær
2540 under stāncleofu,   strenġo ġetruwode
ānes mannes;   ne bið swylċ earges sīð!
Ġeseah ðā be wealle   sē ðe worna fela
gumcystum gōd   gūða ġedīġde,
hildehlemma,   þonne hnitan fēðan,
2545 sto[n]dan stānbogan,   strēam ūt þonan
brecan of beorge;   wæs þǣre burnan wælm
heaðofȳrum hāt,   ne meahte horde nēah
unbyrnende   ǣniġe hwīle
dēop ġedȳġan   for dracan lēġe.
2550 Lēt ðā of brēostum,   ðā hē ġebolgen wæs,
Weder-Ġēata lēod   word ūt faran,
stearcheort styrmde;   stefn in becōm
heaðotorht hlynnan   under hārne stān.
Hete wæs onhrēred,   hordweard oncnīow
2555 mannes reorde;   næs ðǣr māra fyrst
frēode tō friclan.   From ǣrest cwōm
oruð āglǣċean   ūt of stāne,
hāt hildeswāt;   hrūse dynede.
Biorn under beorge   bordrand onswāf
2560 wið ðām gryreġieste,   Ġēata dryhten;
ðā wæs hrinġbogan   heorte ġefȳsed
sæċċe tō sēċeanṇe.   Sweord ǣr ġebrǣd
gōd gūðcyning,   gomele lāfe,
ecgum unslāw;   ǣġhwæðrum wæs
2565 bealohycgendra   brōga fram ōðrum.
Stīðmōd ġestōd   wi(ð) stēapne rond
winia bealdor,   ðā se wyrm ġebēah
snūde tōsomne;   hē on searwum bād.
Ġewāt ðā byrnende   ġebogen scrīðan,

and do a noble deed. I will win the gold
by my valor, or else fearful war
and fatal enmity will take your lord."
   The fierce warrior, hard beneath his helmet,
stood up by his shield, carried his war-shirt
beneath the stone-slope, trusting in the strength
of one man alone: That is by no means
the venture of a coward!
                                  He who had before
in manly fashion survived many battles,
many strokes of war when troops clashed,
saw a stone arch, with a stream
breaking from it out of the barrow.
The running water was hot with hostile fire,
he could get no closer in to the hoard
for any time without being burnt,
because of dragon-fire. Once he was enraged,
the Weder-Geat let the words come
from his breast, the brave-heart shouted.
His voice rang out clearly beneath the grey stone.
It roused hatred, the hoard's guardian
could tell a man's voice. There was no more time
to ask for peace. First the monster's breath
came from the stone, hot and hostile steam.
The earth resounded. The man by the mound,
lord of the Geats, lifted up his shield
against the strange horror. Then was the heart
of the coiled creature stirred to seek battle.
The good war-king had drawn his sword,
an old inheritance, sharp in its edges.
Each of the two intent on fight
knew fear of the other. The lord of the retainers
stood determined behind his curved shield.
He waited in his armor as the worm writhed
quickly towards him. The coiled one came on
wreathed in flame, rushing to its fate.

2570 tō ġescipe scyndan.   Scyld wēl ġebearg
līfe ond līċe   lǣssan hwīle
mǣrum þēodne   þonne his myne sōhte,
ðǣr hē þȳ fyrste   forman dōgore
wealdan mōste   swā him wyrd ne ġescrāf
2575 hrēð æt hilde.   Hond up ābrǣd
Ġēata dryhten,   gryrefāhne slōh
inċġelāfe,   þæt sīo ecg ġewāc
brūn on bāne,   bāt unswīðor
þonne his ðīodcyning   þearfe hæfde
2580 bysigum ġebǣded.   Þā wæs beorges weard
æfter heaðuswenġe   on hrēoųm mōde,
wearp wælfȳre;   wīde sprungon
hildelēoman.   Hrēðsigora ne ġealp
goldwine Ġēata;   gūðbill ġeswāc
2585 nacod æt nīðe,   swā hyt nō sceolde,
īren ǣrgōd.   Ne wæs þæt ēðe sīð,
þæt se mǣra   maga Ecgðeowes
grundwong þone   ofġyfan wolde;
sceolde [ofer] willan   wīċ eardian
2590 elles hwerġen,   swā sceal ǣġhwylċ mon
ālǣtan lǣndagas.

                    Næs ðā long tō ðon
þæt ðā āglǣċean   hȳ eft ġemētton.
Hyrte hyne hordweard,   hreðer ǣðme wēoll,
nīwan stefne;   nearo ðrōwode
2595 fȳre befongen   sē ðe ǣr folce wēold.
Nealles him on hēape   handġesteallan,
æðelinga bearn   ymbe ġestōdon
hildecystum,   ac hȳ on holt bugon,
ealdre burgan.   Hiora in ānum wēoll
2600 sefa wið sorgum;   sibb' ǣfre ne mæġ
wiht onwendan   þām ðe wēl þenċeð.

Wīġlāf wæs hāten,   Wēoxstānes sunu,

The famous lord's shield gave good protection
to life and body a lesser while
than he had thought, or had intended,
when on this occasion, for the first time,
fate did not allow him victory in battle.
The lord of the Geats lifted his hand,
struck the shining terror with his trusted relic,
but the gleaming edge gave way on the bone,
bit less strongly than its king needed,
hard-pressed with cares as he then was.
The mound-guardian was made furious
by the hostile stroke, it spouted deadly fire,
battle-flames flashed out widely.
The Geats' gold-friend could not claim victory.
His drawn war-sword had proved itself weak
in the conflict, as it should not have done,
the proven blade. That was no easy passing,
when the famous son of Ecgtheow
was to leave this world. Against his will
he had to find another dwelling,
as every man must leave these fleeting days.
    It was no long time until the terrible ones
clashed together again. The hoard-guardian rallied,
breath boiled again within his heart.
He who before had ruled the people
suffered hardship, wrapped in flame.
By no means did his picked companions,
children of nobles, cluster valiantly round,
they fled to the wood to save their lives.
The mind of one seethed with grief.
For any person who thinks properly,
nothing can ever put kinship aside.

    He was called Wiglaf, son of Weohstan,

lēofliċ lindwiga,   lēod Scylfinga,
mǣġ Ælfheres;   ġeseah his mondryhten
2605 under heregrīman   hāt þrōwian.
Ġemunde ðā ðā āre   þe hē him ǣr forġeaf,
wīċstede weliġne   Wǣġmundinga,
folcrihta ġehwylċ,   swā his fæder āhte;
ne mihte ðā forhabban,   hond rond ġefēng,
2610 ġeolwe linde,   gomel swyrd ġetēah;
þæt wæs mid eldum   Ēanmundes lāf,
suna Ōhtere[s];   þām æt sæċċe wearð,
wræċċa(n) winelēasum   Wēohstān bana
mēċes ecgum,   ond his māgum ætbær
2615 brūnfāgne helm,   hringde byrnan,
ealdsweord etonisc;   þæt him Onela forġeaf,
his gædelinges   gūðġewǣdu,
fyrdsearo fūsliċ —   nō ymbe ðā fǣhðe sprǣc,
þēah ðe hē his brōðor bearn   ābredwade.
2620 Hē frætwe ġehēold   fela missera,
bill ond byrnan,   oð ðæt his byre mihte
eorlscipe efnan   swā his ǣrfæder;
ġeaf him ðā mid Ġēatum   gūðġewǣda
ǣghwæs unrīm   þā hē of ealdre ġewāt
2625 frōd on forðweġ.   Þā wæs forma sīð
ġeongan cempan   þæt hē gūðe rǣs
mid his frēodryhtne   fremman sceolde.
Ne ġemealt him se mōdsefa,   nē his mǣġes lāf
ġewāc æt wīġe;   þæt se wyrm onfand,
2630 syððan hīe tōgædre   ġegān hæfdon.
     Wīġlāf maðelode,   wordrihta fela
sæġde ġesīðum —   him wæs sefa ġeōmor:
'Iċ ðæt mǣl ġeman,   þǣr wē medu þēgun,
þonne wē ġehēton   ūssum hlāforde
2635 in bīorsele,   ðē ūs ðās bēagas ġeaf,
þæt wē him ðā gūðġetawa   ġyldan woldon
ġif him þyslicu   þearf ġelumpe,

a fine shield-warrior, a man of the Scylfings.
He saw his lord enduring heat
under his war-mask. Then he was mindful
of the honors he had been given,
the fine estate of the Wægmundings,
with all the folk-rights his father had had.
He could not hold back, his hand seized the shield,
the yellow lindenwood, he drew his ancient sword.
Men remembered this as the relic of Eanmund,
the son of Ohthere. With the sword-edge
Weohstan in battle had been the bane
of the friendless exile, and carried off
the shining helmet, the ringed corslet,
and the old sword made by giants
to Eanmund's kinsman. Onela gave it to him,
his nephew's war-gear, the noble armor,
said nothing of revenge, although Weohstan
had been the death of his brother's son.
He kept the booty for many years,
sword and corslet, until his son was able
to do bold deeds like his father.
Then, among the Geats, he gave him the war-gear,
and many other things, when he left his life,
the old man passed away.

                        Now was the first time
for the young champion, that he should face
the rush of battle with his benefactor.
His mind did not melt, nor his father's legacy
grow weak in war. The worm found that out,
once the two of them had clashed together.

  Sad at heart, Wiglaf said many true words
to his companions: "I call to mind the time,
as we drank mead, when in the beer-hall
we promised our lord, who gave us these rings,
that we would repay him for the war equipment,
helmets and hard swords, if this kind of need

helmas ond heard sweord.   Đē hē ūsiċ on herġe ġeċēas
   tō ðyssum sīðfate   sylfes willum,
2640 onmunde ūsiċ mærða,   ond mē þās māðmas ġeaf,
   þē hē ūsiċ gārwīġend   gōde tealde,
   hwate helmberend —   þēah ðe hlāford ūs
   þis ellenweorc   āna āðōhte
   tō ġefremmanne,   folces hyrde,
2645 forðām hē manna mæst   mærða ġefremede,
   dæda dollicra.   Nū is se dæġ cumen
   þæt ūre mandryhten   mæġenes behōfað
   gōdra gūðrinca;   wutun gongan tō,
   helpan hildfruman   þenden hyt sŷ,
2650 glēdeġęsa grim.   God wāt on meċ
   þæt mē is micle lēofre   þæt mīnne līċhaman
   mid mīnne goldġyfan   glēd fæðmie.
   Ne þynċeð mē ġerysne   þæt wē rondas beren
   eft tō earde,   nemne wē æror mæġen
2655 fāne ġefyllan,   feorh ealgian
   Wedra ðēodnes.   Iċ wāt ġeare,
   þæt næron ealdġewyrht   þæt hē āna scyle
   Ġēata duguðe   gnorn þrōwian,
   ġesīgan æt sæċċe;   ūrum sceal sweord ond helm,
2660 byrne ond beaduscrūd   bām ġemæne.'
   Wōd þā þurh þone wælrēċ,   wīġheafolan bær
   frēan on fultum,   fēa worda cwæð:
   'Lēofa Bīowulf,   læst eall tela,
   swā ðū on ġeoguðfēore   ġeāra ġecwæde
2665 þæt ðū ne ālæte   be ðē lifiġendum
   dōm ġedrēosan;   scealt nū dædum rōf,
   æðeling ānhŷdiġ,   ealle mæġene
   feorh ealgian;   iċ ðē fullæstu.'
      Æfter ðām wordum   wyrm yrre cwōm,
2670 atol inwitgæst   ōðre sīðe
   fŷrwylmum fāh   fīonda nīos(i)an,
   lāðra manna.   Līġ ŷðum fōr;

came upon him. He chose us all
out of the army for this expedition
of his own will, remembered our exploits,
and gave me these treasures, because he thought us
good spear-fighters, bold helmet-wearers –
even though the lord, keeper of the people,
meant to carry out this deed of valor
single-handed, because of all men
he had performed the most famous
and reckless deeds. Now the day has come
that our lord has need of the strength
of good warriors. Let us go forward,
help the battle-leader amidst the heat,
grim and fearful fire. God knows of me
that I would much rather have fire and flame
embrace my body with my gold-giver.
It does not seem right to me that we should
carry shields back home, unless we have
been able first to kill our enemy
and protect the life of the lord of Weders.
I know his former deeds do not deserve
that he alone of the Geat war-band
should endure torment, fall in battle.
Both of us must share sword and helmet,
corslet and battle-shirt." He advanced
through deadly reek, carried his helmet
to help his lord, said few words:
"Dear Beowulf, do all things well,
just as you said when you were young,
so long ago, that while you lived
you would not let your fame grow less.
Now, resolute prince, fierce in action,
you must guard your life with all your strength.
I am with you."
            After those words
the worm came again, in wrath once more,
a terrible foe filled with spite,
blazing in gouts of fire, to fall on its enemies,

born bord wiðֿ rond.   Byrne ne meahte
ġeongum gārwigan   ġēoce ġefremman,
2675 ac se maga ġeonga   under his mǣġes scyld
elne ġeēode,   þā his āgen (wæs)
glēdum forgrunden.   Þā ġēn gūðֿcyning
m(ōd) ġemunde,   mæġenstrenġo slōh
hildebille,   þæt hyt on heafolan stōd
2680 nīþe ġenȳded;   Næġling forbærst,
ġeswāc æt sæċċe   sweord Bīowulfes
gomol ond grǣġmǣl.   Him þæt ġifeðe ne wæs
þæt him īrenna   ecge mihton
helpan æt hilde;   wæs sīo hond tō strong,
2685 sē ðe mēċa ġehwane   mīne ġefrǣġe
swenġe ofersōhte   þonne hē tō sæċċe bær
wǣpen wundum heard;   næs him wihte ðē sēl.
     Þā wæs þēodsceaðֿa   þriddan sīðe,
frēcne fȳrdraca   fǣhðֿa ġemyndiġ,
2690 rǣsde on ðone rōfan,   þā him rūm āġeald,
hāt ond heaðֿogrim,   heals ealne ymbefēng
biteran bānum.   Hē ġeblōdegod wearð
sāwuldrīore;   swāt ȳðֿum wēoll.

     Ðā iċ æt þearfe [ġefræġn]   þēodcyninges
2695 andlongne eorl   ellen cȳðֿan,
cræft ond cēnðֿu,   swā him ġecynde wæs.
Ne hēdde hē þæs heafolan,   ac sīo hand ġebarn
mōdiġes mannes   þǣr hē his mǣ*ges* healp,
þæt hē þone nīðֿgæst   nioðֿor hwēne slōh,
2700 secg on searwum,   þæt ðֿæt sweord ġedēaf
fāh ond fǣted,   þæt ðֿæt fȳr ongon
sweðֿrian syðֿðan.   Þā ġēn sylf cyning
ġewēold his ġewitte,   wællseaxe ġebrǣd
biter ond beaduscearp,   þæt hē on byrnan wæġ;
2705 forwrāt Wedra helm   wyrm on middan.
Fēond ġefyldan   — ferh ellen wræc —

the men it hated. Flame came in waves.
The shield burned to its rim. His armor could give
the young warrior no help, but the youth moved quickly
under his kinsman's shield, his own crumbled into coals.
Once again the war-king took heart, struck out
with his war-sword with all his strength,
so that it hit the head, driven by hate.
Nægling shattered, Beowulf's sword,
old and grey-patterned, failed in the fight.
It was not granted to him that iron blades
could help him in battle. His hand was too strong,
he who as I have heard overtaxed with his stroke
any weapon tempered by wounds
when he carried it into combat.
He was never, for them, one whit the better.
    Then the marauder, for the third time,
bold fire-dragon, was bent on violence.
Once it was given room, it rushed at the brave man,
hot and fierce, gripped him by the neck
with bitter fangs. His life-blood
came pouring out, to cover him in it.

    Then in his need I heard that the noble
standing beside him showed his courage,
his strength and boldness, as his birth dictated.
He paid no heed to the dragon's head,
but the brave man's hand was burned
when he came to his kinsman's help;
in his armor he struck the cruel foe
a little lower down, so that the sword
bit deep, and the fire began to subside.
Again the king himself recovered his senses,
drew the battle-seax, sharp and bitter-edged,
which he carried over his armor.
Protector of the Weders, he cut the worm in two.
They felled their enemy, their courage took its life,

ond hī hyne þā bēġen   ābroten hæfdon,
sibæðelingas;   swylċ sceolde secg wesan,
þeġn æt ðearfe!   Þæt ðām þēodne wæs
2710 sīðas[t] siġehwīl*a*   sylfes dǣdum,
worlde ġeweorces.

               Ðā sīo wund ongon,
þē him se eorðdraca   ǣr ġeworhte,
swelan ond swellan;   hē þæt sōna onfand,
þæt him on brēostum   bealonīð(*e*) wēoll
2715 āttor on innan.   Ðā se æðeling ġīong,
þæt hē bī wealle   wīshycgende
ġesæt on sesse;   seah on enta ġeweorc,
hū ðā stānbogan   stapulum fæste
ēċe eorðreċed   innan healde.
2720 Hyne þā mid handa   heorodrēoriġne,
þēoden mǣrne,   þeġn unġemete till,
winedryhten his   wætere ġelafede
hilde sædne   ond his hel(*m*) onspēon.

        Bīowulf maþelode —   hē ofer benne spræc,
2725 wunde wælblēate;   wisse hē ġearwe
þæt hē dæġhwīla   ġedrogen hæfde,
eorðan wyn(ne);   ðā wæs eall sceacen
dōgorġerīmes,   dēað unġemete nēah:
'Nū iċ suna mīnum   syllan wolde
2730 gūðġewǣdu,   þǣr mē ġifeðe swā
ǣniġ yrfeweard   æfter wurde
līċe ġelenġe.   Iċ ðās lēode hēold
fīftiġ wintra;   næs sē folccyning,
ymbęsittendra   ǣniġ ðāra
2735 þe meċ gūðwinum   grētan dorste,
eġesan ðēon.   Iċ on earde bād
mǣlġesceafta,   hēold mīn tela,
ne sōhte searonīðas,   nē mē swōr fela
āða on unriht.   Iċ ðæs ealles mæġ
2740 feorhbennum sēoc   ġefēan habban;

both noble kinsmen had finished him together.
So must a man be, a thane in dire need.
For his lord, that was the last of his victories,
of all the deeds he did in the world.
   Then the neck-wound which the earth-dragon
had given him before began to burn and swell.
He quickly realized that deadly poison
was spreading out from within his breast.
The prince went over, deep in thought,
sat down on a seat by the stone-wall,
looked at the giants' work, how the stone arches,
firm on pillars, held up from within
the ancient earth-hall. His excellent thane
laved his friend and lord, illustrious prince,
covered in blood and battle-weary,
with water in his hands, undid his helmet.
   Beowulf spoke pale-faced, despite his mortal wound;
he knew clearly that he had come
to the end of his days and delight in this world;
his life-span was done, death very close:
"Now I would wish to give my war-gear to my son,
if I had been granted any heir of my body.
I guarded this people for fifty winters.
Not one of the kings of countries round about
dared to attack me with his companions,
threaten me with fear. On earth I lived
my destined time, kept well what was mine.
I did no treacheries, swore no oaths falsely.
Weak with mortal wounds, I can be glad of that,

forðām mē wītan ne ðearf   waldend fīra
morðorbealo māga,   þonne mīn sceaceð
līf of līċe.   Nū ðū lungre ġeong
hord scēawian   under hārne stān,
2745 Wīġlāf lēofa,   nū se wyrm liġeð,
swefeð sāre wund,   sinċe berēafod.
Bīo nū on ofoste,   þæt iċ ǣrwelan,
goldǣht onġite,   ġearo scēawiġe
sweġle searoġimmas,   þæt iċ ðȳ sēft mæġe
2750 æfter māððumwelan   mīn ālǣtan
līf ond lēodscipe,   þone iċ longe hēold.'

Ðā iċ snūde ġefræġn   sunu Wīhstānes
æfter wordcwydum   wundum dryhtne
hȳran heaðosīocum,   hrinġnet beran,
2755 brogdne beaduserċean   under beorges hrōf.
Ġeseah ðā siġehrēðiġ,   þā hē bī sesse ġēong,
magoþeġn mōdiġ   māððumsiġla fealo,
gold glitinian   grunde ġetenġe,
wundur on wealle,   ond þæs wyrmes denn,
2760 ealdes ūhtflogan,   orcas stondan,
fyrnmanna fatu,   feormendlēase,
hyrstum behrorene;   þǣr wæs helm moniġ
eald ond ōmiġ,   earmbēaga fela
searwum ġesǣled.   Sinċ ēaðe mæġ,
2765 gold on grund(e),   gumcynnes ġehwone
oferhīgian,   hȳde sē ðe wylle.
Swylċe hē siomian ġeseah   seġn eall gylden
hēah ofer horde,   hondwundra mǣst,
ġelocen leoðocræftum;   of ðām lēoma stōd,
2770 þæt hē þone grundwong   onġitan meahte,
wrǣtte ġiondwlītan.   Næs ðæs wyrmes þǣr
onsȳn ǣniġ,   ac hyne ecg fornam.
Ðā iċ on hlǣwe ġefræġn   hord rēafian,
eald enta ġeweorc   ānne mannan,

210

because the Ruler of men need not reproach me
with the killing of kinsmen, when life leaves my body.
Now, dear Wiglaf, now the worm is dead,
sleeps sore-wounded, stripped of his treasure,
do you go quickly beneath the grey stone
to look at the hoard. Make haste now,
so I can see the gold, wealth from long ago,
look well at the bright and precious jewels,
so that, because of the wealth of treasures,
I can more easily let go of my life
and the lordship I held so long."

    After these words I heard the son of Weohstan
quickly obeyed his wounded lord,
battle-weary, and went in his ring-mail,
the linked war-shirt, under the barrow-roof.
As he passed the seat, proud and victorious,
the thane could see countless treasures, jewels,
glittering gold, lying on the ground,
wonderful things heaped by the wall,
in the worm's den, the old dawn-flier,
pitchers standing, with none to polish them,
cups of the men of old, their ornaments crumbling.
There was many a rusty old helmet,
many bracelets with twisted ornaments,
Hide it who will, treasure can easily,
gold in the ground, get the better
of any man. He also saw
gleaming there an all-gold standard
high above the hoard, hand-made wondrously,
skilfully linked. A light shone from it,
so that he could see the floor of the cave,
gaze on its treasures, with no glimpse of the worm:
the edge had taken him.
                    Then I was told
that one man robbed the hoard in the mound,

2775 him on bearm hl*a*don   bunan ond discas
sylfes dōme;   seġn ēac ġenōm,
bēacna beorhtost.   Bill ǣr ġescōd
— ecg wæs īren —   ealdhlāfordes
þām ðāra māðma   mundbora wæs
2780 longe hwīle,   līġeġesan wæġ
hātne for horde,   hioroweallende
middelnihtum,   oð þæt hē morðre swealt.
Ār wæs on ofoste,   eftsīðes ġeorn,
frætwum ġefyrðred;   hyne fyrwet bræc,
2785 hwæðer collenferð   cwicne ġemētte
in ðām wongstede   Wedra þēoden
ellensīocne,   þǣr hē hine ǣr forlēt.
Hē ðā mid þām māðmum   mǣrne þīoden,
dryhten sīnne   drīoriġne fand
2790 ealdres æt ende;   hē hine eft ongon
wæteres weorpan,   oð þæt wordes ord
brēosthord þurhbræc.
                    [Biorncyning spræc]
gomel on gioh*ð*e,   gold scēawode:
'Iċ ðāra frætwa   frēan ealles ðanc,
2795 wuldu̯rcyninge   wordum secge,
ēċum dryhtne,   þē iċ hēr on starie,
þæs ðe iċ mōste   mīnum lēodum
ǣr swyltdæġe   swylċ ġestrȳnan.
Nū iċ on māðma hord   mī*n*e bebohte
2800 frōde feorhleġe,   fremmað ġēna
lēoda þearfe;   ne mæġ iċ hēr leng wesan.
Hātað heaðomǣre   hlǣw ġewyrċean
beorhtne æfter bǣle   æt brimes nōsan;
sē scel tō ġemyndum   mīnum lēodum
2805 hēah hlīfian   on Hrones Næsse,
þæt hit sǣlīðend   syððan hātan
Bīowulfes Biorh,   ðā ðe brentingas
ofer flōda ġenipu   feorran drīfað.'

old works of giants, at his own will,
piling the cups and plates in his grasp,
He took the standard too, brightest of ensigns.
The old lord's sword with iron edge
had earlier finished him who was long
keeper of the treasures, had because of the hoard
brought fear to homes with fierce pulses of flame
in the midnights, until he met violent death.
The messenger hurried, eager to get back,
loaded down with precious things;
he needed to know whether he would find
the Weders' bold lord alive on the plain
where he had left him, drained of strength.
With the treasures, he found the famous prince,
his lord, bleeding and close to death.
He splashed him with water, until words broke out
from his breast-hoard.   The old man spoke,
he spoke with pain, gazing at the gold:
"I give my thanks for these treasures
that I look at here to the Lord of all,
the Ruler of Glory, the eternal Lord,
because it has been given me to gain such things
for my people before my passing-day.
Now that I have bought the hoard of treasures
by laying down my life in my old age,
you must look after the needs of the people.
I can be here no longer. Tell the famous ones
to make a shining mound at the sea-shore;
after the cremation. It shall tower high
on Whale Ness as a memorial
for my people, so that sailors call it
Beowulf's Barrow when the boats come
from far away across the dark seas."

Dyde him of healse   hrinġ gyldenne
2810 þīoden þrīsthȳdiġ,   þeġne ġesealde,
ġeongum gārwigan,   goldfāhne helm,
bēah ond byrnan,   hēt hyne brūcan well:
'Þū eart endelāf   ūsses cynnes,
Wæġmundinga;   ealle wyrd forswēop
2815 mīne māgas   tō metodsceafte,
eorlas on elne;   iċ him æfter sceal.'
Þæt wæs þām gomelan   ġinġæste word
brēostġehyġdum,   ær hē bæl cure,
hāte heaðowylmas;   him of hræðre ġewāt
2820 sāwol sēċean   sōðfæstra dōm.

Ðā wæs ġegongen   guman unfrōdum
earfoðlīċe,   þæt hē on eorðan ġeseah
þone lēofestan   līfes æt ende
blēate ġebæran.   Bona swylċe læġ,
2825 eġesliċ eorðdraca   ealdre berēafod,
bealwe ġebæded.   Bēahhordum lenġ
wyrm wōhbogen   wealdan ne mōste,
ac him īrenna   ecga fornāmon,
hearde heaðoscearpe   homera lāfe,
2830 þæt se wīdfloga   wundum stille
hrēas on hrūsan   hordærne nēah.
Nalles æfter lyfte   lācende hwearf
middelnihtum,   māðmæhta wlonc
ansȳn ȳwde,   ac hē eorðan ġefēoll
2835 for ðæs hildfruman   hondġeweorce.
Hūru þæt on lande   lȳt manna ðāh
mæġenāgendra   mīne ġefræġe,
þēah ðe hē dæda ġehwæs   dyrstiġ wære,
þæt hē wið āttọrsceaðan   oreðe ġeræsde,
2840 oððe hringsele   hondum styrede,
ġif hē wæċċende   weard onfunde
būon on beorge.   Bīowulfe wearð

The bold-hearted king took from his neck,
a golden torque, gave it to his thane,
the young spear-warrior, and the helmet,
gleaming with gold, ring and armor,
told him to make good use of them:
"You are the last one left of all our family,
the Wægmundings. Fate has swept away
all my kinfolk to their destiny,
nobles in their pride. I must follow them."
Those were the last words of his heart
from the old man, before he chose the pyre,
the hot flames. From his breast
his soul departed to seek the judgment
of the righteous.
                    Now it had come about
sadly for the young man that he should see
his dearest one on the ground,
lying pitiably, his life over.
The one who killed him lay dead also,
the terrible dragon drawn from his cave,
robbed of life, cut down in battle.
The coiled worm could no longer
own the ring-hoard, but iron edges
had taken him, hard war-sharpened,
forged by hammers, so that the wide-flyer
fell to the earth, made still by wounds,
near the hoard-cave. By no means now
would he sweep at nights sporting in the sky,
show himself off, proud of his treasures,
but he fell to earth from the handiwork
of the war-leader. As I have heard,
few of the world's strongest, however bold
in deeds of every kind, would have succeeded
in facing the breath of the poison-creature,
or would have laid hands on the ring-hall,
if he found its guardian awake in the mound.

dryhtmāðma dǣl   dēaðe forgolden;
hæfde ǣġhwæðer   ende ġefēred
2845 lǣnan līfes.

         Næs ðā lang tō ðon
þæt ðā hildlatan   holt ofġēfan,
tȳdre trēowlogan   tȳne ætsomne,
ðā ne dorston ǣr   dareðum lācan
on hyra mandryhtnes   miclan þearfe;
2850 ac hȳ scamiende   scyldas bǣran,
gūðgewǣdu   þǣr se gomela lǣġ;
wlitan on Wīlāf.   Hē ġewērġad sæt,
fēðecempa   frēan eaxlum nēah,
wehte hyne wætre;   him wiht ne spēow.
2855 Ne meahte hē on eorðan,   ðēah hē ūðe wēl,
on ðām frumgāre   feorh ġehealdan,
nē ðæs wealdendes   wiht onċirran;
wolde dōm Godes   dǣdum rǣdan
gumena ġehwylcum,   swā hē nū ġēn dêð.
2860 Þā wæs æt ðām ġeongan   grim andswaru
ēðbeġēte   þām ðe ǣr his elne forlēas.
Wīġlāf maðelode,   Wēohstānes sunu;
sec sāriġferð   seah on unlēofe:
'Þæt, lā, mæġ secgan   sē ðe wyle sōð specan
2865 þæt se mondryhten,   sē ēow ðā māðmas ġeaf,
ēoredġeatwe   þe ġē þǣr on standað,
þonne hē on ealubenċe   oft ġesealde
healsittendum   helm ond byrnan,
þēoden his þeġnum,   swylċe hē þrȳdlicost
2870 ōwer feor oððe nēah   findan meahte —
þæt hē ġēnunga   gūðgewǣdu
wrāðe forwurpe   ðā hyne wīġ beġet.
Nealles folccyning   fyrdġesteallum
ġylpan þorfte;   hwæðre him God ūðe,
2875 sigora waldend,   þæt hē hyne sylfne ġewræc
āna mid ecge,   þā him wæs elnes þearf.

The death of Beowulf was paid in full
with noble treasures. Each of the two
had come to an end of fleeting life.
    It was only a short while before the shirkers,
ten of them together, came out of the trees,
forsworn from fear, not daring to fight
with spears when their lord had great need of them,
but shamefaced they carried their shields
and their armor to where the old man lay.
They looked at Wiglaf. He sat weary,
the foot-fighter by his lord's side,
reviving him with water. It did not work.
Hard though he tried, he could not hold
his leader's life any longer in the world,
nor could he avert anything of the Ruler.
God's judgment would decide
the deeds of all men, as it still does now.
Then it was not hard for them to hear
the grim reception the young man gave
to each of those who had lost their nerve.
Wiglaf spoke out, son of Weohstan,
grieving, the warrior looked at the disgraced ones:
"Anyone who wishes to speak the truth
may well say this, that the lord who gave you
precious things, the very war-gear
you stand in now, when he often gave out
helmet and mail-shirt to those sitting in hall,
on the ale-bench, as lord to his thanes,
whatever he could find from far or near,
most precious to him, that he pointlessly
and completely wasted all of it,
all the war-gear when battle came upon him.
The king of the people had no cause to boast
about his companions from this levy.
Yet it was granted by God who rules victory,
that he alone might avenge himself
with his own sword, when he needed strength.

Iċ him līfwraðe   lȳtle meahte
ætġifan æt gūðe,   ond ongan swā þēah
ofer mīn ġemet   mǣġes helpan;
2880 symle wæs þȳ sǣmra   þonne iċ sweorde drep
ferhðġenīðlan,   fȳr unswīðor
wēoll of ġewitte.   Werġendra tō lȳt
þrong ymbe þēoden   þā hyne sīo þrāg becwōm.
Nū sceal sinċþego   ond swyrdġifu,
2885 eall ēðelwyn   ēowrum cynne,
lufen ālicgean;   londrihtes mōt
þǣre mǣġburge   monna ǣġhwylċ
īdel hweorfan,   syððan æðelingas
feorran ġefricgean   flēam ēowerne,
2890 dōmlēasan dǣd.   Dēað bið sēlla
eorla ġehwylcum   þonne edwītlīf!'

Heht ðā þæt heaðoweorc   tō hagan bīodan
up ofer ecgclif,   þǣr þæt eorlweorod
morġenlongne dæġ   mōdġiōmor sæt,
2895 bordhæbbende,   bēġa on wēnum,
endedōġores   ond eftcymes
lēofes monnes.   Lȳt swīgode
nīwra spella   sē ðe næs ġerād,
ac hē sōðlīċe   sæġde ofer ealle:
2900 'Nū is wilġeofa   Wedra lēoda,
dryhten Ġēata   dēaðbedde fæst,
wunað wælreste   wyrmes dǣdum;
him on efn liġeð   ealdorġewinna
sexbennum sēoc;   sweorde ne meahte
2905 on ðām āglǣċean   ǣniġe þinga
wunde ġewyrċean.   Wīġlāf siteð
ofer Bīowulfe,   byre Wīhstānes,
eorl ofer ōðrum   unlifiġendum,
healdeð hiġemǣðum   hēafodwearde
2910 lēofes ond lāðes.

I could give his life little protection
in the fight there, but for all that
I helped my kinsman beyond my own measure.
When with my sword I struck the deadly enemy,
he was always weaker, fire welled less strongly
from his head and jaws. Too few protectors
crowded round the lord when the time came for him.
Now for all your families there shall be no more
giving of swords and receiving of treasure,
fine estates and homesteads. All rights to land
will become void for every man
of all your kin, once the princes
from far and wide hear of your flight,
your disgraceful deed. Death is better
for every nobleman than a life of shame!"

   Then he ordered that news of the fight
should be reported to the stockade
up on the cliff-edge, where the band of nobles,
the shield-bearers, had sat all morning,
sad in their hearts, hoping for two things,
the end of the day, and the dear one's return.
He who rode to the headland did not hold back
the news, but said openly and truly:
"Now the lord of the Geats, is laid on his death-bed,
benefactor of the Weders, he rests in blood
by the deeds of the worm. His deadly enemy
lies beside him, lifeless from seax-cuts:
He was not able to inflict wounds
on the monster by any means,
with his sword. Wiglaf now sits,
the son of Weohstan, next to Beowulf,
one noble by the other, no longer living.
Weary in heart, he keeps the death-watch
over friend and foe.

             Nū ys lēodum wēn
orleġhwīle,   syððan under[ne]
Froncum ond Frȳsum   fyll cyninges
wīde weorðeð.   Wæs sīo wrōht scepen
    heard wið Hūgas,   syððan Hiġelāc cwōm
2915 faran flotherġe   on Frēsna land,
    þǣr hyne Hetware   hilde ġenǣġdon,
    elne ġeēodon   mid ofermæġene,
    þæt se byrnwiga   būgan sceolde,
    fēoll on fēðan;   nalles frætwe ġeaf
2920 ealdor dugoðe.   Ūs wæs ā syððan
    Merewīoinges   milts unġyfeðe.
    Nē iċ te Swēoðēode   sibbe oððe trēowe
wihte ne wēne,   ac wæs wīde cūð
    þætte Ongenðīo   ealdre besnyðede
2925 Hæðcen Hrēþling   wið Hrefna Wudu,
    þā for onmēdlan   ǣrest ġesōhton
    Ġēata lēode   Gūð-Scilfingas.
    Sōna him se frōda   fæder Ōhtheres,
    eald ond eġesfull   ondslyht āġeaf,
2930 ābrēot brimwīsan,   brȳd āhredde,
    gomela[n] iōmeowlan   golde berofene,
    Onelan mōdor   ond Ōhtheres,
    ond ðā folgode   feorhġenīðlan
    oð ðæt hī oðēodon   earfoðlīce
2935 in Hrefnes Holt   hlāfordlēase.
    Besæt ðā sinherġe   sweorda lāfe
    wundum wērġe;   wēan oft ġehēt
    earmre teohhe   ondlonge niht,
    cwæð, hē on merġenne   mēċes ecgum
2940 ġētan wolde,   sum' on galgtrēowu[m]
    [fuglum] tō gamene.   Frōfor eft ġelamp
    sāriġmōdum   somod ǣrdæġe,
    syððan hīe Hyġelāces   horn ond bȳman,
    ġealdor onġēaton,   þā se gōda cōm

Now the people must look for
a time of conflict, once the king's fall
becomes openly known to Franks and Frisians.
Bitter grievance was brought about
against the Hugas, when Hygelac
ventured sailing with sea-borne army
into the Frisian land, where the Hetware
beat him in battle, brought it about
that the mailed fighter must bow in death.
The chieftain fell amidst his force,
could give no treasures to tried warriors.
Ever since, the favor of the Merovingian
has been denied us.
                    Nor do I expect
the least friendship or loyalty
from the Swedish nation; for it is well known
that Ongentheow took away the life
of Hæthcyn Hrethling by Ravenswood
when the Geats in their arrogance
first went looking for the War-Scylfings.
Straight away the wise father of Ohthere,
old and terrible, struck a blow in return,
cut down the sea-king; recaptured the old woman,
his wife of former years, stripped of her gold;
mother of Onela and of Ohthere,
and then he pursued his mortal enemies
until with difficulty they made their escape
into Ravenswood without their lord.
Then with a great army he besieged those
whom swords had left, weary and wounded.
Often through the night he promised miseries
to the wretched band, said that in the morning
he would cut them to bits with the blade's edge,
hang some on gallows-trees as sport for the birds.
Relief came with dawn for the grieving ones
when they heard the sound of Hygelac,
his horns and trumpets, as the hero came

2945 lēoda dugoðe   on lāst faran.

Wæs sīo swātswaðu   Sw[ē]ona ond Ġēata,
wælrǣs weora   wīde ġesȳne,
hū ðā folc mid him   fǣhðe tōwehton.
Ġewāt him ðā se gōda   mid his gædelingum,
2950 frōd felaġeōmor   fæsten sēċean,
eorl Ongenþīo   ufor onċirde;
hæfde Hiġelāces   hilde ġefrūnen,
wlonces wīġcræft;   wiðres ne truwode,
þæt hē sǣmannum   onsacan mihte,
2955 heaðolīðendum   hord forstandan,
bearn ond brȳde;   bēah eft þonan
eald under eorðweall.   Þā wæs ǣht boden
Swēona lēodum,   seġn Hiġelāce[s]
freoðowong þone   forð oferēodon,
2960 syððan Hrēðlingas   tō hagan þrungon.
Þǣr wearð Ongenðīo   ecgum sweorda,
blondenfexa   on bid wrecen,
þæt se þēodcyning   ðafian sceolde
Eafores ānne dōm.   Hyne yrringa
2965 Wulf Wonrēding   wǣpne ġerǣhte,
þæt him for swenġe   swāt ǣdrum sprong
forð under fexe.   Næs hē forht swā ðēh,
gomela Scilfing,   ac forġeald hraðe
wyrsan wrixle   wælhlem þone,
2970 syððan ðeodcyning   þyder onċirde.
Ne meahte se snella   sunu Wonrēdes
ealdum ċeorle   ondslyht ġiofan,
ac hē him on hēafde   helm ǣr ġescer,
þæt hē blōde fāh   būgan sceolde,
2975 fēoll on foldan;   næs hē fǣġe þā ġīt,
ac hē hyne ġewyrpte,   þēah ðe him wund hrine.
Lēt se hearda   Hiġelāces þeġn
brād[n]e mēċe,   þā his brōðor læġ,

following their track with the tried and tested
warriors of the people.
                                    It was widely visible,
the bloody swathe of Swedes and Geats,
the deadly onslaught, how these peoples
had whipped up hate between them.
Then, old and grieving, the good man went
with his companions to seek his stronghold;
Ongentheow turned away to higher ground.
He had heard of Hygelac's warfare,
the proud man's prowess in battle;
he did not trust to make resistance,
repel the seamen, defend the hoard,
women and children from the war-voyagers.
The old man fell back beneath an earth-wall.
Then pursuit was given to the people of the Swedes,
Hygelac's banners over-ran the refuge
once the Hrethlings crowded forward
to the enclosure. There Ongentheow,
with his white hair, was brought to bay
by sword-edges, so that the nation's king
had to deal with Eofor's decree alone.
With his weapon Wulf son of Wonred
had struck the king in his fury,
so that from the blow blood spurted forth
out of the veins beneath his hair.
But the old Scylfing was not afraid.
Once he turned to him, the nation's king
swiftly repaid the deadly blow
with worse exchange. Wonred's brave son
could not strike back, give counterstroke
to the old fellow, for he had first
cut through the helmet and into the head,
so that Wulf sank down, stained with blood,
fell to the ground. He was not yet finished,
for he recovered, though the wound hurt him.
As his brother lay there, Hygelac's stern thane

ealdsweord eotonisc   entiscne helm
2980 brecan ofer bordweal;   ðā ġebēah cyning,
folces hyrde,   wæs in feorh dropen.
Ðā wǣron moniġe   þe his mǣġ wriðon,
ricone ārǣrdon,   ðā him ġerȳmed wearð,
þæt hīe wælstōwe   wealdan mōston.
2985 Þenden rēafode   rinċ ōðerne,
nam on Ongenðīo   īrenbyrnan,
heard swyrd hilted,   ond his helm somod,
hāres hyrste   Hiġelāce bær.
Hē (ðām) frætwum fēng   ond him fæġre ġehēt
2990 lēana (mid) lēodum,   ond ġelǣste swā;
ġeald þone gūðrǣs   Ġēata dryhten,
Hrēðles eafora,   þā hē tō hām becōm,
Iofore ond Wulfe   mid ofermāðmum,
sealde hiora ġehwæðrum   hund þūsenda
landes ond locenra bēaga   — ne ðorfte him ðā lēan oðwītan
mon on middanġearde,   syðða[n] hīe ðā mǣrða ġeslōgon —
ond ðā Iofore forġeaf   āngan dohtor,
hāmweorðunge,   hyldo tō wedde.
Þæt ys sīo fǣhðo   ond se fēondscipe,
3000 wælnīð wera,   ðæs ðe iċ [wēn] hafo,
þē ūs sēċeað tō   Swēona lēoda,
syððan hīe ġefricgeað   frēan ūserne
ealdorlēasne,   þone ðe ǣr ġehēold
wið hettendum   hord ond rīċe
3005 æfter hæleða hryre,   hwate Scilfingas,
folcrēd fremede,   oððe furður ġēn
eorlscipe efnde.   *Nū* is ofọst betost
þæt wē þēodcyning   þǣr scēawian
3010 ond þone ġebringan,   þē ūs bēagas ġeaf,
on ādfære.   Ne scel ānes hwæt
meltan mid þām mōdiġan,   ac þǣr is māðma hord,
gold unrīme   grimme ġeċēa(po)d,
ond nū æt sīðestan   sylfes fēore

let his broad blade, an ancient sword
made by ogres, break the helmet,
the work of giants, behind the shield-wall;
then the king sank down, the people's guardian
was mortally stricken. There were many then –
once they had space, so that they could
control the battlefield – who bandaged his kinsman,
lifted him quickly. Then one looted the other,
took from Ongentheow his iron shirt,
his hard hilted sword, and his helmet too,
carried the old man's armor to Hygelac.
He took the gear, gladly promised him
reward before the men, and kept his word.
Once he returned home the child of Hrethel,
lord of the Geats, paid Wulf and Eofor
over and above for the battle-charge,
gave each the worth of a hundred thousand hides
in land and twisted rings – no-one in middle-earth
had any cause to find fault with the payment,
once they had gained fame in battle –
and he gave to Eofor his only daughter
to honor his home, as pledge of favor.
    That is the enmity and the hostility,
so I expect, the deadly spite,
with which the Swedes will assail us,
once they hear our lord is dead, who for so long
after fall of heroes guarded hoard and kingdom
against our enemies, the eager Scylfings,
cared for the profit of the people,
and in addition, did deeds of valor.
Now it is best for us to make haste,
there to look on the people's king,
and bring the one who gave us rings
to the funeral pyre. Nor shall one piece only
burn with the brave one, but there is a hoard,
gold beyond count, a grim bargain,
rings bought in the end with his own life.

  bēagas (ġeboh)te; þā sceall brond fretan,
3015 ǣled þeċċean — nalles eorl wegan
  māððum tō ġemyndum, nē mæġð scȳne
  habban on healse hrinġweorðunge,
  ac sceal ġeōmormōd, golde berēafod
  oft nalles ǣne elland tredan,
3020 nū se herewīsa hleahtor āleġde,
  gamen ond glēodrēam. Forðon sceall gār wesan
  moniġ morgenċeald mundum bewunden,
  hæfen on handa, nalles hearpan swēġ
  wīġend weċċean, ac se wonna hrefn
3025 fūs ofer fǣġum fela reordian,
  earne secgan hū him æt ǣte spēow,
  þenden hē wið wulf wæl rēafode.'
    Swā se secg hwata secggende wæs,
  lāðra spella; hē ne lēag fela
3030 wyrda nē worda. Weorod eall ārās;
  ēodon unblīðe under Earna Næs,
  wollentēare wundṛ scēawian.
  Fundon ðā on sande sāwullēasne
  hlimbed healdan þone þe him hringas ġeaf
3035 ǣrran mǣlum; þā wæs endedæġ
  gōdum ġegongen, þæt se gūðcyning,
  Wedra þēoden wundordēaðe swealt.
  Ǣr hī þǣr ġesēgan syllicran wiht,
  wyrm on wonge wiðerræhtes þǣr
3040 lāðne licgean; wæs se lēġdraca
  grimliċ gry(refāh) glēdum beswǣled;
  sē wæs fīftiġes fōtġemearces
  lang on leġere; lyftwynne hēold
  nihtes hwīlum, nyðer eft ġewāt
3045 dennes niosịan; wæs ðā dēaðe fæst,
  hæfde eorðscrafa ende ġenyttod.
  Him biġ stōdan bunan ond orcas,
  discas lāgon ond dȳre swyrd,

The flames shall take them, the pyre enfold them.
No noble shall carry a precious thing
as a memorial, nor shall fair maid
carry ring-ornaments round her neck,
but in sadness, stripped of gold,
she shall often, not merely once,
tread the path of exile, now the war-leader
has laid down laughter, joy and merriment.
Because of that, shall many a spear
on cold morning be clutched in fist,
raised in hand, no sound of harp
shall waken the warriors, but the dark raven,
ready above corpses will tell the eagle
how he fared well in his feeding
when with the wolf he stripped the carrion."
  So the bold man spoke, a baleful speech.
He was not far wrong in what he said
or what would happen.
                              The war-band all got up,
went unhappily to the Eagles' Ness,
to look at the wonder, eyes welling with tears.
There they found him who in former times
gave them rings, resting lifeless
on his couch of ease. His last day had come
for the good man, the war-king,
lord of the Weders, had died a wondrous death.
They had already seen the stranger-creature,
the hateful worm lying opposite
there on the ground. Grim and shining,
the fire-dragon was burned by flames,
fifty feet long as it lay there.
In the night-times he sported in the air,
swept down again to seek his den.
Now still in death, he had used his earth-cave
for a final time. By him there stood
cups and pitchers, plates lay there

ōmiġe þurhetone,   swā hīe wið eorðan fæðm
3050 þūsend wintra   þǣr eardodon,
þonne wæs þæt yrfe   ēacencræftiġ,
iūmonna gold   galdre bewunden,
þæt ðām hrinġsele   hrīnan ne mōste
gumena ǣniġ,   nefne God sylfa,
3055 sigora sōðcyning   sealde þām ðe hē wolde
— hē is manna ġehyld —   hord openian,
efne swā hwylcum manna   swā him ġemet ðūhte.

Þā wæs ġesȳne   þæt se sīð ne ðāh
þām ðe unrihte   inne ġehȳdde
3060 wrǣtte under wealle.   Weard ǣr ofslōh
fēara sumne;   þā sīo fǣhð ġewearð
ġewrecen wrāðlīċe.   Wundur hwār þonne
eorl ellenrōf   ende ġefēre
līfġesceafta,   þonne lenġ ne mæġ
3065 mon mid his (mā)gum   meduseld būan.
Swā wæs Bīowulfe,   þā hē biorges weard
sōhte, searonīðas   — seolfa ne cūðe
þurh hwæt his worulde ġedāl   weorðan sceolde —
swā hit oð dōmes dæġ   dīope benemdon
3070 þēodnas mǣre   þā ðæt þǣr dydon,
þæt se secg wǣre   synnum scildiġ,
hergum ġeheaðerod,   hellbendum fæst,
wommum ġewītnad,   sē ðone wong strude.
Næs hē goldhwæte,   ġearwor hæfde
3075 āgendes ēst   ǣr ġescēawod.
Wīġlāf maðelode,   Wīhstānes sunu:
'Oft sceall eorl moniġ   ānes willan
wrǣc ādrēogan,   swā ūs ġeworden is.
Ne meahton wē ġelǣran   lēofne þēoden,
3080 rīċes hyrde   rǣd ǣniġne,
þæt hē ne grētte   goldweard þone,
lēte hyne licgean   þǣr hē longe wæs,

and precious swords, eaten with rust,
as they had lain deep in the earth
a thousand winters. It was an inheritance
of great power, the gold of men
from old times, wound round with spells,
so that no one of the children of men
might be allowed to touch the ring-hall,
unless God Himself – humanity's protector,
True King of Victories – had granted access
to open the hoard to whom he wished,
to whichever man he thought deserving.

   Then it was obvious that his attack
had not prospered the one who improperly
hid the valuables beneath the stone wall.
The guardian had killed one man only
before the feud was avenged cruelly.
It is a mystery where a brave man
shall come to an end of life in this world,
when he can no longer live in the mead-hall
with his kinfolk. So it was with Beowulf,
when he went to meet the crafty enmity
of the mound-guardian. He himself did not know
what should bring about his departure from the world.
The famous princes who had placed it there
had declared it deeply till the Day of Doom,
that whoever should plunder that place would be
condemned for sins, confined among the heathen,
fast in hell-bonds, tormented miserably.
He had not looked for a curse on the gold,
rather expected the owner's favor.
   Wiglaf spoke out, son of Weohstan:
"Often many a man must suffer sorrow
from one man's will, as now with us.
We could not give any advice
to our dear lord, keeper of the kingdom,
not to seek out the guardian of the gold,
but let him lie where he had long been,

wīcum wunian   oð woruldende;
hēold on hēahġesceap.   Hord ys ġescēawod,
3085 grimme ġegongen;   wæs þæt ġifeðe tō swīð
þē ðone [þēodcyning]   þyder ontyhte.
Iċ wæs þǣr inne   ond þæt eall ġeondseh,
reċedes ġeatwa,   þā mē ġerȳmed wæs,
nealles swǣslīċe   sīð ālȳfed
3090 inn under eorðweall.   Iċ on ofoste ġefēng
micle mid mundum   mæġenbyrðenne
hordġestrēona,   hider ūt ætbær
cyninge mīnum.   Cwico wæs þā ġēna,
wīs ond ġewittiġ;   worn eall ġespræc
3095 gomol on ġehðo,   ond ēowiċ ġrētan hēt,
bæd þæt ġē ġeworhton   æfter wines dǣdum
in bǣlstede   beorh þone hêan,
miċelne ond mǣrne,   swā hē manna wæs
wīġend weorðfullost   wīde ġeond eorðan,
2100 þenden hē burhwelan   brūcan mōste.
Uton nū efstan   ōðre [sīðe],
sēon ond sēċean   searo[ġimma] ġeþræc,
wundur under wealle;   iċ ēow wīsiġe,
þæt ġē ġenōge   nēon sċēawiað
3105 bēagas ond brād gold.   Sīe sīo bǣr ġearo,
ǣdre ġeæfned,   þonne wē ūt cymen,
ond þonne ġeferian   frēan ūserne,
lēofne mannan   þǣr hē longe sceal
on ðæs waldendes   wǣre ġeþolian.'
3110   Hēt ðā ġebēodan   byre Wīhstānes,
hæle hildedīor   hæleða monegum,
boldāgendra,   þæt hīe bǣlwudu
feorran feredon,   folcāgende,
gōdum tōġēnes: 'Nū sceal glēd fretan
3115   — weaxan wonna lēġ —   wigena strenġel,
þone ðe oft ġebād   īsernsċūre,
þonne strǣla storm   strenġum ġebǣded

to live in his home till the world's end.
Our lord held instead to his high destiny.
The hoard is laid bare, bought grimly.
Too strong was the fate that enticed there
the people's king. Once the way was cleared
for me – by no means was entry granted
easily down under the earth-wall –
I went inside and saw the hall's treasures.
Quickly I took a great load
of hoarded treasures in my hands,
carried them out from there to my king.
He was still alive, in control of his senses;
the old man in sorrow said a great deal,
told me to give you his last greetings,
ordered that in memory of your friend's deeds
you should build a high barrow
on the place of the pyre, a prominent
and famous one, as he was of all fighters
the most honored in all the world,
while he was allowed to enjoy wealth and home.
Let us hasten now once again
to seek out and see the heaped up jewels,
wonder beneath the wall. I will show the way,
so you can look your fill from close at hand
on rings and broad gold. Let the bier be ready,
and let the pyre be prepared,
for when we come back, and then let us carry
the dear man, our lord, to where he shall
long remain in the Ruler's care."
    The son of Weohstan, the bold hero,
then ordered it to be announced
to many heroes, many homesteaders,
and chieftains too, that for the good man
they were to fetch wood from afar:
"Now flame shall devour, dark fire growing,
the chief of warriors, he who often
endured the shower of iron points
when, strongly shot, a storm of arrows

scōc ofer scildweall,   sceft nytte hēold,
fæðerġearwum fūs   flāne fullēode.'
3120   Hūru se snotra   sunu Wīhstānes
āċīġde of corðre   cyniges þeġnas
syfone (tō)somne,   þā sēlestan,
ēode eahta sum   under inwithrōf
hilderinc[a];   sum on handa bær
3125   æledlēoman,   sē ðe on orde ġēong.
Næs ðā on hlytme   hwā þæt hord strude,
syððan orwearde   æniġne dæl
secgas ġesēgon   on sele wunian,
læne licgan;   lȳt æniġ mearn
3130   þæt hī ofostlīċ(e)   ūt ġeferedon
dȳre māðmas;   dracan ēc scufun,
wyrm ofer weallclif,   lēton wēġ niman,
flōd fæðmian   frætwa hyrde.
Þā wæs wunden gold   on wæn hladen,
3135   æġhwæs unrīm,   æþeling boren,
hār hilde[rinċ]   tō Hrones Næsse.

Him ðā ġeġiredan   Ġēata lēode
ād on eorðan   unwāclicne,
helm[um] behongen,   hildebordum,
3140   beorhtum byrnum,   swā hē bēna wæs;
āleġdon ðā tōmiddes   mærne þēoden
hæleð hīofende,   hlāford lēofne.
Ongunnon þā on beorge   bælfȳra mæst
wīġend weċċan;   wud(u)rēċ āstāh
3145   sweart ofer swioðole,   swōgende lēġ
wōpe bewunden   — windblond ġelæġ —
oð þæt hē ðā bānhūs   ġebrocen hæfd(e)
hāt on hreðre.   Hiġum unrōte
mōdċeare mændon,   mondryhtnes cw(e)alm;
3150   swylċe ġiōmorġyd   (Ġē)at(isc) meowle
(æfter Bīowulfe   b)undenheorde

flashed over shield-wall, shaft did its service,
the hurtling feathers urged on the arrow."
   Indeed the wise son of Weohstan
called from the troop seven of the best
of the king's thanes, went one of eight
beneath the enemy's roof. He who went in front
carried a burning torch. No need to cast lots
to plunder the hoard, once in the hall
the men could see any share of it
lying unguarded. Little did any of them
care about carrying treasures out quickly.
They pushed away the dragon also,
worm over cliff-edge, let the waves take him,
the flood embrace the treasure-guardian.
Then twisted gold was loaded on a wagon,
everything beyond count, and the prince carried,
grey-haired warrior, to Whale's Ness.

   The people of the Geats then made a pyre
for him on the ground, a splendid one
hung round with helmets, as he had asked;
with war-shields, and bright mail-shirts.
The lamenting heroes laid down amidst them
the famous prince, their dear lord.
The warriors then kindled on the headland
the greatest of bale-fires. Black wood-smoke
rose from the flame, a roaring fire
mixed with lament – the winds were still –
until hot at core it consumed the body.
Sad in their hearts, they spoke of their grief,
the death of their lord. Likewise a woman
of the Geats sang a lament
sorrowfully, hair bound up,

(sang) sorgċeariġ,   sæ(*id*)e (ġe)neah(*he*)
þæt hīo hyre (here)ġ(eon)gas   hearde ond(r)ēde,
wælfylla wo(*r*)n,   (w)erudes eġesan,
3155 hȳ[n]ðo ond hæf(t)nȳd.   Heofon rēċe swealg.
    Ġeworhton ðā   Wedra lēode
hlǣ(w) on h(ō)e,   sē wæs hēah ond brād,
(w)ēġlīðendum   wīde ġesȳne,
ond beti(m)bredon   on tȳndagum
3160 beadurōf(*e*)s bēcn,   bronda lāfe
wealle beworhton,   swā hyt weorðlicost
foresnotre men   findan mihton.
Hī on beorg dydon   bēg ond siġlu,
eall swylċe hyrsta   swylċe on horde ǣr
3165 nīðhēdiġe men   ġenumen hæfdon;
forlēton eorla ġestrēon   eorðan healdan,
gold on grēote,   þǣr hit nū ġēn lifað,
eldum swā unnyt   swā hyt (ǣro)r wæs.
    Þā ymbe hlǣw riodan   hildedīore,
3170 æþelinga bearn,   ealra twelf(*e*),
woldon (care) cwīðan   (*ond c*)yning mǣnan,
wordġyd wrecan,   ond ymb w(er) sprecan;
eahtodan eorlscipe   ond his ellenweorc
duguðum dēmdon —   swā hit ġedē(fe) bið
3175 þæt mon his winedryhten   wordum herġe,
ferhðum frēoġe,   þonne hē forð scile
of l(ī)ċhaman   (lǣ)ded weorðan.
    Swā begnornodon   Ġeata lēode
hlāfordes (hry)re,   heorðġenēatas;
3180 cwǣdon þæt hē wǣre   wyruldcyning[a]
manna mildust   ond mon(ðw)ǣrust,
lēodum līðost   ond lofġeornost.

said repeatedly she had great fear
of armed invasions, a multitude
of deadly killings, terror from war-bands,
humiliation and slavery. Sky swallowed the smoke.
   Then on the headland the Weder people
made a mound high and broad,
for seafarers to see from afar,
built in ten days for the battle-fierce one
a monument, and enclosed with a wall
what fire had left, as most honorably
wise men could devise. In the mound they placed
rings and jewels, all kinds of accoutrements
stout-hearted men had taken from the hoard.
They let the earth hold the treasures of nobles,
gold in the ground, where it lies still,
as useless to men as it was before.
Then twelve champions, children of princes,
rode round the mound; they all wanted
to utter their sorrow and celebrate the king,
make a song for him and speak of the man;
they gave esteem to his nobility,
spoke to the veterans of his deeds of valor –
as it is proper to praise with words
a friend and lord, and foster him
in inmost heart, when he must go forth,
part from his body.
                So the Geat people,
his close companions, mourned their lord's fall,
they said that he was of all kings in the world
the gentlest of men and the kindest,
most loving to his people and the most generous.

COMMENTARY

§1. **Lines 1-52**: Scyld Scefing is a peculiar figure. The actions attributed to him are plausibly human and even historical: he subjugated neighboring groups, smashed their mead-benches, forced them to pay tribute to the Danes and recognize Danish authority. Something like this probably did happen in Scandinavia in the centuries before the action of the poem is set. Political subjugation through the destruction of an enemy's hall was a real thing, as the archaeology of the period indicates. Yet Scyld Scefing is plainly not a historical or even legendary figure. The story of his mysterious arrival and departure links him to various fertility deities in Germanic and Indo-European traditions, who were believed to arrive miraculously, bring prosperity to their worshippers, and then depart. The nearest analogues suggest, moreover, that the story of Scyld's mysterious arrival and departure belonged originally to his son, Beow, whose name is homophonous with Old English *bēow* ("barley"). What appears to have happened in the pre-history of the poem, then, is that a figure named Scyld was invented through back-formation from the Scylding dynastic name and made a relative of the fertility deities Beow and Scef, the latter's name being homophonous with Old English *scēf* ("sheave" [of grain]). The invented figure of Scyld ("shield" or "protection") then acquired the conventional myth of arrival and departure from the fertility deities with which he was associated. Finally, the myth was made human (or "euhemerized") when Scyld was imagined not as a deity bringing fertility to the land, but as a king who conquered neighbors and departed from the world not on a humble wagon but on a ship loaded with magnificent treasures. Literary and archaeological analogues to Scyld's funeral suggest that the funerary ship would normally have been burned or buried rather than set adrift. Presumably this deviation from the norm was necessitated by Scyld's status as one of these mythical figures who must possess a mysterious departure as well as a mysterious arrival.

Further Reading: Hilda R. Ellis Davidson, *Gods and Myths of Northern Europe* (Harmondsworth: Penguin, 1964), 92–104; R. D. Fulk, "An Eddic Analogue to the Scyld Scefing Story," *Review of English Studies* 40 (1989): 313–322; Clive Tolley, "*Beowulf*'s Scyld Scefing Episode: Some Norse and Finnish Analogues," *Arv* 52 (1996): 7–48; Mercedes Salvador-Bello, "The Arrival of the Hero in a Ship: A Common Leitmotif in OE Regnal Tables and the Story of Scyld Scefing in Beowulf," *SELIM* 8 (1998): 205–221; Joseph Harris, "The Dossier on Byggvir, God and Hero: *Cur deus homo*," *Arv* 55 (1999): 7–23; Alexander Bruce, *Scyld and Scef: Expanding the Analogues* (New York: Routledge, 2002); Judy King, "Launching the Hero: The Case of Scyld and Beowulf," *Neophilologus* 87 (2003): 453–471; David Clark, "Relaunching the Hero: The Case of Scyld and Beowulf Re-Opened," *Neophilologus* 90 (2006): 621–642; Francis Leneghan, "Reshaping Tradition: The Originality of the Scyld Scefing Episode," in *Transmission and Generation in Medieval and*

Renaissance Literature: Essays in Honour of John Scattergood, ed. Karen Hodder and Brendan O'Connell (Dublin: Four Courts Press, 2012), 21–36; Carl Edlund Anderson, "Scyld Scyldinga: Intercultural Innovation at the Interface of West and North Germanic," *Neophilologus* 100 (2016): 461–476.

§2. Lines 53-85: Scyld's Danish empire is passed on to his son, Beow, who passes it on in turn to his son, Healfdene. With the figure of Healfdene, who either kills or is killed by the Heathobardic king Froda in the poem's analogues, we enter the recognizable world of migration-period legend. Healfdene has four children: Heorogar, father of Heoroweard, who rules first and dies young; Halga, father of Hrothulf, who rules next and also dies young; Hrothgar, father of Hrethric and Hrothmund, who rules when the main action of the poem begins; and a daughter who marries the Swedish prince Onela. Scribal carelessness resulted in the omission of the name of Healfdene's daughter from the text, but analogues suggest that it might have been Yrse. Hrothgar decides to punctuate his rise to power by building Heorot ("hart" or "stag"), the greatest mead-hall known to mankind, and distributing treasure to his retinue there. Archaeological evidence suggests that this was indeed what a sixth-century Scandinavian ruler might do to articulate and consolidate his power. Massive halls unearthed at Gammel Lejre, the location of Danish royal power in other sources that relate legends of the Scylding dynasty, provide a possible historical basis for a hall such as Heorot. The statement in line 73 that Hrothgar refrained from distributing slaves to his followers seems, however, to be decidedly ahistorical, as any king contemporary with Hrothgar would probably have engaged in this practice. Here and elsewhere, the poet appears to omit, deny, or alter aspects of his inherited material that he considered distasteful. The passage ends with an allusion to the day when Heorot will burn on account of enmity between father-in-law and son-in-law: the Heathobard prince Ingeld, married to Hrothgar's daughter, will eventually attack Heorot (and kill Hrothgar?) to avenge the killing of Froda (who was killed either by Healfdene or by the tandem of Hrothgar and Halga). A passage in the Old English poem *Widsith* (ll. 45-49) indicates that although Ingeld will burn Heorot, he will lose his life in the attempt and his army will be destroyed.

Further Reading: Kemp Malone, "The Daughter of Healfdene," in *Studies in English Philology: A Miscellany in Honor of Frederick Klaeber*, ed. Kemp Malone and Martin B. Ruud (Minneapolis: University of Minnesota Press, 1929), 135–158; Kemp Malone, "The Tale of Ingeld," in *Studies in Heroic Legend and Current Speech*, ed. Stefán Einarsson and Norman E. Eliason (Copenhagen: Rosenkilde & Bagger, 1959), 1–62; G. N. Garmonsway and Jacqueline Simpson, eds. and trans., *Beowulf and Its Analogues* (New York: Dutton, 1971); Kathryn Hume, "The Concept of the Hall in Old English Poetry," *Anglo-Saxon England* 3 (1974): 63–74; Raymond P. Tripp, Jr., "The Exemplary Role of Hrothgar and Heorot," *Philological Quarterly* 56 (1977): 123–129; Rosemary J. Cramp, "The Hall in *Beowulf* and in Archaeology," in *Heroic Poetry in the Anglo-Saxon Period*, ed. Helen Damico and John Leyerle (Kalamazoo, MI: Medieval Institute Publications, 1993), 331–346; Stefan Jurasinski, *Ancient Privileges: Beowulf, Law and the Making of Germanic Antiquity* (Morgantown: West Virginia University Press, 2006), 49–75; Karl P. Wentersdorf, "The *Beowulf*-Poet's Vision of Heorot," *Studies in Philology* 104 (2007): 409–426; Tom Shippey, "*Hrólfs saga kraka* and the

Legend of Lejre," in *Making History: Essays on the For-naldarsögur*, ed. Martin Arnold and Alison Finlay (London: Viking Society for Northern Research, 2010), 17–32; Stephen Pollington, "The Mead-Hall Community," *Journal of Medieval History* 37 (2011): 19–33; Alfred Bammesberger, "The Meaning of Old English *Folcscaru* and the Compound's Function in *Beowulf*," NOWELE 72 (2019): 1–10; Leonard Neidorf, "The *Beowulf* Poet's Sense of Decorum," *Traditio* 76 (2021): 1–28.

§3. **Lines 86-114**: Grendel, dwelling in darkness on the outskirts of Heorot, is irritated by the sounds of joy that emanate from the hall. The sound of the harp can be heard there, and a poet sings of how the almighty created the earth, the sun, the moon, and every form of plant and animal life. The singer of the song is evidently conceptualized by the poet as an intuitive monotheist, who has inferred from creation the existence of its creator. The creator in question and the story of creation are decidedly Judeo-Christian in orientation, as the native mythology of the pagan Scandinavian peoples appears to have told a very different creation story, according to the accounts preserved in Snorri Sturluson's *Prose Edda* and the Eddic poems (particularly *Vǫluspá* and *Vafþrúðnismál*) on which Snorri's account is based. In this creation myth, the world is created not by a single omnipotent deity but is rather constructed from the corpse of the giant Ymir by the three deities (Óðinn, Vili, and Vé) who killed him. The nature of Grendel is elusive. At his core, he is apparently a giant (Old English *eoten*) derived from the same native mythological tradition that yielded the giants of Norse mythology (Old Norse *jǫtunn*), who are there the adversaries of the gods. Yet Grendel is more than a giant: an aspect of spiritual evil is grafted onto this corporeal monster, who is somehow simultaneously a fiend in hell (*fēond on helle*) and an inhabitant of the land of the giant race (*fīfelcynnes eard*). Grendel is both the ogre of folklore and the demon of hagiography. Furthermore, we are told that Grendel is one of the monstrous progeny that Cain engendered after God sent him into exile for killing Abel. This genealogy connects Grendel to miscellaneous supernatural beings—giants (*eotenas*), zombies (*orcnēas*), and even elves (*ylve*), who are not considered malevolent in Scandinavian tradition—as well as to the biblical giants (identified with the Latin loanword *gīgantas*), who contended with God and were wiped out in the flood. The genealogy thus lends an element of cosmic significance to the poem's narrative, as it makes the hero's combat against Grendel part of a "great feud" between God and his adversaries.

Further Reading: Oliver F. Emerson, "Legends of Cain, Especially in Old and Middle English," *PMLA* 21 (1906): 831–929; Paul Beekman Taylor, "Heorot, Earth, and Asgard: Christian Poetry and Pagan Myth," *Tennessee Studies in Literature* 11 (1966): 119–130; Robert E. Kaske, "*Beowulf* and the Book of Enoch," *Speculum* 46 (1971): 421–431; Stephen C. Bandy, "Cain, Grendel, and the Giants of *Beowulf*," *Papers on Language and Literature* 9 (1973): 235–249; Marijane Osborn, "The Great Feud: Scriptural History and Strife in *Beowulf*," *PMLA* 93 (1978): 973–981; Ruth Mellinkoff, "Cain's Monstrous Progeny in *Beowulf*: Part I, Noachic Tradition," *Anglo-Saxon England* 8 (1979): 143–162; Ruth Mellinkoff, "Cain's Monstrous Progeny in *Beowulf*: Part II, Post-Diluvian Survival," *Anglo-Saxon England* 9 (1980): 183–197; Thalia Phillies Feldman, "Grendel and Cain's Descendants," *Literary Onomastics Studies* 8 (1981): 71–87; Malcolm Andrew, "Grendel in Hell," *English Studies* 62 (1981): 401–410; William Helder, "The Song of Creation in *Beowulf* and the Interpretation of Heorot," *English Studies in Canada* 13 (1987): 243–255; Leonard Neidorf, "Cain, Cam, Jutes, Giants, and the Textual Criticism of *Beowulf*," *Studies in Philology* 112 (2015): 599–632; Margaret Clunies Ross, "Giants," in *The Pre-Christian Religions of the North: History and Structures,* ed. Jens Peter Schjødt, John Lindow, and Anders Andrén, 4 vols (Turnhout: Brepols, 2020), III: 1527–1558.

§4. Lines 115-163: One night, Grendel attacks Heorot and kills thirty men who fell asleep after feasting. Grendel, like many a monster of folklore, can apparently threaten mankind only at night. His nocturnal raids on Heorot prompt the Danes to evacuate the hall every night and find lodging elsewhere. For twelve years, the Danes inhabit Heorot during the day and Grendel takes control of their empty hall every night, killing anyone he should happen to find there. A grim sort of humor is perhaps intended in the ironic description of Grendel as a "hall-thane" (*healðeġn*), as if he were servicing the hall during his visits, and in the observation that the monster both refuses to pay wergild and receive tribute, as if diplomacy could prevail with a demon. The word *helrūnan* is interesting: it literally means "those who know the secrets of hell," and it appears in Old English glossaries as the equivalent of *wicca* ("witch"). The Gothic cognate of this word, *haljarunnae*, is attested in Jordanes's *Getica*, where it is applied to exiled witches, who mate with unclean spirits and thereby engender the Huns, whom Jordanes considers the deformed and ferocious adversaries of the Goths. Grendel is not himself said to be a *helrūne*, but his nocturnal raids prompt the narrator to reflect that mortals cannot know the whereabouts of *helrūnan*. The word and its Gothic cognate suggest something of the native tradition from which Grendel emerges, in which the real or imagined threats on a group's periphery, who do not speak the group's language and do not recognize its norms for conflict resolution, were conceptualized as inscrutable, subhuman, and implacably hostile.

Further Reading: Otto Maenchen-Helfen, "The Legend of the Origin of the Huns," *Byzantion* 17 (1944–1945): 244–251; Nora K. Chadwick, "The Monsters and Beowulf," in *The Anglo-Saxons: Studies in Some Aspects of Their History and Culture Presented to Bruce Dickins*, ed. Peter Clemoes (London: Bowes & Bowes, 1959), 171–203; Stanley M. Wiersma, *A Linguistic Analysis of Words Referring to Monsters in Beowulf* (University of Wisconsin: Unpublished Doctoral Dissertation, 1961), 77–83; Thomas D. Hill, "*Hwyrftum Scriþað: Beowulf*, Line 163," *Mediaeval Studies* 33 (1971): 379–381; Stanley B. Greenfield, "Old English Words and Patristic Exegesis – *hwyrftum scriþað*: A Caveat," *Modern Philology* 75 (1977): 44–48; Jane Roberts, "Understanding Hrothgar's Humiliation: Beowulf Lines 144-74 in Context," in *Text, Image, Interpretation: Studies in Anglo-Saxon Literature and its Insular Context in Honour of Éamonn Ó Carragáin*, ed. Alastair Minnis and Jane Roberts (Turnhout: Brepols, 2007), 355–367; Stephen Pollington, *The Elder Gods: Religion and the Supernatural in Early England* (Ely: Anglo-Saxon Books, 2011), 260–265.

§5. Lines 164-193: Two notable cruces appear within this stretch of text. The first concerns Grendel's inability to approach Hrothgar's *gifstōl* ("gift-stool" or "throne"). The precise meaning of the passage is indeed rather difficult to pin down. Perhaps the simplest conclusion to reach is that the throne is here imagined to possess a certain numinous quality that protects it from desecration or unlawful occupation. The other major crux here concerns the idol worship of the Danes. Made desperate by Grendel's depredations, the Danes engage in idol worship and the poet laments their ignorance of God. Many critics perceive an inconsistency between lines 175-188 and the rest of the poem. Some argue that the passage is a scribal interpolation, while others regard it as an artistic lapse, and others have devised various sophisticated explanations for the temporary inconsistency. There is, however, at least one straightforward way to construe this passage as being consistent with the rest of the poem. The foregrounded characters are represented, it must be stressed, as *intuitive* monotheists, not as Christians. They have intuitions about God, but they do not know God, nor do they know how to praise him; they have not received the Christian revelation and the education in prayer (and explicit prohibition of idol worship) that would come with it. These characters generally follow their better, monotheistic intuitions, but in this instance the depredations of Grendel have driven them to abandon faith in a single deity and resort instead to the temporal expedient of idol worship. The homiletic excursus (ll. 183b-188) acknowledges that this practice imperils the salvation of these otherwise virtuous characters. This excursus does not state that all of the historically pagan characters in the poem are invariably damned. It suggests, rather, that salvation is possible for those who follow their monotheistic intuitions, whereas damnation awaits those who veer toward polytheism. The same logic is evident in Hrothgar's sermon (ll. 1700-1784), where Hrothgar exhorts Beowulf to choose eternal counsels (*ēce rǣdas*) over temporal aggrandizement.

Further Reading: Charles Donahue, "*Beowulf*, Ireland and the Natural Good," *Traditio* 7 (1951): 263–277; Charles Donahue, "*Beowulf* and Christian Tradition: A Reconsideration from a Celtic Stance," *Traditio* 21 (1965): 55–116; Margaret E. Goldsmith, *The Mode and Meaning of Beowulf* (London: Athlone Press, 1970), 183–209; A. D. Horgan, "Religious Attitudes in *Beowulf*," in *Essays and Poems Presented to Lord David Cecil*, ed. W. W. Robson (London: Constable, 1970), 9–17; Betty S. Cox, *Cruces of Beowulf* (The Hague: Mouton, 1971), 56–79 and 102–130; Stanley B. Greenfield, "'Gifstol' and Goldhoard in *Beowulf*," in *Old English Studies in Honour of John C. Pope*, ed. Robert B. Burlin and Edward B. Irving Jr. (Toronto: University of Toronto Press, 1974), 107–117; Karl P. Wentersdorf, "*Beowulf*: The Paganism of Hrothgar's Danes," *Studies in Philology* 78 (1981): 91–119; Robert E. Kaske, "The Gifstol Crux in *Beowulf*," *Leeds Studies in English* 17 (1985): 142–151; Thomas D. Hill, "The Christian Language and Theme of *Beowulf*," in *Companion to Old English Poetry*, ed. Henk Aertsen and Rolf H. Bremmer Jr. (Amsterdam: VU University Press, 1994), 63–77; Dennis Cronan, "*Beowulf*, the Gaels, and the Recovery of the Pre-Conversion Past," *Anglo-Saxon* 1 (2007): 137–180; and Geoffrey Russom, "Historicity and Anachronism in *Beowulf*," in *Epic and History*, ed. David Konstan and Kurt A. Raaflaub (Malden: Wiley-Blackwell, 2010), 243–261; Leonard Neidorf, "*Beowulf* Lines 175-88 and the Transmission of Old English Poetry," *Studies in Philology* 119 (2022): 1–24.

§6. Lines 194-228: Word of Hrothgar's troubles reaches the ears of Beowulf in Geatland. Intent on aiding the distressed king, Beowulf orders a ship to be constructed and assembles a crew of the fourteen bravest men he could find. The wise men of the realm encourage young Beowulf to undertake the dangerous expedition. In our first encounter with Beowulf, we find a hero who, in certain respects, sounds like a conventional hero of folklore. Notably, he is said to be the strongest man alive, and indeed supernatural strength is a standard attribute of the hero of the "bear's son" folktale (among many other folktales). Yet it is made clear from the outset that Beowulf is not a generic hero from the temporally and geographically amorphous world of fairy tales. He is not a bear's son, nor is he a peasant. He is a thegn of the historical king Hygelac, a man of high rank in Geatish society (*gōd mid Ġēatum*). His nobility is no less important to the poet than his prodigious strength; the two qualities are placed on equal footing in the significant pair of adjectives *æþele ond ēacen* ("noble and huge"). After Beowulf and his men sail successfully to Denmark, attention is briefly paid to their martial accoutrements as they exit the ship, and the Geats thank God for their safe passage. We see here two aspects of Beowulf's character that the poet will repeatedly emphasize, namely, his aristocratic status and his monotheistic piety.

Further Reading: Tom Shippey, "The Fairy-Tale Structure of *Beowulf*," *Notes and Queries* 16 (1969): 2–11; Daniel R. Barnes, "Folktale Morphology and the Structure of *Beowulf*," *Speculum* 45 (1970): 416–434; Kemp Malone, "Beowulf the Headstrong," *Anglo-Saxon England* 1 (1972): 139–145; Bruce A. Rosenberg, "Folktale Morphology and the Structure of *Beowulf*: A Counter-proposal," *Journal of the Folklore Institute* 11 (1975): 199–209; J. Michael Stitt, *Beowulf and the Bear's Son: Epic, Saga, and Fairytale in Northern Germanic Tradition* (New York: Garland, 1992); Alfred Bammesberger, "Who Advised Beowulf to Challenge Grendel?" *ANQ* 24 (2011): 244–248.

§7. Lines 229-300: A coastguard confronts the Geats to inquire about their background and purpose. When putting forward his inquiry, he notes the impressive quality of their ship, their armor, and their leader, who is the most formidable man he's ever seen. The coastguard declares that Beowulf has the appearance of a worthy man of a high rank but acknowledges that his peerless appearance alone cannot confirm this to be the case. The coastguard will need to hear Beowulf's words before making up his mind. Beowulf responds by confirming that he is indeed a nobleman: he is one of Hygelac's *heorðgenēatas* ("hearth-retainers"), a significant word in that it indicates regular access to the royal person. Beowulf confirms that he is certainly not a *seldguma* ("hall-man"?), which is evidently a low-status warrior forced to sit in the back of the hall; he is, rather, one of the privileged few with access to the king's hearth. He is, moreover, the son of Ecgtheow, a noble and famous warrior. Beowulf explains that he has heard of the Scyldings' plight and wishes to help. Notably, he does not boast here that he will kill the monster or even fight it. Such assertiveness comes later. In this first speech, Beowulf rather humbly states that he has come merely to offer *rǣd* ("counsel") to Hrothgar. His words impress the coastguard, who replies by stating sententiously that one must know how to judge words and deeds, or rather, that one must know how to properly assess the evidence with which one is presented. He states this apparently to announce that he knows how to weigh evidence, and that he has therefore decided to welcome the Geats into the Danish kingdom. He will guide them to Heorot and his subordinates will guard the Geats' ship.

Further Reading: Margaret W. Pepperdene, "Beowulf and the Coast-Guard," *English Studies* 47 (1966): 409–419;

Stanley B. Greenfield, "Of Words and Deeds: The Coastguard's Maxim Once More," in *The Wisdom of Poetry: Essays in Early English Literature in Honor of Morton W. Bloomfield*, ed. Larry D. Benson and Siegfried Wenzel (Kalamazoo, MI: Medieval Institute Publications, 1982), 45–51; Thomas D. Hill, "Beowulf as Seldguma: *Beowulf*, Lines 247-51," *Neophilologus* 74 (1990): 637–639; Tom Shippey, "Principles of Conversation in Beowulfian Speech," in *Techniques of Description: Spoken and Written Discourse: A Festschrift for Malcolm Coulthard*, ed. John M. Sinclair, Michael Hoey, and Gwyneth Fox (London: Routledge, 1993), 109–126; Jane Roberts, "The Old English Vocabulary of Nobility," in *Nobles and Nobility in Medieval Europe: Concepts, Origins, Transformations*, ed. Anne J. Duggan (Woodbridge, UK: Boydell, 2000), 69–84; Stephen Pollington, *The Mead Hall: The Feasting Tradition in Anglo-Saxon England* (Norfolk: Anglo-Saxon Books, 2003), 79.

§8. Lines 301-331: The poet calls attention to several revealing details in rapid succession. We are told that above the faceguard on Beowulf's helmet there are golden images of boars, which were perhaps believed to possess a totemic ability to protect the helmet's wearer. Boar images are widespread in early Germanic iconography and are even found on several helmets from the early Anglo-Saxon period. We then see, through the eyes of the Geats, the first glimpse of Heorot, which is adorned with gold, and from which emanates a light shining over many lands. The coastguard shows the Geats a road leading to Heorot before announcing that he must leave and expressing his wish that the "all-powerful father" (*fæder alwalda*) should mercifully protect them. Minor though the coastguard is, he too is made out to be an intuitive monotheist.

After his brief departing speech, we are told that a stone-paved street (perhaps a Roman road?) leads to Heorot; the mail-shirts worn by the Geatish men shine and resound as they progress. Upon arrival at Heorot, they set down their war-gear and then sit down on a bench outside of the hall. Having called attention to their spears, shields, and mail-shirts, the poet pronounces the Geatish troop as one that is "made worthy by its weapons" (*wǣpnum ġewurþad*). In other words, their martial gear conveys their high status to observers.

Further Reading: Dorothy Whitelock, *The Audience of Beowulf* (Oxford: Clarendon Press, 1951), 94; A. T. Hatto, "Snake-Swords and Boar-Helms in *Beowulf*," *English Studies* 38 (1957): 145–160; Heinrich Beck, *Das Ebersignum im Germanischen* (Berlin: De Gruyter, 1965); Marijane Osborn, "Laying the Roman Ghost of *Beowulf* 320 and 725," *Neuphilologische Mitteilungen* 70 (1969): 246–255; Maximino Gutiérrez Barco, "The Boar in *Beowulf* and *Elene*: A Germanic Symbol of Protection," *SELIM* 9 (1999): 163–171; Jos Bazelmans, *By Weapons Made Worthy: Lords, Retainers, and their Relationship in Beowulf* (Amsterdam: Amsterdam University Press, 1999); Lindy Brady, "Boars and the Geats in *Beowulf*," in *Early English Poetic Culture and Meter: The Influence of G. R. Russom*, ed. M. J. Toswell and Lindy Brady (Kalamazoo: Medieval Institute Publications, 2016), 61–72.

§9. Lines 331-370: Beowulf is greeted by Wulfgar, the court official, whose first speech would not be out of place in a later medieval Arthurian romance. He is deeply impressed by the knights in shining armor who have arrived at Heorot, proclaiming them to be the most splendidly attired foreigners he has ever seen. He infers from their appearance that the pursuit of glory (*for wlenċo*) motivates their journey abroad rather than desperation (*for wræcsīðum*). Wulfgar states, essentially, that these men are not beggars looking for charity. If they were, they would presumably be turned away. No, these are noble knights in pursuit of adventure. Beowulf's speech confirms Wulfgar's assumption: he announces himself now as one of Hygelac's *bēodġenēatas* ("table-companions"), a word that again stresses his routine proximity to the royal person. Beowulf, asking now for an audience with the Danish king, makes it known that he already enjoys this privilege in his own country; it would therefore not be inappropriate for him to have the same privilege here. Beowulf also reveals his name for the first time in this speech. Perhaps he withheld it earlier because the coastguard is his social inferior, whereas Wulfgar is a nobleman, a Vendel prince (*Wendla lēod*), whom Beowulf regards as a fellow aristocrat. In the same manner, the poet includes Wulfgar's name in the poem, while considering the name of the coastguard too insignificant to mention. The poet's fundamentally aristocratic worldview becomes rather pronounced in this section of the poem. When Wulfgar enters the hall to report Beowulf's arrival to Hrothgar, the poet describes Wulfgar's bodily comportment, as he stands directly before the king. Wulfgar does not shout from the doorway; he "knows the custom of the court" (*cūþe hē duguðe þēaw*). Such details endow *Beowulf* with a quality of courtly realism absent from its folkloric analogues and reveal how important it was to the poet to make *Beowulf* an aristocratic epic, suitable for his presumably courtly audience, rather than a common folktale. Another detail to this effect appears at the end of Wulfgar's speech: he recommends that Hrothgar welcome the new arrivals because *Hȳ on wīġġetawum wyrðe þinċeað / eorla ġeæhtlan.* What these words essentially mean is that the clothing of the Geatish men indicates their aristocratic status and entitles them to an audience with fellow aristocrats.

Further Reading: E. G. Stanley, "Courtliness and Courtesy in *Beowulf* and Elsewhere in English Medieval Literature," in *Words and Works: Studies in Medieval English Language and Literature in Honour of Fred C. Robinson*, ed. Peter S. Baker and Nicholas Howe (Toronto: University of Toronto Press, 1998), 67–104; Michael R. Kightley, "Repetition, Class, and the Nameless Speakers of *Beowulf*," in *Literary Speech Acts of the Medieval North: Essays Inspired by the Works of Thomas A. Shippey*, ed. Eric Shane Bryan and Alexander Vaughan Ames (Tempe, AZ: ACMRS, 2020), 141–156; William Sayers, "Rhetorical Coercion and Heroic Commitment: Beowulf's Reception at Heorot," *English Studies* 101 (2020): 651–664; Leonard Neidorf, *The Art and Thought of the Beowulf Poet* (Ithaca: Cornell University Press, 2022), 66–67 and 75–77.

§10. Lines 371-398: Hrothgar reveals that he is already familiar with Beowulf, having met the young man when he was a boy. He informs us, for the first time, that Beowulf's father, Ecgtheow, was married to Hrethel's only daughter. This detail establishes Beowulf as a true *æþeling*, a man of noble birth, grandson of the dynastic founder and nephew to the current king of Geatland. Hrothgar also reports that he has heard of Beowulf's prodigious strength, seafarers having told him that Beowulf has the strength of thirty men. This pair of details recalls the pair of adjectives that were used when Beowulf was first introduced: *æþele ond ēacen*, noble and preternaturally strong. Hrothgar then attributes Beowulf's arrival to divine intervention, inferring that God sent Beowulf here to kill Grendel (a task that Beowulf has not yet announced his intention to undertake). Following this monotheistic intuition, Hrothgar expresses his readiness to reward the young man with treasures for his undertaking. Two of Hrothgar's most salient qualities are thus revealed: piety and generosity. Wulfgar informs the Geats that Hrothgar knows their lineage, and then welcomes them to enter in their helmets and mail-shirts, insisting however that shields and spears remain outside the hall. The attention paid to court procedure is striking.

Further Reading: Nancy Rose, "Hrothgar, Nestor, and Religiosity as a Mode of Characterization in Heroic Poetry," *Journal of Popular Culture* 1 (1967): 158–165; Hiroto Ushigaki, "The Image of 'God Cyning' in *Beowulf*: A Philological Study," *Studies in English Literature* (Tokyo) 58 (1982): 63–78; Malcolm M. Brennan, "Hrothgar's Government," *Journal of English and Germanic Philology* 84 (1985): 3–15; René Derolez, "Hrothgar, King of Denmark," in *Multiple Worlds, Multiple Words: Essays in Honour of Irène Simon*, ed. Hena Maes-Jelinek, Pierre Michel, and Paulette Michel-Michot (Liège: University of Liège, 1988), 51–58; Edward B. Irving, Jr., *Rereading Beowulf* (Philadelphia: University of Pennsylvania Press, 1989), 49–64; John M. Hill, "Hrothgar's Noble Rule: Love and the Great Legislator," in *Social Approaches to Viking Studies,* ed. Ross Samson (Glasgow: Cruithne, 1991), 169–178; Scott DeGregorio, "Theorizing Irony in Beowulf: The Case of Hrothgar," *Exemplaria* 11 (1999): 309–343.

§11. **Lines 399-455**: Beowulf, standing now in the hearth (*on heorðe*), addresses Hrothgar as his armor shines. The hearth-retainer (*heorðgenēat*) of Hygelac has rightly been granted access to the Danish king. Beowulf explains that the great men of the Geatish realm encouraged him to come to Hrothgar's

aid because they knew of his prowess in the domain of mon-
ster-killing, having witnessed Beowulf kill a family of giants
(*eotenas*) as well as sea-monsters (*niceras*) on the waves. Beo-
wulf thus has experience killing monsters on land and in wa-
ter, yet he addresses Hrothgar very deferentially, speaking to
Hrothgar not as a warrior confident of his future success but
as a humble petitioner asking for a single favor (*ānre bēne*),
that is, the opportunity to occupy Heorot at night and prose-
cute the matter with the monster (*ðing wið þyrse*) on his own.
Ideals of courtesy and courtliness, normally associated with
later medieval literature, are already evident in *Beowulf*, and
especially so in this speech. Following his courteous petition,
Beowulf announces that, in order to make his lord Hygelac
proud of him, he will not use weapons against Grendel, since
that would give him an unfair advantage against a monster
who is reputed to fight without weapons. Perhaps the *Beowulf*
poet invented this detail to rationalize the fact that in his in-
herited folkloric material, Beowulf and other heroes like him
tend to fight without weapons (which are unnecessary when
one possesses supernatural or ursine strength), and this man-
ner of fighting seemed odd for an aristocratic warrior in a cul-
ture where great value is attached to weapons. Here is one of
several explanations the poet will offer for the hero's tendency
not to use weapons in antecedent tradition: he is simply too
chivalrous, too concerned with an ideal of fair-play, to use
them against monsters unfamiliar with such technology. Beo-
wulf concludes his petition by assuring Hrothgar that no fu-
nerary expenses will be incurred in the event of failure, since
Grendel will consume the corpse. Yet Beowulf, still mindful
of his property, does make one request to Hrothgar, namely,
to give his mail-coat to Hygelac. This mail-coat is both a fam-
ily heirloom (the former property of Hrethel) and a product of

supernatural artistry (made by the magical smith Weland). Even this request contributes to the characterization of Beowulf in this speech as a pious, selfless, and dutiful petitioner.

Further Reading: Hilda R. Ellis Davidson, "Weland the Smith," *Folklore* 69 (1958): 145–159; Thomas J. Jambeck, "The Syntax of Petition in *Beowulf* and *Sir Gawain and the Green Knight*," *Style* 7 (1973): 21–29; Michael R. Kightley, "Reinterpreting Threats to Face: The Use of Politeness in *Beowulf*, ll. 407–472," *Neophilologus* 93 (2009): 511–520; Thomas Kohnen, "Understanding Anglo-Saxon 'Politeness': Directive Constructions with *Ic Wille / Ic Wolde*," *Journal of Historical Pragmatics* 12 (2011): 230–254; A. Keith Kelly, "Teaching Good Manners: Civil Discourse Patterns in *Beowulf* and *Sir Gawain and the Green Knight*," in *Literary Speech Acts of the Medieval North: Essays Inspired by the Works of Thomas A. Shippey*, ed. Eric Shane Bryan and Alexander Vaughan Ames (Tempe, AZ: ACMRS, 2020), 223–242.

§12. Lines 456-498: Hrothgar responds by relating a story about Ecgtheow, Beowulf's father, who came to Hrothgar when his own people turned him away due to fear of reprisal from the Wulfings. Ecgtheow had slain the Wulfing prince Heatholaf and the Geats evidently could not afford to pay the massive wergild required to pacify a feud after the fall of a prince. Hrothgar, however, was rich enough to harbor the fugitive Ecgtheow and settle his feud with wealth (*fēo þingode*) in the form of ancient treasures (*ealde mādmas*). Ecgtheow then swore oaths of allegiance to Hrothgar. The episode suggests that the Danes are significantly wealthier and perhaps more powerful than the other migration-period peoples in the poem. Hrothgar appears here to be a sort of overlord. This makes sense, since Hrothgar inherited and aggrandized the empire built by Scyld Scefing, who subjugated neighboring peoples. Hrothgar notes in passing that his business with Ecgtheow occurred when he was a young king, who had just inherited the throne from Heorogar. He states that his older brother was his "better" (*sē wæs betera ðonne ić*), and this is often construed as an elegiac aside, but it might simply be a matter-of-fact acknowledgement of rank: Heorogar ruled before Hrothgar because he had the superior claim to the throne after Healfdene died. Ultimately, the Ecgtheow episode also allows Hrothgar to take pride in his former glory before acknowledging the humiliation (*hȳnðo*) he is currently forced to feel due to Grendel's depredations. He describes a scene of Heorot stained with the blood of those who had previously vowed to fight Grendel, in order to warn Beowulf that success is doubtful, but nevertheless invites the Geats to take a seat and enjoy themselves. An attendant serves them drink while a poet entertains them. The Danes and Geats together experience joy (*drēam*), the same emotion experienced by the Danes (l. 99) prior to Grendel's arrival.

Further Reading: Kemp Malone, "Ecgtheow," *Modern Language Quarterly* 1 (1940): 37–44; R. T. Farrell, *Beowulf, Swedes, and Geats* (London: Viking Society for Northern Research, 1972), 245–250; Sam Newton, *The Origins of Beowulf and the Pre-Viking Kingdom of East Anglia* (Cambridge: D. S. Brewer, 1993), 115–120; Ruth P. M. Lehmann, "Ecgþeow the Wægmunding: Geat or Swede?" *English Language Notes* 31 (1994): 1–5; Erin M. Shaull, "Ecgþeow, Brother of Ongenþeow, and the Problem of Beowulf's Swedishness," *Neophilologus* 101 (2016): 263–275.

§13. Lines 499-528: Unferth, later identified as Hrothgar's *þyle* (orator? counselor?), interrupts the hall-joys to interrogate the newcomer. Sitting at the feet of Hrothgar, who is presumably seated on an elevated throne, Unferth appears to be a prominent and respected figure at the Danish court. He has the same proximity to the royal person denoted in terms such as "hearth-retainer," but his seating suggests a special degree of importance and probably the official role indicated by the term *þyle*. Perhaps it was the job of the *þyle* to question newcomers, gauge their merits, and goad them into stating their intentions more clearly. The poet, however, makes it clear that Unferth is not just a dutiful official perfunctorily questioning Beowulf. He is motivated by genuine jealousy and hostility, we are told, because he cannot tolerate the possibility that another man is more mindful of glory than himself. Unferth's knowledge of Beowulf's swimming contest with Breca suggests, moreover, that his role required him to be informed of noteworthy events abroad. In the *Nibelungenlied*, Hagen has similarly heard of some of Siegfried's exploits before the hero arrived at the Burgundian court; Hagen and Unferth have much in common and perhaps hold essentially the same position at their respective courts. Given the rarity of Beowulf's name in records outside of the poem (it is recorded elsewhere only once, in the *Durham Liber Vitae*, as the name of a seventh-century [?] monk), Unferth's question "Are you the Beowulf...?" seems rather insulting and even slightly humorous. Of course this Beowulf is the same Beowulf.

Further Reading: D. E. Martin Clarke, "The Office of *Thyle* in *Beowulf*," *Review of English Studies* 12 (1936): 61–66; James L. Rosier, "Design for Treachery: The Unferth Intrigue," *PMLA* 77 (1962): 1–7; Norman E. Eliason, "The Þyle and

Scop in *Beowulf*," *Speculum* 38 (1963): 267–284; J. D. A. Ogilvy, "Unferth: Foil to Beowulf?," *PMLA* 79 (1964): 370–375; Joseph L. Baird, "Unferth the *Þyle*," *Medium Ævum* 39 (1970): 1–12; Carroll Y. Rich, "Unferth and Cain's Envy," *South Central Bulletin* 33 (1973): 211–213; Livia Polanyi, "Lexical Coherence Phenomena in Beowulf's Debate with Unferth," *Rackham Literary Studies* 8 (1977): 25–37; John C. Pope, "*Beowulf* 505, 'Gehedde,' and the Pretensions of Unferth," in *Modes of Interpretation in Old English Literature: Essays in Honour of Stanley B. Greenfield*, ed. Phyllis Rugg Brown, Georgia Ronan Crampton, and Fred C. Robinson (Toronto: University of Toronto Press, 1986), 173–187; R. D. Fulk, "Unferth and his Name," *Modern Philology* 85 (1987): 113–127; Leslie A. Donovan, "Þyle as Fool: Revisiting *Beowulf*'s Hunferth," in *Poetry, Place, and Gender: Studies in Medieval Culture in Honor of Helen Damico*, ed. Catherine E. Karkov (Kalamazoo: Medieval Institute Publications, 2009), 75–97; William Sayers, "Cei, Unferth, and Access to the Throne," *English Studies* 90 (2009): 127–141; Leonard Neidorf, "On *Beowulf* and the *Nibelungenlied*: Counselors, Queens, and Characterization," *Neohelicon* 47 (2020): 655–672.

§14. **Lines 529-610**: Beowulf's reply to Unferth does not contradict the basic facts of the swimming contest, as Unferth described it, but offers a very different interpretation of the significance of those facts. Yes, Beowulf admits, he swam with Breca when they were boys, but he did not lose the contest or behave ignominiously; inclement weather separated the boys, and Beowulf went on to gloriously slay the many sea-monsters that harassed him, which was only the proper thing to do (*swā hit ġedēfe wæs*). The competing interpretations of the swimming contest offered by Unferth and Beowulf suggest that we are dealing here with a tale that existed prior to the composition of *Beowulf*. That the tale derives from tradition rather than the poet's invention is likewise suggested by the presence in *Widsith* of Breca, who is said there to rule the Brondings, and who in *Beowulf* hails from the "land of the Brondings" (*lond Brondinga*). The traditionality of their swimming contest is further suggested by the fact the other formalized insult contests (the *flyting* or the *senna*) attested in early Germanic literature tend to feature uncharitable interpretations of past deeds rather than false accusations. In this genre, one does not fabricate allegations, but one tries to interpret the opponent's deeds in the worst possible light. Beowulf seems to follow the rules of this game when he ends his speech by denouncing Unferth for killing his own brothers and condemning him to torment in hellfire for this. Kin-slaying is a widespread phenomenon in early Germanic literature, but it usually occurs under duress: the protagonist, torn between conflicting ethical imperatives (e.g., loyalty to one's lord versus loyalty to one's kindred), is to be pitied and admired for killing a kinsman (and thereby demonstrating unwavering commitment to a heroic ideal) rather than reviled for it. By omitting the circumstances under which Unferth killed his brothers, Beowulf makes it appear that what might have been Unferth's greatest deed is, in fact, a shameful and dishonorable one. In reality, Unferth's deed could not have been so terrible; if it were, he would not be able to hold a respected position at the Danish court. Most likely, Unferth chose loyalty to his lord, Hrothgar, over loyalty to his kindred, and this made him all the more respected as a trustworthy and zealous retainer. Beowulf's tone in this speech, it should be noted, is significantly different from his previous speeches. The flyting genre licenses him to tone down his courtesy and humility and turn up his assertiveness

259

and aggressiveness. He boasts at the outset of his speech that he has more "sea-strength" (*merestrenġo*) than any man alive. He grins, perhaps, as he describes how he "served" (*þēnode*) the sea-monsters, who were intent on feasting on Beowulf's corpse, a rather different meal than the one they expected. He concludes by attributing to Unferth's cowardice Grendel's ability to attack the Danes with impunity, and he boasts, finally, that he will fight and kill the monster. If Unferth were merely playing a game with Beowulf to induce the newcomer to drop the courteous facade and display his heroic resolve, the game has clearly worked. Rejoicing follows the speech, and Hrothgar is pleased by Beowulf's resolute words.

Further Reading: Larry D. Benson, "The Originality of *Beowulf*," in *The Interpretation of Narrative: Theory and Practice*, ed. Morton W. Bloomfield (Cambridge, MA: Harvard University Press, 1970), 1–43; Karl P. Wentersdorf, "Beowulf's Adventure with Breca," *Studies in Philology* 72 (1975): 140–166; Joseph Harris, "The *Senna*: From Description to Literary Theory," *Michigan Germanic Studies* 5 (1979): 65–74; Carol J. Clover, "The Germanic Context of the Unferþ Episode," *Speculum* 55 (1980): 444–468; Peter S. Baker, "Beowulf the Orator," *Journal of English Linguistics* 21 (1988): 3–23; Michael J. Enright, "The Warband Context of the Unferth Episode," *Speculum* 73 (1998): 297–337; Frederick M. Biggs, "Beowulf's Fight with the Nine Nicors," *Review of English Studies* 53 (2002): 311–328; R. D. Fulk, "Afloat in Semantic Space: Old English *sund* and the Nature of Beowulf's Exploit with Breca," *Journal of English and Germanic Philology* 104 (2005): 456–472; Gernot R. Wieland, "The Unferth Enigma: The Þyle between the Hero and the Poet," in *Fact and Fiction from the Middle Ages to Modern Times: Essays Presented to*

Hans Sauer on the Occasion of His 65th Birthday—Part II, ed. Renate Bauer and Ulrike Krischke (Frankfurt am Main: Peter Lang, 2011), 35–46; Leonard Neidorf, "Unferth's Ambiguity and the Trivialization of Germanic Legend," *Neophilologus* 101 (2017): 439–454; Graham Williams, "*Wine Min Unferð*: Courtly Speech and a Reconsideration of (Supposed) Sarcasm in *Beowulf*," *Journal of Historical Pragmatics* 18 (2017): 175–194.

§15. Lines 611-641: Queen Wealhtheow, mindful of courtly etiquette, progresses around the hall with a ceremonial cup, serving alcohol first to her king before giving it to others. Wealhtheow's name, in the form in which it was transmitted, appears to consist of *wealh* ("foreign") and *þēow* ("servant"), which has given rise to the notion that her name means "foreign servant" and designates her as such. An immediate problem with such interpretations is that Wealhtheow appears neither foreign nor servile. She is described as *ides Helminga* ("lady of the Helmings"), and *Widsith* informs us that Helm ruled the Wulfings, an apparently Scandinavian ethnic group. The term *wealh*, however, is normally used in reference to foreigners who do not speak a Germanic language (hence it is used by the English in reference to the Britons or the Romans, but never the Vikings). So Wealhtheow is no *wealh*, and she is certainly not a *þēow*, as she will go on to deliver bold speeches full of imperatives directed at Hrothgar and Beowulf. It is possible that her name was originally *Wælþēow* ("chosen servant" [of a god]) before scribes altered the first element to *wealh* due to this word's association with *þēow* (in England, the enslavement of Britons caused *wealh* to mean both "foreigner" and "slave"). In any event, the etymology of Wealhtheow's name seems to have no meaningful bearing on her

261

characterization. Though many scholars assume that names in Beowulf must reflect meaningfully on their bearers, there are strong linguistic and cultural reasons to doubt the reality of such a relationship. When Wealhtheow brings the mead-cup to Beowulf, she thanks God for bringing her a hero she can believe in. Beowulf responds with a brief speech, reaffirming his commitment to the Danes and stating twice that he will either kill Grendel or die trying. Wealhtheow's words were evidently intended to instigate Beowulf to make a bold and binding vow over the mead-cup. She is pleased with the hero's words and returns to her seat next to Hrothgar.

Further Reading: E. V. Gordon, "Wealhþeow and Related Names," *Medium Ævum* 4 (1935): 169–175; André Crépin, "Wealhtheow's Offering of the Cup to Beowulf: A Study in Literary Structure," in *Saints, Scholars and Heroes: Studies in Medieval Culture in Honour of Charles W. Jones*, ed. Margot H. King and Wesley M. Stevens, 2 vols (Collegeville: Hill Monastic Manuscript Library, Saint John's Abbey and University, 1979), I: 45–58; Helen Damico, *Beowulf's Wealhtheow and the Valkyrie Tradition* (Madison: University of Wisconsin Press, 1984); Thomas D. Hill, "'Wealhtheow' as a Foreign Slave: Some Continental Analogues," *Philological Quarterly* 69 (1990): 106–112; Gabriele Müller-Oberhäuser, "*Cynna Gemyndig*: Sitte und Etikette in der altenglischen Literatur," *Frühmittelalterliche Studien* 30 (1996): 19–59; Michael J. Enright, *Lady with a Mead Cup: Ritual, Prophecy, and Lordship in the European Warband from La Tène to the Viking Age* (Dublin: Four Courts Press, 1996); Stefan Jurasinski, "The Feminine Name *Wealhtheow* and the Problem of Beowulfian Anthroponymy," *Neophilologus* 91 (2007): 701–705; Michael D. C. Drout and Leah Smith, "A Pebble Smoothed by Tradition:

Lines 607-661 of *Beowulf* as a Formulaic Set-piece," *Oral Tradition* 32 (2018): 191–228; Leonard Neidorf, "Wealhtheow and Her Name: Etymology, Characterization, and Textual Criticism," *Neophilologus* 102 (2018): 75–89.

§16. **Lines 642-702a**: Festivities continue until Hrothgar decides that it is time for him to go to bed. Before departing, he briefly addresses Beowulf, explaining that he has never previously entrusted Heorot to any other man and promising abundant reward if he should succeed. Beowulf is now stationed on "giant-watch" (*eotonweard*). The narrator states that Beowulf trusts in both his own strength and in God's protection. As he prepares for bed, Beowulf makes good on his promise not to use technology unavailable to Grendel; he removes his mailcoat, his helmet, and his sword, giving these to an attendant entrusted with the task of holding his war-gear. Before he lays wakefully in bed, Beowulf delivers a final speech, in which he reaffirms his commitment not to use any weapons or war-gear in his fight against Grendel, a monster incapable of wielding such goods. The speech ends with an assertion that God will decide the outcome. The picture of Beowulf as a pious and chivalrous hero is thus strongly reinforced. Additionally, the probable presence in antecedent tradition of a hero fighting a monster without any weapons or armor—an image that must have struck the poet and his aristocratic contemporaries as rather strange—is explained yet again as a consequence of the hero's extraordinary concern for fair-play, which extends even to malevolent and inscrutable monsters. As they lay down to sleep, none of the Geatish men expect to survive and see their homeland again. The narrator notes, however, that their worries were mistaken, since mighty God, who ruled mankind then as now, granted them victory through Beowulf.

263

Further Reading: George Clark, "Beowulf's Armor," *ELH* 32 (1965): 409–441; Brian McFadden, "Sleeping After the Feast: Deathbeds, Marriage Beds, and the Power Structure of Heorot," *Neophilologus* 84 (2000): 629–646; Jane Roberts, "Hrothgar's 'Admirable Courage,'" in *Unlocking the Wordhord: Anglo-Saxon Studies in Memory of Edward B. Irving, Jr.*, ed. Mark C. Amodio and Katherine O'Brien O'Keeffe (Toronto: University of Toronto Press, 2003), 240–251.

§17. **Lines 702b-790**: Grendel approaches Heorot hoping to kill and eat another human victim; little does he know that the strongest man in the world is waiting for him and intending to give him something he does not expect. The poet places great emphasis on the ironic mismatch between Grendel's expectation of easy prey and the outcome that awaits him, apparently finding some humor in it. Grendel is described here as a spectral creature, a "shadow-walker" (*sceadugenga*), and also a diabolical fiend, "God's adversary" (*Godes andsaca*), who wishes to "seek out the company of devils" (*sēċan dēofla ġedræġ*) when he realizes that he cannot break free from Beowulf's grip. At the same time, Grendel is corporeal enough for Beowulf to grapple with him, and he seems to possess the consciousness of a human tyrant who prematurely takes delight in a plan that is about to be foiled (comparable, for instance, to the figure of Holofernes in the Old English *Judith*). Grendel eats the anonymous Geatish warrior who is later identified as Hondscioh. Beowulf watches the monster's movement, evidently determining how best to subdue it. He seizes onto Grendel's arm and refuses to release it. The struggle between the monster and the hero shakes the hall, scattering mead-benches and making frighteningly loud noises. The struggle provides the poet with an occasion to comment on the fine construction of Heorot, which manages to withstand the tumult and will fall only to flames (another allusion to Ingeld's eventual attack on the hall). An interesting detail mentioned in passing is that Beowulf, when grappling with Grendel, is mindful of his "evening-speech" (*æfenspræće*). Beowulf must kill or be killed; should he fail to bring about one of those outcomes, the shame that awaits him would be unbearable.

Further Reading: Alain Renoir, "Point of View and Design for Terror in *Beowulf*," *Neuphilologische Mitteilungen* 63 (1962): 154–167; Richard N. Ringler, "*Him sēo wēn gelēah*: The Design for Irony in Grendel's Last Visit to Heorot," *Speculum* 41 (1966): 49–67; Robert W. Hanning, "Sharing, Dividing, Depriving – The Verbal Ironies of Grendel's Last Visit to Heorot," *Texas Studies in Literature and Language* 15 (1973): 203–213; Katherine O'Brien O'Keeffe, "*Beowulf*, Lines 702b–836: Transformations and the Limits of the Human," *Texas Studies in Literature and Language* 23 (1981): 484–494; Kenneth Florey, "Grendel, Evil, 'Allegory,' and Dramatic Development in *Beowulf*," *Essays in Arts and Sciences* 17 (1988): 83–95; Michael Lapidge, "*Beowulf* and the Psychology of Terror," in *Heroic Poetry in the Anglo-Saxon Period: Studies in Honor of Jess B. Bessinger, Jr.*, ed. Helen Damico and John Leyerle (Kalamazoo: Western Michigan University Press, 1993), 373–402; Andy Orchard, *Pride and Prodigies: Studies in the Monsters of the Beowulf-Manuscript* (Cambridge: D. S. Brewer, 1995); David F. Johnson, "The Gregorian Grendel: *Beowulf* 705b–09 and the Limits of the Demonic," in *Rome and the North: The Early Reception of Gregory the Great in Germanic Europe*, ed. Rolf H. Bremmer Jr., Kees Dekker, and David F. Johnson (Paris: Peeters, 2001), 51–65.

§18. Lines 791-852: While Beowulf continues to apply pressure to Grendel's supernaturally large arm and is apparently perched on it, his Geatish retainers stab at the monster with swords. Their efforts to harm the monster prove futile, however, since Grendel is, in fact, impervious to weapons, having performed a magical spell of invulnerability against them. It would seem that we have here yet another rationalizing explanation, devised by the *Beowulf* poet or one of his predecessors, for an inherited story wherein the hero defeated the monster without using weapons. One explanation for this odd detail is that the hero is too chivalrous to use weapons; another explanation is that the monster is impervious to weapons, so they cannot be used. A third explanation will be mentioned later on in the poem, when we are told that Beowulf is actually too strong to wield weapons, which will only break under the force of his strength. In any event, Grendel's charm against weapons turns out badly for him, as it ends up guaranteeing him a slow and miserable death rather than the quick death that he could have enjoyed from a sword. Grendel departs from Heorot mortally wounded, now anticipating a wretched end in his joyless abode. He hoped to carry back with him the carcass of a slain retainer. Instead, he leaves his own hand, arm, and shoulder in Heorot as a visible sign of Beowulf's victory. In the morning, warriors come from afar to marvel at the remains of Grendel and rejoice at the sight. Hell receives Grendel's "heathen soul" (*hæþene sāwle*). The phrase implies that the poet does not consider Beowulf and the other intuitive monotheists in the poem's foreground to be heathens. Perhaps "heathen" denotes here not someone who is not a Christian, but someone who is actively hostile to God and does not recognize God's authority.

Further Reading: E. D. Laborde, "Grendel's Glove and his Immunity to Weapons," *Modern Language Review* 18 (1923): 202–204; H. L. Rogers, "Beowulf's Three Great Fights," *Review of English Studies* 6 (1955): 339–355; Donald K. Fry, "'Wið Earm Gesæt' And Beowulf's Hammerlock," *Modern Philology* 67 (1970): 364–366; Judson Boyce Allen, "God's Society and Grendel's Shoulder Joint: Gregory and the Poet of the *Beowulf*," *Neuphilologische Mitteilungen* 78 (1977): 239–240; Lana Stone Dietrich, "Syntactic Analysis of Beowulf's Fight with Grendel," *Comitatus* 14 (1983): 5–17; David D. Day, "Hands across the Hall: The Legalities of Beowulf's Fight with Grendel," *Journal of English and Germanic philology* 98 (1999): 313–324; Megan Cavell, "Constructing the Monstrous Body in *Beowulf*," *Anglo-Saxon England* 43 (2014): 151–181; Leonard Neidorf, "Grendel's Blood: On the Translation of *Beowulf* Line 849," *Medium Ævum* 90 (2021): 133–142.

§19. **Lines 853-897**: Beowulf's victory is celebrated by old and young in poetry and games on horseback. High praise is lavished on Beowulf, with many stating that no man could possibly be "worthier of a kingdom" (*rīces wyrðra*) than he. The narrator immediately notes, however, that such praise should not be construed as blame toward Hrothgar, who was nevertheless considered a good king (*ac þæt wæs gōd cyning*). This passage constitutes the first hint of the idea that Beowulf's status as the savior of the Danes might make him a worthy successor to Hrothgar. Perhaps this idea is on the mind of Hrothgar's court poet, who praises Beowulf through implicit comparison with Sigemund of the Volsungs, here said to have slain a dragon, plundered its hoard, and earned lasting glory as a result. Though the *Beowulf* poet omits the details,

Hrothgar's court poet also apparently told the entire story of Sigemund, including the "feuds and crimes" (*fæhðe ond fyrena*) undertaken in connection with Fitela, the son that Sigemund unwittingly conceived with his sister Signý. She slept with her brother in disguise so that their offspring would be able to carry out her plan to kill her husband Siggeir, who had previously killed her father and brothers (excluding Sigemund). Sigemund and Fitela are here referred to as uncle and nephew, which is what Sigemund thinks they are until the vengeance is complete and Signý reveals the truth before committing suicide. It seems that the *Beowulf* poet knows the whole elaborate narrative of Sigemund (Sigmundr), Fitela (Sinfjǫtli), and Signý preserved in *Vǫlsunga saga*, though his sense of decorum allows only for allusions to this story of incest, suicide, and kin-slaying. *Vǫlsunga saga* differs from *Beowulf*, however, in attributing the slaying of a dragon not to Sigemund, but to his son Sigurðr. Given the priority of *Beowulf*, it is likely that the deed was transferred from the father to the son.

Further Reading: Gustav Neckel, "Sigmunds Drachenkampf," *Edda* 13 (1920): 122–140 and 204–229; Adrien Bonjour, *The Digressions in Beowulf* (Oxford: Blackwell, 1950), 46–52; Annelise Talbot, "Sigemund the Dragon-Slayer," *Folklore* 94 (1983): 153–162; M. S. Griffith, "Some Difficulties in *Beowulf*, Lines 874-902: Sigemund Reconsidered," *Anglo-Saxon England* 24 (1995): 11–41; Fred C. Robinson, "Sigemund's *fæhðe ond fyrena*: *Beowulf* 879a," in *To Explain the Present: Studies in the Changing English Language in Honour of Matti Rissanen*, ed. Terttu Nevalainen and Leena Kahlas-Tarkka (Helsinki: Société Néophilologique, 1997), 200–208; James W. Earl, "The Forbidden *Beowulf*: Haunted by Incest,"

PMLA 125 (2010): 289–305; Stephen Harris, "*Beowulf* 881a: *Eam His Nefan*," *ANQ* 26 (2013): 217–218; Catalin Taranu, "Who was the Original Dragon-Slayer of the Nibelung Cycle?" *Viator* 46 (2015): 23–40; Christopher Abram, "Bee-Wolf and the Hand of Victory: Identifying the Heroes of *Beowulf* and *Vǫlsunga saga*," *Journal of English and Germanic Philology* 116 (2017): 387–414; Erin Sebo, "Foreshadowing the End in *Beowulf*," *English Studies* 99 (2018): 836–847.

§20. **Lines 898-915**: The story of Sigemund prompts the court poet (or the narrator?) to reflect that Sigemund was the most glorious hero to emerge after Heremod's glory faded. The story of Heremod's glorious rise and ignominious fall is not preserved outside of *Beowulf*, but a similar story is attributed to a figure named Lotherus in later Danish legendary tradition. In the time immediately prior to the rule of Scyld (Skjøldus), Lotherus seized the throne and ruled tyrannically: he despoiled the people and killed anyone he considered a potential claimant to the throne. Lotherus's abuses prompted an uprising, and according to one very late account, he fled to Jutland in exile before he was finally killed. The story fits well with the story about Heremod that can be inferred from *Beowulf*: ruling before Scyld, Heremod hoards wealth and kills the great men of the realm instead of rewarding them; he is driven into exile among the Jutes and dies a shameful death after tormenting his people. The contrast of Sigemund and Heremod, undertaken by a poet seeking to celebrate Beowulf's victory, is obviously pregnant with meaning, but the precise meaning is difficult to ascertain. Critics inclined to read *Beowulf* as a morality tale have naturally drawn various stern morals from the passage. Perhaps the most straightforward way to read the passage, however, is as a meditation on heroic potential prompted by the extraordinary potential that Beowulf has shown by killing Grendel. In the case of Sigemund, his potential manifested itself in brave deeds that led to lasting fame; in the case of Heremod, the mismanagement of his great potential led only to misery and a shameful demise. The story of Heremod might also offer indirect advice to Hrothgar: whereas Heremod cut down any illustrious man who could be considered a contender for the throne, Hrothgar should freely acknowledge the greatness of such a man and reward him commensurately.

Further Reading: R. W. Chambers, *Beowulf: An Introduction to the Study of the Poem with a Discussion of the Stories of Finn and Offa. With a Supplement by C. L. Wrenn*, 3rd ed. (Cambridge: Cambridge University Press, 1959), 89–97; N. F. Blake, "The Heremod Digressions in *Beowulf*," *JEGP* 61 (1962): 278–287; C. B. Hieatt, "Modþryðo and Heremod: Intertwined Threads in the *Beowulf*-Poet's Web of Words," *Journal of English and Germanic Philology* 83 (1984): 173–182; Scott Gwara, *Heroic Identity in the World of Beowulf* (Leiden: Brill, 2008), 59–134; Leonard Neidorf, "Cain, Cam, Jutes, Giants, and the Textual Criticism of *Beowulf*," *Studies in Philology* 112 (2015): 599–632; Michael Fox, *Following the Formula in Beowulf, Örvar-Odds saga, and Tolkien* (Cham: Palgrave Macmillan, 2020), 101–156; for additional literature on Heremod, see the references in §34.

§21. **Lines 916-956**: Hrothgar, standing on an elevated platform (*on stapole*) presumably reserved for making official announcements, stares at Grendel's hand and delivers one of the poem's pivotal speeches. He gives thanks to God, proclaiming that God can always work wonders and that God must have blessed Beowulf's nameless mother when she conceived him. The crucial moment in the speech comes when Hrothgar declares that he plans to love Beowulf "as a son" (*for sunu*). The statement is followed by an exhortation to Beowulf to maintain their "new kinship" (*nīwe sibbe*), which is in turn followed by a promise of bountiful reward. None of this amounts to an unambiguous statement that Hrothgar has adopted Beowulf and named him as his preferred successor to the Danish throne, but all of it can certainly be interpreted that way. Indeed, Wealhtheow seems to interpret Hrothgar's speech in this manner, as it prompts her to encourage Hrothgar to leave the kingdom to his kinsmen, exclude Beowulf from the succession, and instead reward the foreign hero with portable wealth. Perhaps Hrothgar, in this speech, is merely floating the idea of naming Beowulf as a successor in order to see the reaction it gets. Whereas Heremod kills his most impressive retainers, Hrothgar wishes to reward his greatest champion as generously as possible.

Further Reading: John M. Hill, "Beowulf and the Danish Succession: Gift Giving as an Occasion for Complex Gesture," *Medievalia et Humanistica* 11 (1982): 177–197; Stephanie Hollis, "Beowulf and the Succession," *Parergon* 1 (1983): 39–54; Giovanna Princi Braccini, "Perché Hroðgar *Stod on Stapole* (*Beowulf* 926a)," in *Echi di Memoria: Scritti di varia filologia, critica e linguistica in recordo di Giorgio Chiarini*, ed. Gaetano Chiappini (Florence: Alinea, 1998), 139–157; Haruko Momma, "The Education of Beowulf and the Affair of the Leisure Class," in *Verbal Encounters: Anglo-Saxon and Old Norse Studies for Roberta Frank*, ed. Antonina Harbus and Russell Poole (Toronto: University of Toronto Press, 2005), 163–182; Larry J. Swain, "Of Hands, Halls, and Heroes:

Grendel's Hand, Hroþgar's Power, and the Problem of *stapol* in *Beowulf*," *Anglia* 134 (2016): 260–284; Thomas D. Hill, "Hrothgar's Speech of Adoption: A Danish-Latin Analog," *Notes and Queries* 66 (2019): 163–166; Francis Leneghan, *The Dynastic Drama of Beowulf* (Cambridge: D. S. Brewer, 2020), 63–64.

§22. Lines 957-1008a: Beowulf responds by stating that he wished he could have constrained Grendel so that Hrothgar could marvel at his corpse. Nevertheless, the severed arm of the monster indicates that he is mortally wounded and merely enduring a miserable death elsewhere, after which he will await God's great judgment (*miclan dōmes*). Beowulf's evident awareness of the last judgment is striking, but it must be considered a consistent aspect of the intuitive monotheism attributed to the protagonist. After all, he earlier condemned Unferth to hell for killing his own brothers, and he will later refer to God's posthumous judgment in his final speech. Following Beowulf's speech, we are told that Unferth was then a more silent man (*swīġra secg*). His silence bespeaks embarrassment at his earlier hostility to Beowulf, and there might also be some ironic humor here, since Unferth, as the court orator (*þyle*), might have been expected to give a formal speech on this grand occasion, yet doing so would only augment his embarrassment. While Unferth and others stare at Grendel's hand, servants repair Heorot and restore everything to order. We learn that gold-adorned tapestries hang on the walls. Grendel's death prompts a gnomic reflection on the unavoidability of death, the long sleep after the feast of life.

Further Reading: Adelaide Hardy, "The Christian Hero Beowulf and Unferð Þyle," *Neophilologus* 53 (1969): 55–69; Ida

Masters Hollowell, "Unferð the *Þyle* in *Beowulf*," *Studies in Philology* 73 (1976): 239–265; Rolf H. Bremmer Jr., "Grendel's Arm and the Law," in *Studies in English Language and Literature: 'Doubt Wisely': Papers in Honour of E. G. Stanley*, ed. M. J. Toswell and E. M. Tyler (London: Routledge, 1996), 121–132; for additional literature on Unferth, see the references in §§13 and 14; on the hero's intuitive monotheism, see the references in §5.

§23. Lines 1008b-1062: Beowulf's victory is now celebrated in feasting and ceremonious gift-giving. Hrothgar himself comes to the feast and is seated next to his nephew Hrothulf. This is the first time Hrothulf is mentioned in the poem, and his name is immediately followed by a hint of future strife between members of the Scylding dynasty: at that time (*þenden*), says the narrator, the Scyldings did not at all perform treacherous deeds (*fācenstafas*). Though some scholars attempt to deny it, the obvious import of these words is that there will eventually be some treacherous deed performed in connection with the figure of Hrothulf. This much is clear. Whether Hrothulf is the perpetrator or the victim (or both) is less clear. The controversy is further discussed below. Following the hint of future strife, Hrothgar rewards Beowulf with splendid treasures, including a battle standard, a helmet, a byrnie, a sword, and eight horses. One of the horses bears on it the saddle that had been Hrothgar's own whenever he went into battle. By giving Beowulf an item that the Danes had once used on the battlefield to identify their leader, Hrothgar might be hinting once again at his desire to transfer authority to Beowulf. In this formal scene, Hrothgar is called for the first time the "protector of the friends of Ing" (*eodor Ingwina*). If the title indicates that Hrothgar's authority extends beyond the borders of

273

Denmark and covers all of the peoples who worshipped the deity Ing, then it might be used here to further highlight the honor bestowed on Beowulf. He is receiving gifts of gratitude not from a minor king, but from the greatest king in Scandinavia at the time. Hrothgar then rewards each of Beowulf's men with an item of treasure and pays wergild for his fallen retainer, who is later identified as Hondscioh. The impression created by the scene is that Hrothgar is an ideal king, an exemplar of courtly and regnal behavior. Unfortunately, Hrothgar is old, and troubled times await the Scylding dynasty once he is dead. Perhaps this consideration informs the gnomic reflection on the value of forethought and understanding, which amount to the recognition that periods of good and bad invariably alternate over the course of a long enough life.

Further Reading: M. G. Clarke, *Sidelights on Teutonic History during the Migration Period* (Cambridge: Cambridge University Press, 1911), 95–102; Kemp Malone, "Hrethric," *PMLA* 42 (1927): 268–313; Kenneth Sisam, *The Structure of Beowulf* (Oxford: Clarendon Press, 1965), 34–39 and 80–82; Gerald Morgan, "The Treachery of Hrothulf," *English Studies* 53 (1972): 23–39; Rolf H. Bremmer Jr., "The Importance of Kinship: Uncle and Nephew in *Beowulf*," *Amsterdamer Beiträge zur älteren Germanistik* 15 (1980): 21–38; John M. Hill, *The Anglo-Saxon Warrior Ethic: Reconstructing Lordship in Early English Literature* (Gainesville: University Press of Florida, 2000), 71–73; Michael D. C. Drout, "Blood and Deeds: The Inheritance Systems in *Beowulf*," *Studies in Philology* 104 (2007): 199–226; William Cooke, "Hrothulf: A Richard III, or an Alfred the Great?," *Studies in Philology* 104 (2007): 175–198; Tom Shippey, "*Hrólfs saga kraka* and the Legend of Lejre," in *Making History: Essays on the Fornaldarsögur*, ed.

Martin Arnold and Alison Finlay (London: Viking Society for Northern Research, 2010), 17–32; Marijane Osborn, "The Alleged Murder of Hrethric in *Beowulf*," *Traditio* 74 (2019): 153–177; Rafael J. Pascual, "Hrothgar's Warhorse and the Audience of *Beowulf*," *Medium Ævum* 90 (2021): 123–132.

§24. Lines 1063-1159a: Hrothgar's court poet entertains the revelers in Heorot with a song about a nocturnal ambush and its aftermath: Hildeburh suffered and mourned, and Hengest exacted vengeance months later on those he held responsible for that nocturnal ambush; Danes, Frisians, and Jutes are involved, with the Jutes apparently to blame for the eruption of conflict. Two major questions emerge in connection with this episode: what exactly happens in the story that the court poet relates so allusively? And why is this story told at a feast celebrating Beowulf's victory over Grendel? The effort to answer the first question is aided by the chance preservation of a poem, *The Finnsburg Fragment*, which relates a scene from the nocturnal ambush to which the poet alludes, and by scattered references to characters from this story found in sources such as *Widsith* (ll. 26b-29a). Many reconstructions of the story have been put forward, but perhaps the most plausible is the following:

Tension between Danes and Frisians is pacified by the marriage of the Danish princess Hildeburh to the Frisian king Finn; Hnæf, Hildeburh's brother, visits his sister in Frisia, bringing with him a retinue of champions as well as the son that Hildeburh bore Finn, whom Hnæf had been fostering; Jutish retainers in the service of Finn notice the presence of Jutish warriors in the service of Hnæf; an old rivalry between the Jutes on both sides prompts Finn's Jutish retainers to instigate a nocturnal ambush on Hnæf and his men; during this ambush, Hnæf and his nephew are killed, but so are many of the Jutish and Frisian men who attacked them; Hnæf's champions, led now by Hengest, put up such a fierce resistance that a stalemate is reached; Finn promises to support and maintain Hengest's troop if they will enter into his service and swear oaths to him; Hengest agrees, but the shame of serving the man considered responsible for the death of Hnæf proves unbearable; Hengest resolves to break his oath and kill his current lord in order to avenge his former lord; he and his men kill Finn, murder his bodyguard, loot the palace, and take Hildeburh back to Denmark.

This reconstruction, grounded in the "Jutes on both sides" theory, accounts well for many of the peculiar details of the episode and the associated fragment. It explains, for instance, why the Jutes are apparently to blame for Hildeburh's losses; it also explains why Hengest, fighting on Hnæf's side, is identified as a Jute in sources external to *Beowulf*. It explains, moreover, why Hildeburh is able to remain married to Finn after the nocturnal ambush: Finn did not want the peace between the Danes and the Frisians to be broken; only some zealous Jutes in his employ took it upon themselves to violate the peace and attack their guests, killing Finn's half-Danish son along the way. The story, moreover, is a standard manifestation of migration-period Germanic legend, which tends to focus not on good versus evil but on conflicting ethical imperatives. No one in this story is evil. Even the Jutes who violated the peace likely did so to avenge some past action taken by Hnæf's Jutes. Finn is not evil, but as the lord of the Jutes responsible for the nocturnal ambush, he is ultimately considered the *bana* ("slayer") of Hnæf. Hengest swears an oath of loyalty to Finn, but this oath cannot constrain his need for vengeance. Hengest is reminded of his obligation to avenge

Hnæf first by Hildeburh's mourning, then by the complaints of Guthlaf, Oslaf, and the son of Hunlaf, who, by placing the sword on Hengest's lap, silently indicates what needs to be done. Why is this tragic legend of Hildeburh's shattered happiness and Hengest's anguished revenge recited at a celebration of Beowulf's victory in Heorot? Some readers propose that the legend was chosen to establish a parallel between the Hildeburh and Wealhtheow, two pitiful and helpless Danish queens. But is Wealhtheow actually pitiful and helpless? Another problem with this proposal is that it does not explain why Hrothgar's court poet selected the Finnsburg legend for a celebratory occasion. A better explanation is that the poet chose this tale because it tells of a grievous wrong that was eventually avenged after a period of prolonged suffering. As such, it parallels the situation of the Danes in Heorot, who were violated by Grendel and suffered for twelve years the humiliation of an unsatisfied need for vengeance. Just as Hengest eventually set right the death of Hnæf by killing Finn, Beowulf eventually set right the violation of the Danes by killing Grendel. Viewed in this light, the story suits the occasion well.

Further Reading: William Witherle Lawrence, "Beowulf and the Tragedy of Finnsburg," *PMLA* 30 (1915): 372–431; Nellie S. Aurner, "Hengest: A Study in Early English Hero Legend," *University of Iowa Humanistic Studies* 2 (1921): 1–76; Kemp Malone, "The Finn Episode in *Beowulf*," *Journal of English and Germanic Philology* 25 (1926): 157–172; A. C. Bouman, "The Heroes of the Fight at Finnsburh," *Acta Philologica Scandinavica* 10 (1935): 130–144; Donald K. Fry, ed., *Finnsburh: Fragment and Episode* (London: Methuen, 1974); John F. Vickrey, "The Narrative Structure of Hengest's Revenge in *Beowulf*," *Anglo-Saxon England* 6 (1977): 91–103;

Martin Camargo, "The Finn Episode and the Tragedy of Revenge in *Beowulf*," *Studies in Philology* 78 (1981): 120–134; J. R. R. Tolkien, *Finn and Hengest: The Fragment and the Episode*, ed. A. J. Bliss (London: George Allen & Unwin, 1982); Joyce Hill, "'Þæt Wæs Geomuru Ides!': A Female Stereotype Examined," in *New Readings on Women in Old English Literature*, ed. Helen Damico and Alexandra Hennessey Olsen (Bloomington: Indiana University Press, 1990), 235–247; Richard North, "Tribal Loyalties in the Finnsburh Fragment and Episode," *Leeds Studies in English* 21 (1990): 13–43; Scott Gwara, "The Foreign Beowulf and the 'Fight at Finnsburg,'" *Traditio* 63 (2008): 185–233; Michael Benskin, "The Narrative Structure of the Finnsburh Episode in *Beowulf*," *Amsterdamer Beiträge zur älteren Germanistik* 77 (2017): 37–64; Leonard Neidorf, "Hildeburh's Mourning and *The Wife's Lament*," *Studia Neophilologica* 89 (2017): 197–204; Leonard Neidorf, "Garulf and Guthlaf in the *Finnsburg* Fragment," *Notes & Queries* 66 (2019): 489–492; Leonard Neidorf, "Youth and Age in the *Finnsburg* Fragment," *ANQ* 35 (2022): 4–8.

§25. **Lines 1159b-1191**: A passage in hypermetrics describes an ominous tableau of the Danish court: Wealhtheow walks to where Hrothgar and Hrothulf sit; their kinship (*sib*) was still intact at that time (*þā ġȳt*), each true to the other; Unferth, sitting at Hrothgar's feet, is trusted by both men, though he killed his own kinsmen. The unambiguous implication of the passage is that the current harmony at the Danish court is only temporary, and that the agents responsible for the dissolution of this harmony are those celebrating together at the present moment. It seems that once Hrothgar dies, a dispute over succession will divide the Danish court into factions, with some

favoring Hrothulf and others favoring the children of Hroth-
gar. Wealhtheow will play some role in galvanizing the divi-
sion, and so will Unferth, whose killing of his own kinsmen
reveals not that he is sinister or deceptive, but that he has an
extreme commitment to heroic ideals and will instigate rather
than pacify an emerging conflict. As for Hrothulf, the ana-
logues make it clear that he will eventually be killed by his
cousin Heoroweard, who will in turn be killed by a servant of
Hrothulf, and this will bring the line of Healfdene to its end.
The notion that Hrothulf is a sinister character, who killed his
cousin Hrethric in a treacherous manner, is out of place in
migration-period legend. If Hrothulf killed Hrethric, the ac-
tion was more likely committed under duress, with Hrethric
perhaps attacking Hrothulf at the instigation of Wealhtheow
or Unferth. In any event, Wealhtheow's speech strongly sug-
gests that a dispute over succession is imminent. She tells
Hrothgar that she has heard that he wishes to have Beowulf
"as a son" (*for sunu*) and counsels against this: since Heorot is
cleansed of its monster (*Heorot is ġefǣlsod*), reward the Geats
with gifts but leave the kingdom to your kinsmen (*þīnum
māgum*). She trusts, moreover, that Hrothulf will be good to
her children. Wealhtheow is apparently wrong three times
over: Heorot is not cleansed (Grendel's mother is about to at-
tack); Beowulf was the right candidate to back for the succes-
sion, as he would have protected her children (as he does with
Hygd's children later on); and Hrothulf was the wrong candi-
date, as he will apparently be less kind to her children than
she imagines. The implication need not be that Hrothulf will
kill Wealhtheow's children in the manner of Richard III. What
might actually happen is that Wealhtheow exhorts Hrothulf to
name Hrethric as his co-ruler or subordinate king (the position
that Hrothulf seems currently to have in relation to Hrothgar),

but Hrothulf refuses her request and a battle between the factions at court breaks out. A conflict similar to the one envisioned is described in the Old Norse poem *Hlǫðskviða*, where a king dies and the intransigent demand for shared kingship by the son with a weaker claim to the throne leads to a bloody and tragic war with his half-brother. In this narrative, too, a bellicose counselor prevents a peaceable solution from being achieved, instead instigating the brothers to fight each other. Following Wealhtheow's speech, we are told that Beowulf is seated next to her children. The seating arrangement is possibly another hint that Beowulf is now considered a part of the family by Hrothgar. As such, it helps to explain the boldness and urgency of Wealhtheow's speech.

Further Reading: Tom Shippey, *Beowulf* (London: Arnold, 1978), 32–34; Josephine Bloomfield, "Diminished by Kindness: Frederick Klaeber's Rewriting of Wealhtheow," *Journal of English and Germanic Philology* 93 (1994): 183–203; Gale R. Owen-Crocker, "'Gracious' Hrothulf, 'Gracious' Hrothgar: A Reassessment," *English Language Notes* 38 (2001): 1–9; Jacek Olesiesjko, "Wealhtheow's Peace-Weaving: Diegesis and Genealogy of Gender in *Beowulf*," *Studia Anglica Posnaniensia* 49 (2014): 103–123; Helen Conrad O'Briain, "Listen to the Woman: Reading Wealhtheow as Stateswoman," in *New Readings on Women and Early Medieval English Literature and Culture*, ed. Helene Scheck and Christine E. Kozikowski (Amsterdam: Arc Humanities Press, 2019), 191–207; on Beowulf and the Danish succession, see the references in §21; on the future strife between Scylding kinsmen, see the references in §23.

§26. **Lines 1192-1250**: Wealhtheow gives treasures to Beo-
wulf, including a splendid golden torque, which the narrator
considers the greatest treasure to emerge since the "necklace
of the Brosings" (*Brōsinga men*), which Hama carried away
when he fled Eormenric's persecution. The *Brōsinga men* is
likely related to the *Brísinga men* of Norse mythology, the
necklace of Freyja that is stolen by Loki and apparently recov-
ered by Heimdallr (whose name recalls Hama). A story of
Hama fleeing Eormenric is recorded in the thirteenth-century
saga of Dietrich von Bern (*Þiðreks saga af Bern*), which tells
how Heimir flees the tyrannical Ermenríkr and eventually en-
ters a monastery, to which he donates all of his armor and
treasure in order to repent. A similar story seems to inform
the *Beowulf* poet's allusion. After the torque is compared to
the legendary *Brōsinga men*, we are told that it will be worn by
Hygelac on his fatal expedition in Frisia. It will enter into
Frankish possession after Hygelac falls, but it seems that Beo-
wulf will shortly thereafter avenge Hygelac's death, recover
the torque, and bring it back to Geatland with him. The state-
ment that Hygelac undertook this expedition on account of
wlenco (pride? arrogance? bravado?) is widely interpreted as
an expression of condemnation of Beowulf's uncle, but the
word is used positively by Wulfgar at line 338, and the hero's
unwavering admiration for his lord and uncle suggests that
Hygelac should not be viewed in an excessively negative light.
Wealhtheow's gift of the torque is followed by a speech in
which she exhorts Beowulf to be kind in counsel and appro-
priate in his conduct toward her children. Her speech con-
cludes with an assertion (wrong again) that the men in Heorot
are unified, loyal, and obedient to her will. The import of the
speech is that Beowulf should not disturb the court's harmony
by pursuing the Danish throne, and he should instead be

prepared to support her children in the event of a dispute over succession. Wealhtheow's false sense of security is shared with the rest of the Danes, who drink wine and prepare for sleep, unaware that Grendel's mother is about to attack them.

Further Reading: Howard W. Hintz, "The 'Hama' Reference in *Beowulf*: 1197-1201," *Journal of English and Germanic Philology* 33 (1934): 98–102; Robert E. Kaske, "The Sigemund-Heremod and Hama-Hygelac Passages in *Beowulf*," *PMLA* 74 (1959): 489–494; Lawrence Fast, "Hygelac: A Centripetal Force in *Beowulf*," *Annuale Mediaevale* 12 (1971): 90–98; Tom Shippey, *Old English Verse* (London: Hutchison, 1972), 38–39; Helen Damico, "*Sörlaþáttr* and the Hama Episode in *Beowulf*," *Scandinavian Studies* 55 (1983): 222–235; Hugh Magennis, "The *Beowulf* Poet and his *druncne dryhtguman*," *Neuphilologische Mitteilungen* 86 (1985): 159–164; Tomaki Mizuno, "The Magical Necklace and the Fatal Corselet in *Beowulf*," *English Studies* 80 (1999): 377–397; Dennis Cronan, "Poetic Meanings in the Old English Poetic Vocabulary," *English Studies* 84 (2003): 397–425; Edward Currie, "Hygelac's Raid in Historiography and Poetry: The King's Necklace and *Beowulf* as 'Epic,'" *Neophilologus,* 104 (2020): 391–400; on the political import of Wealhtheow's speeches, see the references in §§15, 23 and 25.

§27. Lines 1250-1320: Grendel's mother attacks the sleeping Danes at night. She is discovered but manages to kill and carry off one man before she hurries back to her underwater dwelling. The man she kills, later identified as Æschere, happens to be Hrothgar's dearest thegn. Was this a lucky choice or did she happen to know that Æschere was the best man in the room to choose to avenge the death of her son? The poet's treatment of Grendel's mother suggests that she is imagined as a somewhat different sort of supernatural being compared to Grendel. As a descendant of Cain, she is forced to live in cold waters. She is less terrifying than Grendel, we are told, and perhaps that is why she kills only one man rather than thirty during her nocturnal raid. She is also apparently less diabolical and demonic than Grendel, as the terms casting Grendel as an embodiment of Satanic evil tend not to be applied to her. Yet the introduction of Grendel's mother is immediately followed by a brief recapitulation of Beowulf's victory over Grendel, which reminds the audience that Grendel's mother begot the "hellish spirit" (*helle gāst*) and the "enemy of mankind" (*mancynnes fēond*) that God permitted Beowulf to defeat. That the poet should apply these terms only to Grendel and not to his mother (or the dragon) is curious. Perhaps the desire for variation at the level of poetic style extends to the level of narrative, with the poet wanting Beowulf's three adversaries to possess three distinctly different monstrous natures. When Grendel's mother attacks, Beowulf is sleeping in outside of Heorot, presumably in more comfortable accommodations reserved for an important guest. Ignorant of what transpired, Beowulf asks Hrothgar the next morning if he had a pleasant night—a minor manifestation of the poet's tendency to foreground the ironic (and grimly humorous?) mismatch between what a character knows and what the audience knows.

Further Reading: Nora K. Chadwick, "The Monsters and Beowulf," in *The Anglo-Saxons: Studies in Some Aspects of Their History and Culture Presented to Bruce Dickins*, ed. Peter Clemoes (London: Bowes & Bowes, 1959), 171–203; Jane C. Nitzsche, "The Structural Unity of *Beowulf*: The Problem of Grendel's Mother," *Texas Studies in Literature and Language*

22 (1980): 287–303; Gwendolyn A. Morgan, "Mothers, Monsters, Maturation: Female Evil in *Beowulf*," *Journal of the Fantastic in the Arts* 4 (1991): 54–68; Keith P. Taylor, "*Beowulf* 1259a: The Inherent Nobility of Grendel's Mother," *English Language Notes* 31 (1994): 13–25; Christine Alfano, "The Issue of Feminine Monstrosity: A Reevaluation of Grendel's Mother," *Comitatus* 23 (1992): 1–16; Paul Acker, "Horror and the Maternal in *Beowulf*," *PMLA* 121 (2006): 702–716; Renée R. Trilling, "Beyond Abjection: The Problem with Grendel's Mother Again," *Parergon* 24 (2007): 1–20; M. Wendy Hennequin, "We've Created a Monster: The Strange Case of Grendel's Mother," *English Studies* 89 (2008): 503–523; Sara Frances Burdorff, "Re-reading Grendel's Mother: *Beowulf* and the Anglo-Saxon Metrical Charms," *Comitatus* 45 (2014): 91–103; Paul Battles, "Dying for a Drink: 'Sleeping after the Feast' Scenes in *Beowulf, Andreas*, and the Old English Poetic Tradition," *Modern Philology* 112 (2015): 435–457; on the descent of Grendel and his mother from Cain, see the references in §3; for additional literature on Grendel's mother, see the references in §31.

§28. **Lines 1321-1382**: Hrothgar, wondering whether God will ever grant him a reversal of fortune, delivers a desperate speech devoid of his usual monotheistic language. In this speech, there are no expressions of confidence in divine providence. Hrothgar laments that the victim of Grendel's mother happened to be Æschere, his beloved counselor, confidante, and shoulder-companion. The gratuitous allusion to Yrmenlaf, Æschere's younger brother, suggests that these two characters were known entities in antecedent legendary tradition, though they are not mentioned in any surviving sources external to *Beowulf*. Hrothgar then conveys to Beowulf frightening reports that he has heard of two monsters, one in the shape of a man (Grendel) and the other in the shape of a woman (Grendel's mother), who live in a terrifying place, where unwelcoming landscape features lead to an ominous body of water, which no man has ever entered and survived. Even a stag pursued by hounds would rather lose its life than enter this water to protect itself. Many features of the description of the mere where Grendel and his mother live, such as the nightly sight of fire on the water (*fȳr on flōde*), appear to reflect the influence of Christian notions of hell and resemble accounts of hell found in early Christian literature. Parallels between the description of Grendel's mere in *Beowulf* and a passage in Blickling Homily 16 raise the possibility of direct influence from one text on the other, but it seems no less possible that both texts are independently indebted to a vernacular literary tradition based on the *Visio Sancti Pauli*, an apocryphal Latin work from the fourth century, in which a vision of hell is attributed to St. Paul. Though Beowulf bravely fought Grendel, Hrothgar seems to doubt whether the hero will agree to risk his life (and his soul?) by journeying into the hellish abode where the monsters dwell. Hrothgar assures the hero that ample rewards will await him if he dares to seek out the terrifying place—and if he lives.

Further Reading: William Witherle Lawrence, "The Haunted Mere in *Beowulf*," *PMLA* 27 (1912): 208–245; W. S. Mackie, "The Demons' Home in *Beowulf*," *Journal of English and Germanic Philology* 37 (1938): 455–461; Sarah L. Higley, "*Aldor on Ofre*, or the Reluctant Hart: A Study of Liminality in *Beowulf*," *Neuphilologische Mitteilungen* 87 (1986): 342–353; Richard Butts, "The Analogical Mere: Landscape and Terror in *Beowulf*," *English Studies* 68 (1987): 113–121;

Charles D. Wright, *The Irish Tradition in Old English Literature* (Cambridge: Cambridge University Press, 1992), 116–136; Margaret Gelling, "The Landscape of *Beowulf*," *Anglo-Saxon England* 31 (2002): 7–11; Geoffrey Russom, "At the Center of *Beowulf*," in *Myth in Early Northwest Europe*, ed. Stephen O. Glosecki (Tempe: ACMRS, 2007), 225–240; Rafael J. Pascual, "Material Monsters and Semantic Shifts," in *The Dating of Beowulf: A Reassessment*, ed. Leonard Neidorf (Cambridge: D. S. Brewer, 2014), 202–218; Paul S. Langeslag, "Monstrous Landscape in *Beowulf*," *English Studies* 96 (2015): 119–138; Michael Bintley, "*Hrinde Bearwas*: The Trees at the Mere and the Root of All Evil in *Beowulf*," *Journal of English and Germanic Philology* 119 (2020): 309–326.

§29. Lines 1383-1441a: Beowulf responds to Hrothgar's despair by stating eternal verities: vengeance is better than mourning; death is inevitable, so the best thing for a worthy man to achieve during this transient life is lasting fame. The statements are gnomic and impersonal, but their meaning is situational, and Beowulf is using them in this situation to affirm in a powerful way to state that *he* is not deterred by the prospect of death. *He* will pursue vengeance and *he* will gain glory or die while doing so. Beowulf then makes it clear that he will immediately search far and wide for Grendel's kinsman. Critics who read *Beowulf* as a critique of heroic values, or as a Christian poet's rueful depiction of benighted pagans, read this speech as the perfect illustration of the hero's tragically limited perspective: if only he knew that heaven, not fame, were the best thing for a man to obtain during his mortal life, and that forgiveness, not vengeance, is the better response to bloodshed. Such readings appear rather doubtful, however, in view of the response that Beowulf's speech elicits: Hrothgar leaps up and thanks God (*Gode þancode*) for the words the man spoke; Beowulf's heroic resolve restores Hrothgar's faith and brings him back to the monotheistic piety that he had briefly forgotten. Following the speech, Beowulf and Hrothgar then lead a hunting party in pursuit of Grendel's mother. Tracing her tracks, they make their way past a series of inhospitable and ominous landscape features, and are distressed to discover Æschere's head, displayed as if it were a warning sign or a boundary marker. Various kinds of sea-monsters inhabit the waters in which Grendel's mother dwells. A Geatish warrior shoots one with an arrow, and the men then use boar-spears to drag it from the water and examine it. The scene makes Beowulf's courage seem all the more impressive: he will have to contend not only with Grendel's mother, but with an untold number of sea-monsters.

Further Reading: Dorothy Whitelock, *The Audience of Beowulf* (Oxford: Clarendon Press, 1951), 13–14; Fred C. Robinson, *Beowulf and the Appositive Style* (Knoxville: University of Tennessee Press, 1985), 10–11; John M. Hill, *The Cultural World in Beowulf* (Toronto: University of Toronto Press, 1995), 35; Gale R. Owen-Crocker, "Horror in *Beowulf*: Mutilation, Decapitation and Unburied Dead," in *Early Medieval English Texts and Interpretations: Studies Presented to Donald G. Scragg*, ed. Elaine Treharne and Susan Rosser (Tempe: ACMRS, 2002), 81–100; Erin Sebo, "*Ne Sorga*: Grief and Revenge in *Beowulf*," in *Anglo-Saxon Emotions: Reading the Heart in Old English Language, Literature and Culture*, ed. Alice Jorgensen, Frances McCormack, and Jonathan Wilcox (Farnham: Ashgate, 2015), 177–192; Helen Appleton, "The Role of Æschere's Head," *Review of English Studies* 68 (2017): 428–447; Thijs Porck and Sander Salk, "Marking Boundaries in

Beowulf: Æschere's Head, Grendel's Arm and the Dragon's Corpse," *Amsterdamer Beiträge zur älteren Germanistik* 77 (2017): 521–540.

§30. Lines 1441b-1491: As Beowulf readies himself, the narrator describes the mail-shirt, helmet, and sword that will accompany him on the mission. Each item has a history and special properties. A notable feature of the hero's helmet is the presence of totemic boar-images, which a smith wondrously forged onto the helmet to ensure that no blade could ever penetrate it. Such a belief would explain why boar-images are found on real helmets from the period. Beowulf's sword for the occasion is Hrunting, lent to him by Unferth, a weapon that has never failed its bearers in battle. Described by another poet, Unferth's decision to lend a family heirloom to Beowulf, a man he formerly criticized, could provide an occasion to make Unferth appear noble and magnanimous. The *Beowulf* poet, however, plainly dislikes Unferth for one reason or another—perhaps the poet considers his kin-slaying unforgiveable, or perhaps the *þyle* was a kind of pagan priest—and so he uses this occasion merely as an opportunity to belittle Unferth, who forgot his earlier words and is too cowardly to undertake the mission on which Beowulf is about to depart. Unferth's reputation for valorous deeds suffers (*hē dōme forlēas*) while Beowulf is on the verge of committing his most valorous deed. Beowulf has taken Unferth's position as the champion of the Danish court; the loan of Hrunting symbolizes Unferth's acceptance of the fact that Beowulf is the better man. Before diving in, Beowulf delivers a heroic and selfless speech. He reminds Hrothgar of his promise to be as a father to him (*on fæder stæle*), but does so merely to urge him to carry out three requests in the event of the hero's untimely demise: be a lord to Beowulf's lordless men; send the treasure that Beowulf won to Hygelac; and return Hrunting to Unferth. Beowulf vows to gain glory or die. His words increase his resolve, as they bind him to this course of action and make the possibility of retreat completely unacceptable.

Further Reading: Geoffrey Hughes, "Beowulf, Unferth and Hrunting: An Interpretation," *English Studies* 58 (1977): 385–395; Barbara Nolan and Morton W. Bloomfield, *"Bēotword, Gilpcwidas*, and the *Gilphlæden* Scop of *Beowulf*," *Journal of English and Germanic Philology* 79 (1980): 499–516; Helen Damico, *"Þrymskviða* and Beowulf's Second Fight: The Dressing of the Hero in Parody," *Scandinavian Studies* 58 (1986): 407–428; Marie Nelson, "Beowulf's Boast Words," *Neophilologus* 89 (2005): 299–310; on the boar-helmet, see the references in §8; on Unferth, see the references in §§13, 14, and 22.

§31. Lines 1492-1569: The fight with Grendel's mother turns out to be much more difficult for Beowulf than the fight with Grendel. The narrator's earlier remark about Grendel's mother inspiring less terror than her son now appears to be yet another ironic incongruity. In this fight, Grendel's mother has all of the advantages that Beowulf previously had. She perceives him before he perceives her. Whereas Beowulf's Geatish retainers previously stabbed (albeit ineffectively) at Grendel, the sea-monsters that inhabit the hostile-hall (*nīðsele*) of Grendel's mother stab at Beowulf with their battle-tusks. Fortunately for Beowulf, his wondrous mail-shirt protects him from the strikes of both Grendel's mother and the sea-monsters. Two excuses are given for the failure of Beowulf's weapon: first, we are told that the conditions of the underwater hall make it impossible for weapons to be wielded there; but then Beowulf somehow manages to take a hard swing at Grendel's mother with Hrunting, only to find out that it cannot harm her. Grendel's mother, it seems, can only be killed by her own weapon—a trait she shares with many a monster from European folklore. Beowulf then tosses the useless sword and, mindful of glory, decides to abandon his chivalrous concern for fair-play. He grabs Grendel's mother by her hair and throws her. The narrator's remark (*nalas for fæhðe mearn*) means, essentially, that he felt no compunction about violating the norms of combat under these circumstances. Beowulf is desperate and the fight is about to take a turn for the worse: Grendel's mother sets upon him, holds him down, and stabs at him. Her blade strikes his shoulder; the hero's life is saved again due to the mail-shirt—and the protection of God. Divine intervention then apparently guides Beowulf, on the verge of defeat, to notice that a wondrous sword, a product of gigantic craftsmanship, is within reach. He seizes the sword, which is too large for any other man to lift, and then thrusts it through the neck of Grendel's mother, finally killing her. The motif of the monster that can only be killed by its own weapon is here combined with the motif of the magical sword that can only be wielded by one man (familiar from, for instance, the Arthurian myth of Excalibur). During the fight, the aquatic nature of Grendel's mother is foregrounded through terms such as "sea-wolf" (*brimwylf*), "outcast of the deep" (*grund-wyrġenne*), and "mighty sea-woman" (*merewīf mihtiġ*). The conception of a supernatural woman living in waters that contain treasures likely originates as a distorted memory of earlier Germanic religious traditions, in which goddesses were associated with bodies of water and goods were ritually deposited in those bodies of waters as sacrificial offerings to their tutelary goddesses.

Further Reading: Martin Puhvel, "The Might of Grendel's Mother," *Folklore* 80 (1969): 81–88; E. G. Stanley, "Did Beowulf Commit 'Feaxfeng' against Grendel's Mother?," *Notes and Queries* 23 (1976): 339–340; Fred C. Robinson, "Did Grendel's Mother Sit on Beowulf?" in *From Anglo-Saxon to Early Middle English: Studies Presented to E. G. Stanley*, ed. Malcolm Godden, Douglas Gray and T. F. Hoad (Oxford: Clarendon Press, 1994), 1–7; Hilda R. Ellis Davidson, *Roles of the Northern Goddess* (London: Routledge, 1998), 21–22; Oren Falk, "Beowulf's Longest Day: The Amphibious Hero in His Element (*Beowulf*, ll. 1495b-96)," *Journal of English and Germanic Philology* 106 (2007): 1–21; William Sayers, "Grendel's Mother (Beowulf) and the Celtic Goddess of Territorial Sovereignty," *Journal of Indo-European Studies* 35 (2007): 31–52; Evelyn Reynolds, "*Beowulf*'s Poetics of Absorption: Narrative Syntax and the Illusion of Stability in the Fight with Grendel's Mother," *Essays in Medieval Studies* 31 (2016): 43–64; Terry Gunnell, "The Goddesses in the Dark Waters," in *Making the Profane Sacred in the Viking Age: Essays in Honour of Stefan Brink*, ed. Irene García Losquiño, Olof Sundqvist, and Declan Taggart (Turnhout: Brepols, 2020), 243–265; on Grendel's mother, see also the references in §27.

§32. Lines 1570-1650: Beowulf, wielding the magical sword that he used to kill Grendel's mother, now uses it to decapitate the corpse of Grendel. The corpse springs apart and its blood melts the blade of the sword. The narrator states that Beowulf's desecration of Grendel's corpse is motivated by a desire to take additional vengeance for the Danes, who were tormented by Grendel on more than one occasion. It is likely, however, that in antecedent tradition Beowulf's deed had been motivated by a belief that the dead Grendel could continue to persecute the Danes unless his head were severed from his corpse: decapitation was believed to be the only guaranteed way to kill a monster and obviate the possibility of its post-mortem return. Although Beowulf sees many treasures in the lair of Grendel's mother, he refrains from plundering it and returns to the surface only with Grendel's head and the giant sword-hilt. This is a curious detail that raises the question: why would he not take more of the treasures with him? One possibility is that Beowulf worried that some of the treasures might be cursed or dangerous. Another possibility is that Grendel's head and the giant sword-hilt were so heavy that he could carry no other gigantic objects with him. Support for the latter possibility emerges when we are told that Grendel's head requires four Geatish men to carry it, and they could only do so with difficulty. In addition to melting the sword-blade, Grendel's blood reddens the water and convinces the Danes that Beowulf perished. They return home while Beowulf's retainers continue to wait for him. The Geats thank God when they see their lord returned safe from his mission. Various forms of Christian symbolism have been discerned in the departure of the Danes, the patience of the Geats, and Beowulf's "resurrected" return from the mere. It is equally possible, though, that the poet has the Danes believe that Beowulf died merely to create another case of the ironic mismatch between what characters believe and what the audience knows to be true. Beowulf and the Geats return triumphantly to Heorot and Grendel's gigantic head, carried disrespectfully by its hair, is presented as a sight for all to admire.

Further Reading: Nora K. Chadwick, "Norse Ghosts (A Study in the *Draugr* and the *Haugbúi*)," *Folklore* 57 (1946): 50–65; Nora K. Chadwick, "Norse Ghosts II," *Folklore* 57 (1946): 106–127; Allen Cabaniss, "*Beowulf* and the Liturgy," *Journal of English and Germanic Philology* 54 (1955): 195–201; M. B. McNamee, "*Beowulf*: An Allegory of Salvation?" *Journal of English and Germanic Philology* 59 (1960): 190–207; Kathryn Hume, "From Saga to Romance: The Use of Monsters in Old Norse Literature," *Studies in Philology* 77 (1980): 1–25; Kent Gould, "*Beowulf* and Folktale Morphology: God as Magical Donor," *Folklore* 96 (1985): 98–103; Rosemary Huisman, "The Three Tellings of Beowulf's Fight with Grendel's Mother," *Leeds Studies in English* 20 (1989): 217–248; Daniel F. Pigg, "Cultural Markers in *Beowulf*: A Re-Evaluation of the Relationship between Beowulf and Christ," *Neophilologus* 74 (1990): 601–607; Dennis Cronan, "The Rescuing Sword," *Neophilologus* 77 (1993): 467–478; Mary Flavia Godfrey, "Beowulf and Judith: Thematizing Decapitation in Old English Poetry," *Texas Studies in Language and Literature* 35 (1993): 1–43.

§33. Lines 1651-1699: Beowulf recounts his exploit. He reveals that Hrunting was useless but is still courteous enough to praise the weapon anyway (*þeah þæt wæpen duge*). He also states that he would have died if God had not intervened in the fight and directed his attention toward the magical sword that was hanging on the wall. It is interesting that Beowulf intuits the intervention of God at precisely the same moment in the fight when the omniscient narrator had mentioned divine intervention in his account. This suggests that there is general (though not complete) alignment between the theological perspectives of the narrator and the characters. The narrator has access to revealed biblical knowledge, whereas the characters merely have their intuitions, yet we can see here that intuition is enough for Beowulf to correctly discern the intervention of God in his life. He is not depicted as a tragically benighted pagan. Beowulf then tells the Danes that they can sleep without any fear of further attacks from Grendel or his mother. This statement, made with Grendel's head in sight, probably alludes to the belief mentioned above that a monster could return as a revenant if it were not decapitated. Following Beowulf's speech, Hrothgar examines the gigantic sword-hilt. The transfer of the sword into Hrothgar's possession (*hit on æht ġehwearf*) after the death of his monstrous persecutors further establishes the finality of their feud: his enemies are vanquished, and this is confirmed by the presence of their plundered wealth. Hrothgar sees on the giant hilt an inscription that recounts "the origin of ancient strife" (*ōr fyrnġewinnes*). Although a normal sword hilt offers limited room for pictorial representations, this gigantic sword hilt is evidently large enough to accommodate a pictorial account of the biblical feud between God and the giants, which began with Cain's killing of Abel and culminated in the flood. The sword-hilt also contains a runic inscription of the name of the person for whom the sword was wrought. Scholars have arrived at no satisfactory explanation of this mysterious detail. In any event, the speech that follows Hrothgar's examination of the hilt suggests that he has acquired new theological insights from it about the suffering he endured. Grendel was not a typical monster; he was an enemy of the eternal lord. Hrothgar, without previously knowing it, had been part of the "great feud" between God and his enemies. This realization appears to inform the spiritual concerns of the following speech, which possesses considerably wider scope than the previous hints of Hrothgar's monotheistic piety.

Further Reading: Hilda R. Ellis Davidson, *The Sword in Anglo-Saxon England: Its Archaeology and Literature* (Woodbridge: Boydell Press, 1962), 135–142; Marijane Osborn, "The Great Feud: Scriptural History and Strife in *Beowulf*," *PMLA* 93 (1978): 973–981; Johann Köberl, "The Magic Sword in *Beowulf*," *Neophilologus* 71 (1987): 120–228; Richard J. Schrader, "The Language on the Giant's Sword Hilt in *Beowulf*," *Neuphilologische Mitteilungen* 94 (1993): 141–184; Dennis Cronan, "The Origin of Ancient Strife in *Beowulf*," *North-Western Language Evolution* 31–32 (1997): 57–68; Dennis Cronan, "Hroðgar and the *Gylden Hilt* in *Beowulf*," *Traditio* 72 (2017): 109–132.

§34. **Lines 1700-1784**: Hrothgar, placed into a reflective mood by the sight of the sword-hilt, delivers the pivotal speech that has come to be known as his sermon or homily. The speech expresses a combination of political and spiritual insights. Recognizing the extraordinary nature of Beowulf's achievement, Hrothgar considers it inevitable that Beowulf will be a king. He now imagines, however, that Beowulf will be ruling among his own people (*lēodum þīnum*). Having seen Wealhtheow's resistance to his plan, Hrothgar has abandoned his hope that Beowulf could inherit the Danish throne. Hrothgar earlier referred to his relationship with Beowulf as one of "new kinship" (*nīwe sibbe*); he now refers to it as one of "friendship" (*frēode*). He states that he intends to fulfill (*ġelǣstan*) the obligations of this friendship, and it soon becomes clear that he plans to do so not by making Beowulf a successor to the Danish throne, but by endowing him with treasures fit only for a royal possessor, which will ensure his eventual kingship in Geatland. Taking Beowulf's future rule for granted, Hrothgar exhorts him not to rule like Heremod, who mismanaged the gifts that God gave him and consequently brought misery to his people and himself. The Heremod exemplum leads Hrothgar into a general reflection on God's wondrous generosity, on his mysterious capacity to endow a fortunate man with extraordinary talent and prosperity. With all of his wishes fulfilled, this hypothetical nobleman might allow an element of pride or arrogance (*oferhyġda dǣl*) to take root and grow within him; his soul becomes vulnerable to the metaphorical arrows of a spiritual assailant. In the end, the man will die, and the wealth he hoarded will just be distributed generously by his successor. This leads into Hrothgar's climactic exhortation to Beowulf: guard yourself against that evil (*Bebeorh þē ðone bealonīð*) and choose the better path, "eternal counsels" (*ēċe rǣdas*). The exhortation appears to be simultaneously temporal and spiritual in its orientation. On the one hand, it can be read as traditional worldly advice to avoid arrogance and ruling generously. On the other hand, the story of the hypothetical nobleman whose "guardian of the soul" (*sāwele hyrde*) neglects his duty makes it clear that Hrothgar has spiritual concerns in mind. The sight of the sword-hilt has apparently caused Hrothgar to ponder the eternal dimensions of human life. He stresses the transience of glory and the inevitability of death not to encourage Beowulf to be mindful of threats to his mortality, but to make him think of the spiritual and eternal consequences of his actions. Hrothgar then relates his message to his own experience, explaining that he felt invulnerable prior to Grendel's arrival. Humbled by his suffering, he gives thanks to the "eternal lord" (*ēċean dryhtne*) that he is able to stare at the decapitated head of his vanquished enemy. Hrothgar's words suggest that he interprets Grendel's persecution as a punishment for his pride, which was alleviated when his pride was replaced by piety. Yet such an interpretation seems merely to be flirted with and presented as the possibly erroneous intuition of a character; the narrator never adopts this perspective with regard to any of the poem's monsters. Beowulf will later worry that the dragon's arrival might indicate God's displeasure, yet the omniscient narrator presents us with no reason to believe that Beowulf has angered God in any way. Perhaps the poet attributes such thoughts to these intuitive monotheists to foreground their humility, their readiness to take responsibility for their actions, and their refusal to blame God for their suffering. Throughout his sermon, Hrothgar maintains the view that God is a purely benevolent being, who doles out gifts to his creations. Hrothgar refrains from stating that God punishes sinful mortals. Instead, he suggests that mortals bring suffering upon themselves through the mismanagement of the gifts that God beneficently gave them. In earlier *Beowulf* scholarship, it was common for scholars to regard Hrothgar's sermon as (partially or wholly) a Christian interpolation in an otherwise pagan poem. It is now clear, however, that the passage is linguistically and theologically consistent with the rest of the poem. There is no compelling reason to doubt its authenticity.

Further Reading: Charles Donahue, "*Beowulf* and Christian Tradition: A Reconsideration from a Celtic Stance," *Traditio* 21 (1965): 55–116; Betty S. Cox, *Cruces of Beowulf* (The Hague: Mouton, 1971), 131–153; John F. Vickrey, "*Egesan ne gymeð* and the Crime of Heremod," *Modern Philology* 71 (1974): 295–300; Elaine Tuttle Hansen, "Hrothgar's 'Sermon' in *Beowulf* as Parental Wisdom," *Anglo-Saxon England* 10

(1981): 53–67; Mark Atherton, "The Figure of the Archer in *Beowulf* and the Anglo-Saxon Psalter," *Neophilologus* 77 (1993): 653–657; Paul Cavill, "Christianity and Theology in *Beowulf*," in *The Christian Tradition in Anglo-Saxon England: Approaches to Current Scholarship and Teaching*, ed. Paul Cavill (Woodbridge, UK: D. S. Brewer, 2004), 15–40; Scott Gwara, *Heroic Identity in the World of Beowulf* (Leiden: Brill, 2008), 181–238; Raymond P. Tripp, Jr., "Heremod's Sin, Hrothgar's Sermon, and Beowulf's Choice," *Geardagum* 30 (2011): 59–77; Leonard Neidorf, "The Language of Hrothgar's Sermon," *Studia Neophilologica* 91 (2019): 1–10; James H. Morey, "The Fourth Fate of Men: Heremod's Darkened Mind," in *Darkness, Depression, and Descent in Anglo-Saxon England*, ed. Ruth Wehlau (Berlin: de Gruyter, 2019), 155–166; for additional literature on Heremod, see the references in §20.

§35. Lines 1785-1839: Having achieved lasting fame, Beowulf sleeps exceedingly well. Prior to sleep, he is waited on by a hall-attendant, who sees to the guest's needs with fitting reverence. This minor detail recalls Beowulf's earlier interactions with Danish personnel (the coastguard, Wulfgar) and contributes to the courtly realism of the narrative. Cumulatively, these details help to distance the main story of *Beowulf* from its folkloric origins and recast it as a rather subtle and sophisticated political drama. The next morning, Beowulf orders Hrunting to be brought to Unferth and he praises the weapon despite its manifest uselessness. The poet praises Beowulf in turn for his exceptional courtesy toward his humiliated rival, calling him a *mōdig* man, a term that must mean "magnanimous" in the present context. The incident illustrates Beowulf's courtly *savoir faire*, his ability to finesse the dangerous

298

political predicament in which he found himself at Heorot. He successfully navigated the threats posed by Unferth and Wealhtheow and he managed to win the firm friendship of Hrothgar, the poem's wealthiest and most powerful king. Beowulf then delivers a speech thanking Hrothgar and offering military support in the form of a thousand thegns should Hrothgar ever find himself under attack. He then suggests that Hrethric, Hrothgar's son, could visit the Geatish court and find friends there. A gnomic statement on the suitability of travel for worthy travelers softens the political acuteness of Beowulf's remark. Beowulf's offer of military aid for Hrothgar and asylum for Hrethric evidently reflects his apprehension of threats on the horizon: the former likely alludes to the feud between the Danes and the Heathobards and the inevitable failure of Hrothgar's plan to pacify the feud through a diplomatic marriage; the latter surely alludes to the peril in which Hrethric will find himself after Hrothgar dies and a dispute over succession arises.

Further Reading: Tom Shippey, "Maxims in Old English Narrative: Literary Art or Traditional Wisdom?," in *Oral Tradition, Literary Tradition: A Symposium*, ed. Hans Bekker-Nielsen et al. (Odense: Odense University Press, 1977), 28–46; Susan E. Deskis, *Beowulf and the Medieval Proverb Tradition* (Tempe: ACMRS, 1996), 126–128; on the narrative's courtliness, see the references in §9; on the future strife between Scylding kinsmen, see the references in §23.

§36. Lines 1840-1887: Impressed by the hero's words, Hrothgar declares them a product of divine inspiration. He praises Beowulf for his ability to conduct diplomacy (*þingian*), for his strength, his wisdom, and his eloquence. Hrothgar then requites Beowulf's perspicacity in regard to Danish politics by demonstrating his own perspicacity in regard to Geatish politics: he states that if Hygelac should happen to die prematurely (as, in fact, will happen), then the Geats could do no better than to appoint Beowulf as king (as, in fact, will also happen). Beowulf himself apparently does not expect such an end for Hygelac, as he just expressed his faith in Hygelac ruling long enough to support any military venture undertaken to aid Hrothgar. Beowulf's misapprehension regarding Hygelac's longevity mirrors Hrothgar's own misapprehension regarding the Heathobard feud. Hrothgar then announces that Beowulf's achievement will forever end military tensions between the Danes and the Geats, and that the relationship between them now will be one characterized by trade and gift exchange. This allusion to a former feud between Danes and Geats is surprising: it had not been mentioned previously in the poem and it is not clarified by the poem's analogues. Following his speech, Hrothgar gives twelve treasures to Beowulf and then kisses and embraces him. Tears fall from Hrothgar's eyes as he doubts that he will see Beowulf again after they part. The narrator reports that a "secret longing" or "unexpressed desire" (*dyrne langað*) burned in Hrothgar's blood at their moment of parting: the expression probably alludes to Hrothgar's thwarted plan to make Beowulf his successor. Hrothgar wishes that Beowulf could remain in Denmark, assume the throne, and prevent the dispute over succession that will eventually claim the lives of most of the Scylding princes. He accepts, however, that this is not politically feasible, and so he does not express his desire; he must allow Beowulf to return home and fulfill his destiny there. As Hrothgar's gifts are carried out and admired, the narrator praises Hrothgar as an altogether flawless king. Such praise must cast doubt on any interpretation wherein the poet is allegedly criticizing Hrothgar for one failing or another. Hrothgar's plans do not always succeed: his attempt to pacify the Heathobard feud will fail; his attempt to name Beowulf as a successor was thwarted; and his attempts to rebuff Grendel were unsuccessful. Yet political failure is not necessarily a sign of moral failure in a world where there are forces beyond one's control. Hrothgar is consistently presented as an exemplar of courtesy and generosity; he is, moreover, the poem's principal mouth-piece for monotheistic wisdom. Here and elsewhere, the narrator goes out of his way to ensure that we regard Hrothgar as a good king.

Further Reading: Thomas L. Wright, "Hrothgar's Tears," *Modern Philology* 65 (1967): 39–44; Tom Shippey, *Beowulf* (London: Arnold, 1978), 32–34; Teresa Pàroli, "The Tears of the Heroes in Germanic Epic Poetry," in *Helden und Heldensage: Otto Gschwantler zum 60. Geburtstag*, ed. Hermann Reichert and Günter Zimmermann (Wien: Fassbaender, 1990), 233–266; Mary Dockray-Miller, "*Beowulf*'s Tears of Fatherhood," *Exemplaria* 10 (1998): 1–28; Kristen Mills, "Emotion and Gesture in Hroðgar's Farewell to Beowulf," in *Anglo-Saxon Emotions: Reading the Heart in Old English Language, Literature and Culture*, ed. Alice Jorgensen, Frances McCormack, and Jonathan Wilcox (Farnham: Ashgate, 2015), 163–176; Leonard Neidorf, *The Art and Thought of the Beowulf Poet* (Ithaca: Cornell University Press, 2022), 93–94.

§37. **Lines 1888-1924**: Returning to the coast with their treasures and horses in tow, Beowulf and the Geats encounter the coastguard who interrogated them when they first arrived. This time around, there is no inquiry into their motives; the Geats are treated as honored guests. Beowulf rewards the coastguard for watching their vessel by giving him a sword bound with gold, which makes the coastguard the worthier thereafter among his peers on the mead-bench. The sword commands respect and elevates the social status of its owner. This splendid gift, which must have exceeded its recipient's expectation of reward, reinforces the characterization of Beowulf as a magnanimous hero, respectful toward those of higher rank and courteous toward those beneath him. Beowulf's ship, loaded with his winnings, departs for Geatland and is greeted there by a Geatish coastguard, who has eagerly awaited its arrival. Attention is paid throughout this passage on treasure and its movement from land to vessel to land. One gets the impression that the transportation of the treasures is almost as important as the transportation of the men themselves. The impression is not quite wrong, since the treasure is the proof of Beowulf's achievement, and it is about to play a pivotal role in elevating Beowulf's status among the Geats.

Further Reading: Ernst Leisi, "Gold und Manneswert im *Beowulf*," *Anglia* 71 (1953): 259–273; Paul Beekman Taylor, "The Traditional Language of Treasure in *Beowulf*," *Journal of English and Germanic Philology* 85 (1986): 191–205; David C. Van Meter, "The Ritualized Presentation of Weapons and the Ideology of Nobility in *Beowulf*," *Journal of English and Germanic Philology* 95 (1996): 175–189; Peter S. Baker, *Honour, Exchange and Violence in Beowulf* (Cambridge: D. S. Brewer, 2013), 35–76; Rory Naismith, "The Economy of *Beowulf*," in *Old English Philology: Studies in Honour of R. D. Fulk*, ed. Leonard Neidorf, Rafael J. Pascual, and Tom Shippey (Cambridge: D. S. Brewer, 2016), 371–391.

§38. Lines 1925-1962: Though Beowulf is eager to see Hygelac, the narrator digresses to comment on the virtues of Hygd, Hygelac's young queen, which are contrasted with the vices displayed by Offa's queen before her marriage. This passage, known as the Offa digression, contains notable difficulties. The transition from the praise of Hygd to the criticism of Offa's queen is sufficiently abrupt and the overall justification for the passage is sufficiently opaque for many critics to have deemed the passage an interpolation intended to flatter king Offa of Mercia (r. 757-796), who was named after the legendary (fourth century?) Offa, king of the continental Angles. There is, however, no compelling linguistic reason to consider the passage inauthentic, and various thematic justifications for the passage have been devised. It is somewhat likely, though, that eye-skip between the verses comprising line 1931 has resulted in the loss of text, which might have included the name of Offa's queen. The line is not metrically defective, but it is difficult to believe that the poet would abruptly transition from praising Hygd to condemning an ostensibly anonymous character. Many scholars have interpreted the word *mōdþrȳðo* as the name of Offa's queen, but this is entirely implausible: *mōdþrȳðo wæġ* ("bore arrogance") is a formulaic verse (closely paralleled by *hiġeþrȳðo wæġ* in *Genesis A*, l. 2240b) that begins with a feminine abstract noun in an oblique case, not a proper name. It is not impossible that *fremu* ("excellent") is the name of the queen, but there are difficulties with this explanation as well. It appears that, as it stands, the transmitted text simply lacks the name of Offa's queen. Beyond the problem of the queen's name is the problem of the passage's relevance. Since Offa's queen is reformed by her marriage, the passage seems intended less to condemn her temporarily flawed character than to praise the invariably excellent character of Offa. The

contrast of the queens thus enables a transition into an enco-
mium on the virtues of Offa, who is here praised as the greatest
king who ever lived. Perhaps the poet mentions Offa in order
to provoke the audience to compare Beowulf with Offa and
view the hero as a figure cut from the same folkloric cloth:
legends of Offa record that he was considered unpromising in
his childhood (due to a disability), yet he went on to surprise
everyone and achieve greatness while still young; the same
basic outline fits the career of Beowulf, who was considered
unpromising in his childhood, yet suddenly proved himself
throne-worthy as a young man through the monster-slaying
adventure in Denmark. Naturally, many other explanations
for the passage's rationale have been devised, with some con-
struing the praise of Offa as a form of indirect criticism di-
rected at either Beowulf or Hygelac. Such interpretations ap-
pear rather strained. It is possible, moreover, that the passage
contains minimal moral significance and is merely intended,
along with other digressions, to provide the narrative in the
foreground with a rich and variegated heroic-legendary back-
ground.

Further Reading: Kemp Malone, "Hygd," *Modern Language
Notes* 56 (1941): 356–358; Bruce Moore, "The Thryth-Offa
Digression in *Beowulf*," *Neophilologus* 64 (1980): 127–133;
Norman E. Eliason, "The Thryth-Offa Digression in *Beowulf*,"
in *Franciplegius: Medieval and linguistic studies in honor of
Francis Peabody Magoun, Jr.*, ed. Jess B. Bessinger, Jr. and
Robert P. Creed (New York: New York University Press,
1965), 124–138; C. B. Hieatt, "Modþryðo and Heremod: In-
tertwined Threads in the *Beowulf*-Poet's Web of Words," *Jour-
nal of English and Germanic Philology* 83 (1984): 173–182;
Gillian R. Overing, *Language, Sign, and Gender in Beowulf*

(Carbondale: Southern Illinois Press, 1990), 101–112; Mary Dockray-Miller, "The Masculine Queen of Beowulf," *Women and Language* 21 (1998): 31–38; Marijane Osborn, "The Wealth They Left Us: Two Women Author Themselves Through Others' Lives in Beowulf," *Philological Quarterly* 78 (1999): 49–76; R. D. Fulk, "The Name of Offa's Queen: Beowulf 1931-2," *Anglia* 122 (2004): 614–639; Stacy S. Klein, *Ruling Women: Queenship and Gender in Anglo-Saxon Literature* (Notre Dame: University of Notre Dame Press, 2006), 105–111; Francis Leneghan, "The Poetic Purpose of the Offa-Digression in *Beowulf*," *Review of English Studies* 60 (2009): 538–560; Eric Weiskott, "Three Beowulf Cruces: *Healgamen, Fremu, Sigemunde*," *Notes and Queries* 58 (2011): 5–6; Erin Sebo and Cassandra Schilling, "Modthryth and the Problem of Peace-Weavers: Women and Political Power in Early Medieval England," *English Studies* 102 (2021): 637–650.

§39. Lines 1963-1998: Beowulf is finally reunited with Hygelac. He and his retainers are seated in Hygelac's hall. Hygd serves them mead and Hygelac asks Beowulf how his adventure went. Though Hygelac is a prominent figure in *Beowulf*, who is named by the hero on multiple occasions and mentioned in several digressions concerning his demise, he plays a role in the poem's narrative present only during the scene of hero's home-coming. In all other cases, his actions take place in the past or the future. Additionally, it is worth noting that lines 1987-1998 are the only lines spoken by Hygelac in the poem. Interpretations of Hygelac as a foolish or arrogant king abound in the critical literature, yet such interpretations are not supported by the one speech that this character delivers. In this speech, Hygelac is depicted as a concerned kinsman and an intuitive monotheist, who thanks God for Beowulf's safe return. Before the end of the homecoming scene, Hygelac will also show himself to be a generous lord and kinsman to his nephew, and the narrator will praise their fidelity.

Further Reading: Arthur G. Brodeur, *The Art of Beowulf* (Berkeley: University of California Press, 1959), 78–87; Robert E. Kaske, "Hygelac and Hygd," in *Studies in Old English Literature in Honor of Arthur G. Brodeur*, ed. Stanley B. Greenfield (Eugene: University of Oregon Press, 1963), 200–206; Edward B. Irving Jr., "Heroic Role-Models: Beowulf and Others," in *Heroic Poetry in the Anglo-Saxon Period: Studies in Honor of Jess B. Bessinger, Jr.*, ed. Helen Damico and John Leyerle (Kalamazoo: Western Michigan University Press, 1993), 347–372; Leonard Neidorf, "King Hygelac of the Geats: History, Legend, and *Beowulf*," *Neophilologus* 106 (2022): 461–477.

§40. **Lines 1999-2151**: Beowulf's homecoming speech is the longest speech in the poem. Though long dismissed as a scribal interpolation or a perfunctory summary, the speech is now recognized as a sophisticated rhetorical performance that is integral to the political drama of *Beowulf*. In this speech, Beowulf does not merely relate what transpired in Denmark. He goes out of his way to demonstrate his worldliness, his wisdom, and ultimately his readiness to rule a kingdom. The piety and humility that Beowulf had previously exhibited are here toned down: he now attributes his successes to his own valor rather than to divine intervention. This is the time for Beowulf to take credit for his achievements. It eventually becomes clear that Beowulf's aim is to use his experience in Denmark to convince Hygelac to recognize his worth and elevate his standing. Beowulf thus emphasizes at the beginning of his speech that Hrothgar recognized his worth: when Beowulf arrived in Denmark, he was seated next to Hrothgar's son. Beowulf also relates various details about the courtly etiquette and the high culture maintained at Hrothgar's court. Such details convey to Hygelac the wealth and nobility of the foreign king whose undying gratitude Beowulf has won. Noting the royal women circulating at Heorot, Beowulf takes the opportunity to demonstrate his political perspicacity: he correctly predicts that the diplomatic marriage between Freawaru, Hrothgar's daughter, and Ingeld, the son of the enemy of Hrothgar's father, will fail. This marriage was arranged by Hrothgar in the hope that it would pacify an old and acrimonious feud between the Danes and the Heathobards. Beowulf imagines a scenario in which an old Heathobard goads a young Heathobard to violate the peace by pointing out that a Danish warrior in Freawaru's retinue carries a sword that had been plundered from the corpse of the young man's father (a similarly inciting speech is delivered in the context of the Ingeld story by the legendary hero Starcatherus in Saxo Grammaticus's *Gesta Danorum*). This incitement will lead to murder and then to the collapse of the marriage. The rectitude of Beowulf's prediction is confirmed by the allusions in *Beowulf* and *Widsith* to Ingeld's failed attack on his father-in-law at Heorot. Beowulf then recounts his struggle with Grendel and two revelations emerge in his retelling: Grendel possessed a magical glove into which he wished to thrust Beowulf; and the name of Geatish retainer whom Grendel killed was Hondscioh, a word that means "glove." Hondscioh's name is anomalous in the context of Beowulfian nomenclature: no other character bears a name like his, which does not consist of elements that were used to form early Germanic personal names. Many critics interpret that the proximity between Hondscioh and Grendel's glove, two details revealed within ten lines of each other, as a sign that Hondscioh's name was intended as some kind of humorous pun. Yet Beowulf is here giving the name of his slain retainer, a man who was dear to him; this is not a jocular moment. A more plausible explanation for Hondscioh's anomalous name and its proximity to Grendel's glove is that Hondscioh became the name of Beowulf's slain retainer through an aural misunderstanding of an earlier poem in the *Beowulf* tradition wherein both *glof* ("glove") and *hondscioh* ("glove") had been used in reference to Grendel's glove. An auditor mistook *hondscioh* as the name of Grendel's victim and thus a character named Hondscioh was born. After recounting his victories over Grendel and Grendel's mother, Beowulf concludes his speech by praising Hrothgar's generosity, noting that he was amply rewarded for his achievements, and ceding ownership of all his winnings to Hygelac, on whom all his favor will ultimately depend. Given the earlier allusions to treachery among kinsmen and Heremod's killing of his most prominent retainers (for fear that they might usurp him), there is an element of suspense as the speech ends and Beowulf puts his future in Hygelac's hands. Beowulf has achieved lasting fame, earned the support of Hrothgar, and performed valorous deeds that far exceed those of his uncle. How will Hygelac treat his formidable nephew?

Further Reading: Marilyn M. Carens, "Handscóh and Grendel: The Motif of the Hand in *Beowulf*," in *Aeolian Harps: Essays in Literature in Honor of Maurice Browning Cramer*, ed. Donna G. Fricke and Douglas C. Fricke (Bowling Green: Bowling Green University Press, 1976), 39–55; Edward B. Irving Jr., "Beowulf Comes Home," in *Acts of Interpretation: The Text in Its Contexts, 700–1600: Essays on Medieval and*

Renaissance Literature in Honor of E. Talbot Donaldson, ed. Mary J. Carruthers and Elizabeth D. Kirk (Norman, OK: Pilgrim Books, 1982), 129–143; Robin Waugh, "Competitive Narrators in the Homecoming Scene of *Beowulf*," *Journal of Narrative Technique* 25 (1995): 202–222; John W. Schwetman, "Beowulf's Return: The Hero's Account of His Adventures among the Danes," *Medieval Perspectives* 13 (1998): 136–148; Frederick M. Biggs, "Hondscioh and Æschere in *Beowulf*," *Neophilologus* 87 (2003): 635–652; Haruko Momma, "The Education of Beowulf and the Affair of the Leisure Class," in *Verbal Encounters: Anglo-Saxon and Old Norse Studies for Roberta Frank*, ed. Antonina Harbus and Russell Poole (Toronto: University of Toronto Press, 2005), 163–182; John M. Hill, *The Narrative Pulse of Beowulf: Arrivals and Departures* (Toronto: University of Toronto Press, 2008), 65–69; Andrew M. Pfrenger, "Grendel's *Glof*: *Beowulf* line 2085 Reconsidered," *Philological Quarterly* 87 (2008): 209–235; Edward Currie, "Political Ideals, Monstrous Counsel, and the Literary Imagination in *Beowulf*," in *Imagination and Fantasy in the Middle Ages and Early Modern Time: Projections, Dreams, Monsters, and Illusions*, ed. Albrecht Classen, vol. 24 (Berlin: De Gruyter, 2020), 275–302; Leonard Neidorf, "The Origin of Hondscioh: Grendel's Glove and the *Beowulf* Tradition," *Studia Neophilologica* 95 (2023): 342-350.

§41. Lines 2152-2199: Following his speech, Beowulf orders a standard, a helmet, a mail-shirt, and a sword to be presented to Hygelac. He then explains that these items constitute the war-gear of Heorogar, the man who ruled Denmark prior to Hrothgar. When Heorogar died, he gave these items not to his own son Heoroweard but to his brother Hrothgar. As it happens, the Danish throne also passed directly from Heorogar to

Hrothgar. The implication is clear: the possessor of these items has been designated as the king's preferred successor for the Danish throne. Hrothgar's gift of them to Beowulf expresses his desire to reward the hero with royal authority. Beowulf's speech, though indirect and courteous (it is called a *ġyd*, a word applied to riddles and parables), nevertheless makes clear to Hygelac the magnitude of the reward that his achievements deserve. Hygelac comprehends the message: at the end of this passage, after Hygelac has received numerous horses and treasures and Hygd has received Wealhtheow's fabulous torque, Hygelac essentially establishes Beowulf as a subordinate king of the Geatish realm. Hygelac gives to Beowulf the sword of Hrethel, a kingdom of seven thousand hides, a hall, and a throne. Hygelac will remain the primary king of the realm, but Beowulf will be his subordinate co-ruler. It appears that Beowulf now holds in relation to Hygelac the position that Hrothulf holds in relation to Hrothgar. A comparison between these two pairs of uncles and nephews is perhaps implicit in the narrator's comment that the behavior of Beowulf and Hygelac illustrates the correct way for kinsmen to behave toward each other (lines 2166b–2171). Hygelac's decision to endow Beowulf with royal authority is made all the more remarkable by the revelation that Beowulf was considered unpromising in his youth (lines 2183b–2189). The hero's "inglorious youth," as it has come to be called, is a familiar folkloric motif, and some critics argue that its introduction at this point in the narrative contradicts the earlier statement that Geatish elders recognized Beowulf's strength and encouraged his trip to Denmark. The apparent contradiction is resolved if the passage is understood to mean that Beowulf was not initially considered a promising candidate for kingship. There were other noblemen in the Geatish royal family with better claims to

COMMENTARY

kingship. Yet Beowulf's adventure in Denmark demonstrated that he deserves to be king, and thus the period of the hero's youth satisfactorily concludes with his ascension to a position of royal authority in Geatland.

Further Reading: Kemp Malone, "Young Beowulf," *Journal of English and Germanic Philology* 36 (1937): 21–23; Adrien Bonjour, "Young Beowulf's Inglorious Period," *Anglia* 70 (1951): 339–344; George J. Engelhardt, "On the Sequence of Beowulf's *Geogoð*," *Modern Language Notes* 68 (1953): 91–95; Norman E. Eliason, "Beowulf's Inglorious Youth," *Studies in Philology* 76 (1979): 101–108; Stephanie Hollis, "Beowulf and the Succession," *Parergon* 1 (1983): 39–54; Raymond P. Tripp, Jr., "Did Beowulf Have an 'Inglorious Youth'?," *Studia Neophilologica* 61 (1989): 129–143; Frederick M. Biggs, "The Politics of Succession in *Beowulf* and Anglo-Saxon England," *Speculum* 80 (2005): 709–741; Scott Gwara, "Paradigmatic Wisdom and the Native Genre *Giedd* in Old English," *Studi Medievali* 53 (2012): 783–852; Francis Leneghan, *The Dynastic Drama of Beowulf* (Cambridge: D. S. Brewer, 2020), 129–134.

§42. Lines 2200-2311: *Beowulf* is widely considered a work with a bipartite structure. Part I (lines 1-2199) focuses on the hero's youth and his rise to kingship; Part II (lines 2200-3182) focuses on the hero's old age and his death. The narrative style of Part II differs from that of Part I in that it becomes even less linear and more temporally disjointed. In the space of ten lines, fifty years elapse and the narrative is suddenly resituated in a time when Beowulf is an old man and the sole king of Geatland, having ascended to the throne after Heardred died (the circumstances of the death of Heardred and the other

311

Geatish kings are revealed later). Things went well in Beo-
wulf's kingdom, we are told, until it was threatened by a
dragon. The narrator then digresses to explain both the history
of the dragon's hostility and the history of the dragon's treas-
ure. The text is exceptionally damaged at this point, but the
essence of the narrative remains fairly clear: a slave breaks into
the dragon's hoard and steals a precious cup; the slave, who
had previously gotten into some trouble, presents the cup to
his master in the hope that it would save him from a flogging;
the master and the slave return to the hoard and are detected
by the dragon, who will express his displeasure at the disturb-
ance by ravaging Geatland and burning down Beowulf's hall.
As these details are gradually revealed, the narrator digresses
to relate the origins of the dragon's treasure: it was deposited
in the barrow three hundred years earlier by the last survivor
of an exterminated race, who delivers an elegiac speech com-
manding the earth to hold his people's treasures; the dragon
finds the last survivor's treasure-hoard and guards it for the
next three centuries. Although the *Beowulf* poet represents the
last survivor and the dragon as two distinct entities, it is likely
that in the antecedent legendary tradition the last survivor ac-
tually became the dragon after his death. The somewhat cen-
sorious author of *Beowulf* was evidently uncomfortable with
the idea of a man posthumously morphing into a dragon and
consequently obscured this aspect of the poem's tradition. The
poet's concern about the pagan connotations of the last survi-
vor, his burial of treasure, and his draconic nature is perhaps
registered in the description of his wealth as "heathen gold"
(*hæðen gold*). The use of this word, which had previously been
applied to Grendel, suggests that the last survivor is heathen
in a way that Beowulf and the other intuitive monotheists are
not. Though familiar today, the poet's conception of the

dragon as a flying and fire-breathing creature, intent on ter-
rorizing an entire populace, is rather uncommon in medieval
literature and thus results in a creature that is significantly dif-
ferent from some of its nearest analogues.

Further Reading: G. V. Smithers, *The Making of Beowulf*
(Durham: University of Durham, 1961); Hilda R. Ellis Da-
vidson, *Gods and Myths of Northern Europe* (Harmondsworth,
UK: Penguin, 1964), 161; Kathryn Hume, "The Theme and
Structure of *Beowulf*," *Studies in Philology* 72 (1975): 1–27;
Thomas Pettitt, "Beowulf: The Mark of the Beast and the Bal-
ance of Frenzy," *Neuphilologische Mitteilungen* (1976): 526-
535; Raymond P. Tripp, Jr., *More about the Fight with the
Dragon: Beowulf, 2208b-3182: Commentary, Edition, and
Translation* (Lanham, MD: University Press of America,
1983), 60; Theodore M. Andersson, "The Thief in *Beowulf*,"
Speculum 59 (1984): 493–508; Peter C. Braeger, "Connota-
tions of (Earm) Sceapen: *Beowulf* ll. 2228-2229 and the Shape-
Shifting Dragon," *Essays in Literature* 13 (1986): 327–328;
Tom Shippey, "Structure and Unity," in *A Beowulf Handbook*,
ed. Robert E. Bjork and John D. Niles (Lincoln: University of
Nebraska Press, 1997), 149–174; Christine Rauer, *Beowulf and
the Dragon: Parallels and Analogues* (Cambridge: D. S. Brewer,
2000); Joseph Harris, "Heroic Poetry and Elegy: *Beowulf*'s Lay
of the Last Survivor," in *Heldenzeiten—Heldenräume: Wann
und wo spielen Heldendichtung und Heldensage?*, ed. Johannes
Keller and Florian Kragl (Wien: Fassbaender, 2007), 27–41;
Thomas Klein, "*Stonc æfter stane* (*Beowulf*, l. 2288a): Philol-
ogy, Narrative Context, and the Waking Dragon," *Journal of
English and Germanic Philology* 106 (2007): 22–44; Sophie
Marshall, "Digression, Coherence, and a Missing Cup in

Beowulf," Zeitschrift Für Literaturwissenschaft Und Linguistik 48 (2018): 167–192.

§43. Lines 2312-2354a: Like Grendel and Grendel's mother, the dragon attacks at night and then returns to its lair in the belief that it would be safe there. The narrator, always keen to identify points of irony, notes that the dragon's expectation would soon be proven false. During the dragon's nocturnal attack, it burned down the houses of many of the Geats and it even destroyed Beowulf's own hall, the symbol of his rule and authority (recall that Scyld Scefing subordinated neighboring peoples by taking away their mead-benches—in other words, destroying their halls). The loss of his hall inspires in Beowulf uncharacteristically dark thoughts: he wonders if he has angered God by transgressing "against the old law" (*ofer ealde riht*). The phrase *eald riht* is evidently the poet's name for the code of intuitive morality to which virtuous pagans could adhere without access to biblical knowledge. What the poet terms "old law" here appears essentially to be the concept of natural law; it is the behavior that the poem's intuitive monotheists imagine to be pleasing to the singular deity presiding over human affairs. Significantly, the text offers no reason to believe that Beowulf has actually violated natural law or angered God. He simply does not yet know the real cause of the dragon's enmity (he learns it at line 2403). Beowulf's inclination to take responsibility and consider the possibility of his own guilt is best construed as a sign of this character's humility and piety, not a sign of his genuine guilt. His next reaction is to resolve to fight the dragon in single combat. He will risk his own life in this dangerous endeavor without risking the lives of his men. This reaction is likewise best construed not as a sign of the hero's arrogance or imprudence, but as a sign of his courage and selflessness.

Further Reading: Charles Donahue, "*Beowulf*, Ireland and the Natural Good," *Traditio* 7 (1951): 263–277; Morton W. Bloomfield, "Patristics and Old English Literature: Notes on Some Poems," *Comparative Literature* 14 (1962): 36–43; Joseph L. Baird, "The Uses of Ignorance: *Beowulf* 435, 2330," *Notes and Queries* 14 (1967): 6–8; Dennis Cronan, "*Beowulf*, the Gaels, and the Recovery of the Pre-Conversion Past," *Anglo-Saxon* 1 (2007): 137–180; Ruth Wehlau, "Beowulf's Dark Thoughts: Heremod, Hrethel, and Exempla of the Mind," in *Darkness, Depression, and Descent in Anglo-Saxon England*, ed. Ruth Wehlau (Berlin: de Gruyter, 2019), 135–154; Francis Leneghan, *The Dynastic Drama of Beowulf* (Cambridge: D. S. Brewer, 2020), 215–216.

§44. Lines 2354b-2424: The narrator digresses to recount other conflicts that Beowulf survived after cleansing Heorot of its monsters. Beowulf, we now learn, was present at the failed raid in Frisia in which Hygelac was killed. Though Beowulf lost his beloved uncle and king on this occasion, he still managed to emerge heroically from the battle, swimming back to Geatland with thirty sets of armor on his arm. The detail suggests that Beowulf suitably avenged his king's death by killing an appropriate number of lesser men (thirty) and plundering their corpses. The valuable war-gear with which he returns establishes that Hygelac's death was not in vain and was not left unavenged. We then learn that Beowulf, upon his return to Geatland, was offered the throne, but could not be persuaded to rule before Heardred, the son of Hygelac, and opted instead to serve as an advisor to the young king. A contrast is probably implied between the peaceful Geatish succession following Hygelac's death and the tumultuous Danish succession following Hrothgar's death. Beowulf will not become sole king of Geatland until Heardred loses his life due to his involvement in a feud between members of the Swedish royal family: Heardred permits Eanmund and Eadgils, the exiled sons of Ohthere, to take refuge from the Swedish king Onela (Ohthere's brother) at the Geatish court; then Onela's forces invade Geatland and Heardred is killed for his hospitality (Eanmund, we later learn, was also killed in this invasion and by the hand of Weohstan, the father of Wiglaf). In the aftermath, Onela is said to have allowed (*let*) Beowulf to rule Geatland. The words can be construed to mean that he installed Beowulf on the throne, but the humiliation implied is somewhat difficult to credit; the words may simply mean that by killing Heardred, Onela cleared the path for Beowulf's kingship. In any event, Beowulf soon avenges the death of his cousin: he provides Eadgils, the surviving son of Ohthere, with the men and weapons required for him to kill Onela and take the Swedish throne. Whether Beowulf himself accompanied Eadgils on this mission is not made clear here or elsewhere. The narrator, having explained that Beowulf both survived the battles in which Hygelac and Heardred lost their lives and successfully avenged his kinsmen, returns to the narrative present by acknowledging that Beowulf would not survive on this occasion. The slave that stole the treasure is forced to lead Beowulf and the eleven warriors comprising his retinue to the dragon's lair, described as an underground barrow (*hlæw*) near the ocean and full of treasures. Beowulf sits on the headland and senses that his death is imminent. The narrator confirms that his expectation is correct. The hero's decision to fight valiantly despite his recognition that he is fated to die is paralleled elsewhere in Germanic heroic literature, for instance, by Sigmundr in *Vǫlsunga saga* and Hagen in the *Nibelungenlied*.

Further Reading: Francis P. Magoun, Jr., "Béowulf and King Hygelác in the Netherlands: Lost Anglo-Saxon Verse Stories about this Event," *English Studies* 35 (1954): 193–204; Sherman Kuhn, "*Beowulf* and the Life of Beowulf: A Study in Epic Structure," in *Studies in the Language, Literature, and Culture of the Middle Ages and Later*, ed. E. Bagby Atwood and Archibald A. Hill (Austin: University of Texas Press, 1969), 243–264; R. T. Farrell, *Beowulf, Swedes and Geats* (London: Viking Society for Northern Research, 1972); John McNamara, "Beowulf and Hygelac: Problems for Fiction in History," *Rice University Studies* 62 (1976): 55–63; Richard North, "Saxo and the Swedish Wars in *Beowulf*," in *Saxo Grammaticus: Tra storiografia e letteratura*, ed. Carlo Santini (Roma: Il calamo, 1992), 175–188; Augustine Thompson, "Rethinking Hygelac's Raid," *English Language Notes* 38 (2001): 9–16; Frederick M. Biggs, "*Beowulf* and Some Fictions of the Geatish Succession," *Anglo-Saxon England* 32 (2003): 55–77; Frederick M. Biggs, "History and Fiction in the Frisian Raid," in *The Dating of Beowulf: A Reassessment*, ed. Leonard Neidorf (Cambridge: D. S. Brewer, 2014), 138–156; James W. Earl, "The Swedish Wars in *Beowulf*," *Journal of English and Germanic Philology* 114 (2015): 32–60.

§45. Lines 2425-2537: Sensing that his own death is near, Beowulf delivers a lengthy speech reflecting on the deaths of the earlier Geatish kings. At age seven, Beowulf entered into a relationship of fosterage with Hrethel, the dynastic founder, who loved him no less than his own sons, Herebeald,

Hæthcyn, and Hygelac. Hrethel's oldest son, Herebeald, was the first to die: his tragic death occurred when Hæthcyn accidentally missed his mark and shot his older brother with an arrow. Hrethel resented Hæthcyn, but still could not bring himself to avenge Herebeald's accidental death on his own son. The combination of grief and shame causes Hrethel to die of sadness. Beowulf states that Hrethel "chose God's light" (*Godes lēoht ġecēas*), a phrase that might suggest that Hrethel merited heavenly reward for restraining himself from an act of kin-slaying (recall that Unferth is condemned to hell by Beowulf for killing his own brothers). The story of Hæthcyn's accidental killing of Herebeald is almost certainly related in some way to the story of Hǫðr's inadvertent killing of Baldr recounted in Snorri Sturluson's *Prose Edda* and other sources. The stories not only share a similarity of names (Hǫðr is cognate with the first element of Hæthcyn, Baldr is cognate with the second element of Herebeald), but also a similarity of results, with the death of Baldr bringing unprecedented grief to his father and the other gods. After Herebeald and Hrethel die, hostility between the Swedes and the Geats takes the life of Hæthcyn. Fortunately, Hæthcyn's death at the hands of Ongentheow would go on to be avenged by Hygelac and his men (Wulf and Eofor, as we later learn in the speech of the Geatish messenger). Hygelac's death, in turn, would go on to be avenged by Beowulf himself, who takes pride in recalling how he served his lord well, obviated the need for him to recruit mercenaries, and crushed the life out of Dæghrefn with his bare hands. Dæghrefn, bearer of a characterristically Frankish name, is apparently the Frankish champion who killed Hygelac and plundered his corpse of the golden torque that Wealhtheow had given to Beowulf. Here we learn that Beowulf recovered this torque (*brēostweorðung*) from the corpse of

Dæghrefn, preventing him from delivering it and other treasures to the Frisian king. Beowulf concludes his speech by declaring that he will fight the dragon and acknowledging, with regret, that he will have to use a sword and a shield in this conflict, as he sees no other way to contend with a fire-breathing dragon. He rules out the possibility of retreat and vows to win gold or die. The speech reflects the somber and resolute character of Beowulf's mind at this moment. It is elegiac in its recollection of the deaths of loved ones, yet it is also a formal boast that commits Beowulf to a course of action and is intended to inspire its speaker through the recollection of prior achievements.

Further Reading: Ursula Dronke, "*Beowulf* and Ragnarǫk," *Saga-Book* 17 (1969): 302–325; John C. Pope, "Beowulf's Old Age," in *Philological Essays: Studies in Old and Middle English Language and Literature in Honour of Herbert Dean Meritt*, ed. James L. Rosier (The Hague: Mouton, 1970), 55–64; John McNamara, "*Beowulf*, 2490-2508a," *The Explicator* 32 (1974): 1–2; Rosemary Woolf, "The Ideal of Men Dying with their Lord in the *Germania* and *The Battle of Maldon*," *Anglo-Saxon England* 5 (1976): 63–81; Paul Cavill, "A Note on *Beowulf*, Lines 2490-2509," *Neophilologus* 67 (1983): 599–604; Linda Georgianna, "King Hrethel's Sorrow and the Limits of Heroic Action in *Beowulf*," *Speculum* 62 (1987): 829–850; Thomas D. Hill, "The 'Variegated Obit' as an Historiographic Motif in Old English Poetry and Anglo-Latin Historical Literature," *Traditio* 44 (1988): 101–124; Joseph Harris, "Beowulf's Last Words," *Speculum* 67 (1992): 1–32; Joseph Harris, "A Nativist Approach to *Beowulf*: The Case of Germanic Elegy," in *Companion to Old English Poetry*, ed. Henk Aertsen and Rolf H. Bremmer Jr. (Amsterdam: VU University Press, 1994), 45–62;

Heather O'Donoghue, "What Has Baldr to Do with Lamech? The Lethal Shot of a Blind Man in Old Norse Myth and Jewish Exegetical Traditions," *Medium Ævum* 72 (2003): 82–107; Andy Orchard, *A Critical Companion to Beowulf* (Cambridge: D. S. Brewer, 2003), 116–119; Richard North, *The Origins of Beowulf: From Vergil to Wiglaf* (Oxford: Oxford University Press, 2006), 198–202; Gale R. Owen-Crocker, "Beast Men: Wulf and Eofor and the Mythic Significance of Names in *Beowulf*," in *Myth in Early Northwest Europe*, ed. Stephen O. Glosecki (Tempe: Arizona Center for Medieval and Renaissance Studies, 2007), 257–280; Leonard Neidorf, "The Gepids in *Beowulf*," *ANQ* 34 (2021): 3–6.

§46. **Lines 2538-2601**: Beowulf's fight with the dragon occurs over the course of three rounds. The narration of the fight is more complex and more difficult to follow than the narration of the hero's fights against Grendel or Grendel's mother. In the first round, Beowulf approaches the dragon's barrow and finds that a brook emanates from it. The brook, which is heated by the dragon's fire, is too hot to be traversed and so prevents Beowulf from entering the barrow and fighting the dragon there. The hero makes his presence known through a resounding utterance and thereby lures the dragon out of the inner recesses of his barrow. The dragon's fiery breath is first released from the barrow; Beowulf swings his shield in response; then the dragon itself emerges to fight its human challenger. Beowulf's iron shield successfully protects him from the dragon's flames, but his sword fails to penetrate the dragon's bone. Enraged by the failed strike, the dragon responds by releasing his fiery breath and engulfing the hero in flames. Beowulf is not killed in the flames, but the sight of him surrounded by flames nevertheless convinces all of his retainers (with the exception of Wiglaf) that the battle is hopeless. The cowardly retainers retreat to the woods to preserve their lives, while Wiglaf steps forward to aid his lord and kinsman.

Further Reading: William Witherle Lawrence, "The Dragon and His Lair in *Beowulf*," *PMLA* 33 (1918): 547–583; Kenneth Sisam, "Beowulf's Fight with the Dragon," *Review of English Studies* 9 (1958): 129–140; Thomas L. Keller, "The Dragon in *Beowulf* Revisited," *Aevum* 55 (1981): 218–228; Michael Lapidge, "*Beowulf*, Aldhelm, the *Liber Monstrorum* and Wessex," *Studi Medievali* 23 (1982): 151–192; Paul Sorrell, "The Approach to the Dragon-Fight in *Beowulf*, Aldhelm, and the 'traditions folkloriques' of Jacques Le Goff," *Parergon* 12 (1994): 57–87; Maria Elena Ruggerini, "L'eroe germanico contro avversari mostruosi: tra testo e iconografia," in *La funzione dell'eroe germanico: storicità, metafora, paradigma; Atti del Convegno internazionale di studio Roma, 6–8 maggio 1993*, ed. Teresa Pàroli (Rome: Calamo, 1995), 201–257; Howard Shilton, "The Nature of Beowulf's Dragon," *Bulletin of the John Rylands Library* 79 (1997): 67–78; Christine Rauer, *Beowulf and the Dragon: Parallels and Analogues* (Cambridge: D. S. Brewer, 2000).

§47. Lines 2602-2668: Wiglaf is introduced as the son of Weohstan, the kinsman of Ælfhere, and a prince of the Scylfings (*lēod Scylfinga*). Weohstan is the slayer of Eanmund; Ælfhere is unknown (the father of Walther of Aquitaine bore the same name, but there is no reason to connect him to Wiglaf); and as a *lēod Scylfinga*, Wiglaf is evidently both a Swedish nobleman and a Geatish retainer, who is about to become the next king of Geatland. He is also a member of the

Wægmundings, a kin group to which Beowulf belongs as well. It has been speculated that Wiglaf is Beowulf's sister's son, and that this relationship helps to explain the extraordinary strength of their bond. In any event, all of the details about Wiglaf suggest his derivation from antecedent legendary tradition, in particular, from heroic narratives about strife between kinsmen in the Swedish and the Geatish royal families. He is far from the simplistic figure of the devoted thegn and kinsman that could have been invented for his role in the present narrative. Wiglaf's sword is identified, moreover, as the "heirloom of Eanmund" (*Ēanmundes lāf*): it was plundered from Eanmund's corpse by Weohstan, who went on to present it to Onela, the uncle of Eanmund, from whom Eanmund had taken refuge in Geatland; Onela, grateful that Weohstan slew his kinsman, rewards Weohstan for the deed by granting him possession of Eanmund's war-gear. Weohstan held onto it until his son was ready to use it; Wiglaf is now about to bear it into battle for the first time. Before he enters into battle, Wiglaf delivers a fairly conventional speech of incitement to the other retainers. He reminds them of the generosity of Beowulf, who provided them with mead and rings and war-gear, and surely expected their undying loyalty in return. The faithless retainers have broken their oaths to risk their lives in the service of Beowulf. Wiglaf affirms that he would rather be killed by the dragon's flames than shamefully return home bearing the war-gear that his dead lord gave him. Wiglaf then enters the fray and exhorts Beowulf to remember a boast from his youth in which he swore never to allow his glory to falter (*dōm ġedrēosan*). Since Wiglaf is a young man and Beowulf would have delivered this boast fifty years ago, it would appear that Wiglaf is familiar with tales of Beowulf's youthful exploits, which included the same sort of speeches that were depicted in Part I of the present poem.

Further Reading: Robert E. Kaske, "Weohstan's Sword," *Modern Language Notes* 75 (1960): 465–468; Norman E. Eliason, "Beowulf, Wiglaf and the Wægmundings," *Anglo-Saxon England* 7 (1978): 95–105; Rolf H. Bremmer Jr., "The Importance of Kinship: Uncle and Nephew in *Beowulf*," *Amsterdamer Beiträge zur älteren Germanistik* 15 (1980): 21–38; Dennis Cronan, "Wiglaf's Sword," *Studia Neophilologica* 65 (1993): 129–139; Michael D. C. Drout, "Blood and Deeds: The Inheritance Systems in *Beowulf*," *Studies in Philology* 104 (2007): 199–226; James W. Earl, "The Swedish Wars in *Beowulf*," *Journal of English and Germanic Philology* 114 (2015): 32–60.

§48. Lines 2669-2723: In the second round (*ōðre sīðe*) of the fight, the dragon lets out a surge of flames that destroys Wiglaf's shield and forces him to take cover under Beowulf's iron shield. Beowulf strikes the dragon with the sword Nægling (perhaps to be identified as Hrethel's old sword, which Hygelac gave to Beowulf during his homecoming) only to find out that the sword breaks under the pressure of his strength. The narrator's remark that Beowulf's hand was too strong to swing swords without breaking them recalls the several earlier passages concerning his refusal to use swords and his opponents' immunity to swords. The whole collection of passages seems to reflect the rationalizing effort of an aristocratic poet (or earlier aristocratic poets in the same tradition), who placed great value and emphasis on swords yet needed to explain why the hero in these folkloric narratives should repeatedly triumph without a storied sword in hand. In the third round (*þriddan sīðe*) of the fight, the dragon's fangs connect with Beowulf's neck, biting him in the exposed area between his helmet and his mail-shirt. Wiglaf thrusts his sword into the dragon's abdomen, allowing his hand to be burnt while doing so. Beowulf, though wounded, delivers the fatal blow: he takes a dagger (*wællseaxe*) out of his mail-shirt and uses it to carve the dragon through its middle (probably not cutting the dragon into two pieces, but making a large enough incision across the abdominal region to end its life). Bloodied and poisoned, Beowulf recognizes that he is about to die. He takes a seat near a wall and, with his mortality at its limit, surveys the ancient and enduring "works of giants" (*enta geweorc*) that surround him. Wiglaf sprinkles water on Beowulf to revive him as he prepares to deliver his final speech. The reference to the works of giants prior to Beowulf's final speech recalls the allusions to these constructions (Roman ruins? Prehistoric earthworks?) in other Old English elegiac poems such as *The Wanderer* and *The Ruin*, where they function as symbols of the world's mutability.

Further Reading: J. R. Hulbert, "Surmises Concerning the *Beowulf* Poet's Source," *Journal of English and Germanic Philology* 50 (1951): 11–18; Taylor Culbert, "The Narrative Function of Swords in Beowulf," *Journal of English and Germanic Philology* 59 (1960): 13–20; P. J. Frankis, "The Thematic Significance of *Enta Geweorc* and Related Imagery in *The Wanderer*," *Anglo-Saxon England* 2 (1973): 253–269; Emily Thornbury, "*Eald Enta Geweorc* and the Relics of Empire: Revisiting the Dragon's Lair in *Beowulf*," *Quaestio Insularis* 1 (2000): 82–92; Christopher Grocock, "*Enta Geweorc*: *The Ruin* and its Contexts Reconsidered," in *The Material Culture of the Built Environment in the Anglo-Saxon World*, ed.

Maren Clegg Hyer and Gale R. Owen-Crocker (Liverpool: Liverpool University Press, 2017), 13–36; on the nature of the dragon and the fight against him, see the references in §46.

§49. Lines 2724-2792a: Beowulf begins his final speech, which has notable affinities to other "death songs" in early Germanic poetry, by reflecting on his life. He wishes he had a son to inherit his war-gear at this moment. Though Beowulf will soon designate Wiglaf as the inheritor of his property and his presumed successor, several critics have perceived Beowulf's childlessness as a serious character flaw, a sign that he failed to make provisions for his country's future. It seems likelier, however, that Beowulf's apparent failure to marry and procreate simply reflects the fact that he is an originally fictional hero, who had been inserted into a historical milieu and made the kinsman of genuinely historical figures. A poet with some respect for historical and dynastic facts might consequently hesitate to introduce further complications into the record by attaching a wife and descendants to a fictional character. Another reason for the omission of a wife and child from Beowulf's life could be the poet's evident intention to make Beowulf a wholly admirable and rather uncomplicated and unconventional hero. The typical hero in migration-period legend is compelled by circumstances to kill kinsmen or break oaths. Caught between conflicting ethical imperatives, the hero is neither good nor bad, but simply does what duty demands, no matter how horrific it may be. In this speech, Beowulf rejoices that he lived a life unstained by the two standard heroic transgressions: he broke no oaths and killed no kinsmen. He is pleased, moreover, that God need not blame him for such transgressions when he dies. The notion that God finds kin-slaying particularly objectionable, and that

325

posthumous reward depends on whether one commits this transgression, resonates with various other passages in the poem (the digressions on Cain and Abel, the hero's condemnation of Unferth to hell for killing his brothers, Hrethel's heavenly reward for his restraint). It is possible, moreover, that the very decision to construct an epic around a folkloric hero like Beowulf, rather than a legendary and transgressive hero like Hengest or Ingeld, reflects the poet's discomfort with the prospect of relating an amoral narrative that culminates in a justified transgression. After reflecting on his unconventional life, Beowulf instructs Wiglaf to plunder the dragon's hoard so that the sight of the treasures won might help him to die more easily. Wiglaf hurries to the hoard and finds it full of ancient valuables—the fantasy of a culture that prizes such objects above all other material goods. A golden standard illuminates the floor of the hall and enables him to see the extraordinary riches it contains. Wiglaf fills his arms with items "at his own discretion" (*sylfes dōme*); the phrase contrasts his unconstrained plundering of the hoard with the ritual gifting of treasure from lord to retainer that would normally occur at the lord's discretion and involve a single item. Wiglaf hurries back to Beowulf and sprinkles him with water again to revive him.

Further Reading: Bertha S. Phillpotts, "Wyrd and Providence in Anglo-Saxon Thought," *Essays and Studies* 13 (1928): 7–27; Thomas D. Hill, "The Confession of Beowulf and the Structure of *Volsunga Saga*," in *The Vikings: Papers from the Cornell Lecture Series Held to Coincide with the Viking Exhibition 1980–1981*, ed. Robert T. Farrell (London: Phillimore, 1982), 165–179; Stephanie Hollis, "Beowulf and the Succession," *Parergon* 1 (1983): 39–54; Theodore M. Andersson, *A Preface to the Nibelungenlied* (Stanford: Stanford

University Press, 1987), 3–16; Joseph Harris, "Beowulf's Last Words," *Speculum* 67 (1992): 1–32; Susan E. Deskis, "An Addendum to Beowulf's Last Words," *Medium Ævum* 63 (1994): 301–305; Frederick M. Biggs, "*Beowulf* and Some Fictions of the Geatish Succession," *Anglo-Saxon England* 32 (2003): 55–77; Leonard Neidorf, "Beowulf and Freawaru," *The Explicator* 79 (2021): 182–187.

§50. Lines 2793b-2820: Beowulf thanks God for permitting him to see the treasure, using three different terms for the deity (*frēa, wuldurcyning, ēce dryhten*) over the course of three lines. The hymnic quality of these lines reiterates the characterization of Beowulf as a pious hero and an intuitive monotheist—significantly so, given their proximity to the poem's most significant suggestion of the hero's salvation. He then instructs Wiglaf to arrange for the construction of a massive grave-mound on the promontory, which will be known as "Beowulf's Barrow" (*Bīowulfes Biorh*) and will serve as a landmark for seafarers. The conception of Beowulf's Barrow reflects the reality of such landmarks in the English and Scandinavian landscape. Beowulf then takes a "golden ring" (*hring gyldenne*) from his neck and gives it to Wiglaf along with his helmet and mail-shirt. Perhaps this golden ring is the same torque that Wealhtheow gave to Beowulf, and which Beowulf subsequently gave to Hygd, who gave it to Hygelac, who lost it briefly to Dæghrefn, who lost it in turn to Beowulf, who held onto it for the next fifty years. In any event, the gesture recalls Heorogar's gifting of his war-gear to Hrothgar (his successor) rather than Heoroweard (his son), wherein the transfer of property symbolizes the transfer of authority. Beowulf is thus apparently designating Wiglaf as his successor, and this suggestion is reinforced by his statement to Wiglaf that he is his only surviving kinsman. Implicit in the statement is that an idea that kinship imposes certain obligations on Wiglaf that need not be stated. When Beowulf dies, the narrator states that his soul departed from his breast to seek "the judgment of the righteous" (*sōðfæstra dōm*). The phrase has attracted considerable debate. Had it appeared in an explicitly Christian context, there would be little doubt that it indicated the soul's salvation. Because Beowulf is not a Christian, doubt can be raised about the theological plausibility of his soul reaching heaven. Regardless of the notion's orthodoxy, the *Beowulf* poet seems comfortable suggesting that his intuitive monotheists could reach heaven if they followed their better intuitions and chose eternal counsels.

Further Reading: Marie Padgett Hamilton, "The Religious Principle in Beowulf," *PMLA* 61 (1946): 309–330; Hilda R. Ellis Davidson, "The Hill of the Dragon: Anglo-Saxon Burial Mounds in Literature and Archaeology," *Folklore* 61 (1950): 169–185; E. G. Stanley, "*Hæþenra Hyht* in *Beowulf*," in *Studies in Old English Literature in Honor of Arthur G. Brodeur*, ed. Stanley B. Greenfield (Eugene: University of Oregon Books, 1963), 136–151; Stanley B. Greenfield, "Beowulf and the Judgement of the Righteous," in *Learning and Literature in Anglo-Saxon England: Studies Presented to Peter Clemoes*, ed. Michael Lapidge and Helmut Gneuss (Cambridge: Cambridge University Press, 1985), 393–407; Sam Newton, *The Origins of Beowulf and the Pre-Viking Kingdom of East Anglia* (Cambridge: D. S. Brewer, 1993), 43–53; Paul Cavill, "Christianity and Theology in *Beowulf*," in *The Christian Tradition in Anglo-Saxon England: Approaches to Current Scholarship and Teaching*, ed. Paul Cavill (Woodbridge, UK: D. S. Brewer, 2004), 15–40; James Cahill, "Reconsidering Robinson's Beowulf,"

English Studies 89 (2008): 251–262; on the golden torque, see the references in §26.

§51. Lines 2821-2891: The narrator reflects on what has transpired. Beowulf lies died; the dragon lies dead as well. A sense emerges from the passage that this was a fitting death for the greatest of mortal heroes. He found a worthy adversary and he managed to protect his people. Beowulf died, the narrator notes, in a battle that few men would ever dare to undertake, regardless of how bold they may be. After killing Grendel and Grendel's mother, it would be anticlimactic for Beowulf to meet his end in battle against a Swedish prince. Beowulf died well, losing his life while simultaneously killing the most fearsome creature known to the mythological imagination. Additionally, the hero's death is immediately compensated through the winning of a suitable "quantity of splendid treasures" (*dryhtmāðma dæl*). Beowulf's killer is dead and a royal wergild was paid; the wrong of his death was thus set right twice over. The theme of justice continues to be pursued when the cowardly retainers emerge from the woods and are suitably chastised by Wiglaf, who is first seen splashing water on the dead Beowulf in a poignant and futile attempt to revive his dead lord. God's decision, the narrator remarks, was irreversible—Beowulf died at the time appointed by God. Though the allusion to God's will encourages an attitude of resignation, Wiglaf prefers indignation as he addresses the retainers. He proclaims that the war-gear given by Beowulf to these men—all of it given in the expectation that it would be put to use in their unwavering service to their lord—was clearly wasted when it was given to cowards. Wiglaf states that though he could provide limited support to Beowulf, and though God granted Beowulf the ability to avenge his own death, he still rushed to the aid of his imperiled lord and provided some assistance in the battle. Since the deserters failed to do that, they will be deprived all the privileges they formerly enjoyed, stripped of their land and estates, and exiled from Geatland along with their family members. This harsh punishment for desertion reflects the intense and sacrosanct character of the bond between lord and retainer as depicted in early Germanic poetry, yet parallels in legal writings suggest its historical plausibility as well. Wiglaf's concluding remark, namely that death is better than a life of shame for a warrior, captures well the ethos that pervades the poetry, where those who die valiantly in an honorable cause are celebrated and those who shamefully desert their obligations are treated with contempt.

Further Reading: J. R. R. Tolkien, "*Beowulf*: The Monsters and the Critics," *Proceedings of the British Academy* 22 (1936): 245–295; Adrien Bonjour, "Monsters Crouching and Critics Rampant: Or the *Beowulf* Dragon Debated," *PMLA* 68 (1953): 304–312; Rosemary Woolf, "The Ideal of Men Dying with their Lord in the *Germania* and *The Battle of Maldon*," *Anglo-Saxon England* 5 (1976): 63–81; Joseph Harris, "Love and Death in the *Männerbund:* An essay with special reference to the *Bjarkamál* and *The Battle of Maldon*," in *Heroic Poetry in the Anglo-Saxon Period: Studies in Honor of Jess B. Bessinger, Jr.*, ed. Helen Damico and John Leyerle (Kalamazoo: Medieval Institute Publications, 1993), 77–114; Peter R. Richardson, "Making Thanes: Literature, Rhetoric, and State Formation in Anglo-Saxon England," *Philological Quarterly* 78 (1999): 215–232; Paul Battles, "'Contending Throng' Scenes and the Comitatus Ideal in Old English Poetry, with special attention to *The Battle of Maldon* 122a," *Studia Neophilologica* 83 (2011): 41–53.

§52. Lines 2892-3027: Wiglaf commands a messenger to convey the news of Beowulf's death to the council of warriors who remained behind and hoped for their lord's return. The messenger briefly conveys the essential facts—Beowulf is dead and so is the dragon that killed him—and then launches into a lengthy speech predicting trouble for the Geats from the Franks, Frisians, and Swedes. Now that the formidable king Beowulf is dead, the peoples who have been harboring grudges against the Geats are sure to express their pent-up hostility by bringing invasion, subjugation, enslavement, and exile to their Geatish enemies. The messenger recounts the past events responsible for the Geats' present predicament. Enmity from the Franks and Frisians was earned during Hygelac's failed raid on their territory, an event to which the poem has alluded on several earlier occasions. This event caused the Frankish emperor, here identified as "the Merovingian" (*Merewīoing*), to withdraw his favor from the Geats—a phrase that likely implies cutting them off from trade or gift exchange. Enmity from the Swedes, moreover, dates back at least to the time when Geats and Swedes fought at the battle of Ravenswood: there Ongentheow killed Hæthcyn and threatened to massacre (and perhaps sacrifice) the surrounded Geats, but Hygelac and his army arrived just in time to save the Geats and avenge his brother. The old and fierce king Ongentheow, now on the retreat, puts up a valiant defense but eventually falls in battle against Wulf and Eofor, two of Hygelac's men, though not before he wounded Wulf. Hygelac rewards the men lavishly for their deed, even arranging for his only daughter to marry Eofor—a gesture that has been interpreted as a political miscalculation, though it seems better construed as a sign of the king's laudable generosity. Eofor, after all, killed a man who was not only an enemy king but was also the bane of Hygelac's brother. The dire predictions of national disaster at the end of messenger's speech raise the question: are the Geats about to experience a merely temporary setback or are they about to suffer a more or less permanent loss of their political autonomy? Whatever the exact history of the sixth-century Geats might have been, it seems likely that poets conceptualized this national disaster as a form of annihilation. Stories of a people's annihilation captivated the imaginations of poets during the migration period and after. The destruction of the Burgundians in 436, for instance, inspired legends related in *Vǫlsunga saga*, the *Nibelungenlied*, and the heroic poems of the Poetic Edda.

Further Reading: Stanley B. Greenfield, "Geatish History: Poetic Art and Epic Quality in *Beowulf*," *Neophilologus* 47 (1963): 211–217; Kenneth Sisam, *The Structure of Beowulf* (Oxford: Clarendon Press, 1965), 54–58; Thomas A. Carnicelli, "The Function of the Messenger in *Beowulf*," *Studies in Philology* 72 (1975): 246–257; John Gardner, "Guilt and the World's Complexity: The Murder of Ongentheow and the Slaying of the Dragon," in *Anglo-Saxon Poetry: Essays in Appreciation for John C. McGalliard*, ed. Lewis E. Nicholson and Delores Warwick Frese (Notre Dame: University of Notre Dame Press, 1975), 14–22; Fred C. Robinson, "History, Religion, Culture: The Background Necessary for Teaching *Beowulf*," in *Approaches to Teaching Masterpieces of World Literature*, ed. Jess B. Bessinger Jr. and Robert F. Yeager (New York: Modern Language Association of America, 1984), 107–122; Tom Shippey, "The Merow(ich)ingian Again: *damnatio memoriae* and the *usus scholarum*," in *Latin Learning and English Lore: Studies in Anglo-Saxon Literature for Michael Lapidge*, ed. Katherine O'Brien O'Keeffe and Andy Orchard, 2 vols.

(Toronto: University of Toronto Press, 2005), I: 389–406; Alaric Hall, "Hygelac's Only Daughter: A Present, a Potentate and a Peaceweaver in *Beowulf*," *Studia Neophilologica* 78 (2006): 81–87; Tom Shippey, "'The Fall of King Hæðcyn': Or, Mimesis 4a, the Chapter Auerbach Never Wrote," in *On the Aesthetics of Beowulf and Other Old English Poems*, ed. John M. Hill (Toronto: University of Toronto Press, 2010), 247–265; Peter S. Baker, *Honour, Exchange and Violence in Beowulf* (Cambridge: D. S. Brewer, 2013), 232–239; Leonard Neidorf, "Hygelac and His Daughter: Rereading *Beowulf* Lines 2985-98," *Medium Ævum* 89 (2020): 350–355; on the Geats' conflicts with the Franks and the Swedes, see also the references in §44.

§53. Lines 3028-3075: These lines are exceptionally burdened with difficulties. In the narrative present, the only event that occurs is the men of the Geatish council travel to where the corpses of Beowulf and the dragon were located. The sight of the corpses prompts two reactions from the narrator: first, sententious moralizing about the ineluctability of mortality, which is straightforward enough; second, revelations about a curse (or curses?) that had been placed on the treasure, which are far from straightforward and rank among the most obscure passages in the poem. Regarding the curse, the first comment states that it would prevent anyone from obtaining the treasure unless God himself wanted someone to find it. Since Beowulf successfully obtained the treasure, it seems that we can assume that God must have wanted Beowulf to get the treasure. Does this mean, essentially, that God had nullified the heathen curse that had been placed on the treasure? The second comment about a curse follows a comment about Beowulf's mortality and appears there to imply that Beowulf died because the treasure was cursed. Some take these lines to mean, additionally, that the curse has consigned Beowulf to an eternity in hell. Yet it seems doubtful that a heathen curse could result in Christian damnation. Doubts are furthermore raised by the general inconsistency of such an implication with the rest of the poem, which nowhere else affirms the hero's damnation and in several places strongly suggests his salvation. An alternative way of construing the second comment about the curse is that it refers not to the curse placed on the treasure prior to Beowulf finding it but refers rather to a curse that the Geats are placing on the treasure they are about to bury with Beowulf. The curse would then be intended to offer supernatural discouragement to anyone who considered breaking into Beowulf's barrow. Whatever is made of the curse (or curses) placed on the treasure, it seems best to avoid identifying any passage in this stretch of text as a key to the interpretation of the poem. The curse on the treasure seems, above all, to be a vestigial motif retained from antecedent tradition yet not fully integrated into the present poem.

Further Reading: E. G. Stanley, "*Hæþenra Hyht* in *Beowulf*," in *Studies in Old English Literature in Honor of Arthur G. Brodeur*, ed. Stanley B. Greenfield (Eugene: University of Oregon Books, 1963), 136–151; Margaret E. Goldsmith, *The Mode and Meaning of Beowulf* (London: Athlone Press, 1970), 95–96; Earl R. Anderson, "Treasure Trove in *Beowulf*: A Legal View of the Dragon's Hoard," *Mediaevalia* 3 (1977): 141–164; Willem Helder, "Beowulf and the Plundered Hoard," *Neuphilologische Mitteilungen* 78 (1977): 317–325; A. J. Bliss, "*Beowulf*, Lines 3074-3075," in *J. R. R. Tolkien, Scholar and Storyteller: Essays in Memoriam*, ed. Mary Salu and Robert T. Farrell (Ithaca: Cornell University Press, 1979), 41–63; Bruce

Mitchell, *On Old English* (Oxford: Blackwell, 1988), 30–40; Claus-Dieter Wetzel, "*Beowulf* 3074 f. – ein *locus desperatus?*" in *Anglo-Saxonica: Beiträge zur Vor- und Frühgeschichte der englischen Sprache und zur altenglischen Literatur: Festschrift für Hans Schabram zum 65 Geburtstag,* ed. Klaus R. Grinda and Claus-Dieter Wetzel (München: Fink, 1993), 113–166; Paul Beekman Taylor, "The Dragon's Treasure in *Beowulf,*" *Neuphilologische Mitteilungen* 98 (1997): 229–240; John Tanke, "Beowulf, Gold-Luck, and God's Will," *Studies in Philology* 99 (2002): 356–379; William Cooke, "Who Cursed Whom, and When? The Cursing of the Hoard and Beowulf's Fate," *Medium Ævum* 76 (2007): 207–224; Scott Gwara, "*Beowulf* 3074-75: Beowulf Appraises His Reward," *Neophilologus* 92 (2008): 333–338; Cameron Hunt McNabb, "'Eldum Unnyt': Treasure Spaces in *Beowulf,*" *Neophilologus* 95 (2011): 145–164; Richard North, "Gold and the Heathen Polity in *Beowulf,*" in *Gold in der europäischen Heldensage,* ed. Wilhelm Heizmann, Victor Millet, and Heike Sahm (Berlin: de Gruyter, 2019), 72–114.

§54. Lines 3076-3136: Wiglaf laments that Beowulf could not be dissuaded from fighting the dragon. His comment that many people often suffer on account of "the will of one man" (*ānes willan*) has been construed as a critique of Beowulf's decision to fight the dragon alone. This speech (or, rather, mainly its first two lines) has thus fed into a reading of Beowulf wherein the hero is broadly criticized for risking his life by fighting the dragon. According to this reading, Beowulf should have simply refused to fight the dragon so that he could remain alive and continue to protect his people from foreign enemies. Yet Beowulf is already an old man, who will not live forever, and it is difficult to believe that Beowulf could have been expected to do nothing while a dragon terrorizes his people. Furthermore, Wiglaf does not go on to attribute what has transpired to any defect in Beowulf's character; he sees the tragic death of his lord, rather, as a consequence of the "fate" (*hēahgesceap*, *ġifeðe*) to which Beowulf was compelled to respond. Beowulf had no choice but to fight the dragon. Of course, he could not be persuaded to turn away from his destiny. Wiglaf then describes how he brought some of the dragon's treasure to the dying Beowulf, who asked for a barrow to be constructed in his memory. He then orders the best of the newly arrived men to aid him in the preparation of the pyre and the barrow. It is interesting Wiglaf's speech concludes with the conviction that the soul of Beowulf, after a thoroughly pagan funeral, will dwell thereafter in "the protection of the omnipotent God" (*on ðæs waldendes wære*). The presence of an expression of intuitive monotheism at this moment in the narrative suggests that the funerary practices accorded Beowulf were not considered by the poet to be problematically pagan. They could be regarded dispassionately as historical details provided that the pagan beliefs motivating them went unexpressed. After his speech, Wiglaf and seven others plunder the dragon's hoard and fill a wagon with treasure. They also push the dragon over a cliff into the ocean. The significance of the gesture is not explained. Perhaps it is intended, like the posthumous decapitation of Grendel, to ensure that the monster does not come back to life. Alternatively, the unceremonious disposal of the unloved, treasure-hoarding dragon might merely be intended to contrast with the elaborate ceremonies accorded the magnanimous Beowulf by his adoring followers.

Further Reading: J. R. R. Tolkien, "The Homecoming of Beorhtnoth Beorhthelm's Son," *Essays and Studies* 6 (1953): 1–18; John Leyerle, "Beowulf the Hero and the King," *Medium Ævum* 34 (1965): 89–102; G. N. Garmonsway, "Anglo-Saxon Heroic Attitudes," in *Franciplegius: Medieval and Linguistic Studies in Honor of Francis Peabody Magoun, Jr.*, ed. Jess B. Bessinger and Robert P. Creed (New York: New York University Press, 1965), 139–146; G. V. Smithers, "Destiny and the Heroic Warrior in *Beowulf*," in *Philological Essays: Studies in Old and Middle English Literature in Honour of Herbert Dean Meritt*, ed. J. L. Rosier (The Hague: Mouton, 1970), 65–81; Kemp Malone, "Beowulf the Headstrong," *Anglo-Saxon England* 1 (1972): 139–145; Deborah S. Frisby, "'Daring' and 'Foolish' Renderings: On the Meaning of *Dollic* in *Beowulf*," *ANQ* 4 (1991): 59–63; C. E. Fell, "Paganism in *Beowulf*: A Semantic Fairy-Tale," in *Pagans and Christians: The Interplay between Christian Latin and Traditional Germanic Cultures in Early Medieval Europe*, ed. T. Hofstra, L. A. J. R. Houwen, and A. A. MacDonald (Groningen: Egbert Forsten, 1995), 9–34; Andy Orchard, *A Critical Companion to Beowulf* (Cambridge: D. S. Brewer, 2003), 262–264; J. A. Burrow, *The Poetry of Praise* (Cambridge: Cambridge University Press, 2008), 54–60; Leonard Neidorf, "An Old Norse Analogue to Wiglaf's Lament (*Beowulf* Lines 3077-3086)," *Neophilologus* 102 (2018): 515–524; Thijs Porck, *Old Age in Early Medieval England: A Cultural History* (Woodbridge: Boydell, 2019), 177–211; on the intuitive monotheism of the foregrounded characters, see the references in §5.

§55. **Lines 3137-3182**: The Geats construct a funeral pyre onto which they place the corpse of Beowulf along with helmets and mail-shirts. As they commit his body to the flames, a female mourner recites a dirge for Beowulf, in which she expresses fear of invasion and enslavement. A great deal of speculation has been forward regarding the identity of this female mourner (is she Beowulf's queen? Is she Hygd?), but there is no compelling reason to assume that she is not simply an anonymous female mourner performing a role that women conventionally performed at funerals. The pyre portion of Beowulf's funeral is punctuated by a suggestive verse, "heaven swallowed the smoke" (*Heofon rēce swealg*), which might constitute another hint of his salvation. Ten days after the cremation of Beowulf's corpse, the Geats commit his remains to a barrow they constructed in the intervening period. They also bury within the barrow all of the treasure that had been obtained from the dragon's hoard. With the barrow completed, the Geats conduct a second funeral for Beowulf, in which they ride around his barrow and sing his praises. The elaborate nature of the funeral that Beowulf receives in two phases over the course of ten days raises questions about the purpose that such a ritual might have possessed in earlier tradition. Does it reflect an attempt to deify Beowulf and retain his spirit's protection? If so, the Christian author has understandably refrained from making such implications clear. The final words of the poem eulogize Beowulf as the mildest, kindest, and gentlest king, as well as the "most eager for glory" or the "most generous" (*lofġeornost*). The use of the same word (*lofġeorn*) in homiletic contexts with a negative meaning such as "vainglorious" has encouraged various critics to interpret the final word of the poem as a stinging indictment of the hero. In the present context, however, the word is almost certainly intended to reflect positively on the hero's character, given its status as the fourth item in a catalogue preceded by three unambiguously positive terms. The summarizing assessment of the hero's character with which the poem concludes recalls the assessment that had appeared at the end of the narrative of the hero's youth (ll. 2177-2183a), which likewise praised Beowulf for his kindness and gentleness.

Further Reading: Fr. Klaeber, "Attila's and Beowulf's Funeral," *PMLA* 42 (1927): 255–267; John C. Pope, *"Beowulf* 3150-3151: Queen Hygd and the Word 'Geomeowle,'" *Modern Language Notes* 70 (1955): 77–87; Paul Beekman Taylor, *"Heofon Riece Swealg*: A Sign of Beowulf's State of Grace," *Philological Quarterly* 42 (1963): 257–259; Margaret E. Goldsmith, *The Mode and Meaning of Beowulf* (London: Athlone Press, 1970), 224–228; M. P. Richards, "A Reexamination of *Beowulf* ll. 3180–3182," *English Language Notes* 10 (1973): 163–167; Martin Puhvel, "The Ride Around Beowulf's Barrow," *Folklore* 94 (1983): 108–112; Gernot R. Wieland, *"Manna Mildost*: Moses and Beowulf," *Pacific Coast Philology* 23 (1988): 86–93; Dennis Cronan, *"Lofgeorn*: Generosity and Praise," *Neuphilologische Mitteilungen* 92 (1991): 187–194; Helen Bennett, "The Female Mourner at Beowulf's Funeral: Filling in the Blanks / Hearing the Spaces," *Exemplaria* 4 (1992): 35–50; George Clark, *"Beowulf*: The Last Word," in *Old English and New: Studies in Language and Linguistics in Honor of Frederic G. Cassidy*, ed. Joan H. Hall, Nick Doane, and Dick Ringler (New York: Garland, 1992), 15–30; Fred C. Robinson, "The Tomb of Beowulf," in his *The Tomb of Beowulf and Other Essays* (Cambridge: Blackwell, 1993), 3–17; Gale R. Owen-Crocker, *The Four Funerals in Beowulf and the Structure of the Poem* (Manchester: Manchester University Press, 2000), 104–105; Thomas D. Hill, "Beowulf's Roman Rites: Roman Ritual and Germanic Tradition," *Journal of English and Germanic Philology* 106 (2007): 325–335; Tauno F.

Mustanoja, "The Unnamed Woman's Song of Mourning over Beowulf and the Tradition of Ritual Lamentation," *Neuphilologische Mitteilungen* 108 (2007): 153–179.

APPENDIX I
Tolkien and *Beowulf*—A Lifelong Involvement

We do not know when Tolkien first encountered *Beowulf*. He must have been introduced to the poem during his undergraduate career at Oxford (1911-15), and he lectured on the poem many times during his professorial career at Oxford (1925-59), and almost certainly earlier on, at Leeds (1920-25). The first visible sign of his involvement with the poem indeed comes from 1923, when he published a poem in *The Gryphon* (a Leeds University journal), with the title "Iumonna Gold Galdre Bewunden." These four words form line 3052 of *Beowulf*, and Tolkien translated them later as "the gold of bygone men [...] wound about with spells."[1] Tolkien was not strictly accurate here, for *galdre* is singular, not plural. More interesting is the question, "what kind of spell was meant in *Beowulf*?", and this had already caused scholars some uncertainty.

Tolkien was, however, different from other scholars, both earlier and later, in two respects. One is that while they considered issues like line 3052 as purely textual problems, Tolkien tried to probe deeper to find both mythical meanings and real-world meanings. The other is that he found solutions of this kind not only in the poem itself, but in the scholarship which had built up over many years, rarely if ever providing definite answers, but creating a range of possibilities.

Setting the line in context, it occurs late in the poem, and the "gold" is the hoard of the dragon, which Beowulf has just killed at the cost of his own life. But that is not what the line says: it says the gold is "the gold of bygone men," and earlier on there has been a scene in which a man, usually described as "the Last Survivor" of a fallen people, commits his people's gold to the earth, since he no longer has the power to guard it. How, then, did it pass to the dragon? And since the "spell" was clearly put on the gold by the "bygone men," what was it supposed to do? If it was meant to shield the gold from discovery, it didn't work. So it must have been a curse, laid on whoever should take the gold. Did it work on the dragon? Did it work, or would it have worked, on Beowulf, who lived long enough only to see the gold? These are not scholarly questions, being purely speculative, but they are suggestive ones.

One further complication (unless it is in fact a clue) is that while it is very clear that the Last Survivor commits the treasure to the earth (line 2247), before wandering off in some way to die (2269-70), the dragon immediately comes upon it and finds it "standing open," *opene standan* (line 2271).[2] This contradicts everything we all know about the procedure for burying treasure, which is (first stage), dig a hole, (second stage), deposit treasure in the hole, and (vital third stage) *fill the hole in again*: just what does not happen in *Beowulf*, if one relies simply on the text.

The thought struck scholars very quickly that perhaps (in some earlier version of the story), the disappearance of the Last Survivor and the appearance of the dragon had been one and the same thing: the Last Survivor *became* the dragon. Old Norse sagas contain hints of the idea that if a man "lay down on his gold," *lagðisk a gullit*, in his own funeral barrow, then he would turn into a dragon.[3] That would explain, for one thing, why dragons are to be found in mounds or barrows, as declared firmly by another Anglo-Saxon poem, *draca sceal on hlæwe*, "dragon must be in mound," and also where their gold comes from: it has been buried with the dead man, or rather, the not-dead man.

What does the spell or curse do, then? This is the question Tolkien answered in his poem of 1923, an answer which remained consistent through several minor and major reworkings of the poem all the way to its appearance as "The Hoard" in *The Adventures of Tom Bombadil* in 1962. Briefly, just as the Last Survivor is the dragon, so the curse is the hoard itself. What it does is destroy successive owners morally, and eventually physically, cursing them with avarice and blindness.

In the 1923 version—Tolkien tinkered with details for nearly forty years, without losing the main shape and point of the poem[4]—the gold was originally elvish, until the fall of the elf-kingdoms. It then passed to "an old dwarf," who became a miser, counting his hoard, and not noticing the dragon who found his cave. In turn the dragon became old and failed to hear the approach of a "fearless warrior," who called him to come out and fight for the gold. And the warrior became "an old king," brooding on his riches and neglecting his kingdom, until he too was displaced and killed. Now the hoard is lost, and will remain so till the elves return: if they do, for the 1923 version ends with the word "awake," the 1962 one with the word "sleep."

The "spell" which winds inextricably round the hoard is, then, what Tolkien in *The Hobbit* would call "the dragon-sickness." At the end of the story this affects first Thorin, through "the power that gold has upon which a dragon has long brooded," and then kills the Master of Laketown, who flees with the gold he has been given and (like the dwarf, dragon and king in the poem) dies miserably, in his case "of starvation in the Waste, deserted by his companions."

"Dragon-sickness," then, began as an interpretation of a difficult line in *Beowulf*, but the poem made other contributions to *The Hobbit*. In chapter 2 Tolkien surely remembered the crux of line 3052, when he noted that the dwarfs put "a great many spells" over the pots of gold they had just won from the trolls, "in case they ever had the chance to come back and recover them," as Bilbo and Gandalf eventually do.

More important is the way that chapters 12 and then 14 follow the outline of *Beowulf* lines 2280 ff. In *Beowulf* an unknown person—the word is obscured in the MS, but it looks like three or four letters beginning þe-, so þeo(w), "slave," or þegn, "retainer," but Tolkien clearly preferred þeof, "thief"— steals a cup from the sleeping dragon, and hands it over to his lord. The dragon wakes, immediately notices the missing cup, cannot find the thief and flies off "to burn the bright halls." In just the same way Bilbo (the professional "burglar," or thief) steals a cup, hands it over to Thorin, and cannot be caught by the dragon's first attempt at revenge, after which the dragon flies off to attack Laketown with fire from the air.

But perhaps the most unexpected borrowing from the poem stems, again, not from the poem itself, but from the cluster of different opinions and analogues brought up by many decades of scholarship. In this case the problem for scholars was what Beowulf's own extremely unusual name meant. And by Tolkien's time (things have changed since) general opinion was solid: it meant "Bee-wolf," "Enemy of the Bees," and the enemy of the bees was the notoriously honey-loving bear (the Russian word for "bear" being, as every *Beowulf*-scholar knew, *medved*, "honey-eater"). But why did the hero have such a strange name?

Once again, scholarship had found a solution in a close analogue of the poem, the Old Norse *Saga of Hrolf Kraki,* which not only mentioned a number of the legendary/historical characters of the poem, but also had a hero called Böthvarr Bjarki, one of the champions of King Hrolf.[5] There was no doubt about him. His father was called Björn = "bear," his mother was Bera = "lady bear," and his own nickname, Bjarki, means "little bear." He was both a bear's son—for his father had been placed under an enchantment—and a were-bear. In the final battle of the saga, King Hrolf's men are fighting against great odds, much assisted by a giant bear which appears in their own ranks. Bjarki, however, is nowhere to be seen, and one of the warriors runs back to the hall, where he finds Bjarki sitting motionless. He urges Bjarki to come and join the fight, and Bjarki does so, but says it would have been better for him to be undisturbed. As he joins the fight, the great bear disappears. Bjarki, then, was clearly *eigi einhamr*, "not of one skin," and could be either man or bear: but not both at the same time.

Also once again, Tolkien turned a scholarly puzzle in *Beowulf* into a character in *The Hobbit*: Beorn, who takes up most of chapter 7 and reappears in chapter 17. He is Tolkien's image of what a were-bear would be like, with his beehives and bee-pastures, his night-shape and day-shape, his hospitality and his ferocity. In the Battle of the Five Armies, he appears suddenly, "alone, and in bear's shape" (just like Bjarki), "and he seemed to have grown almost to giant-size in his wrath."

Tracing all the sources of Tolkien's inspiration is notoriously impossible (he knew too much), but certainly a large part of the structure of *The Hobbit* derives from thoughts on

Beowulf—along with entirely original features, like hobbits themselves, and features from other ancient texts, like the name and character of Smaug.

Tolkien's best-known interaction with *Beowulf* is, however, his 1936 lecture to the British Academy, "*Beowulf*: the Monsters and the Critics." This is one of the most frequently cited articles in the whole field of English literature, and is generally agreed to have inaugurated a new era in *Beowulf*-studies.

In it Tolkien had three main, linked goals. First, he wanted people to see the poem as a whole, as an integrated and purposeful work by a single poet who had a very good idea of what he was doing—not, as had been the case for much of the preceding century, mostly by German scholars, as a mishmash, hodgepodge, or *Wirrwarr* of different stories tacked together by a whole sequence of incompetent bunglers. Second, he wanted to argue for the right to write fantasy, and in that mode to create something valuable and autonomous. And in order to make that case, third, he was obliged to argue down the powerfully-expressed opinion of, for instance, R. W. Chambers (whom Tolkien greatly respected, and with whom he was on very good personal terms) that in the Ingeld legend, which the *Beowulf*-poet only alluded to, and which no-one has ever been able to reconstruct fully, "we have a situation which the old heroic poets loved, and would not have sold for a wilderness of dragons."[6]

Tolkien argued, in short, that fantasy was valuable for itself, not just as a preserver of legend—or a distraction from history, as German scholars had often complained. Much quoted have been Tolkien's remarks near the start of his lecture that "The illusion of historical truth and perspective [in *Beowulf*] is largely a product of art," and further that "the seekers after history must beware lest the glamour of Poesis overcome them."[7] Ever since, the consensus opinion has been that *Beowulf* is useless as a historical document.

What has not been sufficiently noted by followers of Tolkien is Tolkien's personal situation at the time. He delivered his British Academy lecture on 25th November 1936. Just over six weeks earlier, on 5th October 1936, his publishers Allen & Unwin had received the typescript of *The Hobbit*, which they would bring out the following year. One might ask, who in the world at this point had a stronger personal motive for asserting the value of fantasy than Tolkien? He had been writing about dragons and trolls and elves and dwarves for at least twenty years, but in secret. Now he was going public. In his argument about the interpretation of *Beowulf* he was, then, laying the grounds for future interpretations of his own work.

This does not mean that Tolkien was wrong. But the uncritical acceptance of his lecture has had two bad effects which I am sure Tolkien would have regretted. First, there is no doubt that he actually took *Beowulf* very seriously as a historical document, as shown by remarks in his "Commentary" on the poem, not published till 2014, and even more by his book *Finn and Hengest*, published posthumously in 1982 (see further below). The other was that while, in his title, it was clear that Tolkien preferred the "monsters" to the "critics," the critics he meant and named were people like W. P. Ker and R. W. Chambers, scholars of his own type, as knowledgeable as he was, even if he happened to disagree with them. But by his arguments for unity and autonomy, he opened the gate for a very different set of interpretations, produced by Tolkien's lifetime professional enemies, the New Critics, the literary critics.

Seeing literary works "as a whole" was something which such critics were very ready to do, perhaps because it wasn't too difficult. After World War II a whole industry grew up of books and essays which demonstrated that *Beowulf* was a work of great "organic unity" (a favorite phrase), and that all the many bits which had been taken as "digressions" or insertions actually played an important part in the poet's conception, and might well be seen as (another favorite word in the critical vocabulary) "ironic." As time went by such interpretations, often moralistic, often detached from any historical or linguistic context, grew ever more fanciful, to the point of raising eyebrows, if no more, among serious scholars from other disciplines.[8] Some would say nowadays, with the advantage of hindsight, and while conceding that it was not in any way Tolkien's fault, nevertheless his essay, in spite of its warmth, humor and persuasiveness, in the long term did study of the poem more harm than good.

Be that as it may, Tolkien's attention now turned to the composition of what began as a *Hobbit* sequel, and would become *The Lord of the Rings*. This contains several echoes of *Beowulf*. To begin with, Tolkien did not forget his poem of 1923 when writing *The Lord of the Rings*, for Aragorn says in *The Two Towers* that the short swords taken from the Wight's barrow are "work of Westernesse, *wound about with spells* for the bane of Mordor," repeating exactly Tolkien's own translation of his poem's title. Much more generally, Anglo-Saxon civilization as a whole and the Old English language are the basis for the Riders of Rohan, as many have noted.

Beowulf specifically is however a source for Book 3, chapter 6, of *The Two Towers*, "The King of the Golden Hall," and one may think that once again inspiration came from the puzzle of a single word. At one point in the poem King Hrothgar has eight horses brought to be presented to Beowulf as a reward, and they are brought *on flet ... (in) under eodoras* (lines 1036-7). The *flet* is the hall, or the floor of the hall, but what are the *eodoras*, and does that mean something different? The K4 editors suggest that the latter word means "shelter, enclosure," though it is also a more familiar word for "leader." But do *on flet* and *(in) under eodoras* mean the same thing?

As usual, Tolkien dealt with these issues economically and convincingly. In the first place, he rewrote the word as "Edoras"—nothing to do with leaders—and as for what it meant, that is explained by Gandalf. In Book 3, chapter 6 of *The Two Towers*, Legolas sees a green hill at the mouth of a valley: "A dike and mighty wall and thorny fence encircle it. Within there rise the roofs of houses; and in the midst, set upon a green terrace, there stands aloft a great hall of Men." Gandalf explains, "Edoras those courts are called [...] and Meduseld is that golden hall." *Meduseld* is another word from *Beowulf*, but its relationship with *e(o)doras* in now perfectly clear. Edoras is the name of the whole stockaded precinct, which has many buidlings inside it, and Meduseld is the name of the great hall itself. So, if one accepts Tolkien's reading, Hrothgar's horses were brought into the precinct, and then into the hall.

Be that as it may (and there are objections to such a reading), what is absolutely clear is that Tolkien modelled the whole sequence of the approach to Meduseld by Gandalf, Legolas and Gimli, point for point on Beowulf's approach to Heorot. In the poem, Beowulf is challenged first by the unnamed Danish coastguard, and then, when the Geats reach Heorot, by Wulfgar the door-ward, where they are eventually allowed in after stacking their spears and shields outside. In the same way Gandalf, Aragorn and Gimli, in Tolkien's fiction, are challenged first by an unnamed guard at the gates of

Edoras, the outer precinct of the royal dwelling, and then, once they reach the hall itself, by Hama the door-ward, who likewise tells them to deposit their weapons. Just like the coastguard in Beowulf, the unnamed guard in *The Lord of the Rings* is impressed by the appearance of the strangers, though in Tolkien what really impresses the guardsman is Shadowfax.

Going on, the resemblance becomes even closer, for Tolkien clearly thought deeply about the meaning of the coastguard's proverbial statement in lines 287b-89, which has proved puzzling to many translators. The statement is clear enough in context. The coastguard has to make his mind up about Beowulf and his companions: friend or foe?, and the only evidence he has to go on is what Beowulf has just said. But (as we all know) "actions speak louder than words" and the coastguard has no actions (*worca*) to guide him, only words (*worda*). Just the same, he says, a "sharp shield-warrior" must be able, not to tell the *difference* between words and actions (as some have suggested, which is nonsense, for any fool can do that), but to make decisions *on the basis of either*: which is what he does: they are friends. Tolkien presents a similar dilemma for the door-ward Hama, over whether Gandalf's staff should be considered as a weapon or not, and has him say eventually, "In doubt a man of worth will trust to his own wisdom," a good paraphrase of the Beowulfian proverb, if actually a good deal clearer. Hama also uses his judgement in favor of the strangers.

Three other links between Tolkien and *Beowulf* deserve to be mentioned (no doubt there are more to be discovered). One of the three is important only for students of *Beowulf*, who have however for the most part chosen to ignore it. This is the book published posthumously as edited by A. J. Bliss, *Finn and Hengest*.[9] This offers a new explanation for a legend elliptically told within *Beowulf* (and in another Old English poem of which we have only a fragment), the story of "The Fight at Finnsburg." No section of the poem has caused more dispute and confusion.

The core of the problem is that the story involves three groups. There are the "Half-Danes," led by Hnæf. He and they are on a visit to King Finn of the Frisians, who has married Hnæf's sister Hildeburh, when they are attacked at night by the Jutes, who appear to be in Finn's service. One perplexing and even embarrassing complication is that after Hnæf has been killed in the fighting against the Jutes, he is succeeded as leader of the Half-Danes by a man called Hengest. This is a rare name, borne only by one other man in our records, and that is the man who invaded Kent in the mid-fifth century and began the whole process of turning Britannia into England. But the invader of Kent is recorded early and firmly as being a Jute!

Moreover, the whole story involves both those staples of Germanic legend, kin-slaying and oath-breaking, and there is a strong sense that *someone* must have behaved very badly. But (thought both English and American scholars) surely not *our* Hengest, Founding Father of England, and a man whose image still figures on the Great Seal of the United States of America! Excuses and explanations became ever more complex.

Once again, as with Edoras, Tolkien cut the whole Gordian knot. The real-world explanation, he argued was this. The event must have taken place in the first half of the fifth century (which checks very well with the chronology of *Beowulf*) at a time when the Danes under their ruling dynasty of the Scyldings were expanding out of the Danish islands to the Jutish mainland, ending Jutish independence and displacing the

Jutish royal dynasty, whether by force or by marriage. "Half-Danes" is then a pejorative term for those Jutes who have accepted the situation and come to an accommodation with the Danish incomers.

Meanwhile, however, other Jutes, who have *not* accepted the situation, and perhaps have rallied round a surviving member of their royal dynasty, have taken shelter at the Frisian court—the Frisians being by this time also alarmed at Danish expansion. In World War II terms, then, we have a "collaborator" group, the Half-Danes, including Hengest, and what we might call the "Free Jutes in Exile." These two groups obviously hate and despise each other more than anyone else, and when they encounter each other on neutral territory there is bound to be trouble—into which their host Finn is reluctantly drawn. As for Hengest, if he was the invader of Kent (and Tolkien was sure he was), then whatever his role in the whole story, which ends in the death of Finn, he must have been unpopular and distrusted by virtually everyone along the North Sea coast from Jutland to Frisia, and setting off to make a new life in England would make good sense.

There is much more to be said about the theory, but the important point, for us, is Tolkien's imaginative and unexpected solution to an unresolved problem. Once again, he took a whole bundle of textual issues and gave them a real-world explanation.

While most of the above has been concerned with legendary and mythical elements in the poem, Tolkien's second "reconstruction" was a folk-tale or "wonder-tale." Tolkien clearly accepted the notion that *Beowulf* was based on a folk-tale about a "bear's son," and to make his point, he wrote the folk-tale as he thought it must once have existed. He did so in the early 1940s, but it was not published until 2014,[10] and there entitled "Sellic Spell": another phrase from *Beowulf* which Tolkien took to mean "wonder-tale." (Tolkien moreover wrote it—just to show it could be done?—in both modern and, in part, in Old English.)

The idea that the poem is based on an incompletely assimilated wonder-tale does explain several otherwise awkward features, long-noted by scholars. Such as:

- The death of Hondscioh, in section #17 above. It does seem strange that Beowulf lies quiet and allows his companion to be killed, even if the poet assures us that it all happened very quickly. Too quickly for Beowulf to move, or shout a warning?

- The abandonment of Beowulf at the monsters' lake by the Scyldings (not the Geats). They leave, the poet tells, because they see blood in the water. But they knew he was diving in to fight and kill the monster. So why do they assume the blood must be the hero's?

- Then there is the case of Unferth and his sword Hrunting. This seems to take up disproportionate space, given that the sword turns out to be useless. Yet it is borrowed, kept, and returned with thanks. This provides Beowulf with an easy score over the man who challenged him, and moreover allows him to show his own magnanimity. But is that a good enough explanation?

- Finally, there is the sword with which Beowulf beheads both Grendel and his mother. In folk-tale a common motif is that the giant/monster has put a spell on all weapons—as Grendel has, indeed—so that none of them can hurt him *except his own sword*. And that is the one that kills him. But it should be stressed that the poet says carefully that this is *not* a magic sword, not a sword exempt from a spell, it is just a *very big* sword, which only a very strong man could handle. And that is why it works. No magic involved.

Having said so much, how are these questions to be explained, and what was the shape of the tale that the poet, in theory, might have known? It would, of course, be rash to try to reconstruct it. So that is what Tolkien did. Like his reconstruction of *Finn and Hengest*, and like his chronology of events mentioned above in the Introduction, there has been no comment on this by modern scholars, of *Beowulf* or of Tolkien. His readiness to test a theory by example, and to present it in fiction, has proved too shocking.

The main features of "Sellic Spell", however, go like this:

- The hero is called "Beewolf."
- He is neither a bear's son nor a were-bear, but was fostered by bears (like Mowgli by wolves).
- Once rescued and adopted by a king, he grows up very strong, but "surly" and "lumpish," slow to learn to talk. (This corresponds to the unexpected remark in the poem, line 2187, that Beowulf was considered *sleac* in youth, not "slack" but "slow" or "lazy.")
- He is a very strong swimmer, competes with "Breaker," and kills "nixes" in the sea.
- He sets off to fight a hall-haunting ogre, and on the way encounters, first "Handshoe," a man who has gloves which give him enormous strength; and then "Ashwood," a character who (like the coastguard in *Beowulf*) brandishes a great spear. This spear is a magic one which can "put to flight a host of men."
- Arrived at the haunted hall, first Ashwood and then Handshoe try their luck against Grendel, but both are defeated. Ashwood's head remains (like Æschere's in the poem), but Handshoe is carried off to be devoured.

- Beewolf then defeats "Grinder," tearing off his arm, but "Unfriend" insists that is not good enough, and leads Beewolf to Grinder's lair in a deep ravine, a cave behind a waterfall. Beewolf takes his former companions' magic aids with him, Ashwood's spear and Handshoe's gloves.
- Unfriend is left guarding the rope by which Beewolf descends into the ravine. In the fight that follows, Ashwood's spear fails him, but Beewolf kills Grinder's dam with the giant sword he finds. Handshoe's gloves however prove useful to roll aside a great stone, so Beewolf can find and behead Grinder.
- Unfriend however sees blood in the water and loosens the rope, so Beewolf has difficulty climbing out.
- Unfriend is then humbled in the hall, and Beewolf gains prestige back home.
- There is no dragon episode.

One can see that Tolkien's main aim in the story was to deal with the "awkward features" in *Beowulf* mentioned above, explained away as hangovers from the original folktale. It has to be said, though, that the tale itself is not inspiring. It feels like an explanation rather than a narrative.

It is quite likely, by contrast—though these thoughts are now purely speculative—that *Beowulf* in fact contributed very vital elements of Tolkien's own personal mythology: while once again these derived from textual issues, one of them, this time, so minor as to have passed without comment in the scholarly literature.

Two matters arise out of the first few lines of *Beowulf*. Line 4 begins *Oft Scyld Scefing*, and entirely characteristically, scholars have been stumped ever since by the word *Scefing* (only sixteen words into the poem and trouble already). Does it mean Scyld is "the son of Scef" or does it mean "Scyld with the sheaf"? Neither explanation makes much sense. For Tolkien, however, it was "Sheaf" or "Sheave" which was important, King Scyld being a complete invention, created by back-formation from what early Danes called themselves, the "Shieldings," the Men of the Shield. In his poem "King Sheave," Tolkien presented this figure as a myth, the creator of a kind of "eucatastrophe" for the heathen Danes: in fact, though there is no theologically secure way to say it, as a kind of image/parallel/forerunner of Christian revelation.[11] "King Sheave" left the Danes (just as they are in *Beowulf*, and just like Tolkien's own heroes of Middle-earth) outside the Christian revelation, but also definitely not "heathen": a word which occurs only twice in *Beowulf* in reference to human beings, and only twice in *The Lord of the Rings*.

Meanwhile, and going on only forty lines into the poem, there is a word, a very insignificant word, which may nevertheless have triggered Tolkien's thoughts about the very basis of his own mythology. The word is *þa*, and in that line it means the demonstrative pronoun "those." Whoever "those" are, they are the ones who sent Scyld (or was it Sheave) as a comfort to the Danes—a Providential comfort. But the word is definitely plural: it can't mean "God." So who, or what, are God's agents? In Tolkien's terms they would be the Valar, and their home would be in the Undying Lands, across the Western Ocean: to which there was once (in Tolkien's mythology) a Lost Road, and from which "those" sent the baby Scyld (or Sheave), floating in a boat (or maybe a shield), to save the Danes from their distress.

The start of *Beowulf* moreover shows the Danes putting Scyld's body into a funeral ship, and not setting it alight, but pushing it out to sea—where it will find the Lost Road? The idea of the Undying Lands across the ocean was perhaps the most persistent element in Tolkien's whole mythology, and the source of it may well be exactly here. Was some awareness of this, perhaps—probably Tolkien thought so—what lay behind the pre-Christian Northern custom of boat-burial, or of no boat was available, burial within a ring of stones shaped like a boat? The soul had to go somewhere. Where but across the western ocean?

By contrast, there is one point where Tolkien thought the *Beowulf*-poet had got it wrong—not his fault, no doubt, but he had been misinformed. This is at lines 111-12, where it says that all *untydras* (i.e., "unnatural creatures," like Grendel) are of the race of Cain, and they include *eotenas ond ylfe ond orcneas*. The second half-line here is defective, having only three syllables, but that is readily explained (it happens elsewhere in *Beowulf*) by the loss of an original -h in the middle of the word, so *orc-neahas*. What an *orc-neah* was we do not know, but the second element seems to mean "corpse," so it was obviously something monstrous. Tolkien has now brought the word "orc" back into the language, but what he could not accept was having them lumped together with *ylfe*, or "elves": chalk and cheese, to Tolkien. In his 2014 translation, he just took the elves out: the "unnatural creatures" are now "evil broods," and the giants and elves and orc-creatures are now "ogres and goblins and haunting shapes of hell." The *Beowulf*-poet must have been a bit like Eomer in *Lord of the Rings*, who also got the wrong idea about the nature of Galadriel. Tolkien was always interested in the way stories got garbled, like the tales of "Mad Baggins" in the Shire, and the story about Frodo and Sam which Ioreth relates as "the tale in the City" after the Ring has been destroyed.

Finally, there is no doubt that Tolkien was involved with the poem of *Beowulf* for most of his professional career, from at least 1923 until at least the time when he composed *The Lord of the Rings*, but probably both earlier and later: we do not know exactly when some of the works mentioned here were written, and they may well have been adapted and re-written repeatedly before being published posthumously. I would end by saying one thing more: I feel sure that Tolkien, in his heart of hearts, felt that he and the *Beowulf*-poet were kindred spirits: both Englishmen, both aware of ancient myth and legend, both devout Christians, but not willing to turn their backs on their pre-Christian ancestors, both happy to write about trolls and dragons as well as kings and heroes. How deeply this identification went and how far it was responsible for the unequalled success of Tolkien's work, we shall never know. More, no doubt, than this brief appendix has been able to prove.

NOTES

[1] See J. R. R. Tolkien, *Beowulf: A Translation and Commentary, together with Sellic Spell*, edited by Christopher Tolkien (Boston: Houghton Mifflin Harcourt, 2014), 102.

[2] Tolkien noticed the implausibility, and tried to moderate it by translating "standing unprotected." See Tolkien, *Beowulf: A Translation and Commentary*, 79.

[3] There is a very clear fictional example in C. S. Lewis's "Narnia" novel, *The Voyage of the Dawn-Treader* (1952), in which the boy Eustace, lying down on a dragon's gold with dragonish thoughts of greed in his heart, wakes up to find he has turned into a dragon. It's highly likely that Lewis got the idea from Tolkien.

[4] See Tom Shippey, "The Versions of 'The Hoard,'" *Lembas* 100 (2001): 3–7.

[5] See Jesse Byock, trans., *The Saga of King Hrolf Kraki* (London: Penguin, 1998).

[6] See R. W. Chambers, ed., *Widsith: A Study in Old English Heroic Legend* (Cambridge: Cambridge University Press, 1912), 79–80.

[7] J. R. R. Tolkien, *"Beowulf*: The Monsters and the Critics," *Proceedings of the British Academy* 22 (1936): 245–295, at 247, 248.

[8] See Tom Shippey, *"Beowulf* Studies from Tolkien to Fulk," in *Old English Philology: Studies in Honour of R. D. Fulk*, edited by Leonard

Neidorf, Rafael J. Pascual and Tom Shippey (Cambridge: D. S. Brewer, 2016), 392–414, especially 398 ff.

[9] J. R. R. Tolkien, *Finn and Hengest: The Fragment and the Episode*, edited by A. J. Bliss (London: George Allen & Unwin, 1982).

[10] Tolkien, *Beowulf: A Translation and Commentary*, 360–414.

[11] For a more detailed summary, see Tom Shippey, "'King Sheave' and 'The Lost Road,'" in *The Great Tales Never End: Essays in Memory of Christopher Tolkien*, edited by Richard Ovenden and Catherine McIlwaine (Oxford: Bodleian Library Publishing, 2022), 166–80.

APPENDIX II: *Finnsburg, Waldere, Hildebrandslied*

Introduction

The three fragmentary poems translated here are the relics of what must at one time have been a powerful and widespread tradition of heroic poetry, probably composed and recited orally to begin with—as was the case in pre-Classical Greece, in medieval Celtic societies, and even into modern times in the Balkan countries. Once upon a time it was thought that these poems, presumably oral, therefore presumably short, might have been (so to speak) stitched together to form poems of epic length like *Beowulf*. They were *Lieder*, or "lays," or "ballads," which developed in time into epic. But we now know that this was a misunderstanding of the nature of oral poetry, which in some traditions is capable of producing poems of considerable length. Nor, indeed, can you create an epic by cut-and-paste.

Be that as it may, these three poems, in their different ways, bear witness to carelessness and abandonment, tempered now and then by what may have been a lingering affection. There is, however, no such affection apparent in the provenance of *Waldere*. Its fragments consist of two vellum folds, dating from about the year 1000, discovered in the Royal

Library of Denmark among a miscellaneous pile of papers. They survived only because they had been cut out and used as stiffening for the cover of an Elizabethan prayer book. Originally they may well have been part of a much longer work, but if that is so, whoever cut them out must have thrown the rest away, or used it for some other ignominious purpose. To him, whoever he was, the old epic was valuable only as scrap paper.

In the case of *Finnsburh*, we do not even have a manuscript any more, and the poem is known only from a transcript made by George Hickes, an eighteenth-century antiquarian, or by someone he employed to copy its original. Whoever made the copy did not know much (or perhaps anything) about Old English, so the text is often suspect. And having made the copy, whoever did so must once more have thrown the original away. We do know that it consisted of a single leaf attached to a book of homilies in the Lambeth Palace Library of the Archbishop of Canterbury, but the leaf isn't there any more, though the homilies are.

Just the same, at least someone, perhaps the person copying the book of homilies, thought enough of the poem to write it down, probably unofficially and maybe from memory, which is proof of a kind of affection: and this may be true as well of the *Hildebrandslied*. In this case the manuscript survives, but like *Finnsburh* it was copied on to two spare leaves on the outside of a religious codex from the library of the monastery of Fulda, around the year 830. The two scribes who made the copy presumably copied religious texts as their main job: but seeing some spare space, they decided to add something they knew and liked. One imagines it must have been a strong liking to risk the wrath of the abbot by preserving something so non-monastic.

Three poems then, far apart in provenance, probably in date, are all preserved by chance or whim or accident. Nevertheless, the three are similar in substance. All deal with legends for which we have other evidence. Not much in the case of *Finnsburh*, but weighty evidence just the same, consisting of a long passage in *Beowulf* (1063-1159b), which paraphrases a song said to be sung in the great Danish hall of Heorot, and is normally known as "the Finnsburg Episode." The story of *Waldere* meanwhile is told in several versions: a long Latin poem called *Waltharius*, written in the ninth or tenth century; a Middle High German epic, written some 300 years later, now surviving only in fragments and allusions; the Old Norse *Þiðrikssaga*; and both a Polish and an Italian chronicle. Hildebrand also figures prominently in *Þiðrikssaga*, while there is a much later Middle High German poem ("The Younger *Hildebrandslied*") recounting the same event, and an Old Norse poem ("Hildebrand's Death Song") incorporated into an Old Norse saga (*Ásmundar saga kappabana*), in which Hildebrand regrets the killing of his son. The different versions are markedly discrepant in what they think was the outcome of the duel, as is the case with the different versions of the Walther legend.

More importantly, all three turn on what we might call "the heroic dilemma," in which a hero is confronted with a situation that can only end in kin-slaying or oath-breaking: honour requires him to do something dishonorable, one way or another. But which will he choose? In *Finnsburh* there must be an element of kinslaying. The Beowulfian paraphrase says that Hildeburh, a Danish princess married to the Frisian king Finn, lost in the fighting both her brother Hnæf and her son by Finn, who was then Hnæf's sister's son, an especially close relationship in Germanic culture. Was he fighting with his father against his uncle? Or the other way round? In the *Fragment* itself we hear that there is a man called Guthlaf inside the hall, with the defenders, but Garulf the son of Guthlaf is among the attackers, and the first to fall. Two different men? Before he starts his attack Garulf is careful to ask whom he is facing—to be sure it is not his father? And how did this come about? According to *Beowulf*, the whole episode ends with deliberate oath-breaking (dishonourable) for the purpose of revenge (honourable): Hengest must kill his current lord (Finn) to avenge his previous lord (Hnæf). No easy solution.

In the case of Hildebrand, the poem looks as if it is building up to a fight between father and son, which will lead to the killing of the son. The strange thing here (to modern eyes) is what is not said. It seems that Hildebrand, the father, does not know who his antagonist is until his son gives his name and his father's. This would be the moment, one might think, for Hildebrand to say, "I'm your father!" and call the duel off. Why doesn't he? Presumably, because it might just look as if he was calling off the fight out of fear; and the pair are "between the armies," with everyone watching. So Hildebrand tries to hint at what he means, only for his son Hadubrand, it seems, to understand the hint, but refuse to believe it. Much of the tension in the poem comes from the two characters stepping warily round the boundaries of what is and is not heroically acceptable. Here an easy solution is obvious, but ruled out as unheroic.

In *Waldere* the dilemma (as reconstructed from the other versions) is this. Waldere has been a hostage of Attila, king of the Huns, but has escaped with another hostage, Hildegyð, to whom he is betrothed. They are then ambushed, on their way home (to Spain) by Guðhere the Burgundian king and a cohort of his companions, among them Hagena, a famous champion. Waldere gets himself into a narrow defile and kills the king's companions as they come at him one at a time. In the end only Guðhere and Hagena are left. It is clearly Hagena's duty to fight now for his lord, as so far he has refrained from doing so. But the reason he held back was that while in captivity among the Huns, he and Waldere became blood-brothers. So Hagena has to break either the oath of blood-brotherhood with Waldere or the oath of loyalty to Guðhere.

No-one seems able to decide how this tangle could be solved—partly because in our surviving fragments, it is not clear who is speaking. Hildegyð encouraging Waldere in the speech in fragment 1, certainly, and Waldere taunting Guðhere in the second speech in the second fragment. But who says the not-quite ten lines at the start of the second fragment, praising a sword not yet used? It seems unlikely to be Hildegyð, who has already handed over Mimming—unless for some reason she kept a better sword back? Of the three men present, it could be Guðhere, as Waldere is clearly addressing him in the next speech. But why would Guðhere keep his best sword in reserve? Could it be Waldere, praising Mimming, which Hildegyð has given him? But it has been "hidden in a jeweled scabbard," which you might expect a man to do, rather than a woman. Perhaps the speech comes from Hagena, warning his lord that there is only one sword better than Mimming, one which Hagena owns but has not yet drawn? If Hagena has just said also that he does not intend to intervene, even with this pre-eminent sword, then that would explain Waldere's speech in reply, which in effect says to Guðhere, "It's just you and me now." Scholars have argued this puzzle many ways, and have had to work hard even to imagine a tolerable end to this tangled situation.

Despite the confusion, the uncertainties, the loss of context for all three poems, they do give evidence of a powerful tradition, with a central theme, based on many legends, existing in several languages, with many admirers, and abandoned—at least by some—only reluctantly. We can only feel grateful to the long-dead monastics who took the time to record some scraps: though none at all to the vandal who cut up the original *Waldere*-poem to use as scrap paper.

Further Reading

Braune, Wilhelm, ed. *Althochdeutsches Lesebuch*. Revised by Ernst A. Ebbinghaus, 17th ed. Tübingen: Max Niemeyer, 1994.

Bostock, J. Knight. "The Lay of Hildebrand." In *A Handbook on Old High German Literature*, revised by K. C. King and D. R. McLintock, 2nd ed., 43–82. Oxford: Clarendon Press, 1976.

Himes, Jonathan B., ed. *The Old English Epic of Waldere*. Newcastle upon Tyne: Cambridge Scholars Publishing, 2009.

Kratz, Dennis M., ed. and trans. *Waltharius and Ruodlieb*. New York: Garland, 1984.

Lühr, Rosemarie. *Studien zur Sprache des Hildebrandliedes*. Frankfurt am Main: Peter Lang, 1982.

Gentry, Francis G., and James K. Walter, ed. and trans. *German Epic Poetry: The Nibelungenlied, the Older Lay of Hildebrand, and Other Works*. New York: Continuum, 1995.

Gillespie, George T. "Heroic Lays: Survival and Transformation in Ballad." *Oxford German Studies* 9 (1978): 1–18.

Magoun, Francis P., Jr. "A Note on Old West Germanic Poetic Unity." *Modern Philology* 43 (1945): 77-82.

Neidorf, Leonard. "Garulf and Guthlaf in the *Finnsburg* Fragment." *Notes & Queries* 66 (2019): 489–492.

Neidorf, Leonard. "Youth and Age in the *Finnsburg* Fragment." *ANQ* 35 (2022): 4–8.

Norman, Frederick. *Three Essays on the Hildebrandslied*, edited by A. T. Hatto. London: University of London, 1973.

Phillpotts, Bertha S. "Wyrd and Providence in Anglo-Saxon Thought." *Essays and Studies* 13 (1928): 7–27.

Smyser, H. M., and Francis P. Magoun Jr., ed. and trans. *Walther of Aquitaine: Materials for the Study of His Legend*. New London: Connecticut College, 1950.

Tolkien, J. R. R. *Finn and Hengest: The Fragment and the Episode*. Edited by A. J. Bliss. London: George Allen & Unwin, 1982.

THE FIGHT AT FINNSBURG

      *   *   * [hor]nas byrnað.'
[H]næf hlēoþrode ðā   heaþoġeong cyning:
'Nē ðis ne dagað ēastan,   nē hēr draca ne flēogeð,
nē hēr ðisse healle   hornas ne byrnað;
5 ac hēr forþ berað,   fugelas singað,
ġylleð grǣġhama,   gūðwudu hlynneð,
scyld scefte oncwyð.   Nū scȳneð þes mōna
waðol under wolcnum;   nū ārīsað wēadǣda
ðe ðisne folces nīð   fremman willað.
10 Ac onwacniġeað nū,   wīġend mīne,
habbað ēowre linda,   hicgeaþ on ellen,
winnað on orde,   wesað on mōde!'
Ðā ārās mæniġ goldhladen ðeġn,   gyrde hine his swurde;
ðā tō dura ēodon   drihtliċe cempan,
15 Siġeferð and Eaha,   hyra sword ġetugon,
and æt ōþrum durum   Ordlāf and Gūþlāf
and Henġest sylf,   hwearf him on lāste.
Ðā ġȳt Gārulf[e]   Gūðere stȳrde,
ðæt hē swā frēoliċ feorh   forman sīþe
20 tō ðǣre healle durum   hyrsta ne bǣre,
nū hyt nīþa heard   ānyman wolde;
ac hē fræġn ofer eal   undearninga,
dēormōd hæleþ,   hwā ðā duru hēolde.
'Siġeferþ is mīn nama,' cweþ hē;   'iċ eom Secgena lēod,
25 wreċċea wīde cūð;   fæla iċ wēana ġebād,

THE FIGHT AT FINNSBURG

... gables are burning."
Hnæf spoke,   the young war-king:
"This is not day from the east,   nor a dragon flying,
nor are the gables   of this hall burning,
but here they are carrying forward,   the birds are singing,
the grey-coat howls,   the war-wood rings,
shield speaks to shaft.   Now the moon shines,
fitful through the clouds,   now sad deeds must follow,
which will bring about   disaster for this people.
But wake now, my warriors,   pick up your shields,
think of valour,   fight in the front,
be courageous.   Then many a thane got up,
laden with gold,   girded on his sword.
Then Sigeferth and Eaha,   veteran champions,
went to the door,   drawing their swords,
and at the other doors   Ordlaf and Guthlaf,
and Hengest himself   turned in their track.
Then again Guthhere   urged Garulf
not to bear his armour   and his valuable life
for the first time   to the hall-doors,
now that the battle-hardened   wished to take it.
But the brave-hearted hero   demanded openly,
over everything, who it was   who held the door.
He said, "Sigeferth is my name,   a man of the Secge,
a famous adventurer.   I have lived through

heordra hilda;   ðē is ġȳt hēr witod
swæþer ðū sylf tō mē   sēċean wylle.'
Ðā wæs on healle   wælslihta ġehlyn,
sceolde celæs bord   cēnum on handa,
30 bānhelm berstan,   — buruhðelu dynede —
oð æt ðǣre gūðe   Gārulf ġecrang
ealra ǣrest   eorðbūendra,
Gūðlāfes sunu,   ymbe hyne gōdra fæla,
hwearflatra hrǣw.   Hræfen wandrode
35 sweart and sealobrūn.   Swurdlēoma stōd,
swylċe eal Finn[e]s Buruh   fȳrenu wǣre.
Ne ġefræġn iċ nǣfre wurþlicor   æt wera hilde
sixtiġ siġebeorna   sēl ġebǣran,
nē nēfre swānas hwītne medo   sēl forġyldan,
40 ðonne Hnæfe guldan   his hæġstealdas.
Hiġ fuhton fīfdagas,   swā hyra nān ne fēol,
drihtġesīða,   ac hiġ ðā duru hēoldon.
   Ðā ġewāt him wund hæleð   on wæġ gangan,
sǣde þæt his byrne   ābrocen wǣre,
45 heresceorp unhrōr,   and ēac wæs his helm ðȳr[e]l.
Ðā hine sōna fræġn   folces hyrde
hū ðā wīġend hyra   wunda ġenǣson,
oððe hwæþer ðǣra hyssa   * * * * *

many troubles,   many hard battles.
For you it will now be seen   which of the two things
you yourself will get   from me here."
Then in the hall   there was a din of death-strokes,
hollow shields broke   in the hands of brave ones,
and the helmets   that protected skulls,
the planks of the hall   re-echoed with the din,
until in the battle   the first to fall
of all those   who lived on earth
was Garulf son of Guthlaf,   round him many good men,
mortal bodies.   The raven hovered,
black and shining.   Sparks flew from swords,
as if all Finnsburg   were on fire.
I have never heard   of sixty warriors
who bore themselves better,   more nobly in battle
between men,   nor ever followers
who better repaid   their white mead,
than his young men   paid to Hnæf.
They fought for five days,   so that none fell
of the companions,   but they held the doors.
    Then a wounded hero   turned away,
said his armour was broken,   his war-sword blunted,
his helmet pierced.   Then the shepherd of the people
asked him immediately   how the warriors
were bearing their wounds,   or whether any of the young men ...

WALDERE

A

* * * * *   hyrde hyne ġeorne:
'Hūru Wēland(es)   worc ne ġeswīceð
monna ǣnigum   ðāra ðe Mimming can
hear[d]ne ġehealdan;   oft æt hilde ġedrēas
5 swātfāg ond sweordwund   sec[g] æfter ōðrum.
Ætlan ordwyga,   ne lǣt ðīn ellen nū ġȳ(t)
ġedrēosan tō dæġe,   dryhtscipe * * *
* * * * *   (Nū) is se dæġ cumen
þæt ðū scealt āninga   ōðer twēġa,
10 līf forlēosan   oððe lang[n]e dōm
āgan mid eldum,   Ælfheres sunu.
Nalles iċ ðē, wine mīn,   wordum ċīde,
(ð)ȳ iċ ðē ġesāwe   æt ðām sweordplegan
ðurh edwītscype   ǣniġes monnes
15 wīġ forbūgan   oððe on weal flēon,
līċe beorgan,   ðēah þe lāðra fela
ðīnne byrnhomon   billum hēowun;
ac ðū symle furðor   feohtan sōhtest,
mǣl ofer mearce;   ðȳ iċ ðē metod ondrēd,
20 þæt ðū tō fyrenlīċe   feohtan sōhtest
æt ðām ætstealle   ōðres monnes,
wīġrǣdenne.   Weorða ðē selfne
gōdum dǣdum   ðenden ðīn God reċċe.

WALDERE

A

... heard him gladly.
"The work of Wayland   will surely not fail
any man who can hold   Mimming, the hard one.
Often one man   after another
fell in battle,   stained with blood,
wounded by the sword.   Warrior of Attila,
do not let your valour   and nobility fail today ...
Son of Ælfhere,   now the day has come
when you must surely   do one or the other:
lose your life, or gain   lasting glory among men.
My friend, I am not   blaming you with words
because I saw you   in the sword-play,
disgracefully   flinch from battle
or flee to the wall   to save your life,
though many foes   cut at your armour
with their blades;   but you always wanted
to go forward   in the fighting,
overstepping the mark.   That is the reason
I fear fate for you,   you fought too willfully,
on your enemy's ground,   giving him vantage.
While God cares for you,   gain yourself honour
by noble deeds.   Do not mourn for your sword.

Ne murn ðū for ðī mēċe;   ðē wearð māðma cyst

25 ġifeðe tō [ġ]ēoce,   (mit) ðȳ ðū Gūðhere[s] scealt

bēot forbīġan,   ðæs ðe hē ðās beaduwe ongan

mid unryhte   ǣrest sēċan.

Forsōc hē ðām swurde   ond ðām synċfatum,

bēaga mæniġo;   nū sceal bēġa lēas

30 hworfan from ðisse hilde,   hlāfurd sēċan,

ealdne ēðel,   oððe hēr ǣr swefan,

ġif hē ðā' * * * * * * *

B

* * * *   'swilċeı bæteran

būton ðām ānum   ðe iċ ēac hafa

on stānfate   stille ġehīded.

Iċ wāt þæt [h]it ðōhte   Ðēodrīċ Widian

5 selfum onsendon,   ond ēac sinċ miċel

māðma mid ðī mēċe,   moniġ ōðres mid him

golde ġeġirwan;   iūlēan ġenam,

þæs ðe hine of nearwum   Nīðhādes mǣġ,

Wēlandes bearn,   Widia ūt forlēt;

10 ðurh fīfẹla ġe(wea)ld   forð ōnette.'

Waldere mað(e)lode,   wiga ellenrōf,

hæfde him on handa   hildefrō[f]re,

gūðbilla gripe,   ġyddode wordum:

'Hwæt, ðū hūru wēndest,   wine Burgenda,

15 þæt mē Hagenan hand   hilde ġefremede,

ond ġetwǣmde fēðewiġġes.   Feta, ġyf ðū dyrre,

æt ðus heaðuwērịgan   hāre byrnan!

Standeð mē hēr on eaxelum   Ælfheres lāf,

gōd ond ġēapneb,   golde ġeweorðod,

20 ealles unscende   æðelinges rēaf

tō habbanne   þonne ha[n]d wereð

feorhhord fēondum;   neı bið fāh wið mē

þonne (mē) unmǣgas   eft onġynnað,

The best of treasures   has been given to help you,
with it you shall humble   the boast of Guthhere,
because from the start   he sought this battle
without just cause.   He refused the sword
and the treasures, many rings.   Now he will leave
this battle with no rings,   to seek out his lord
and his old homeland,   or sleep here first,
if he ..."

B

"... any better
than the one I have here,   hidden secretly
in jeweled scabbard.   I know that Theodoric
meant to send it   to Widia himself,
much treasure as well,   many valuable things,
to deck with gold   many another;
he got this reward   because Widia,
Wayland's child,   Nithhad's son
from his hardships,   hurried him out
of the grasp   of the giants."
Waldere spoke,   the bold warrior,
he had in his hand   the hilt of a war-blade,
a solace in battle,   he spoke these words:
"Friend of the Burgundians,   you no doubt expected
the hand of Hagena   to give me battle,
and put an end   to my fighting on foot.
Fetch, if you dare,   the grey armour
from a war-weary man!   On my shoulders
lies Ælfhere's legacy,   large and splendid,
adorned with gold,   fit to be without shame
in every way   a prince's plunder,
to have when hand   defends life-hoard
from enemies.   It will not fail me

mēċum ġemētað,   swā ġē mē dydon.
25 Ðēah mæġ siġe syllan   sē ðe symle byð
recon ond rǣdfest   ryhta ġehwilċes.
Sē ðe him tō ðām hālgan   helpe ġelīfeð,
tō Gode ġīoce,   hē þǣr ġearo findeð,
ġif ðā earnunga   ǣr ġeðenċeð.
30 Þonne mōten wlance   welan britnian,
ǣhtum wealdan;   þæt is * * * *

376

when foes begin again   to meet me with swords,
as you have just done.   He who is always
prompt and just   in every right
can still give victory.   He who believes
in help from the Holy One,   succor from God,
will find it soon,   if he has thought in time
how to deserve it.   Then the proud ones
will have the right   to divide treasure,
take hold of wealth.   That is ..."

HILDEBRANDSLIED

Ik gihōrta ðat seggen,
ðat sih urhēttun   ǣnon muotīn,
Hiltibrant enti Haðubrant,   untar heriun tuēm
sunufatarungo.   Iro saro rihtun,
5 garutun se iro gūðhamun,   gurtun sih iro suert ana,
helidos, ubar [h]ringā,   dō sie tō dero hiltiu ritun.
Hiltibrant gimahalta — Heribrantes sunu —
                        her uuas hērōro man,
ferahes frōtōro;   her frāgēn gistuont
fōhēm uuortum,   [h]wer sīn fater wāri
10 fireo in folche, * * * *
                        'eddo [h]welīhhes cnuosles dū sīs;
ību dū mī ẹ̄nan sagēs,   ik mī dē ōdre uuēt,
chind, in chunincrīche;   chūd ist mir al irmindeot.'
    Hadubrant gimahalta,   Hiltibrantes sunu:
15 'Dat sagētun mī ūsere liuti,
alte anti frōte,   dea ērhina wārun,
dat Hiltibrant hǣtti mīn fater;   ih heittu Hadubrant.
Forn her ōstar giuueit,   flōh her Ōtachres nīd,
hina miti Theotrīhhe,   enti sīnero degano filu.
20 Her furlaet in lante   luttila sitten
prūt[i] in būre,   barn unwahsan,
arbeo laosa;   he[r] raet ōstar hina,
de[s] sīd Dētrīhhe   darbā gistuontun
fatereres mīnes: dat uuas sō friuntlaos man.

378

HILDEBRANDSLIED

I heard it said   that the warriors
Hildebrand and Hadubrand,   father and son,
met alone,   between the two armies.
The heroes made their gear ready,   girded on their swords
over the ring-mail,   when they rode to the battle.
Hildebrand spoke,   son of Heribrand –
he was the older man,   wiser in mind.
He began to ask   the other in few words
who among men   in the people
might be his father ...
                  "or of what family you are.
If you tell me one, young man,   I will know the others.
All great people   are known to me."
  Hadubrand spoke,   son of Hildebrand:
"Old and wise men   of our people,
who lived in former times,   told me that my father
was called Hildebrand.   I am called Hadubrand.
Long ago he went   away to the east,
fled from the enmity   of Odoacer,
along with Theodoric   and many of his thanes.
He left in the land   little ones sitting,
a bride in her bower,   an ungrown child
with no inheritance.   He rode off to the east,
once Theodoric   stood in need
of my father;   he was such a friendless man.

25 Her was Ōtachre   ummett[i] irri,
   degano dechisto   unti Deotrīchhhe darba gistontun.
   Her was eo folches at ente,   imo was eo fehta ti leop;
chūd was her chōnnēm mannum; ni wāniu ih iū līb habbe.'
   'Wēttu irmingot,' quad Hiltibrant,   'obana ab heuane,
dat dū neo dana halt mit sus sippan man   dinc ni gileitōs.'
   Want her dō ar arme   wuntane baugā,
   cheisuringu gitān,   sō imo se der chuning gap,
   Hūneo truhtīn: 'Dat ih dir it nū bi huldī gibu.'
35   Hadubrant gima[ha]lta,   Hiltibrantes sunu:
   'Mit gēru scal man   geba infāhan,
   ort wider orte. * * * * *
   Dū bist dir altēr Hūn,   ummet spāhēr,
spenis mih mit dīnēm wortun,   wili mih dīnu speru werpan;
40   pist alsō gialtēt man,   sō dū ēwīn inwit fortōs.
   Dat sagētun mī   sēolīdante
   westar ubar Wentilsēo,   dat inan wīc furnam:
   tōt ist Hiltibrant,   Heribrantes suno.'
   Hiltibrant gimahalta,   Heribrantes suno:
45 'Wela gisihu ih   in dīnēm hrustim,
   dat dū habēs hēme   hērron gōten,
   dat dū noh bi desemo rīche   reccheo ni wurti.'
'Welaga nū, waltant got,' quad Hiltibrant,   'wēwurt skihit.
   Ih wallōta sumaro enti wintro   sehstic ur lante,
50   dār man mih eo scerita   in folc sceotantero;
   sō man mir at burc ēnīgeru   banun ni gifasta,
   nū scal mih suāsat chind   suertu hauwan,
   bretōn mit sīnu billiu,   eddo ih imo ti banin werdan.
   Doh maht dū nū aodlīhho,   ibu dir dīn ellen taoc,
55   in sus hēremo man   hrusti giwinnan,
   rauba birahanen,   ibu dū dār ēnīc reht habēs.'

He was angry   with Odoacer
beyond measure,   but the most loyal of thanes
to Theodoric when   need came upon him.
He was always   in the forefront
of the army,   battle was always
too dear to him,   he was well-known
among brave men.   I do not believe he is still alive."
    Hildebrand said,   "May great God from heaven above
bear witness that you have never   had anything to do
with any man   more closely related."
    He took from his arm   twisted rings,
rings of imperial gold   which the king,
the lord of the Huns,   had given to him.
"I give you this now   as a sign of friendship."
    Hadubrand spoke,   son of Hildebrand,
"A man should get   gifts with a spear,
point against point.   Old Hun, you are crafty
beyond measure,   lure me with your words,
mean to throw your spear at me.   You have reached old age,
because always   you use cunning.
Seafarers from the west   over the Wendel-sea
told me that war   had taken him.
Hildebrand is dead,   son of Heribrand."
    Hildebrand spoke,   son of Heribrand,
"I can well see   from your war-gear
 that you have at home   a good lord,
that under his rule   you have never needed
to become a wanderer.   Almighty God,
sixty summers and winters   have I wandered,
exiled out of this land,   always counted
among the army   of the shooters,
yet even so no man ever   dealt me death in any encampment.
    Now my own child   must cut at me with sword,
strike me with his blade,   or else I will be his bane.
Still, now you can easily,   if your valour is up to it,
win the armour   from such an aged man,
seize the plunder,   if you have any right to it.

'Der sī doh nū argōsto,' quad Hiltibrant, 'ōstarliuto,
  der dir nū wīges warne, nū dih es sō wel lustit,
  gūdea gimeinūn; niuse dē mōtti,
  [h]werdar sih hiutu der hregilo hru[o]men muotti
60 erdo desero brunnōno bēdero uualtan.'
    Dō lēttun se ǣrist asckim scrītan,
  scarpēn scūrun, dat in dēm sciltim stōnt.
  Dō stōpun tōsamane, staimbort chlubun,
  heuwun harmlīcco huīttę scilti,
65 unti im iro lintūn luttilo wurtun,
  giwigan miti wābnum * * * *

May he now be most craven   of the easterners,
who should now refuse you battle,   fight between us,
since it pleases you so much.   Let him have it who may,
whichever of us shall today   be able to take pride
in the armor,   become the owner
of both the mail-shirts."
    Then they let fly   first with ash-spears,
in sharp showers,   so they stood in the shields.
Then they closed together,   clove the battle-boards,
hacked furiously   at the white shields,
until the linden-shields   grew smaller
from the strokes   of the weapons ...

ABOUT THE AUTHORS

TOM SHIPPEY received his PhD from the University of Cambridge. In an academic teaching career lasting 43 years (1965-2008), he taught at six universities, including Oxford and Harvard. His first published article, more than fifty years ago, was "The Fairy-Tale Structure of *Beowulf*" (1969), while his first published book was *Old English Verse* (1972). Since then, he has published well over a hundred academic articles, and more than twenty monographs and edited collections, notably (with Andreas Haarder) *The Critical Heritage: Beowulf* (1998), and most recently, *Beowulf and the North before the Vikings* (2022). He also written more than 200 reviews on fantasy and science fiction for *The Wall Street Journal*, as well as many contributions, often on archaeology, to *The London Review of Books*. He is well known for books that have reached a wider community of readers outside academia, such as *Laughing Shall I Die* (2018) and his much-reprinted and often-translated books on Tolkien, *The Road to Middle-earth* (1981) and *J. R. R. Tolkien: Author of the Century* (2000).

LEONARD NEIDORF received his PhD from Harvard University. He has been Professor of English at Nanjing University since 2016. He is the author of two monographs on *Beowulf*: *The Transmission of Beowulf* (2017) and *The Art and Thought of the Beowulf Poet* (2022), both of which were published by Cornell University Press. He is the editor of *The Dating of Beowulf: A Reassessment* (2014), which was named an Outstanding Academic Title by *CHOICE*, and the co-editor (with Rafael J. Pascual and Tom Shippey) of *Old English Philology: Studies in Honour of R. D. Fulk* (2016). Neidorf has published more than 90 papers, which have appeared in a wide range of prominent journals, including *ELH, Folklore, Traditio, Nature Human Behaviour*, and *Journal of Germanic Linguistics*. For his research on *Beowulf*, Neidorf was awarded the Beatrice White Prize from the English Association in 2020.

BIBLIOGRAPHY

Abram, Christopher. "Bee-Wolf and the Hand of Victory: Identifying the Heroes of *Beowulf* and *Vǫlsunga saga.*" *Journal of English and Germanic Philology* 116 (2017): 387–414.

Acker, Paul. "Horror and the Maternal in *Beowulf.*" *PMLA* 121 (2006): 702–716.

Alfano, Christine. "The Issue of Feminine Monstrosity: A Reevaluation of Grendel's Mother." *Comitatus* 23 (1992): 1–16.

Allen, Judson Boyce. "God's Society and Grendel's Shoulder Joint: Gregory and the Poet of the *Beowulf.*" *Neuphilologische Mitteilungen* 78 (1977): 239–240.

Anderson, Carl Edlund. "Scyld Scyldinga: Intercultural Innovation at the Interface of West and North Germanic." *Neophilologus* 100 (2016): 461–476.

Anderson, Earl R. "Treasure Trove in *Beowulf*: A Legal View of the Dragon's Hoard." *Mediaevalia* 3 (1977): 141–164.

Andersson, Theodore M. *A Preface to the Nibelungenlied.* Stanford: Stanford University Press, 1987.

——. "The Thief in *Beowulf.*" *Speculum* 59 (1984): 493–508.

Andrew, Malcolm. "Grendel in Hell." *English Studies* 62 (1981): 401–410.

Appleton, Helen. "The Role of Æschere's Head." *Review of English Studies* 68 (2017): 428–447.

Atherton, Mark. "The Figure of the Archer in *Beowulf* and the Anglo-Saxon Psalter." *Neophilologus* 77 (1993): 653–657.

Aurner, Nellie S. "Hengest: A Study in Early English Hero Legend." *University of Iowa Humanistic Studies* 2 (1921): 1–76.

Babcock, Michael A. *The Stories of Attila the Hun's Death: Narrative, Myth, and Meaning.* Lewiston: Edwin Mellen Press, 2001.

Baird, Joseph L. "Unferth the Þyle." *Medium Ævum* 39 (1970): 1–12.

——. "The Uses of Ignorance: *Beowulf* 435, 2330." *Notes and Queries* 14 (1967): 6–8.

Baker, Peter S. "Beowulf the Orator." *Journal of English Linguistics* 21 (1988): 3–23.

——. *Honour, Exchange and Violence in Beowulf.* Cambridge: D. S. Brewer, 2013.

Bammesberger, Alfred. "The Meaning of Old English *Folcscaru* and the Compound's Function in *Beowulf.*" *NOWELE* 72 (2019): 1–10.

——. "Who Advised Beowulf to Challenge Grendel?" *ANQ* 24 (2011): 244–248.

Bandy, Stephen C. "Cain, Grendel, and the Giants of *Beowulf.*" *Papers on Language and Literature* 9 (1973): 235–249.

Barco, Maximino Gutiérrez. "The Boar in *Beowulf* and *Elene*: A Germanic Symbol of Protection." *SELIM* 9 (1999): 163–171.

Barnes, Daniel R. "Folktale Morphology and the Structure of *Beowulf.*" *Speculum* 45 (1970): 416–434.

Bately, Janet. "Linguistic Evidence as a Guide to the Authorship of Old English Verse: A Reappraisal, with Special Reference to *Beowulf*." In *Learning and Literature in Anglo-Saxon England: Studies Presented to Peter Clemoes on the Occasion of His Sixty-Fifth Birthday*, edited by Michael Lapidge and Helmut Gneuss, 409–431. Cambridge: Cambridge University Press, 1985.

Battles, Paul. "'Contending Throng' Scenes and the Comitatus Ideal in Old English Poetry, with special attention to *The Battle of Maldon* 122a." *Studia Neophilologica* 83 (2011): 41–53.

———. "Dying for a Drink: 'Sleeping after the Feast' Scenes in *Beowulf, Andreas*, and the Old English Poetic Tradition." *Modern Philology* 112 (2015): 435–457.

Bazelmans, Jos. *By Weapons Made Worthy: Lords, Retainers, and their Relationship in Beowulf*. Amsterdam: Amsterdam University Press, 1999.

Beck, Heinrich. *Das Ebersignum im Germanischen*. Berlin: De Gruyter, 1965.

Bennett, Helen. "The Female Mourner at Beowulf's Funeral: Filling in the Blanks / Hearing the Spaces." *Exemplaria* 4 (1992): 35–50.

Benskin, Michael. "The Narrative Structure of the Finnsburh Episode in *Beowulf*." *Amsterdamer Beiträge zur älteren Germanistik* 77 (2017): 37–64.

Benson, Larry D. "The Originality of *Beowulf*." In *The Interpretation of Narrative: Theory and Practice*, edited by Morton W. Bloomfield, 1–43. Cambridge, MA: Harvard University Press, 1970.

———. "The Pagan Coloring of *Beowulf*." In *Old English Poetry: Fifteen Essays*, edited by Robert P. Creed, 193–213. Providence: Brown University Press, 1967.

Biggs, Frederick M. "*Beowulf* and Some Fictions of the Geatish Succession." *Anglo-Saxon England* 32 (2003): 55–77.

——. "Beowulf's Fight with the Nine Nicors," *Review of English Studies* 53 (2002): 311–328.

——. "History and Fiction in the Frisian Raid." In *The Dating of Beowulf: A Reassessment*, edited by Leonard Neidorf, 138–156. Cambridge: D. S. Brewer, 2014.

——. "Hondscioh and Æschere in *Beowulf*." *Neophilologus* 87 (2003): 635–652.

——. "The Politics of Succession in *Beowulf* and Anglo-Saxon England." *Speculum* 80 (2005): 709–741.

Bintley, Michael. "*Hrinde Bearwas*: The Trees at the Mere and the Root of All Evil in *Beowulf*." *Journal of English and Germanic Philology* 119 (2020): 309–326.

Blake, N. F. "The Heremod Digressions in *Beowulf*." *JEGP* 61 (1962): 278–287.

Bliss, A. J. "*Beowulf*, Lines 3074-3075." In *J. R. R. Tolkien, Scholar and Storyteller: Essays in Memoriam*, edited by Mary Salu and Robert T. Farrell, 41–63. Ithaca: Cornell University Press, 1979.

Bloomfield, Josephine. "Diminished by Kindness: Frederick Klaeber's Rewriting of Wealhtheow." *Journal of English and Germanic Philology* 93 (1994): 183–203.

Bloomfield, Morton W. "Patristics and Old English Literature: Notes on Some Poems." *Comparative Literature* 14 (1962): 36–43.

Bonjour, Adrien. *The Digressions in Beowulf*. Oxford: Blackwell, 1950.

——. "Monsters Crouching and Critics Rampant: Or the *Beowulf* Dragon Debated." *PMLA* 68 (1953): 304–312.

——. "Young Beowulf's Inglorious Period." *Anglia* 70 (1951): 339–344.

Bouman, A. C. "The Heroes of the Fight at Finnsburh." *Acta Philologica Scandinavica* 10 (1935): 130–144.

Braccini, Giovanna Princi. "Perché Hroðgar *Stod on Stapole* (*Beowulf* 926a)." In *Echi di Memoria: Scritti di varia filologia, critica e linguistica in recordo di Giorgio Chiarini*, edited by Gaetano Chiappini, 139–157. Florence: Alinea, 1998.

Brady, Caroline. *The Legends of Ermanaric.* Berkeley: University of California Press, 1943.

Brady, Lindy. "Boars and the Geats in *Beowulf.*" In *Early English Poetic Culture and Meter: The Influence of G. R. Russom*, edited by M. J. Toswell and Lindy Brady, 61–72. Kalamazoo: Medieval Institute Publications, 2016.

Braeger, Peter C. "Connotations of (Earm) Sceapen: *Beowulf* ll. 2228-2229 and the Shape-Shifting Dragon." *Essays in Literature* 13 (1986): 327–328.

Bremmer, Rolf H., Jr. "Grendel's Arm and the Law." In *Studies in English Language and Literature: 'Doubt Wisely': Papers in Honour of E. G. Stanley*, edited by M. J. Toswell and E. M. Tyler, 121–132. London: Routledge, 1996.

——. "The Importance of Kinship: Uncle and Nephew in *Beowulf.*" *Amsterdamer Beiträge zur älteren Germanistik* 15 (1980): 21–38.

Brennan, Malcolm M. "Hrothgar's Government." *Journal of English and Germanic Philology* 84 (1985): 3–15.

Brodeur, Arthur G. *The Art of Beowulf.* Berkeley: University of California Press, 1959.

Bruce, Alexander. *Scyld and Scef: Expanding the Analogues.* New York: Routledge, 2002.

Burdorff, Sara Frances. "Re-reading Grendel's Mother: *Beowulf* and the Anglo-Saxon Metrical Charms." *Comitatus* 45 (2014): 91–103.

Burrow, J. A. *The Poetry of Praise*. Cambridge: Cambridge University Press, 2008.

Butts, Richard. "The Analogical Mere: Landscape and Terror in *Beowulf*." *English Studies* 68 (1987): 113–121.

Byock, Jesse, trans. *The Saga of King Hrolf Kraki*. London: Penguin, 1998.

Cabaniss, Allen. "*Beowulf* and the Liturgy." *Journal of English and Germanic Philology* 54 (1955): 195–201.

Cahill, James. "Reconsidering Robinson's Beowulf." *English Studies* 89 (2008): 251–262.

Camargo, Martin. "The Finn Episode and the Tragedy of Revenge in *Beowulf*." *Studies in Philology* 78 (1981): 120–134.

Carens, Marilyn M. "Handscóh and Grendel: The Motif of the Hand in *Beowulf*." In *Aeolian Harps: Essays in Literature in Honor of Maurice Browning Cramer*, edited by Donna G. Fricke and Douglas C. Fricke, 39–55. Bowling Green: Bowling Green University Press, 1976.

Carnicelli, Thomas A. "The Function of the Messenger in *Beowulf*." *Studies in Philology* 72 (1975): 246–257.

Cavell, Megan. "Constructing the Monstrous Body in *Beowulf*." *Anglo-Saxon England* 43 (2014): 151–181.

Cavill, Paul. "A Note on *Beowulf*, Lines 2490-2509." *Neophilologus* 67 (1983): 599–604.

——. "Christianity and Theology in *Beowulf*." In *The Christian Tradition in Anglo-Saxon England: Approaches to Current Scholarship and Teaching*, edited by Paul Cavill, 15–40. Woodbridge, UK: D. S. Brewer, 2004.

Chadwick, Nora K. "The Monsters and Beowulf." In *The An-glo-Saxons: Studies in Some Aspects of Their History and Culture Presented to Bruce Dickins*, edited by Peter Clemoes, 171–203. London: Bowes & Bowes, 1959.

——. "Norse Ghosts (A Study in the *Draugr* and the *Haugbúi*)." *Folklore* 57 (1946): 50–65.

——. "Norse Ghosts II." *Folklore* 57 (1946): 106–127.

Chambers, R. W. *Beowulf: An Introduction to the Study of the Poem with a Discussion of the Stories of Finn and Offa. With a Supplement by C. L. Wrenn*, 3rd ed. Cambridge: Cambridge University Press, 1959.

Chance, Jane. "The Structural Unity of *Beowulf*: The Problem of Grendel's Mother." In *New Readings on Women in Old English Literature*, edited by Helen Damico and Alexandra Hennessy Olsen, 248–261. Bloomington: Indiana University Press, 1990.

Chickering, Howell D., Jr., ed. and trans. *Beowulf: A Dual-Language Edition*, 2nd ed. New York: Anchor Books, 2006.

Clark, David. *Beowulf in Contemporary Culture*. Newcastle upon Tyne: Cambridge Scholars, 2020.

——. "Relaunching the Hero: The Case of Scyld and Beowulf Re-Opened." *Neophilologus* 90 (2006): 621–642.

Clark, George. "*Beowulf*: The Last Word." in *Old English and New: Studies in Language and Linguistics in Honor of Frederic G. Cassidy*, edited by Joan H. Hall, Nick Doane, and Dick Ringler, 15–30. New York: Garland, 1992.

——. "Beowulf's Armor." *ELH* 32 (1965): 409–441.

——. "The Hero and the Theme." In *A Beowulf Handbook*, edited by Robert E. Bjork and John D. Niles, 271–290. Lincoln: University of Nebraska Press, 1997.

Clarke, D. E. Martin. "The Office of *Thyle* in *Beowulf*." *Review of English Studies* 12 (1936): 61–66.

Clarke, M. G. *Sidelights on Teutonic History during the Migration Period*. Cambridge: Cambridge University Press, 1911.

Clover, Carol J. "The Germanic Context of the Unferþ Episode." *Speculum* 55 (1980): 444–468.

Cooke, William. "Hrothulf: A Richard III, or an Alfred the Great?" *Studies in Philology* 104 (2007): 175–198.

——. "Who Cursed Whom, and When? The Cursing of the Hoard and Beowulf's Fate." *Medium Ævum* 76 (2007): 207–224.

Cox, Betty S. *Cruces of Beowulf*. The Hague: Mouton, 1971.

Cramp, Rosemary J. "The Hall in *Beowulf* and in Archaeology." In *Heroic Poetry in the Anglo-Saxon Period*, edited by Helen Damico and John Leyerle, 331–346. Kalamazoo, MI: Medieval Institute Publications, 1993.

Crépin, André. "Wealhtheow's Offering of the Cup to Beowulf: A Study in Literary Structure." In *Saints, Scholars and Heroes: Studies in Medieval Culture in Honour of Charles W. Jones*, edited by Margot H. King and Wesley M. Stevens, 2 vols., I: 45–58. Collegeville: Hill Monastic Manuscript Library, Saint John's Abbey and University, 1979.

Grocock, Christopher. "*Enta Geweorc*: *The Ruin* and its Contexts Reconsidered." In *The Material Culture of the Built Environment in the Anglo-Saxon World*, edited by Maren Clegg Hyer and Gale R. Owen-Crocker, 13–36. Liverpool: Liverpool University Press, 2017.

Cronan, Dennis. "*Beowulf*, the Gaels, and the Recovery of the Pre-Conversion Past." *Anglo-Saxon* 1 (2007): 137–180.

——. "*Eotena*, Eotenum 'Jutes' in the Finnsburg Episode in *Beowulf*." *Modern Philology* 116 (2018): 1–19.

——. "Hroðgar and the *Gylden Hilt* in *Beowulf*." *Traditio* 72 (2017): 109–132.

——. "*Lofgeorn*: Generosity and Praise." *Neuphilologische Mitteilungen* 92 (1991): 187–194.

——. "The Origin of Ancient Strife in *Beowulf*." *North-Western Language Evolution* 31–32 (1997): 57–68.

——. "Poetic Meanings in the Old English Poetic Vocabulary." *English Studies* 84 (2003): 397–425.

——. "Poetic Words, Conservatism, and the Dating of Old English Poetry." *Anglo-Saxon England* 33 (2004): 23–50.

——. "The Rescuing Sword." *Neophilologus* 77 (1993): 467–478.

——. "Wiglaf's Sword." *Studia Neophilologica* 65 (1993): 129–139.

Culbert, Taylor "The Narrative Function of Swords in Beowulf." *Journal of English and Germanic Philology* 59 (1960): 13–20.

Currie, Edward. "Hygelac's Raid in Historiography and Poetry: The King's Necklace and *Beowulf* as 'Epic.'" *Neophilologus,* 104 (2020): 391–400.

——. "Political Ideals, Monstrous Counsel, and the Literary Imagination in *Beowulf*." In *Imagination and Fantasy in the Middle Ages and Early Modern Time: Projections, Dreams, Monsters, and Illusions*, edited by Albrecht Classen, vol. 24, 275–302. Berlin: De Gruyter, 2020.

Damico, Helen. *Beowulf's Wealhtheow and the Valkyrie Tradition*. Madison: University of Wisconsin Press, 1984.

——. "*Sörlaþáttr* and the Hama Episode in *Beowulf*." *Scandinavian Studies* 55 (1983): 222–235.

——. "*Þrymskviða* and Beowulf's Second Fight: The Dressing of the Hero in Parody." *Scandinavian Studies* 58 (1986): 407–428.

Davidson, Hilda R. Ellis. *Gods and Myths of Northern Europe.* Harmondsworth: Penguin, 1964.

——. "The Hill of the Dragon: Anglo-Saxon Burial Mounds in Literature and Archaeology." *Folklore* 61 (1950): 169–185.

——. *Roles of the Northern Goddess.* London: Routledge, 1998.

——. *The Sword in Anglo-Saxon England: Its Archaeology and Literature.* Woodbridge: Boydell Press, 1962.

——. "Weland the Smith." *Folklore* 69 (1958): 145–159.

Day, David D. "Hands across the Hall: The Legalities of Beowulf's Fight with Grendel." *Journal of English and Germanic philology* 98 (1999): 313–324.

DeGregorio, Scott. "Theorizing Irony in Beowulf: The Case of Hrothgar." *Exemplaria* 11 (1999): 309–343.

Derolez, René. "Hrothgar, King of Denmark." In *Multiple Worlds, Multiple Words: Essays in Honour of Irène Simon*, edited by Hena Maes-Jelinek, Pierre Michel, and Paulette Michel-Michot, 51–58. Liège: University of Liège, 1988.

Deskis, Susan E. "An Addendum to Beowulf's Last Words." *Medium Ævum* 63 (1994): 301–305.

——. *Beowulf and the Medieval Proverb Tradition.* Tempe: ACMRS, 1996.

Dietrich, Lana Stone. "Syntactic Analysis of Beowulf's Fight with Grendel." *Comitatus* 14 (1983): 5–17.

Dockray-Miller, Mary. "*Beowulf*'s Tears of Fatherhood." *Exemplaria* 10 (1998): 1–28.

——. "The Masculine Queen of Beowulf." *Women and Language* 21 (1998): 31–38.

Donahue, Charles. "*Beowulf* and Christian Tradition: A Reconsideration from a Celtic Stance." *Traditio* 21 (1965): 55–116.

——. "*Beowulf*, Ireland and the Natural Good." *Traditio* 7 (1951): 263–277.

Donoghue, Daniel. "On the Non-Integrity of *Beowulf*." *SELIM* 1 (1991): 29–44.

Donovan, Leslie A. "Þyle as Fool: Revisiting *Beowulf*'s Hunferth." In *Poetry, Place, and Gender: Studies in Medieval Culture in Honor of Helen Damico*, edited by Catherine E. Karkov, 75–97. Kalamazoo: Medieval Institute Publications, 2009.

Dronke, Ursula. "*Beowulf* and Ragnarǫk." *Saga-Book* 17 (1969): 302–325.

Drout, Michael D. C. "Blood and Deeds: The Inheritance Systems in *Beowulf*." *Studies in Philology* 104 (2007): 199–226.

——, and Leah Smith. "A Pebble Smoothed by Tradition: Lines 607-661 of *Beowulf* as a Formulaic Set-piece." *Oral Tradition* 32 (2018): 191–228.

——, and Nelson Goering. "The Emendation *Eorle* (Heruli) in *Beowulf*, Line 6a: Setting the Poem in 'The Named Lands of the North.'" *Modern Philology* 117 (2020): 285–300.

Dumville, David N. "Beowulf Come Lately: Some Notes on the Paleography of the Nowell Codex." *Archiv für das Studium der neueren Sprachen und Literaturen* 225 (1988): 49–63.

Earl, James W. "The Forbidden *Beowulf*: Haunted by Incest." *PMLA* 125 (2010): 289–305.

——. "The Swedish Wars in *Beowulf*." *Journal of English and Germanic Philology* 114 (2015): 32–60.

Ecay, Aaron, and Susan Pintzuk. "The Syntax of Old English Poetry and the Dating of *Beowulf*." In *Old English Philology: Studies in Honour of R. D. Fulk*, edited by Leonard Neidorf, Rafael J. Pascual, and Tom Shippey, 144–171. Cambridge: D. S. Brewer, 2016.

Eliason, Norman E. "Beowulf, Wiglaf and the Wægmundings." *Anglo-Saxon England* 7 (1978): 95–105.

——. "Beowulf's Inglorious Youth." *Studies in Philology* 76 (1979): 101–108.

——. "The Thryth-Offa Digression in Beowulf." In *Franciplegius: Medieval and linguistic studies in honor of Francis Peabody Magoun, Jr.,* edited by Jess B. Bessinger, Jr. and Robert P. Creed, 124–138. New York: New York University Press, 1965.

——. "The Þyle and Scop in *Beowulf*." *Speculum* 38 (1963): 267–284.

Emerson, Oliver F. "Legends of Cain, Especially in Old and Middle English." *PMLA* 21 (1906): 831–929.

Engelhardt, George J. "On the Sequence of Beowulf's *Geogoð*." *Modern Language Notes* 68 (1953): 91–95.

Enright, Michael J. *Lady with a Mead Cup: Ritual, Prophecy, and Lordship in the European Warband from La Tène to the Viking Age*. Dublin: Four Courts Press, 1996.

——. "The Warband Context of the Unferth Episode." *Speculum* 73 (1998): 297–337.

Falk, Oren. "Beowulf's Longest Day: The Amphibious Hero in His Element (*Beowulf*, ll. 1495b-96)." *Journal of English and Germanic Philology* 106 (2007): 1–21.

Farrell, R. T. *Beowulf, Swedes and Geats*. London: Viking Society for Northern Research, 1972.

Fast, Lawrence. "Hygelac: A Centripetal Force in *Beowulf*." *Annuale Mediaevale* 12 (1971): 90–98.

Feldman, Thalia Phillies. "Grendel and Cain's Descendants." *Literary Onomastics Studies* 8 (1981): 71–87.

Fell, C. E. "Paganism in *Beowulf*: A Semantic Fairy-Tale." In *Pagans and Christians: The Interplay between Christian Latin and Traditional Germanic Cultures in Early Medieval Europe*, edited by T. Hofstra, L. A. J. R. Houwen, and A. A. MacDonald, 9–34. Groningen: Egbert Forsten, 1995.

Florey, Kenneth. "Grendel, Evil, 'Allegory,' and Dramatic Development in *Beowulf*." *Essays in Arts and Sciences* 17 (1988): 83–95.

Forni, Kathleen. *Beowulf's Popular Afterlife in Literature, Comic Books, and Film.* New York: Routledge, 2018.

Fox, Michael. *Following the Formula in Beowulf, Örvar-Odds saga, and Tolkien* (Cham: Palgrave Macmillan, 2020), 101–156.

Frankis, P. J. "The Thematic Significance of *Enta Geweorc* and Related Imagery in *The Wanderer*," *Anglo-Saxon England* 2 (1973): 253–269.

Frisby, Deborah S. "'Daring' and 'Foolish' Renderings: On the Meaning of *Dollic* in *Beowulf*," *ANQ* 4 (1991): 59–63.

Fry, Donald K, ed. *Finnsburh: Fragment and Episode* (London: Methuen, 1974).

——. "'Wið Earm Gesæt' And Beowulf's Hammerlock." *Modern Philology* 67 (1970): 364–366.

Fulk, R. D. *A History of Old English Meter.* Philadelphia: University of Pennsylvania Press, 1992.

——. "An Eddic Analogue to the Scyld Scefing Story." *Review of English Studies* 40 (1989): 313–322.

——. "Afloat in Semantic Space: Old English *sund* and the Nature of Beowulf's Exploit with Breca." *Journal of English and Germanic Philology* 104 (2005): 456–472.

——. "Archaisms and Neologisms in the Language of *Beowulf*." In *Studies in the History of the English Language III*, edited by Christopher M. Cain and Geoffrey Russom, 267–287. Berlin: Mouton de Gruyter, 2007.

——, ed. and trans. *The Beowulf Manuscript: Complete Texts and The Fight at Finnsburg*. Cambridge: Harvard University Press, 2010.

——. "Inductive Methods in the Textual Criticism of Old English Verse." *Medievalia et Humanistica* 23 (1996): 1–24.

——. "The Name of Offa's Queen: Beowulf 1931-2." *Anglia* 122 (2004): 614–639.

——. "Old English *Þa* 'Now that' and the Integrity of *Beowulf*." *English Studies* 88 (2007): 623–631.

——. "The Textual Criticism of Frederick Klaeber's *Beowulf*." In *Constructing Nations, Reconstructing Myths: Essays in Honour of T. A. Shippey*, edited by Andrew Wawn with Graham Johnson and John Walter, 131–153. Turnhout: Brepols, 2007.

——. "Unferth and his Name." *Modern Philology* 85 (1987): 113–127.

——. Robert E. Bjork, and John D. Niles, ed., *Klaeber's Beowulf and The Fight at Finnsburg*, 4th ed. Toronto: University of Toronto Press, 2008.

Gardner, John. "Guilt and the World's Complexity: The Murder of Ongentheow and the Slaying of the Dragon." In *Anglo-Saxon Poetry: Essays in Appreciation for John C. McGalliard*, edited by Lewis E. Nicholson and Delores

Warwick Frese, 14–22. Notre Dame: University of Notre Dame Press, 1975.

Garmonsway, G. N. "Anglo-Saxon Heroic Attitudes." In *Franciplegius: Medieval and Linguistic Studies in Honor of Francis Peabody Magoun, Jr.*, edited by Jess B. Bessinger and Robert P. Creed, 139–146. New York: New York University Press, 1965.

——, and Jacqueline Simpson, eds. and trans. *Beowulf and Its Analogues*. New York: Dutton, 1971.

Gelling, Margaret. "The Landscape of *Beowulf*." *Anglo-Saxon England* 31 (2002): 7–11.

Georgianna, Linda. "King Hrethel's Sorrow and the Limits of Heroic Action in *Beowulf*." *Speculum* 62 (1987): 829–850.

Ghosh, Shami. *Writing the Barbarian Past: Studies in Early Medieval Historical Narrative*. Leiden: Brill, 2016.

Gilchrist, Bruce, and Britt Mize, ed. *Beowulf as Children's Literature*. Toronto: University of Toronto Press, 2021.

Godfrey, Mary Flavia. "Beowulf and Judith: Thematizing Decapitation in Old English Poetry." *Texas Studies in Language and Literature* 35 (1993): 1–43.

Goldsmith, Margaret E. *The Mode and Meaning of Beowulf*. London: Athlone Press, 1970.

Gordon, E. V. "Wealhþeow and Related Names." *Medium Ævum* 4 (1935): 169–175.

Gould, Kent. "*Beowulf* and Folktale Morphology: God as Magical Donor." *Folklore* 96 (1985): 98–103.

Gräslund, Bo. "Fimbulvintern, Ragnarök och klimatkrisen år 536–537 e. Kr." *Saga och Sed* (2007): 93–123.

Greenfield, Stanley B. "Beowulf and the Judgement of the Righteous." In *Learning and Literature in Anglo-Saxon England: Studies Presented to Peter Clemoes*, edited by

Michael Lapidge and Helmut Gneuss, 393–407. Cambridge: Cambridge University Press, 1985.

——. "Did Beowulf Commit 'Feaxfeng' against Grendel's Mother?" *Notes and Queries* 23 (1976): 339–40.

——. "Geatish History: Poetic Art and Epic Quality in *Beowulf*." *Neophilologus* 47 (1963): 211–217.

——. "'Gifstol' and Goldhoard in *Beowulf*." In *Old English Studies in Honour of John C. Pope*, edited by Robert B. Burlin and Edward B. Irving Jr., 107–117. Toronto: University of Toronto Press, 1974.

——. "Old English Words and Patristic Exegesis – *hwyrftum scriþað*: A Caveat." *Modern Philology* 75 (1977): 44–48.

——. "Of Words and Deeds: The Coastguard's Maxim Once More." In *The Wisdom of Poetry: Essays in Early English Literature in Honor of Morton W. Bloomfield*, edited by Larry D. Benson and Siegfried Wenzel, 45–51. Kalamazoo, MI: Medieval Institute Publications, 1982.

Griffith, M. S. "Some Difficulties in *Beowulf*, Lines 874-902: Sigemund Reconsidered." *Anglo-Saxon England* 24 (1995): 11–41.

Gunnell, Terry. "The Goddesses in the Dark Waters." In *Making the Profane Sacred in the Viking Age: Essays in Honour of Stefan Brink*, edited by Irene García Losquiño, Olof Sundqvist, and Declan Taggart, 243–265. Turnhout: Brepols, 2020.

Gwara, Scott. "*Beowulf* 3074-75: Beowulf Appraises His Reward." *Neophilologus* 92 (2008): 333–338.

——. "The Foreign Beowulf and the 'Fight at Finnsburg.'" *Traditio* 63 (2008): 185–233.

——. *Heroic Identity in the World of Beowulf*. Leiden: Brill, 2008.

——. "Paradigmatic Wisdom and the Native Genre *Giedd* in Old English." *Studi Medievali* 53 (2012): 783–852.

Hall, Alaric. "Hygelac's Only Daughter: A Present, a Potentate and a Peaceweaver in *Beowulf*." *Studia Neophilologica* 78 (2006): 81–87.

Hamilton, Marie Padgett. "The Religious Principle in Beowulf." *PMLA* 61 (1946): 309–330.

Hanning, Robert W. "Sharing, Dividing, Depriving – The Verbal Ironies of Grendel's Last Visit to Heorot." *Texas Studies in Literature and Language* 15 (1973): 203–213.

Hansen, Elaine Tuttle. "Hrothgar's 'Sermon' in *Beowulf* as Parental Wisdom." *Anglo-Saxon England* 10 (1981): 53–67.

Hardy, Adelaide. "The Christian Hero Beowulf and Unferð Þyle." *Neophilologus* 53 (1969): 55–69.

Harris, Joseph. "A Nativist Approach to *Beowulf*: The Case of Germanic Elegy." In *Companion to Old English Poetry*, edited by Henk Aertsen and Rolf H. Bremmer Jr., 45–62. Amsterdam: VU University Press, 1994.

——. "Beowulf's Last Words." *Speculum* 67 (1992): 1–32.

——. "The Dossier on Byggvir, God and Hero: *Cur deus homo*." *Arv* 55 (1999): 7–23.

——. "Elegy in Old English and Old Norse: A Problem in Literary History." In *The Old English Elegies: New Essays in Criticism and Research*, edited by Martin Green, 46–56. Rutherford: Fairleigh Dickinson University Press, 1983.

——. "Hadubrand's Lament: On the Origin and Age of Elegy in Germanic." In *Heldensage und Heldendichtung im Germanischen*, edited by Heinrich Beck, 81–114. Berlin: Walter de Gruyter, 1988.

——. "Heroic Poetry and Elegy: *Beowulf*'s Lay of the Last Survivor." In *Heldenzeiten—Heldenräume: Wann und wo spielen Heldendichtung und Heldensage?*, edited by Johannes Keller and Florian Kragl, 27–41. Wien: Fassbaender, 2007.

——. "Love and Death in the *Männerbund:* An essay with special reference to the *Bjarkamál* and *The Battle of Maldon*," In *Heroic Poetry in the Anglo-Saxon Period: Studies in Honor of Jess B. Bessinger, Jr.*, edited by Helen Damico and John Leyerle, 77–114. Kalamazoo: Medieval Institute Publications, 1993.

——. "The *Senna*: From Description to Literary Theory." *Michigan Germanic Studies* 5 (1979): 65–74.

Harris, Stephen. "*Beowulf* 881a: *Eam His Nefan*." *ANQ* 26 (2013): 217–218.

Hatto, A. T. "Snake-Swords and Boar-Helms in *Beowulf*." *English Studies* 38 (1957): 145–160.

Haydock, Nickolas, and E. L. Risden. *Beowulf on Film: Adaptations and Variations.* Jefferson: McFarland, 2013.

Haymes, Edward, and Susann T. Samples. *Heroic Legends of the North: An Introduction to the Nibelung and Dietrich Cycles.* New York: Garland, 1996.

Hedeager, Lotte. *Iron-Age Societies: from Tribe to State in Northern Europe, 500 BC to AD 700*, translated by John Hines. Oxford: Blackwell, 1992.

Helder, Willem. "Beowulf and the Plundered Hoard." *Neuphilologische Mitteilungen* 78 (1977): 317–325.

Helder, William. "The Song of Creation in *Beowulf* and the Interpretation of Heorot." *English Studies in Canada* 13 (1987): 243–255.

Hennequin, M. Wendy. "We've Created a Monster: The Strange Case of Grendel's Mother." *English Studies* 89 (2008): 503–523.

Herschend, Frands. *The Idea of the Good in Late Iron Age Society*. Uppsala: Institutionen för arkeologi och antikens historia, Uppsala Universitet, 1998.

Hieatt, C. B. "Modþryðo and Heremod: Intertwined Threads in the *Beowulf*-Poet's Web of Words." *Journal of English and Germanic Philology* 83 (1984): 173–182.

Higley, Sarah L. "*Aldor on Ofre*, or the Reluctant Hart: A Study of Liminality in *Beowulf*." *Neuphilologische Mitteilungen* 87 (1986): 342–353.

Hill, John M. *The Anglo-Saxon Warrior Ethic: Reconstructing Lordship in Early English Literature*. Gainesville: University Press of Florida, 2000.

——. "Beowulf and the Danish Succession: Gift Giving as an Occasion for Complex Gesture." *Medievalia et Humanistica* 11 (1982): 177–197.

——. *The Cultural World in Beowulf*. Toronto: University of Toronto Press, 1995.

——. "Hrothgar's Noble Rule: Love and the Great Legislator." In *Social Approaches to Viking Studies,* edited by Ross Samson, 169–178. Glasgow: Cruithne, 1991.

——. *The Narrative Pulse of Beowulf: Arrivals and Departures*. Toronto: University of Toronto Press, 2008.

Hill, Joyce. "'Þæt Wæs Geomuru Ides!': A Female Stereotype Examined." In *New Readings on Women in Old English Literature*, edited by Helen Damico and Alexandra Hennessey Olsen, 235–247. Bloomington: Indiana University Press, 1990.

Hill, Thomas D. "Beowulf as Seldguma: *Beowulf*, Lines 247-51." *Neophilologus* 74 (1990): 637–639.

——. "Beowulf's Roman Rites: Roman Ritual and Germanic Tradition." *Journal of English and Germanic Philology* 106 (2007): 325–335.

——. "The Christian Language and Theme of *Beowulf*." In *Companion to Old English Poetry*, edited by Henk Aertsen and Rolf H. Bremmer Jr., 63–77. Amsterdam: VU University Press, 1994.

——. "The Confession of Beowulf and the Structure of *Volsunga Saga*." In *The Vikings: Papers from the Cornell Lecture Series Held to Coincide with the Viking Exhibition 1980–1981*, edited by Robert T. Farrell, 165–179. London: Phillimore, 1982.

——. "Hrothgar's Speech of Adoption: A Danish-Latin Analog." *Notes and Queries* 66 (2019): 163–166.

——. "*Hwyrftum Scripað*: *Beowulf*, Line 163." *Mediaeval Studies* 33 (1971): 379–381.

——. "The 'Variegated Obit' as an Historiographic Motif in Old English Poetry and Anglo-Latin Historical Literature." *Traditio* 44 (1988): 101–124.

——. "'Wealhtheow' as a Foreign Slave: Some Continental Analogues." *Philological Quarterly* 69 (1990): 106–112.

Himes, Jonathan B., ed. *The Old English Epic of Waldere*. Newcastle upon Tyne: Cambridge Scholars Publishing, 2009.

Hintz, Howard W. "The 'Hama' Reference in *Beowulf*: 1197-1201." *Journal of English and Germanic Philology* 33 (1934): 98–102.

Hollis, Stephanie. "Beowulf and the Succession." *Parergon* 1 (1983): 39–54.

Hollowell, Ida Masters. "Unferð the Þyle in *Beowulf*." *Studies in Philology* 73 (1976): 239–265.

Horgan, A. D. "Religious Attitudes in *Beowulf*." In *Essays and Poems Presented to Lord David Cecil*, edited by W. W. Robson, 9–17. London: Constable, 1970.

Hughes, Geoffrey. "Beowulf, Unferth and Hrunting: An Interpretation." *English Studies* 58 (1977): 385–395.

Huisman, Rosemary. "The Three Tellings of Beowulf's Fight with Grendel's Mother." *Leeds Studies in English* 20 (1989): 217–248.

Hulbert, J. R. "Surmises Concerning the *Beowulf* Poet's Source." *Journal of English and Germanic Philology* 50 (1951): 11–18.

Hume, Kathryn. "The Concept of the Hall in Old English Poetry." *Anglo-Saxon England* 3 (1974): 63–74.

———. "From Saga to Romance: The Use of Monsters in Old Norse Literature." *Studies in Philology* 77 (1980): 1–25.

———. "The Theme and Structure of *Beowulf*." *Studies in Philology* 72 (1975): 1–27.

Irving, Edward B., Jr. "Beowulf Comes Home." In *Acts of Interpretation: The Text in Its Contexts, 700–1600: Essays on Medieval and Renaissance Literature in Honor of E. Talbot Donaldson*, edited by Mary J. Carruthers and Elizabeth D. Kirk, 129–143. Norman, OK: Pilgrim Books, 1982.

———. "Christian and Pagan Elements." In *A Beowulf Handbook*, edited by Robert E. Bjork and John D. Niles, 175–192. Lincoln: University of Nebraska Press, 1997.

———. "Heroic Role-Models: Beowulf and Others." In *Heroic Poetry in the Anglo-Saxon Period: Studies in Honor of Jess B. Bessinger, Jr.*, edited by Helen Damico and John Leyerle, 347–372. Kalamazoo: Western Michigan University Press, 1993.

——. "The Nature of Christianity in *Beowulf*." *Anglo-Saxon England* 13 (1984): 7–21.

——. *Rereading Beowulf*. Philadelphia: University of Pennsylvania Press, 1989.

Jambeck, Thomas J. "The Syntax of Petition in *Beowulf* and *Sir Gawain and the Green Knight*." *Style* 7 (1973): 21–29.

Johnson, David F. "The Gregorian Grendel: *Beowulf* 705b–09 and the Limits of the Demonic." In *Rome and the North: The Early Reception of Gregory the Great in Germanic Europe*, edited by Rolf H. Bremmer Jr., Kees Dekker, and David F. Johnson, 51–65. Paris: Peeters, 2001.

Jurasinski, Stefan. *Ancient Privileges: Beowulf, Law and the Making of Germanic Antiquity*. Morgantown: West Virginia University Press, 2006.

——. "The Feminine Name *Wealhtheow* and the Problem of Beowulfian Anthroponymy." *Neophilologus* 91 (2007): 701–705.

Kaske, Robert E. "*Beowulf* and the Book of Enoch." *Speculum* 46 (1971): 421–431.

——. "The Gifstol Crux in *Beowulf*." *Leeds Studies in English* 17 (1985): 142–151.

——. "Hygelac and Hygd." In *Studies in Old English Literature in Honor of Arthur G. Brodeur*, edited by Stanley B. Greenfield, 200–206. Eugene: University of Oregon Press, 1963.

——. "The Sigemund-Heremod and Hama-Hygelac Passages in *Beowulf*." *PMLA* 74 (1959): 489–494.

——. "Weohstan's Sword." *Modern Language Notes* 75 (1960): 465–468.

Keller, Thomas L. "The Dragon in *Beowulf* Revisited." *Aevum* 55 (1981): 218–228.

Kelly, A. Keith. "Teaching Good Manners: Civil Discourse Patterns in *Beowulf* and *Sir Gawain and the Green Knight.*" In *Literary Speech Acts of the Medieval North: Essays Inspired by the Works of Thomas A. Shippey*, edited by Eric Shane Bryan and Alexander Vaughan Ames, 223–242. Tempe, AZ: ACMRS, 2020.

Kelly, Birte. "The Formative Stages of *Beowulf* Textual Scholarship: Part I." *Anglo-Saxon England* 11 (1982): 247–274.

———. "The Formative Stages of Beowulf Textual Scholarship: Part II." *Anglo-Saxon England* 12 (1983): 239–275.

Kiernan, Kevin S. *Beowulf and the Beowulf Manuscript*, 2nd ed. Ann Arbor: University of Michigan Press, 1996.

Kightley, Michael R. "Reinterpreting Threats to Face: The Use of Politeness in *Beowulf*, ll. 407–472." *Neophilologus* 93 (2009): 511–520.

———. "Repetition, Class, and the Nameless Speakers of *Beowulf*." In *Literary Speech Acts of the Medieval North: Essays Inspired by the Works of Thomas A. Shippey*, edited by Eric Shane Bryan and Alexander Vaughan Ames, 141–156. Tempe, AZ: ACMRS, 2020.

King, Judy. "Launching the Hero: The Case of Scyld and Beowulf." *Neophilologus* 87 (2003): 453–471.

Kisor, Yvette. "Numerical Composition and *Beowulf*: A Reconsideration." *Anglo-Saxon England* 38 (2009): 41–76

Klaeber, Fr. "Attila's and Beowulf's Funeral." *PMLA* 42 (1927): 255–267.

Klein, Stacy S. *Ruling Women: Queenship and Gender in Anglo-Saxon Literature*. Notre Dame: University of Notre Dame Press, 2006.

Klein, Thomas. "*Stonc æfter stane* (*Beowulf*, l. 2288a): Philology, Narrative Context, and the Waking Dragon."

Journal of English and Germanic Philology 106 (2007): 22–44.

Kohnen, Thomas. "Understanding Anglo-Saxon 'Politeness': Directive Constructions with *Ic Wille / Ic Wolde.*" *Journal of Historical Pragmatics* 12 (2011): 230–254.

Köberl, Johann. "The Magic Sword in *Beowulf.*" *Neophilologus* 71 (1987): 120–228.

Kuhn, Sherman. "*Beowulf* and the Life of Beowulf: A Study in Epic Structure." In *Studies in the Language, Literature, and Culture of the Middle Ages and Later*, edited by E. Bagby Atwood and Archibald A. Hill, 243–264. Austin: University of Texas Press, 1969.

Laborde, E. D. "Grendel's Glove and his Immunity to Weapons." *Modern Language Review* 18 (1923): 202–204.

Langeslag, Paul S. "Monstrous Landscape in *Beowulf.*" *English Studies* 96 (2015): 119–138.

Lapidge, Michael. "The Archetype of *Beowulf.*" *Anglo-Saxon England* 29 (2000): 5–41.

——. "*Beowulf*, Aldhelm, the *Liber Monstrorum* and Wessex." *Studi Medievali* 23 (1982): 151–192.

——. "*Beowulf* and the Psychology of Terror." In *Heroic Poetry in the Anglo-Saxon Period: Studies in Honor of Jess B. Bessinger, Jr.*, edited by Helen Damico and John Leyerle, 373–402. Kalamazoo: Western Michigan University Press, 1993.

Larrington, Carolyne. "Eddic Poetry and Heroic Legend." In *A Handbook to Eddic Poetry: Myths and Legends of Early Scandinavia*, edited by Carolyne Larrington, Judy Quinn, and Brittany Schorn, 147–172. Cambridge: Cambridge University Press, 2016.

Lawrence, William Witherle. "Beowulf and the Tragedy of Finnsburg." *PMLA* 30 (1915): 372–431.

——. "The Dragon and His Lair in *Beowulf*." *PMLA* 33 (1918): 547–583.

——. "The Haunted Mere in *Beowulf*." *PMLA* 27 (1912): 208–245.

Lehmann, Ruth P. M. "Ecgþeow the Wægmunding: Geat or Swede?" *English Language Notes* 31 (1994): 1–5.

Leisi, Ernst. "Gold und Manneswert im *Beowulf*." *Anglia* 71 (1953): 259–273.

Leneghan, Francis. *The Dynastic Drama of Beowulf*. Cambridge: D. S. Brewer, 2020.

——. "The Poetic Purpose of the Offa-Digression in *Beowulf*." *Review of English Studies* 60 (2009): 538–560.

——. "Reshaping Tradition: The Originality of the Scyld Scefing Episode." In *Transmission and Generation in Medieval and Renaissance Literature: Essays in Honour of John Scattergood*, edited by Karen Hodder and Brendan O'Connell, 21–36. Dublin: Four Courts Press, 2012.

Leyerle, John. "Beowulf the Hero and the King." *Medium Ævum* 34 (1965): 89–102.

——. "The Interlace Structure of *Beowulf*." *University of Toronto Quarterly* 37 (1967): 1–17.

Mackie, W. S. "The Demons' Home in *Beowulf*." *Journal of English and Germanic Philology* 37 (1938): 455–461.

Maenchen-Helfen, Otto. "The Legend of the Origin of the Huns." *Byzantion* 17 (1944–1945): 244–251.

Magennis, Hugh. "The *Beowulf* Poet and his *druncne dryhtguman*." *Neuphilologische Mitteilungen* 86 (1985): 159–164.

Magoun, Francis P., Jr. "Béowulf and King Hygelác in the Netherlands: Lost Anglo-Saxon Verse Stories about this Event." *English Studies* 35 (1954): 193–204.

Malone, Kemp. "Beowulf the Headstrong." Anglo-Saxon England 1 (1972): 139–145.

——. "The Daughter of Healfdene." In *Studies in English Philology: A Miscellany in Honor of Frederick Klaeber*, edited by Kemp Malone and Martin B. Ruud, 135–158. Minneapolis: University of Minnesota Press, 1929.

——. "Ecgtheow." *Modern Language Quarterly* 1 (1940): 37–44.

——. "The Finn Episode in *Beowulf*." *Journal of English and Germanic Philology* 25 (1926): 157–172.

——. "Hrethric." *PMLA* 42 (1927): 268–313.

——. "Hygd." *Modern Language Notes* 56 (1941): 356–358.

——. "The Tale of Ingeld." In *Studies in Heroic Legend and Current Speech*, edited by Stefán Einarsson and Norman E. Eliason, 1-62. Copenhagen: Rosenkilde & Bagger, 1959.

——. "Young Beowulf." *Journal of English and Germanic Philology* 36 (1937): 21–23.

Marshall, Sophie. "Digression, Coherence, and a Missing Cup in *Beowulf*." *Zeitschrift Für Literaturwissenschaft Und Linguistik* 48 (2018): 167–192.

McFadden, Brian. "Sleeping After the Feast: Deathbeds, Marriage Beds, and the Power Structure of Heorot." *Neophilologus* 84 (2000): 629–646.

McNabb, Cameron Hunt. "'Eldum Unnyt': Treasure Spaces in *Beowulf*." *Neophilologus* 95 (2011): 145–164.

McNamara, John. "Beowulf and Hygelac: Problems for Fiction in History." *Rice University Studies* 62 (1976): 55–63.

——. "*Beowulf*, 2490-2508a." *The Explicator* 32 (1974): 1–2.

McNamee, M. B. "*Beowulf*: An Allegory of Salvation?" *Journal of English and Germanic Philology* 59 (1960): 190–207.

Mellinkoff, Ruth. "Cain's Monstrous Progeny in *Beowulf*: Part I, Noachic Tradition." *Anglo-Saxon England* 8 (1979): 143–162.

——. "Cain's Monstrous Progeny in *Beowulf*: Part II, Post-Diluvian Survival." *Anglo-Saxon England* 9 (1980): 183–197.

Van Meter, David C. "The Ritualized Presentation of Weapons and the Ideology of Nobility in *Beowulf*." *Journal of English and Germanic Philology* 95 (1996): 175–189.

Mills, Kristen. "Emotion and Gesture in Hroðgar's Farewell to Beowulf." In *Anglo-Saxon Emotions: Reading the Heart in Old English Language, Literature and Culture*, edited by Alice Jorgensen, Frances McCormack, and Jonathan Wilcox, 163–176. Farnham: Ashgate, 2015.

Mitchell, Bruce. *On Old English*. Oxford: Blackwell, 1988.

Mizuno, Tomaki. "The Magical Necklace and the Fatal Corselet in *Beowulf*." *English Studies* 80 (1999): 377–397.

Momma, Haruko. "The Education of Beowulf and the Affair of the Leisure Class." In *Verbal Encounters: Anglo-Saxon and Old Norse Studies for Roberta Frank*, edited by Antonina Harbus and Russell Poole, 163–182. Toronto: University of Toronto Press, 2005.

Moore, Bruce. "The Thryth-Offa Digression in *Beowulf*." *Neophilologus* 64 (1980): 127–133.

Morey, James H. "The Fourth Fate of Men: Heremod's Darkened Mind." In *Darkness, Depression, and Descent in Anglo-Saxon England*, edited by Ruth Wehlau, 155–166. Berlin: De Gruyter, 2019.

Morgan, Gerald. "The Treachery of Hrothulf." *English Studies* 53 (1972): 23–39.

Morgan, Gwendolyn A. "Mothers, Monsters, Maturation: Female Evil in *Beowulf.*" *Journal of the Fantastic in the Arts* 4 (1991): 54–68.

Mustanoja, Tauno F. "The Unnamed Woman's Song of Mourning over Beowulf and the Tradition of Ritual Lamentation." *Neuphilologische Mitteilungen* 108 (2007): 153–179.

Müller-Oberhäuser, Gabriele. "*Cynna Gemyndig*: Sitte und Etikette in der altenglischen Literatur." *Frühmittelalterliche Studien* 30 (1996): 19–59.

Naismith, Rory. "The Economy of *Beowulf.*" In *Old English Philology: Studies in Honour of R. D. Fulk*, edited by Leonard Neidorf, Rafael J. Pascual, and Tom Shippey, 371–391. Cambridge: D. S. Brewer, 2016.

Neckel, Gustav. "Sigmunds Drachenkampf." *Edda* 13 (1920): 122–140, 204–229.

Neidorf, Leonard. "An Old Norse Analogue to Wiglaf's Lament (*Beowulf* Lines 3077-3086)." *Neophilologus* 102 (2018): 515–524.

——. "The Archetype of Beowulf." *English Studies* 99 (2018): 229–242.

——. *The Art and Thought of the Beowulf Poet.* Ithaca: Cornell University Press, 2022.

——. "*Beowulf.*" In *Books to Film*: *Cinematic Adaptations of Literary Works*, vol. 1, edited by Barry Keith Grant, 21–24. Farmington Hills: Gale-Cengage, 2018.

——. "Beowulf and Freawaru." *The Explicator* 79 (2021): 182–187.

——. "Beowulf before *Beowulf*: Anglo-Saxon Anthroponymy and Heroic Legend." *Review of English Studies* 64 (2013): 553–573.

——. "*Beowulf* Lines 175-88 and the Transmission of Old English Poetry." *Studies in Philology* 119 (2022): 1–24.

——. "The *Beowulf* Poet's Sense of Decorum." *Traditio* 76 (2021): 1–28.

——. "Cain, Cam, Jutes, Giants, and the Textual Criticism of *Beowulf*." *Studies in Philology* 112 (2015): 599–632.

——, ed. *The Dating of Beowulf: A Reassessment*. Cambridge: D. S. Brewer, 2014.

——. "Garulf and Guthlaf in the *Finnsburg* Fragment." *Notes & Queries* 66 (2019): 489–492.

——. "The Gepids in *Beowulf*." *ANQ* 34 (2021): 3–6.

——. "Goths, Huns, and *The Dream of the Rood*." *Review of English Studies* 72 (2021): 821–835.

——. "Grendel's Blood: On the Translation of *Beowulf* Line 849." *Medium Ævum* 90 (2021): 133–142.

——. "Hildeburh's Mourning and *The Wife's Lament*." *Studia Neophilologica* 89 (2017): 197–204.

——. "Hygelac and His Daughter: Rereading *Beowulf* Lines 2985-98." *Medium Ævum* 89 (2020): 350–355.

——. "King Hygelac of the Geats: History, Legend, and *Beowulf*." *Neophilologus* 106 (2022): 461–477.

——. "The Language of Hrothgar's Sermon." *Studia Neophilologica* 91 (2019): 1–10.

——. "Lexical Evidence for the Relative Chronology of Old English Poetry." *SELIM* 20 (2013–2014): 7–48.

——. "On *Beowulf* and the *Nibelungenlied*: Counselors, Queens, and Characterization." *Neohelicon* 47 (2020): 655–672.

——. "The Origin of Hondscioh: Grendel's Glove and the *Beowulf* Tradition." *Studia Neophilologica* 95 (2023): 342-350.

——. "Philology, Allegory, and the Dating of *Beowulf.*" *Studia Neophilologica* 88 (2016): 97–115.

——. *The Transmission of Beowulf: Language, Culture, and Scribal Behavior.* Ithaca: Cornell University Press, 2017.

——. "Unferth's Ambiguity and the Trivialization of Germanic Legend." *Neophilologus* 101 (2017): 439–454.

——. "Wealhtheow and Her Name: Etymology, Characterization, and Textual Criticism." *Neophilologus* 102 (2018): 75–89.

——. "Youth and Age in the *Finnsburg* Fragment." *ANQ* 35 (2022): 4–8.

——, and Rafael J. Pascual, "The Language of *Beowulf* and the Conditioning of Kaluza's Law." *Neophilologus* 98 (2014): 657–673.

Nelson, Marie. "Beowulf's Boast Words." *Neophilologus* 89 (2005): 299–310.

Newton, Sam. *The Origins of Beowulf and the Pre-Viking Kingdom of East Anglia.* Cambridge: D. S. Brewer, 1993.

Nitzsche, Jane C. "The Structural Unity of *Beowulf*: The Problem of Grendel's Mother." *Texas Studies in Literature and Language* 22 (1980): 287–303.

Nolan, Barbara, and Morton W. Bloomfield, "*Bēotword, Gilpcwidas*, and the *Gilphlæden* Scop of *Beowulf.*" *Journal of English and Germanic Philology* 79 (1980): 499–516.

North, Richard. "Gold and the Heathen Polity in *Beowulf.*" In *Gold in der europäischen Heldensage*, edited by Wilhelm Heizmann, Victor Millet, and Heike Sahm, 72–114. Berlin: De Gruyter, 2019.

——. *Heathen Gods in Old English Literature*. Cambridge: Cambridge University Press, 1997.

——. *The Origins of Beowulf: From Vergil to Wiglaf*. Oxford: Oxford University Press, 2006.

——. "Saxo and the Swedish Wars in *Beowulf*." In *Saxo Grammaticus: Tra storiografia e letteratura*, edited by Carlo Santini, 175–188. Roma: Il calamo, 1992.

——. "Tribal Loyalties in the Finnsburh Fragment and Episode." *Leeds Studies in English* 21 (1990): 13–43.

Ogilvy, J. D. A. "Unferth: Foil to Beowulf?" *PMLA* 79 (1964): 370–375.

O'Briain, Helen Conrad. "Listen to the Woman: Reading Wealhtheow as Stateswoman." In *New Readings on Women and Early Medieval English Literature and Culture*, edited by Helene Scheck and Christine E. Kozikowski, 191–207. Amsterdam: Arc Humanities Press, 2019.

O'Donoghue, Heather. "What Has Baldr to Do with Lamech? The Lethal Shot of a Blind Man in Old Norse Myth and Jewish Exegetical Traditions." *Medium Ævum* 72 (2003): 82–107.

O'Keeffe, Katherine O'Brien. "*Beowulf*, Lines 702b-836: Transformations and the Limits of the Human." *Texas Studies in Literature and Language* 23 (1981): 484–494.

Olesiesjko, Jacek. "Wealhtheow's Peace-Weaving: Diegesis and Genealogy of Gender in *Beowulf*." *Studia Anglica Posnaniensia* 49 (2014): 103–123.

Orchard, Andy. *A Critical Companion to Beowulf*. Cambridge: D. S. Brewer, 2003.

——. *Pride and Prodigies: Studies in the Monsters of the Beowulf-Manuscript*. Cambridge: D. S. Brewer, 1995.

Osborn, Marijane. "The Alleged Murder of Hrethric in *Beowulf*." *Traditio* 74 (2019): 153–177.

——. "The Great Feud: Scriptural History and Strife in *Beowulf*." *PMLA* 93 (1978): 973–981.

——. "Laying the Roman Ghost of *Beowulf* 320 and 725." *Neuphilologische Mitteilungen* 70 (1969): 246–255.

——. "The Wealth They Left Us: Two Women Author Themselves Through Others' Lives in Beowulf." *Philological Quarterly* 78 (1999): 49–76.

Overing, Gillian R. *Language, Sign, and Gender in Beowulf.* Carbondale: Southern Illinois Press, 1990.

Owen-Crocker, Gale R. "Beast Men: Wulf and Eofor and the Mythic Significance of Names in *Beowulf*." In *Myth in Early Northwest Europe*, edited by Stephen O. Glosecki, 257–280. Tempe: Arizona Center for Medieval and Renaissance Studies, 2007.

——. *The Four Funerals in Beowulf and the Structure of the Poem.* Manchester: Manchester University Press, 2000.

——. "'Gracious' Hrothulf, 'Gracious' Hrothgar: A Reassessment." *English Language Notes* 38 (2001): 1–9.

——. "Horror in *Beowulf*: Mutilation, Decapitation and Unburied Dead." In *Early Medieval English Texts and Interpretations: Studies Presented to Donald G. Scragg*, edited by Elaine Treharne and Susan Rosser, 81–100. Tempe: ACMRS, 2002.

Pascual, Rafael J. "Hrothgar's Warhorse and the Audience of *Beowulf*." *Medium Ævum* 90 (2021): 123–132.

——. "Material Monsters and Semantic Shifts." In *The Dating of Beowulf: A Reassessment*, edited by Leonard Neidorf, 202–218. Cambridge: D. S. Brewer, 2014.

Pàroli, Teresa. "The Tears of the Heroes in Germanic Epic Poetry." In *Helden und Heldensage: Otto Gschwantler zum 60. Geburtstag*, edited by Hermann Reichert and Günter Zimmermann, 233–266. Wien: Fassbaender, 1990.

Pepperdene, Margaret W. "Beowulf and the Coast-Guard." *English Studies* 47 (1966): 409–419.

Pettitt, Thomas. "Beowulf: The Mark of the Beast and the Balance of Frenzy." *Neuphilologische Mitteilungen* (1976): 526–535.

Pfrenger, Andrew M. "Grendel's *Glof*: *Beowulf* line 2085 Reconsidered." *Philological Quarterly* 87 (2008): 209–235.

Phillpotts, Bertha S. "Wyrd and Providence in Anglo-Saxon Thought." *Essays and Studies* 13 (1928): 7–27.

Pigg, Daniel F. "Cultural Markers in *Beowulf*: A Re-Evaluation of the Relationship between Beowulf and Christ." *Neophilologus* 74 (1990): 601–607.

Polanyi, Livia. "Lexical Coherence Phenomena in Beowulf's Debate with Unferth." *Rackham Literary Studies* 8 (1977): 25–37.

Pollington, Stephen. *The Elder Gods: Religion and the Supernatural in Early England*. Ely: Anglo-Saxon Books, 2011.

——. "The Mead-Hall Community." *Journal of Medieval History* 37 (2011): 19–33.

——. *The Mead Hall: The Feasting Tradition in Anglo-Saxon England*. Norfolk: Anglo-Saxon Books, 2003.

——. *Religion and the Supernatural in Early England*. Ely: Anglo-Saxon Books, 2011.

Pope, John C. "*Beowulf* 505, 'Gehedde,' and the Pretensions of Unferth." In *Modes of Interpretation in Old English Literature: Essays in Honour of Stanley B. Greenfield*, edited by Phyllis Rugg Brown, Georgia Ronan Crampton, and Fred C. Robinson. Toronto: University of Toronto Press, 1986.

——. "*Beowulf* 3150-3151: Queen Hygd and the Word 'Geomeowle.'" *Modern Language Notes* 70 (1955): 77–87.

——. "Beowulf's Old Age." In *Philological Essays: Studies in Old and Middle English Language and Literature in Honour of Herbert Dean Meritt*, edited by James L. Rosier, 55–64. The Hague: Mouton, 1970.

Porck, Thijs. *Old Age in Early Medieval England: A Cultural History*. Woodbridge: Boydell, 2019.

——, and Sander Salk, "Marking Boundaries in *Beowulf*: Æschere's Head, Grendel's Arm and the Dragon's Corpse." *Amsterdamer Beiträge zur älteren Germanistik* 77 (2017): 521–540.

Puhvel, Martin. "The Might of Grendel's Mother." *Folklore* 80 (1969): 81–88.

——. "The Ride Around Beowulf's Barrow." *Folklore* 94 (1983): 108–112.

Rauer, Christine. *Beowulf and the Dragon: Parallels and Analogues*. Cambridge: D. S. Brewer, 2000.

Renoir, Alain. "Point of View and Design for Terror in *Beowulf*." *Neuphilologische Mitteilungen* 63 (1962): 154–167.

Reynolds, Evelyn. "*Beowulf*'s Poetics of Absorption: Narrative Syntax and the Illusion of Stability in the Fight with Grendel's Mother." *Essays in Medieval Studies* 31 (2016): 43–64.

Rich, Carroll Y. "Unferth and Cain's Envy." *South Central Bulletin* 33 (1973): 211–213.

Richards, M. P. "A Reexamination of *Beowulf* ll. 3180–3182." *English Language Notes* 10 (1973): 163–167.

Richardson, Peter R. "Making Thanes: Literature, Rhetoric, and State Formation in Anglo-Saxon England." *Philological Quarterly* 78 (1999): 215–232.

Ringler, Richard N. "*Him sēo wēn gelēah*: The Design for Irony in Grendel's Last Visit to Heorot." *Speculum* 41 (1966): 49–67.

Roberts, Jane. "Hrothgar's 'Admirable Courage.'" In *Unlocking the Wordhord: Anglo-Saxon Studies in Memory of Edward B. Irving, Jr.*, edited by Mark C. Amodio and Katherine O'Brien O'Keeffe, 240–251. Toronto: University of Toronto Press, 2003.

——. "The Old English Vocabulary of Nobility" In *Nobles and Nobility in Medieval Europe: Concepts, Origins, Transformations*, edited by Anne J. Duggan, 69–84. Woodbridge, UK: Boydell, 2000.

——. "Understanding Hrothgar's Humiliation: *Beowulf* Line 144-74 in Context." In *Text, Image, Interpretation: Studies in Anglo-Saxon Literature and its Insular Context in Honour of Éamonn Ó Carragáin*, edited by Alastair Minnis and Jane Roberts, 355–367. Turnhout: Brepols, 2007.

Robinson, Fred C. *Beowulf and the Appositive Style.* Knoxville: University of Tennessee Press, 1985.

——. "Did Grendel's Mother Sit on Beowulf?" In *From Anglo-Saxon to Early Middle English: Studies Presented to E. G. Stanley*, edited by Malcolm Godden, Douglas Gray and T. F. Hoad, 1–7. Oxford: Clarendon Press, 1994.

——. "History, Religion, Culture: The Background Necessary for Teaching *Beowulf*." In *Approaches to Teaching Masterpieces of World Literature*, edited by Jess B. Bessinger Jr. and Robert F. Yeager, 107–122. New York: Modern Language Association of America, 1984.

——. "Sigemund's *fæhðe ond fyrena*: *Beowulf* 879a." In *To Explain the Present: Studies in the Changing English Language in Honour of Matti Rissanen*, edited by Terttu Nevalainen and Leena Kahlas-Tarkka, 200–208. Helsinki: Société Néophilologique, 1997.

——. "The Tomb of Beowulf." *The Tomb of Beowulf and Other Essays*, 3–17. Cambridge: Blackwell, 1993.

Rogers, H. L. "Beowulf's Three Great Fights." *Review of English Studies* 6 (1955): 339–355.

Rose, Nancy. "Hrothgar, Nestor, and Religiosity as a Mode of Characterization in Heroic Poetry." *Journal of Popular Culture* 1 (1967): 158–165.

Rosenberg, Bruce A. "Folktale Morphology and the Structure of *Beowulf*: A Counterproposal." *Journal of the Folklore Institute* 11 (1975): 199–209.

Rosier, James L. "Design for Treachery: The Unferth Intrigue." *PMLA* 77 (1962): 1–7.

Ross, Margaret Clunies. "Giants." In *The Pre-Christian Religions of the North: History and Structures,* edited by Jens Peter Schjødt, John Lindow, and Anders Andrén, 4 vols, III: 1527–1558. Turnhout: Brepols, 2020.

Ruggerini, Maria Elena. "L'eroe germanico contro avversari mostruosi: tra testo e iconografia." In *La funzione dell'eroe germanico: storicità, metafora, paradigma; Atti del Convegno internazionale di studio Roma, 6–8 maggio 1993*, edited by Teresa Pàroli, 201–257. Rome: Calamo, 1995.

Rundkvist, Martin. *Mead-halls of the Eastern Geats: Elite Settlements and Political Geography AD 375–1000 in Östergötland, Sweden.* Stockholm: KVHAA, Royal Swedish Academy, 2012.

Russom, Geoffrey. "At the Center of *Beowulf*." In *Myth in Early Northwest Europe*, edited by Stephen O. Glosecki, 225–240. Tempe: ACMRS, 2007.

——. "Historicity and Anachronism in *Beowulf*." In *Epic and History*, edited by David Konstan and Kurt A. Raaflaub, 243–261. Malden: Wiley-Blackwell, 2010.

Salvador-Bello, Mercedes. "The Arrival of the Hero in a Ship: A Common Leitmotif in OE Regnal Tables and the Story of Scyld Scefing in Beowulf." *SELIM* 8 (1998): 205–221.

Sayers, William. "Cei, Unferth, and Access to the Throne." *English Studies* 90 (2009): 127–141.

——. "Grendel's Mother (Beowulf) and the Celtic Goddess of Territorial Sovereignty." *Journal of Indo-European Studies* 35 (2007): 31–52.

——. "Rhetorical Coercion and Heroic Commitment: Beowulf's Reception at Heorot." *English Studies* 101 (2020): 651–664.

Schrader, Richard J. "The Language on the Giant's Sword Hilt in *Beowulf*." *Neuphilologische Mitteilungen* 94 (1993): 141–184.

Schwetman, John W. "Beowulf's Return: The Hero's Account of His Adventures among the Danes." *Medieval Perspectives* 13 (1998): 136–148.

Sebo, Erin. "Foreshadowing the End in *Beowulf*." *English Studies* 99 (2018): 836–847.

——. "*Ne Sorga*: Grief and Revenge in *Beowulf*." In *Anglo-Saxon Emotions: Reading the Heart in Old English Language, Literature and Culture*, edited by Alice Jorgensen, Frances McCormack, and Jonathan Wilcox, 177–192. Farnham: Ashgate, 2015.

——, and Cassandra Schilling. "Modthryth and the Problem of Peace-Weavers: Women and Political Power in Early Medieval England." *English Studies* 102 (2021): 637–650.

Shaull, Erin M. "Ecgþeow, Brother of Ongenþeow, and the Problem of Beowulf's Swedishness." *Neophilologus* 101 (2016): 263–275.

Shilton, Howard. "The Nature of Beowulf's Dragon." *Bulletin of the John Rylands Library* 79 (1997): 67–78.

Shippey, Tom. *Beowulf*. London: Arnold, 1978.

——. *Beowulf and the North before the Vikings*. Leeds: Arc Humanities Press, 2022.

——. "The Fairy-Tale Structure of *Beowulf*." *Notes and Queries* 16 (1969): 2–11.

——. "'The Fall of King Hæðcyn': Or, Mimesis 4a, the Chapter Auerbach Never Wrote." In *On the Aesthetics of Beowulf and Other Old English Poems*, edited by John M. Hill, 247–265. Toronto: University of Toronto Press, 2010.

——. "*Hrólfs saga kraka* and the Legend of Lejre." In *Making History: Essays on the Fornaldarsögur*, edited by Martin Arnold and Alison Finlay, 17–32. London: Viking Society for Northern Research, 2010.

——. "'King Sheave' and 'The Lost Road.'" In *The Great Tales Never End: Essays in Memory of Christopher Tolkien*, edited by Richard Ovenden and Catherine McIlwaine, 166–180. Oxford: Bodleian Library Publishing, 2022.

——. "Maxims in Old English Narrative: Literary Art or Traditional Wisdom?" In *Oral Tradition, Literary Tradition: A Symposium*, edited by Hans Bekker-Nielsen et al., 28–46. Odense: Odense University Press, 1977.

——. "The Merow(ich)ingian Again: *damnatio memoriae* and the *usus scholarum*." In *Latin Learning and English Lore:*

Studies in Anglo-Saxon Literature for Michael Lapidge, edited by Katherine O'Brien O'Keeffe and Andy Orchard, 2 vols., 1: 389–406. Toronto: University of Toronto Press, 2005.

——. "Names in *Beowulf* and Anglo-Saxon England." In *The Dating of Beowulf: A Reassessment*, edited by Leonard Neidorf, 58–78. Cambridge: D. S. Brewer, 2014.

——. "Old English Poetry: The Prospects for Literary History." In *Proceedings of the Second International Conference of SELIM (Spanish Society for English Medieval Language and Literature)*, edited by A. León Sendra, 164–179. Córdoba: SELIM, 1993.

——. *Old English Verse.* London: Hutchison, 1972.

——. "Principles of Conversation in Beowulfian Speech." In *Techniques of Description: Spoken and Written Discourse: A Festschrift for Malcolm Coulthard*, edited by John M. Sinclair, Michael Hoey, and Gwyneth Fox, 109–126. London: Routledge, 1993.

——. "Review Article: Klaeber's *Beowulf* Eighty Years On: A Triumph for a Triumvirate." *Journal of English and Germanic Philology* 108 (2009): 360–376.

——. *The Road to Middle Earth: How J. R. R. Tolkien Created a New Mythology*, 4th ed. Boston: Houghton Mifflin, 2003.

——. "Structure and Unity." In *A Beowulf Handbook*, edited by Robert E. Bjork and John D. Niles, 149–174. Lincoln: University of Nebraska Press, 1997.

——. "The Versions of 'The Hoard.'" *Lembas* 100 (2001): 3–7.

——, and Andreas Haarder, ed. *Beowulf: The Critical Heritage.* London: Routledge, 1998.

Sisam, Kenneth. "Beowulf's Fight with the Dragon." *Review of English Studies* 9 (1958): 129–140.

——. *The Structure of Beowulf.* Oxford: Clarendon Press, 1965.

Smithers, G. V. "Destiny and the Heroic Warrior in *Beowulf.*" In *Philological Essays: Studies in Old and Middle English Literature in Honour of Herbert Dean Meritt*, edited by J. L. Rosier, 65–81. The Hague: Mouton, 1970.

——. *The Making of Beowulf.* Durham: University of Durham, 1961.

Sorrell, Paul. "The Approach to the Dragon-Fight in *Beowulf*, Aldhelm, and the 'traditions folkloriques' of Jacques Le Goff." *Parergon* 12 (1994): 57–87.

Stitt, J. Michael. *Beowulf and the Bear's Son: Epic, Saga, and Fairytale in Northern Germanic Tradition.* New York: Garland, 1992.

Stanley, E. G. "Courtliness and Courtesy in *Beowulf* and Elsewhere in English Medieval Literature." In *Words and Works: Studies in Medieval English Language and Literature in Honour of Fred C. Robinson*, edited by Peter S. Baker and Nicholas Howe, 67–104. Toronto: University of Toronto Press, 1998.

——. "Did Beowulf Commit 'Feaxfeng' against Grendel's Mother?" *Notes and Queries* 23 (1976): 339–340.

——. "*Hæþenra Hyht* in *Beowulf.*" In *Studies in Old English Literature in Honor of Arthur G. Brodeur*, edited by Stanley B. Greenfield, 136–151. Eugene: University of Oregon Books, 1963.

Sundquist, John D. "Relative Clause Variation and the Unity of *Beowulf.*" *Journal of Germanic Linguistics* 14 (2002): 243–269.

Swain, Larry J. "Of Hands, Halls, and Heroes: Grendel's Hand, Hroþgar's Power, and the Problem of *stapol* in *Beowulf.*" *Anglia* 134 (2016): 260–284.

Talbot, Annelise. "Sigemund the Dragon-Slayer." *Folklore* 94 (1983): 153–162.

Tanke, John. "Beowulf, Gold-Luck, and God's Will." *Studies in Philology* 99 (2002): 356–379.

Taranu, Catalin. "Who was the Original Dragon-Slayer of the Nibelung Cycle?" *Viator* 46 (2015): 23–40.

Taylor, Keith P. "*Beowulf* 1259a: The Inherent Nobility of Grendel's Mother." *English Language Notes* 31 (1994): 13–25.

Taylor, Paul Beekman. "The Dragon's Treasure in *Beowulf.*" *Neuphilologische Mitteilungen* 98 (1997): 229–240.

——. "*Heofon Riece Swealg*: A Sign of Beowulf's State of Grace." *Philological Quarterly* 42 (1963): 257–259.

——. "Heorot, Earth, and Asgard: Christian Poetry and Pagan Myth." *Tennessee Studies in Literature* 11 (1966): 119–130.

——. "The Traditional Language of Treasure in *Beowulf.*" *Journal of English and Germanic Philology* 85 (1986): 191–205.

Thompson, Augustine. "Rethinking Hygelac's Raid." *English Language Notes* 38 (2001): 9–16.

Thornbury, Emily. "*Eald Enta Geweorc* and the Relics of Empire: Revisiting the Dragon's Lair in *Beowulf.*" *Quaestio Insularis* 1 (2000): 82–92.

Tolkien, J. R. R. "*Beowulf*: The Monsters and the Critics." *Proceedings of the British Academy* 22 (1936): 245–295.

——. *Finn and Hengest: The Fragment and the Episode.* Edited by A. J. Bliss. London: George Allen & Unwin, 1982.

——. "The Homecoming of Beorhtnoth Beorhthelm's Son." *Essays and Studies* 6 (1953): 1–18.

——, trans. *Beowulf: A Translation and Commentary, together with Sellic Spell*. Edited by Christopher Tolkien. Boston: Houghton Mifflin Harcourt.

Tolley, Clive. "*Beowulf*'s Scyld Scefing Episode: Some Norse and Finnish Analogues." *Arv* 52 (1996): 7–48.

Trilling, Renée R. "Beyond Abjection: The Problem with Grendel's Mother Again." *Parergon* 24 (2007): 1–20.

Tripp, Raymond P., Jr. "Did Beowulf Have an 'Inglorious Youth'?" *Studia Neophilologica* 61 (1989): 129–143.

——. "The Exemplary Role of Hrothgar and Heorot." *Philological Quarterly* 56 (1977): 123–129.

——. "Heremod's Sin, Hrothgar's Sermon, and Beowulf's Choice." *Geardagum* 30 (2011): 59–77.

——. *More about the Fight with the Dragon: Beowulf, 2208b-3182: Commentary, Edition, and Translation*. Lanham, MD: University Press of America, 1983.

Turville-Petre, E. O. G. *Myth and Religion of the North: The Religion of Ancient Scandinavia*. New York: Holt, Reinhart and Winston, 1964.

Ushigaki, Hiroto. "The Image of 'God Cyning' in *Beowulf*: A Philological Study." *Studies in English Literature* (Tokyo) 58 (1982): 63–78.

Vickrey, John F. "*Egesan ne gymeð* and the Crime of Heremod." *Modern Philology* 71 (1974): 295–300.

——. "The Narrative Structure of Hengest's Revenge in *Beowulf*." *Anglo-Saxon England* 6 (1977): 91–103.

Waugh, Robin. "Competitive Narrators in the Homecoming Scene of *Beowulf*." *Journal of Narrative Technique* 25 (1995): 202–222.

Wehlau, Ruth. "Beowulf's Dark Thoughts: Heremod, Hrethel, and Exempla of the Mind." In *Darkness, Depression, and Descent in Anglo-Saxon England*, edited by Ruth Wehlau, 135–154. Berlin: De Gruyter, 2019.

Weiskott, Eric. "Three Beowulf Cruces: *Healgamen, Fremu, Sigemunde.*" *Notes and Queries* 58 (2011): 5–6.

Wentersdorf, Karl P. "*Beowulf*: The Paganism of Hrothgar's Danes." *Studies in Philology* 78 (1981): 91–119.

——. "The *Beowulf*-Poet's Vision of Heorot." *Studies in Philology* 104 (2007): 409–426.

——. "Beowulf's Adventure with Breca." *Studies in Philology* 72 (1975): 140–166.

Wetzel, Claus-Dieter. "*Beowulf* 3074 f. – ein *locus desperatus?*" In *Anglo-Saxonica: Beiträge zur Vor- und Frühgeschichte der englischen Sprache und zur altenglischen Literatur: Festschrift für Hans Schabram zum 65 Geburtstag*, edited by Klaus R. Grinda and Claus-Dieter Wetzel, 113–166. München: Fink, 1993.

Whitelock, Dorothy. *The Audience of Beowulf.* Oxford: Clarendon Press, 1951.

Wieland, Gernot R. "*Manna Mildost*: Moses and Beowulf." *Pacific Coast Philology* 23 (1988): 86–93.

——. "The Unferth Enigma: The Þyle between the Hero and the Poet." In *Fact and Fiction from the Middle Ages to Modern Times: Essays Presented to Hans Sauer on the Occasion of His 65th Birthday—Part II*, edited by Renate Bauer and Ulrike Krischke, 35–46. Frankfurt am Main: Peter Lang, 2011.

Wiersma, Stanley M. *A Linguistic Analysis of Words Referring to Monsters in Beowulf.* University of Wisconsin: Unpublished Doctoral Dissertation, 1961.

Williams, Graham. "*Wine Min Unferð*: Courtly Speech and a Reconsideration of (Supposed) Sarcasm in *Beowulf.*" *Journal of Historical Pragmatics* 18 (2017): 175–194.

Woolf, Rosemary. "The Ideal of Men Dying with their Lord in the *Germania* and *The Battle of Maldon.*" *Anglo-Saxon England* 5 (1976): 63–81.

Wright, Charles D. *The Irish Tradition in Old English Literature.* Cambridge: Cambridge University Press, 1992.

Wright, Thomas L. "Hrothgar's Tears." *Modern Philology* 65 (1967): 39–44.

www.ingramcontent.com/pod-product-compliance
Lightning Source LLC
Chambersburg PA
CBHW020915140626
46545CB00015B/52